S0-BYH-909

EZEKIEL 18 AND THE RHETORIC
OF MORAL DISCOURSE

SOCIETY
OF BIBLICAL
LITERATURE

DISSERTATION SERIES
David L. Petersen, Old Testament Editor
Charles Talbert, New Testament Editor

Number 126

EZEKIEL 18 AND THE RHETORIC
OF MORAL DISCOURSE

by
Gordon H. Matties

Gordon H. Matties

EZEKIEL 18 AND THE RHETORIC OF MORAL DISCOURSE

Scholars Press
Atlanta, Georgia

BS
1545.6
.E8
M37
1990

EZEKIEL 18 AND THE RHETORIC OF MORAL DISCOURSE

Gordon H. Matties

Ph.D., 1989
Vanderbilt University

Advisor:
Douglas A. Knight

© 1990
The Society of Biblical Literature

Library of Congress Cataloging in Publication Data

Matties, Gordon.
  Ezekiel 18 and the rhetoric of moral discourse / Gordon Matties.
  p. cm. -- (Dissertation series / Society of Biblical
  Literature ; no. 126)
  Includes bibliographical references.
  ISBN 1-55540-458-8 (alk. paper). -- ISBN 1-55540-459-6 (pbk. :
  alk. paper)
  1. Bible. O.T. Ezekiel XVIII--Criticism, interpretation, etc.
2. Ethics in the Bible. I. Title. II. Title: Ezekiel eighteen and the
rhetoric of moral discourse in the book of Ezekiel.
III. Series: Dissertation series (Society of Biblical Literature) ;
no. 126.
BS1545.6.E8M37 1990
224'.4066--dc20   90-44548
                                                   CIP

Printed in the United States of America
on acid-free paper

CONTENTS

ACKNOWLEDGMENTS

This dissertation is a result of the vision and inspiration of teachers who have nurtured my study of the Hebrew Bible. I think particularly of my first Hebrew teachers, Dr. Paul Mosca and Dr. Bruce Waltke. I am also especially grateful to two faculty members at Vanderbilt University: Dr. Walter Harrelson for his consistent encouragement and for his initial suggestion that sparked my interest in Ezekiel 18; and my advisor, Dr. Douglas Knight, who inspired and helped to shape my interest in ethics in the Hebrew Bible.

I also appreciate my fellow students, Dr. Lloyd M. Barré and Dr. Paul N. Franklyn, who proved to be valuable conversation partners and supporters.

Most of all I value the support, confidence and encouragement of Lorraine, my wife, who helped to keep my vision focused and who persistently prodded until the task was complete.

I dedicate this work to Zoe Esther, our daughter, whose birth has been a sign of grace. I hope she lives to experience a community that lives authentically in the light of the biblical story of faithfulness.

LIST OF ABBREVIATIONS

AB	Anchor Bible
AnBib	Analecta biblica
AJSL	*American Journal of Semitic Languages and Literature*
ANET	J. B. Pritchard (ed.), *Ancient Near Eastern Texts Relating to the Old Testament*
ASTI	Annual of the Swedish Theological Institute
ATAbh	Alttestamentliche Abhandlungen
BA	*Biblical Archaeologist*
BBB	Bonner biblische Beiträge
Bib	*Biblica*
BibS(N)	Biblische Studien (Neukirchen)
BHT	Beiträge zur historischen Theologie
Bib	*Biblica*
BJRL	*Bulletin of the John Rylands University Library of Manchester*
BWANT	Beiträge zur Wissenschaft vom Alten und Neuen Testament
BZ	*Biblische Zeitschrift*
BZAW	Beihefte zur *ZAW*
CahRB	Cahiers de la Revue biblique
CBQ	*Catholic Biblical Quarterly*
D	Deuteronomistic tradition
DtrH	Deuteronomistic History
DTT	*Dansk teologisk tidsskrift*
EstBib	*Estudios bíblicos*
ExpTim	*Expository Times*
FB	Forschung zur Bibel
FRLANT	Forschungen zur Religion und Literatur des Alten und Neuen Testaments
GKC	Gesenius' Hebrew Grammar, ed. E. Kautzsch, tr. A. E. Cowley
H	Holiness Code
HAT	Handbuch zum Alten Testament
HKAT	Handkommentar zum Alten Testament
HSM	Harvard Semitic Monographs
HUCA	*Hebrew Union College Annual*
ICC	International Critical Commentary
Int	*Interpretation*
JAOS	*Journal of the American Oriental Society*

JBL	*Journal of Biblical Literature*
JETS	*Journal of the Evangelical Theological Society*
JNES	*Journal of Near Eastern Studies*
JSOT	*Journal for the Study of the Old Testament*
JSOTSup	Journal for the Study of the Old Testament, Supplement Series
JTS	*Journal of Theological Studies*
LXX	The Septuagint
MT	The Masoretic Text
NCB	New Century Bible
OBO	Orbis biblicus et orientalis
OBT	Overtures to Biblical Theology
OLZ	*Orientalische Literaturzeitung*
OTL	Old Testament Library
P	Priestly tradition
RB	*Revue biblique*
RSR	*Recherches de science religieuse*
SBB	Stuttgarter biblische Beiträge
SBLDS	Society of Biblical Literature Dissertation Series
SBLMS	Society of Biblical Literature Monograph Series
SBT	Studies in Biblical Theology
ScEccl	*Sciences ecclésiastiques*
SJLA	Studies in Judaism in Late Antiquity
SJT	*Scottish Journal of Theology*
TBü	Theologische Bücherei
TDOT	G. J. Botterweck and H. Ringgren (eds.), *Theological Dictionary of the Old Testament*
TGl	*Theologie und Glaube*
THAT	E. Jenni and C. Westermann (eds.), *Theologisches Handwörterbuch zum Alten Testament*
TLZ	*Theologische Literaturzeitung*
TRu	*Theologische Rundschau*
TynBul	*Tyndale Bulletin*
TZ	*Theologische Zeitschrift*
UF	*Ugarit-Forschungen*
WMANT	Wissenschaftliche Monographien zum Alten und Neuen Testament
VT	*Vetus Testamentum*
VTSup	Vetus Testamentum, Supplements
ZEE	*Zeitschrift für evangelische Ethik*
ZAW	*Zeitschrift für die alttestamentliche Wissenschaft*
ZThK	*Zeitschrift für Theologie und Kirche*

1

INTRODUCTION

THE PROBLEM

More than fifty years ago G. A. Cooke wrote: "No one who has worked at Ezekiel can feel satisfied that all the problems have been solved."[1] Since then no consensus has emerged, in spite of several well-defined positions on a variety of issues. The literary-historical discussion remains at the forefront of Ezekiel research, as the recently edited book by J. Lust illustrates.[2] And two masterful commentaries by W. Zimmerli and M. Greenberg dominate the horizon, yet demonstrate marked methodological divergence.[3]

Ezekiel also continues to elicit a variety of responses from readers. Most recently Elie Wiesel commented:

> No prophet was endowed with such vision—no other vision was as extreme. . . .
> No messenger has hurt us more—none has offered us such healing words.[4]

---

[1]Review of G. Hölscher, *Hesekiel: der Dichter und das Buch* (BZAW 39; Giessen: Töpelmann, 1924), *JTS* 27 (1925-26) 202.

[2]*Ezekiel and His Book: Textual and Literary Criticism and their Interrelation* (Leuven: Leuven University Press/Peeters, 1986). Research on Ezekiel in this century has been well documented. See, e.g., G. A. Cooke, "New Views on Ezekiel," *Theology* 24 (1932) 61-69; C. Kuhl, "Zur Geschichte der Hesekiel-Forschung," *TRu* 5 (1933) 92-118; idem, "Neuere Hesekiel-Literatur," *TRu* 20 (1952) 1-26; W. A. Irwin, "Ezekiel Research Since 1943," *VT* 3 (1953) 54-66; H. H. Rowley, "The Book of Ezekiel in Modern Study," *BJRL* 36 (1953-54) 146-90; C. Kuhl, "Zum Stand der Hesekiel-Forschung," *TRu* 24 (1956-57) 1-53; G. Fohrer, "Das Symptomatische der Ezechielforschung," *TLZ* 83 (1958) 241-50; idem, "Zehn Jahre Literatur zur alttestamentlichen Prophetie (1950-1960): VIII Ezechiel," *TRu* 28 (1962) 261-67; H. Bardtke, "Der Prophet Ezekiel in der modernen Forschung," *TLZ* 96 (1971) 721-34; G. Fohrer, "Neue Literatur zur alttestamentlichen Prophetie: VIII Ezechiel," *TRu* 45 (1980) 121-29.

[3]Zimmerli, *Ezekiel 1* (Hermeneia; Philadelphia: Fortress, 1979); idem, *Ezekiel 2* (Hermeneia; Philadelphia, 1983); Greenberg, *Ezekiel 1-20* (AB 22; Garden City, NY: Doubleday, 1983).

[4]"Ezekiel," *Congregation: Contemporary Writers Read the Jewish Bible* (ed. David

In the face of scholarly methodological differences, and in recognition of Ezekiel's extremes, I enter the fray cautiously, yet expectantly. I am aware of the dangers of using the prophet's book to serve specific interests, yet the treasure has not been fully found.

One area of Ezekiel research that has not been explored fully is the ethics of Ezekiel.[5] In this matter we face a problem. In the last century the prophets were hailed as ethical reformers. In this century the biblical theology movement sought to highlight the theological content of the prophets and to ascribe the moral dimension to the prophets' restatement of ancient tradition—although in new and transformed theological shapes. In the light of recent literary approaches to biblical literature, we may be in a position to recognize the integral function of moral discourse in prophetic literature. The dissertation will explore the shape of moral discourse in the book of Ezekiel. Ezekiel 18 will provide the point of entry into the book.[6]

THE TASK

The purpose of this dissertation has a twofold orientation. The first task is to analyze Ezekiel 18 using the literary-historical tools of form criticism (Chapter 3) and traditio-historical investigation (Chapter 4). Building on that base, the second task is to investigate three traditional moral problems raised by the text of Ezekiel 18: 1) the shaping of the moral community and the place of the individual in that community (Chapter 5); 2) the identity of the human moral agent and the function of law (Chapter 6); and 3) the relationship of ethics to theodicy (Chapter 7). The work will be preceded by a discussion of the relationship of the Book of Ezekiel to Israelite tradition (Chapter 2).

Rosenberg; San Diego, New York, London: Harcourt Brace Jovanovich, 1987) 167.

[5]The last monograph on the subject was by P. Patricius Herzog (*Die ethischen Anschauungen des Propheten Ezechiel* [ATAbh, Band 9, Heft 2/3; Münster i. W.: Verlag der Aschendorffschen Verlagsbuchhandlung, 1923]). Herzog sought to integrate the ethical and cultic dimensions of the Book of Ezekiel.

[6]The chapter has been the subject of a number of shorter studies, among which are: H. Junker, "Ein Kernstück der Predigt Ezechiels," *BZ* NF 7 (1963) 173-85; J. N. Carreira, "Raizes da linguagem profética de Ezequiel. A proposito de Ez 18, 5-9," *EstBib* 26 (1967) 275-86; K. D. Sakenfeld, "Ez 18:25-32." *Int* 32 (1978) 295-300; J. B. Geyer, "Ezekiel 18 and a Hittite Treaty of Mursilis II," *JSOT* 12 (1979) 31-46; R. M. Hals, "Methods of Interpretation: Old Testament Texts [Ezekiel 18]," *Studies in Lutheran Hermeneutics* (ed. J. Reumann; Philadelphia, PA: Fortress, 1979) 271-82; P. M. Joyce, "Individual Responsibility in Ezekiel 18?" *Studia Biblica 1978: Papers on Old Testament and Related Themes* (JSOTSup 11; ed. E. A. Livingstone; Sheffield: JSOT, 1979) 185-96; E. Hammershaimb, "De Sure Druer: Nogle Overvejelser til Ez Kap 18," *DTT* 43 (1980) 225-34.

MORAL DISCOURSE ANALYSIS AND THE STUDY OF EZEKIEL

Problems of doing this kind of study in conjunction with traditional biblical exegesis are many. What does the category "moral discourse" mean in relation to the book of Ezekiel? Is it possible to analyze the "ethics in Ezekiel" descriptively?[7] And how do the literary, historical, and theological dimensions of the text intersect with the ethical task? According to J. Barton, a description of Old Testament ethics must be informed by astute sociological observations.[8] How is that possible with Ezekiel, in view of the literary problems faced by the exegete? Can one get behind the literature to the sociological facets of the book? Beyond that, how are we to deal with the diversity in the *book* of Ezekiel? Specifically, how is it possible to speak of ethics in the book of Ezekiel in the light of recent redaction-critical research that posits a variety of sociological settings for the book of Ezekiel? What is the relationship of form criticism and tradition criticism to the study of ethics?[9] Finally, is it possible to distinguish between the ethics of exilic Israel and the ethics of Ezekiel?[10]

My task here is to begin with the exegetical disciplines themselves and then to ask questions of the function of form and tradition in the service of moral discourse. I fully recognize, with Barton, that in studying ethics in the Hebrew Bible, as in other areas of scripture study, "simple answers falsify."[11]

---

[7]John Goldingay (*Approaches to Old Testament Interpretation* [Downers Grove, IL: InterVarsity, 1981] 64) suggests that "ethics, like theology, is not really a biblical category." What we find, rather, are "various concrete observations about how things are and concerning how men should live. Theology and ethics take these as their raw material and look behind the concrete statements for principles and generalities, which sometimes are actually on or very near the surface, at other times are much less obvious" (54).

[8]J. Barton, "Understanding Old Testament Ethics," *JSOT* 9 (1978) 53. R. E. Clements (*A Century of Old Testament Study* [Guildford and London: Lutterworth, 1976] 107) remarked in an aside in his discussion of wisdom literature that "the subject of Old Testament ethics has proved to be a most difficult one to deal with, and has in fact generally been treated as a subsidiary part of the wider study of Old Testament theology. The literature devoted to it has been surprisingly sparse, and the complex interaction of historical, sociological and religious factors has made it a subject in which it has been difficult to avoid the merely superficial."

[9]Part of the question concerns the relationship between Ezekiel and Israel's legal tradition. For example, concerning the relationship between Ezekiel and the Holiness Code Zimmerli (*Ezekiel 1*, 48) stated that "the question needs further intensive study in monographs."

[10]So suggests H. McKeating, "Sanctions Against Adultery in Ancient Israelite Society, with some Reflections on Methodology in the Study of Old Testament Ethics," *JSOT* 11 (1979) 57-72.

[11]"Understanding Old Testament Ethics," 61.

The study of ethics in relation to Israelite tradition has contributed greatly to our understanding of the prophets.[12] With regard to Ezekiel, for example, ancient Israelite legal traditions have been studied in relation to their contribution to Ezekiel's work.[13] The danger we face, of course, is the assumption that once the origin of a literary or traditional element has been discovered we have also articulated the meaning of that element in its present context. That is exactly the problem that recent redaction-critical discussions have explored. To orient the discussion around concerns of ethics and moral discourse poses the questions differently. Perhaps we can combine a holistic approach (Greenberg) with an awareness of a complex process of formation (Zimmerli).

Specifically, the study of ethics in Ezekiel 18 asks questions about the suasive function of the text's literary shape in particular social settings.[14] Chapter 2 sets the stage for this task by introducing the current debate about Ezekiel's use of Israelite tradition, and by positing a thesis that will be explored throughout the dissertation in a variety of ways.

INTRODUCTION TO THE EXEGESIS

The exegesis of Ezekiel 18 in Chapters 3 and 4 serves two purposes. First, it will enable us to enter the world of the text analytically. Second, the depth of that analysis will allow us to explore the dimensions of ethical discourse in the Book of Ezekiel. Thus, the exegesis prevents superficiality but is not an end in itself. The exegesis of Ezekiel 18 points to the broader discussion of issues within the Book of Ezekiel. The place of the exegetical portion of this study, then, is primary both for the entire movement of the work from beginning to end, and for the definition of categories that determine the choice of issues for discussion in Chapters 5, 6, and 7.

Particularly important for the purposes of this study is the recognition of the limitations of exegetical method. A holistic approach demands that the exercise of critical methodology be kept in perspective, that is, with a view toward the horizon of the task of this study.[15] The exegesis takes

---

[12]One recent example is the book by E. W. Davies (*Prophecy and Ethics: Isaiah and the Ethical Tradition of Israel* [JSOTSup 16; Sheffield: JSOT, 1981], which begins with an extensive survey of traditio-historical research on the prophets.

[13]See Chapter 2 below for a survey of recent work.

[14]This encompasses my use of the term "rhetoric." As Terry Eagleton (*Literary Theory: An Introduction* [Minneapolis, MN: University of Minnesota Press, 1983] 205) writes: "rhetoric . . . examine[s] the way discourses are constructed in order to achieve certain effects."

[15]As G. Fohrer ("Das Symptomatische der Ezechielforschung," 242) notes: "Es geht darum, ob . . . in der richtigen und notwendigen Anwendung der motiv-, form- und überlieferungsgeschichtlichen Untersuchung das richtige Mass eingehalten und die Grenze

into consideration the significant work in form-critical and traditio-historical research.[16]

This study will attempt to bring together the literary, historical, and theological approaches to Ezekiel. I view those three facets as necessary partners in the task of describing the modes and content of moral discourse within the Book of Ezekiel. Focusing on Ezekiel 18 provides boundaries within which to work. The literary-historical study of chap. 18 will provide the necessary diachronic facets in a study that might otherwise tend toward the synchronic.

In view of that, I should stress that the study of ethics in literature must take numerous factors into account. Naturally, content is not the only indicator. Forms and types of literature are laden with meaning by virtue of the specificity of formal characteristics. That is especially true in terms of the specific settings, functions, and intentions of the text. Equally important is the relation of the text to the theological tradition to which it belongs. For the Book of Ezekiel, the matter of tradition is the most difficult. Diversity of traditions and forms within the book have generated much redaction-critical research during the last decade. But it is, in fact, just this mixture of forms and traditions that makes discourse and communication possible. That mixture has been the subject of most Ezekiel research in this century.

ANALYSIS OF TRADITIONAL MOTIFS AND MORAL PROBLEMS

This dissertation seeks to open new ground in the investigation of the Book of Ezekiel by focusing attention on moral discourse, and particularly on the function of legal language and conceptions within moral discourse. I shall seek to offer new perspectives on the moral vision of Ezekiel.[17] The intersection of perspective and intuition often leads to fresh possibilities.

I shall focus on three theological-ethical problems that illustrate the way Ezekiel 18 charts a course within the available ethical categories of traditional thought: (1) the matter of responsibility in community, (2) the human moral agent and the function of law, and (3) the divine moral agent

---

dieser Methoden beachtet wird."

[16]I have placed the discussion of the smaller units that have been incorporated into chap. 18 within a discussion of traditional conventions (Chapter 4). They are distinct formally defined units, sub-elements of the larger composition. Zimmerli's alternative is to join the two, as in his article "The Special Form- and Traditio-Historical Character of Ezekiel's Prophecy," *VT* 15 (1965) 515-27.

[17]L. Boadt (Review of J. Lust, ed., *Ezekiel and His Book, CBQ* 50 [1988] 557) notes that "further work on the rhetorical power hidden in the message of the book is called for."

in relation to human responsibility, human community, and theodicy. Discussion of those moral problems addressed by Ezekiel 18 will take into account the wider context of ancient Israelite ethics and biblical literature.[18] In each case exegetical analysis from Chapters 3 and 4 will inform the discussion in Chapters 5, 6, and 7. Those latter chapters, therefore, will press the specifics of the exegetical discoveries in order to propose new or different juxtapositions of content and contexts by which we can better understand not only the text but the problems and concerns of the community in which these texts formed a basis for dialogue and formation.

In Chapter 5 I shall deal with traditional questions concerning the responsibility of the individual within the orbit of the community. I shall ask about the identity of the moral agent and the context in which the moral agent operates. Are the notions of life and death as presented in Ezekiel 18 ultimate ontological categories, are they moral categories that apply to individual human beings, or are they communal categories within which individuals find orientation?

In Chapter 6 I ask about the character of the moral agent.[19] What are the norms and values that shape the moral vision of the human moral agent? How does moral reasoning happen? What are the catalysts that engage human beings toward action? And what are the goals of ethical reflection and action? I will be interested in discovering the meaning of "doing/establishing righteousness and justice," and the understanding of following laws and observing/performing judgments. Of particular concern will be discovering the function of law in moral discourse.[20]

In Chapter 7 I focus on the way Yahweh is depicted as a moral agent. That is, what role does Yahweh play in moral formation and discourse? How is Yahweh viewed as a participant and therefore as a moral agent in the experience of the people? Ezekiel speaks several times about the new heart. In chap. 18 the reader is encouraged to get a new heart, and in chaps.

---

[18]What I call "traditional motifs and moral problems" belongs properly within the traditio-historical task. On investigating a particular moral or theological "problem" as part of traditio-historical study see D. A. Knight, *Rediscovering the Traditions of Israel* (rev. ed.; SBLDS 9; Missoula, MT: Scholars Press, 1975) 16-17.

[19]In Chapters 6 and 7 I shall be using the expression "moral agent" as it is defined by Stanley Hauerwas, *The Peaceable Kingdom: A Primer in Christian Ethics* (Notre Dame, IN: University of Notre Dame Press, 1983) 38-44.

[20]According to R. Hutton ("Declaratory Formulae: Forms of Authoritative Pronouncement in Ancient Israel" [Ph.D. diss., Claremont Graduate School, 1983] 106-107), law has social functions that are not to be subsumed under morality. J. Barton (commenting on the relationship between law and ethics in Ezekiel 18 in "Understanding Old Testament Ethics," 56-57) suggests that one should not begin with the legal material but with the audiences. I am suggesting, however, that law does not function simply to describe what the audience does, but what it is and might become. And that, I submit, is an integral function of ethics.

11 and 36 it is Yahweh who promises to give a new heart. This reflects a tension between moral responsibility and divine enablement. I shall explore the function of responsibility in chap. 18, and relate that to the rest of the book of Ezekiel. This, of course, ties in closely to the matter of the relationship between the individual and the community.

My thesis is that Ezekiel 18 seeks the formation of a community of character and understands that the community forms itself through the self-conscious acts of individuals.[21] Hence, the moral deliberation of the individual effects the shaping of the moral community. But Ezekiel's theological orientation permits no simple community formation without the divine agent, whom I shall also describe as a moral agent. It is Ezekiel's own understanding of the divine presence or divine absence, juxtaposed with his concept of the character of the community (expressed theologically as holiness), that necessitates that we do not create an artificial opposition between the human moral act and the divine moral enablement.

Ezekiel's view of Yahweh as a moral agent raises the question of theodicy. Ezekiel 18 debates the justice of Yahweh, along with the practice of justice in the moral community of Israel. Theodicy and anthropodicy meet for Ezekiel in the community where Yahweh dwells.

The dissertation will close with a concluding sketch of the way the literature, theology, and ethical issues intersect in Ezekiel 18 and the book of Ezekiel.

---

[21]On the expression "community of character" see Stanley Hauerwas, *A Community of Character: Toward a Constructive Christian Social Ethic* (Notre Dame, IN: University of Notre Dame Press, 1981).

2

TRADITION AND MORAL DISCOURSE
IN EZEKIEL

INTRODUCTION

Most discussions of the theological traditions in exilic and postexilic Israel begin with a host of decisions made on the basis of literary analysis. Since we know very little about the historical and socio-religious world of exilic Israel, we depend on textual witnesses for reconstructing that ancient context. Traditio-historical investigation and redaction criticism of the book of Ezekiel have been closely aligned in that enterprise. Since Zimmerli suggested the concept of *Nachinterpretation* as a way of describing the process of shaping the Ezekiel tradition, scholars have been using the traditio-historical tool to reconstruct the character of the Ezekiel "school(s)" responsible for shaping the book of Ezekiel.[1]

It is my intent in what follows to survey briefly the connections between Ezekiel and the Priestly and Deuteronomistic traditions. The two chapters that follow will present an analysis of the text of Ezekiel 18. Then, in Chapters 5, 6, and 7 I shall focus on specific traditional moral problems or issues addressed in Ezekiel 18. By asking how Ezekiel 18 in particular,

---

[1]W. Zimmerli, "Das Phänomen der 'Fortschreibung' im buche Ezechiel," *Prophecy: Essays Presented to G. Fohrer*, pp. 174-91 (ed. J. A. Emerton; BZAW 150; Berlin/New York: de Gruyter, 1980). For an analysis of Zimmerli's concept see Pamela D. J. Scalise, "From Prophet's Word to Prophetic Book: A Study of Walter Zimmerli's Theory of Nachinterpretation." Ph.D. Dissertation, Yale University, 1982. Among those who use tradition history as a tool for recovering the compositional history of the book and the character of the Ezekiel school are: Horacio Simian, *Die Theologische Nachgeschichte der Prophetie Ezechiels. Form- und Traditionskritische Untersuchung zu Ez 6; 35; 36* (FB 14; Würzburg: Echter Verlag, 1974); F. Hossfeld, *Untersuchungen zu Komposition und Theologie des Ezechielbuches* (FB 20; Würzburg: Echter Verlag, 1977); G. Bettenzoli, *Geist der Heiligkeit: Traditionsgeschichtliche Untersuchung des QDŠ Begriffes im Buch Ezechiel* (Quaderni di Semitistica 8; Florence: Istituto di Linguistica e di Lingue Orientali Università di Firenze, 1979); R. Liwak, "Überlieferungsgeschichtliche Probleme des Ezechielbuches: eine Studie zu postexilischen Interpretationen und Komposition" (Inauguraldissertation, Ruhr-Universität Bochum, 1976).

and the book of Ezekiel in general, treat three major theological-ethical concerns, I hope to illustrate that the book of Ezekiel charts an independent course among existing traditions. In that respect, Ezekiel reflects a distinct tradition that has been shaped in dialogue with earlier traditionists and in response to a unique historical moment.[2]

My thesis is that for Ezekiel the old theological patterns and ideological dependencies no longer work. Therefore it may not be adequate simply to find a traditio-historical slot into which Ezekiel fits. It may be more helpful to consider whether Ezekiel lives eclectically within the range of traditional formulations, and in so doing transforms them into a new program of restoration that looks different from the old foundational Deuteronomistic and Priestly traditions. I shall argue that Ezekiel is drawing on a rather fluid and dynamic tradition complex that commands no loyalties. Ezekiel forges a new path within Israel.

What is clear is that Ezekiel 18 is heir to a long tradition. But it is not the slave of that tradition. A matrix of factors has made Ezekiel 18 a new entity that builds on the past, but that moves creatively into the future. As R. E. Clements puts it, Ezekiel is "remembered and applied to a particular situation at the hands of a very distinctive theological circle."[3] I intend to explore the theological and especially the ethical interests of that distinctive circle. Those interests may be partially discerned by understanding how the laws, themes, and language in Ezekiel 18 are related to those of the Priestly and Deuteronomistic traditions. We need to be careful, however, not to assume that once we have discovered traditional affinities we have also described the meaning and function of the particular text. Beyond that, we may also discern the nuances of how the traditional material in Ezekiel 18 functions within its new setting.

In the following introductory survey of Ezekiel and Israelite tradition I shall focus specifically on the way Ezekiel 18 intersects with the various tradition complexes.[4]

---

[2]On this matter O. H. Steck ("Theological Streams of Tradition," *Tradition and Theology in the Old Testament* [ed. D. A. Knight; Philadelphia: Fortress, 1977] 205-206) suggests that the prophets "alter tradition in characteristic ways." Their work "evinces both reference to and contingent separation from ruling traditions." Knight (*Rediscovering*, 18-19) also warns that since the prophets often upset or altered the tradition, diversity ought not to be overshadowed by the search for continuity in a stream of tradition. See also H. Barth and O. H. Steck, *Exegese des Alten Testaments: Leitfaden der Methodik* (9th ed.; Neukirchen-Vluyn: Neukirchener Verlag, 1980) 77-78.

[3]"The Ezekiel Tradition: Prophecy in a Time of Crisis," *Israel's Prophetic Tradition: Essays in Honour of Peter R. Ackroyd* (eds. R. Coggins, A. Phillips, and M. Knibb; Cambridge/New York: Cambridge University Press, 1982) 129.

[4]For a wider and more comprehensive survey of Ezekiel's affinities with Israelite tradition see R. Liwak, "Überlieferungsgeschichtliche Probleme," 5-43; M. Burrows, *The Literary*

EZEKIEL AND THE PRIESTLY TRADITION

It has become commonplace to assign Ezekiel to the Priestly group, not only because of his birthright, but because the book that bears his name is filled with Priestly terminology and forms.[5] A reading of the book of Ezekiel as a product of an exclusively Priestly (or Zadokite) perspective would interpret the book as reflecting an attempt to articulate both a theodicy based on a concept of Yahweh as a transcendent deity, and a program for restoration based on temple ideology. Ezekiel, in that case, would represent a theocratic perspective in the face of the breakdown of social order and cultic practice.

Clements, for example, articulates the commonly held view that just as the Book of Jeremiah reflects the situation in Judah during the sixth century B.C.E., so the book of Ezekiel reflects the situation of the Babylonian exiles. Just as the book of Jeremiah is connected with the Deuteronomic movement, the book of Ezekiel finds its theological connections with the work of the Priestly school (the Holiness Code of Lev 17-26 and the Priestly document).[6] According to Clements, we must not think of simple dependence in literary terms, but of a common dependence on the Jerusalem cult tradition.[7] That Priestly alliance has been investigated

---

Relations of Ezekiel (Philadelphia: Jewish Publication Society, 1925); J. W. Miller, *Das Verhältnis Jeremias und Hesekiels sprachlich und theologisch untersucht* (Assen: Van Gorcum, 1955); Zimmerli, *Ezechiel: Gestalt und Botschaft* (BibS[N] 62; Neukirchen-Vluyn: Neukirchener Verlag, 1972); K. Carley, *Ezekiel among the Prophets: A Study of Ezekiel's Place in Prophetic Tradition* (SBT, Second Series 31; Naperville, Il: Allenson, 1975).

[5] G. von Rad (*Old Testament Theology* [2 vols.; London: SCM, 1962-65]. 2. 224] commented: "The world of ideas in which he lives, the standards which he applies, and the categories according to which he sees Israel's existence ordered before Yahweh, are expressly those of a priest." See von Rad's traditio-historical observations on pp. 223-37. He adds that Ezekiel's "message went far beyond priestly theology, and, indeed, can easily be shown to have shattered its bases at certain points" (225).

[6] "The Ezekiel Tradition," 126.

[7] Ibid., 128. The literature generated by the question of Ezekiel's relationship to the priestly tradition is massive. The following represent some of the major works. L. Horst, *Leviticus xvii-xxvi und Hezekiel: ein Beitrag zur Pentateuchkritik* (Colmar: Barth, 1881); A. Klostermann, "Ezechiel und das Heiligkeitsgesetz," *Der Pentateuch: Beiträge zu seinem Verständnis und seiner Entstehungsgeschichte* (Leipzig: Böhme, 1893) 368-418; L. B. Paton, "The Holiness Code and Ezekiel," *Presbyterian and Reformed Review* 7 (January, 1896) 98-115; E. König, "Die letzte Pentateuchschicht und Hesekiel," *ZAW* 28 (1908) 174-79; H. G. Reventlow, *Wächter über Israel: Ezechiel und seine Tradition* (BZAW 82; Berlin: Töpelmann, 1962); A. Hurvitz, "The Evidence of Language in Dating the Priestly Code: A Linguistic Study in Technical Idioms and Terminology," *RB* 81 (1974) 24-56; B. A. Levine, *In the Presence of the Lord: A Study of Cult and some Cultic Terms in Ancient Israel* (SJLA 5; Leiden: Brill, 1974); A. Hurvitz, *A Linguistic Study of the Relationship between the Priestly Source and the Book*

on two fronts: the Holiness Code and the Priestly Pentateuchal tradition.[8] But as Carley notes, "virtually every possibility of relating the prophecy and the law code has been advocated by one scholar or another in the course of the last century." Some argued for the priority of Ezekiel, others for the priority of the law code, and still others for common sources.[9]

Reventlow analyzed the elements shared between Ezekiel and the Holiness Code and concluded that literary dependence was not the major factor, but that, as Carley writes, "the prophecy and the code are independent expressions of the same liturgy of covenant renewal."[10] Whether or not a liturgy is shared, the formal affinities with the Holiness Code, and Leviticus 26 in particular, are evident. And as Driver notes, Ezekiel regards the laws of the Holiness Code "as an authoritative basis of moral and religious life."[11] Using Ezekiel 18 as a starting point, I hope to illustrate how Ezekiel's "authoritative basis" in Israel's legal tradition functioned in his program of reconstruction.

For Ezekiel 18 particularly, the affinities with the Holiness Code and the Priestly tradition are numerous. As von Rad notes, sin is described in Ezekiel as offenses against sacral orders. Ezekiel does not, however, distinguish between sacral and moral transgressions. Rather, and here von Rad's comments are appropriate, "the cause of Israel's approaching fall lay quite indubitably in a failure in the sphere of the holy."[12] The sacral tradition offered Ezekiel the categories of the holy and the profane, and the expression of those categories in legal terminology and form is most prominent in the repeated reference to the standards "by which those who

---

of Ezekiel: A New Approach to an Old Problem (CahRB 20; Paris: Gabalda, 1982).

[8] For surveys of literary affinities with Ezekiel see Carley, Ezekiel among the Prophets, 62-65; G. Fohrer, Die Hauptprobleme des Buches Ezechiel (BZAW 72; Berlin: Töpelmann, 1952) 144ff.; Burrows, Literary Relations, 28-36; S. R. Driver, An Introduction to the Literature of the Old Testament (New York: Meridian, 1957) 49-50, 131-35, 145-57.

[9] Ezekiel among the Prophets, 62. Most recent work argues for the priority of P. For example: R. Friedman, The Exile and Biblical Narrative: The Formation of the Deuteronomistic and Priestly Works (HSM 22; Chico, CA: Scholars Press, 1981) 61-64; Hurvitz, The Priestly Source and the Book of Ezekiel; M. Haran, Temples and Temple Service in Ancient Israel: An Inquiry into the Character of Cult Phenomena and the Historical Setting of the Priestly School (Oxford: Oxford University Press, 1978). Haran argues for P's priority on pp. 45-46, 72-76, 93-96, 102-111, 125-128, 187, 193-94, 225, 288, 296-298. See also M. Haran, "The Law Code of Ezekiel XL-XLVII and its Relation to the Priestly School," HUCA 50 (1979) 45-71. The lack of scholarly consensus with regard to the dating of P allows Ezekiel to stand on its own independent of a date for P. Thus Ezekiel 18 can easily be dated before or after P without altering the interpretation of Ezekiel 18, or the use and significance of law in Ezekiel.

[10] Reventlow, Wächter über Israel. Carley, Ezekiel among the Prophets, 63.

[11] Introduction, 146.

[12] Old Testament Theology. 2. 224.

were in contact with the holy had to live."[13] Thus, both in the oracles of judgment and in the oracles of salvation the legal covenant tradition is central. In the one the violation of Yahweh's order served notice on Israel's history and called for an end. And in the other the saving acts of Yahweh are envisioned as "the re-creation of a people able to obey the commandments perfectly."[14] This is the heart of Ezekiel's hope—a faithful people. The land, the temple, and the restored Davidic line are all servants of that larger hope symbolized by the Sinai tradition through the motifs of holiness and knowledge of Yahweh within a faithful community where Yahweh is actively present.

EZEKIEL AND THE DEUTERONOMISTIC TRADITION

The emphasis on Ezekiel's relationship to the priestly tradition needs to be balanced by another traditional connection that has frequently been overlooked. The book of Ezekiel also bears many marks of having been shaped by interaction with Deuteronomistic thinking.[15] Although the dominant linguistic similarities are not as prevalent as in the book of Jeremiah, a considerable number of Deuteronomisms are found in the book of Ezekiel.[16] Unlike many of the recent works on Jeremiah, only a few have suggested that the book of Ezekiel has been reworked by a Deuteronomistic redactor.[17] Robert R. Wilson, however, thinks a Deuteronomistic

---

[13]Ibid., 225.

[14]Ibid., 235.

[15]G. von Rad (ibid., 224) notes that legal terminology dominates the chapter, deriving from both the Priestly and the Deuteronomistic traditions. P. R. Ackroyd (*Exile and Restoration: A Study of Hebrew Thought of the Sixth Century B.C.* [OTL; Philadelphia: Westminster, 1968] 108-9) notes that the hortatory emphasis in Ezekiel 18 is characteristic of Deuteronomy, but that Ezekiel moves beyond the tendency to moral exhortation.

[16]See Burrows, *Literary Relations*, 19-28, 44-47; Miller, *Das Verhältnis*; Zimmerli, *Ezechiel: Gestalt und Botschaft*, 62-79; idem, *Ezekiel 1*, 46; Carley, *Ezekiel among the Prophets*, 8-12, 48-62; Fohrer, *Hauptprobleme*, 140ff.; Haag, *Was lehrt die literarkritische Untersuchung des Ezechieltextes?* (Frieburg in der Schweiz: Paulusdruckerie, 1943) 137-41.

[17]Already Hölscher (*Hesekiel: der Dichter und das Buch*) suggested that the inauthentic portions of Ezekiel were composed under Deuteronomistic influence. See also S. Herrmann, *Die prophetischen Heilserwartungen im Alten Testament* (BWANT 85; Stuttgart: Kohlhammer, 1965); W. Thiel, "Erwägungen zum Alter des Heiligkeitsgesetzes," *ZAW* 81 (1969) 69-70; R. Liwak, "Überlieferungsgeschichtliche Probleme." See Liwak (27-31) for a survey of scholarship on the relationship between Ezekiel and Deuteronomy. Liwak (246, n. 292) mentions E. Sehmsdorf ("Studien zur Redaktionsgeschichte von Jesaja I [Jes 65,16b-25; 66,1-4; 56,1-8]," *ZAW* 84 [1972] 517-61) and K.-H. Bernhardt ("Prophetie und Geschichte," *Congress Volume, Uppsala, 1971* [VTSup 22; Leiden: Brill, 1972] 20-46), who also suggest Deuteronomistic reworking of Ezekiel.

editing is unlikely "because the Ephraimite features are an integral part of the book at all redactional levels. It is not possible to isolate a specifically Deuteronomic editorial layer."[18]

Wilson suggests that "although Ezekiel's language and theology clearly reflect his Zadokite background, there are also a number of Deuteronomistic characteristics in the book." He points out two specifically Ephraimite factors. First, in both Ezekiel and D we find an emphasis on the word of Yahweh as the mode of revelation. That is particularly evident in the reception formula "the word of the Lord came to me."[19] Second, in Ezekiel's prophetic activity as depicted in 14:3 and 20:1 elders come to the prophet to "seek Yahweh," which is characteristic behaviour for an Ephraimite Mosaic prophet.[20]

Carley notes a number of other similarities between Ezekiel and Deuteronomy.[21] First, some of the legislation is similar. Although many of the laws in Ezekiel 18 parallel legislation in the Holiness Code, one law in Ezek 18:6 parallels Deut 12:1ff.[22] The vision of a restored community organized around a single sanctuary may reflect Deuteronomistic influence (Ezek 40:1-42:20).

Second, the imagery of harlotry in Ezekiel 16 and 23, along with the punishment of stoning, may be drawn from texts like Deut 13:10 and 22:21.

Third, certain phrases and expressions find parallels in Deuteronomy and Ezekiel. Two examples will illustrate. First, the description of the fruitful land in Ezek 36:29-30 bears marked similarities to Deuteronomy.[23] The similarities here are striking in part because of the differences. Ezekiel and Deuteronomy link fruitfulness to Israel's faithful response. In Ezekiel Yahweh's concern for Israel is motivated by concern for Yahweh's name, whereas in Deuteronomy Yahweh is motivated by love ('āhēb) and kindness (ḥesed). Carley suggests that the emphasis in Ezekiel belongs to the interest in showing Yahweh as a God of compassion and grace. The name theology in Ezekiel serves to vindicate the compassionate and forgiving character of Yahweh, which is balanced by his wrath against those who do not respond. In this regard, Ezek 18:23, 32 and 33:11 combine those two aspects of grace and wrath.[24]

---

[18]*Prophecy and Society in Ancient Israel* (Philadelphia: Fortress, 1980) 284.

[19]Ibid., 283. See Zimmerli, "The Special Form- and Traditio-historical Character of Ezekiel's Prophecy."

[20]Wilson, *Prophecy and Society*, 283.

[21]*Ezekiel among the Prophets*, 57-62.

[22]Chapter 5 will deal with specific legal similarities.

[23]See also Haag (*Was Lehrt?*, 48) and Simian (*Die theologische Nachgeschichte der Prophetie Ezechiels*) on the traditio-historical background of chap. 36.

[24]*Ezekiel among the Prophets*, 59.

Another example is the promise to the exiles in Ezek 11:14-21 (cf. Ezek 11:16 with Deut 4:27; 11:17 with 30:3-5; 11:20 with 7:6 and 26:16-19). The similarities may be simply a reflection of the common theology of the day, as G. Fohrer suggests.[25] Reventlow, however, uses the same text to show dependence on the Holiness Code.[26] He notes the words "countries" ('ărāṣôt) and "nations" (gôyîm) in Ezek 11:16 instead of Deuteronomy's "peoples" ('ammîm; 4:27). He also notes that in Ezek 11:20 "they will walk in my statutes" is closer to Lev 26:3 than to Deut 26:16. The use of "heart" in Ezek 11:19 is certainly Deuteronomic, and not Priestly,[27] yet the heart motif in Ezekiel is different from its Deuteronomic and even Jeremianic settings. For Ezekiel the new heart is a more radical gift from Yahweh, which enables Israel to keep the commandments.[28]

For Zimmerli the connections with Deuteronomy are fortuitous (e.g. the polemic against high places in Ezekiel 6). He states: "It is striking how the most important elements and formulations of the Deuteronomic language and preaching are absent in Ezekiel."[29] Liwak takes on himself the challenge, as Zimmerli poses it, to examine more carefully the contacts with Deuteronomy.[30] His solution, however, is to depart from looking for exact parallels with the book of Deuteronomy. Rather, he suggests affinities with a broad range of Deuteronomistic texts that were composed during the exilic period.[31] His suggestion is based on a hesitancy to ascribe Ezekiel's relationship to tradition to literary dependency. In this regard he seeks another explanation for the tradition-bound character of the book than (1) that Ezekiel eclectically chose diverse aspects of the current theological ethos in order to construct his own system, or (2) that a redactor within a particular tradition stream shaped the book to give it the character of that tradition.[32]

Liwak attempts, then, to restore the integrity of the book, which has been "taken apart" by division into tradition-bound components. His solution is to subsume the diverse traditional elements into a Deuteronomistic "common denominator."[33] To bolster his suggestion he cites recent scholarship that finds Deuteronomistic echoes nearly everywhere, and suggests that the book of Ezekiel may well exhibit the same tendency.[34] This pan-deuteronomism in the exilic period would explain the

---

[25]G. Fohrer *Ezechiel* (HAT 13; Tübingen: Mohr-Siebeck, 1955) 61-62.

[26]*Wächter über Israel*, 50ff.

[27]The only occurrence of "heart" in the book of Leviticus is 26:41.

[28]See Carley, *Ezekiel among the Prophets*, 56, 60.

[29]*Ezekiel 1*, 46.

[30]Liwak, "Überlieferungsgeschichtliche Probleme," 30. Zimmerli, *Ezekiel 1*, 8.

[31]Liwak, ibid., 238, n. 220.

[32]Ibid., 38.

[33]Ibid., 39.

[34]Ibid., 245-56, n. 291.

diversity of expression in the book.[35] He suggests simply that the levites are the bearers of the tradition, which takes different shapes and emphases depending on the base material available in the transmission process. In this case the Ezekiel material would presumably have given primary direction to the way in which the levites gave shape to the book as a whole. But theological consistency and continuity with the Ezekiel material is not to be expected.

Liwak carefully avoids a formalistic definition of Deuteronomism, but allows for a focus on content, which is served by form.[36] His analysis encompasses Ezek 2:2b-3:11; 5:4b-17; 6; 11:14-21; and 20, and leads him to the conclusion that "dtr Sprach- und Vorstellungsstrukturen auf einen Priesterkreis gewirkt haben, der sie interpretierend in den Kontext von Priestertradition (Ez, vermutlich auch H) einbaute."[37] It is specifically a Priestly circle that is the bearer of the Deuteronomistic tradition evidenced in the book of Ezekiel.

Liwak denies that literary dependency can be proved on the basis of a unified and constant vocabulary.[38] Deuteronomism, therefore, seems to be an ideological premise concerning a structured view of history that is expressed through a bundle of terms and expressions, which, by themselves, however, do not prove Deuteronomism. For example, disobedience can be expressed by reference to idolatry or failure to follow commandments. Thus,

> Dtr sind die Formulierungen erst, wenn sie in das dtr Schema eingeordnet sind. Paradigma für das Ezechielbuch ist das Begriffspaar ḥqwt wmšptym, das in Kap 18 den dtr Vorstellungszusammenhang vermissen lässt, der aber in Kap 20 (und in der dtr Interpretation in Kap 5) existiert.[39]

Liwak isolates the following topoi as central to the Deuteronomistic interpretation in the book of Ezekiel. First, the entire history of the people is given the verdict of "disobedient" (2:3; 20:5ff.; cf. 5:5ff). That spans from the "fathers" to "this day" (2:3), from the Exodus to the present (chap.

---

[35]Liwak (ibid., 40) writes: "Damit scheint zugleich angedeutet, was aus einem breit gestreuten Kommunikationsvorgang notwendig resultiert: die Pluralität der Ausdrucksformen und -inhalte, die nicht notwendig mit einer Mehrzahl von Autoren bzw. Trägernkreisen korrespondieren muss."

[36]Ibid., 41.

[37]Ibid., 194.

[38]Liwak (ibid., 207) writes: "Gebunden waren sie an einen vorgegebenen, auf die pauschale Skizzierung der Volksgeschichte abzielenden Vorstellungsrahmen, in dem sie sich mit entsprechend pauschalen Formulierungen bewegen konnten, die vorzugsweise nur diesen Texten innewohnen."

[39]Ibid., 327, n. 14.

20). Second, the retrospective historical analysis is schematized into three phases (20:5-9, 10-17, 18-26). Third, the disobedience is characterized primarily as rebellion and apostasy (2:3).[40] Fourth, the judging actions of Yahweh are experienced because of the people's disobedience through pestilence, sword, hunger, and exile (5:12). Fifth, those who escape the devastation depicted in chaps. 5 and 6 will ultimately acknowledge (*zākar*) their complicity in the evil of the past and hence also the justification of Yahweh's action (6:8-10). That recognition is the prerequisite for Yahweh's restorative action in 11:15ff. and 20:39ff. Yet it is for the sake of his name that Yahweh acts (20:44). The Deuteronomistic historical portrait is expressed most concretely by the concept of the "heart." According to Liwak the "hard heart" symbolizes the disobedience (3:7), the broken heart (6:9) the reflective phase, and the "other heart" (11:19) a phase of obedience.[41]

As helpful as it is to isolate Priestly and Deuteronomistic tendencies and affinities in Ezekiel, Ezekiel continues to be viewed as a product of tradition rather than as a shaper of it. What follows is a suggestion that Ezekiel could profitably be understood as an independent synthesizer and shaper of tradition.

EZEKIELIAN SYNTHESIS OF TRADITION

Almost all traditio-historical work on Ezekiel assumes a kind of discontinuity between Ezekiel the prophet and the circles responsible for the preservation and transmission process. According to many, the changed situation of a later time calls for an interpretation of the prophetic tradition. That interpretive process inevitably alters the original fund of prophetic material. That much is a given, having accepted the assumptions inherent in affirming a transmission process. To determine, however, that certain formulations and content could not belong to Ezekiel, or are foreign to Ezekiel's thought, is to fall into the formalistic trap. Without arguing for authorship by the prophet himself, it ought to be possible to allow the book of Ezekiel to determine the parameters of the Ezekiel tradition. In that way the adjective "Ezekielian" would designate not genetic but descriptive factors. That would allow the Ezekiel tradition to be fluid and dynamic without being either literarily dependent on other tradition complexes (D, H, P, Jer), nor completely independent of them. It would also allow the Ezekiel tradition to offer its own statement on the events of 597/587 B.C.E.

---

[40]Among other expressions are "to be rebellious" (2:5; 5:6; 20:8, 13, 21), not to be willing to hear (3:7), disobedience of commandments (5:6, 7; 20:13, 21), and idolatry (6:3ff., 9; 20:8). Only child sacrifice is mentioned as a specific offense (20:26, 31).

[41]"Überlieferungsgeschichtliche Probleme," 210.

and its own prospects for recovery after that. It is my intent, therefore, to suggest a reading of the Ezekiel tradition that moves within ancient Israelite traditions, yet offers a significant and independent program.

Several scholars have offered suggestions about how the Ezekiel tradition moves among the various traditional options in exilic Israel to chart an independent course.

Zimmerli dismissed the Deuteronomistic connection by noting how many of the central Deuteronomistic theological motifs are absent in Ezekiel. For example, we find in Ezekiel no reference to the love of/for Yahweh, or to the fear of God. The term *miṣwâ* is not in Ezekiel, and *tôrâ* is not used for "law" in general. Ezekiel articulates no explicit covenant theology with the patriarchal and Horeb covenants. The term *bāhar* occurs only in Ezek 20:5; *šākaḥ* only in 22:12 and 23:35; and *zākar* only in 6:9.[42]

The similarities between Ezekiel and H are predominantly with Leviticus 17, 18, 20, and 26, and slight with Leviticus 21-25. Concerning Leviticus 26 Zimmerli discovers "a confused and many-sided picture, which in any case forbids a hasty formula for the mutual relationship of H and Ezekiel."[43]   And after pointing out the similarities and differences between Leviticus and Ezekiel, he suggests that "the circles which must have given to H its (pre-P Document) form must not be sought too far from the circles which transmitted the book of Ezekiel."[44]   But Zimmerli observes that in spite of the linguistic connection we ought to note Ezekiel's lack of P's theological outline: "creation (with man made in God's image, and a sabbath instituted at creation), the fixed systematizing of a covenant theology, whereby the tradition of a covenant at Sinai is eliminated in a revolutionary way, find no echo in Ezekiel." All Zimmerli chooses to say is that "P drew from the great stream of priestly tradition, from which also the priest-prophet Ezekiel (at an earlier point of time) had also been nourished."[45]

J. S. Park's traditio-historical study of the judgment speeches in Ezekiel comes to the conclusion that Ezekiel incorporated and synthesized Priestly and Deuteronomic traditions.[46]   Park analyses five traditional ele-

---

[42]*Ezekiel 1*, 46. Similarly W. Eichrodt (*Ezekiel: A Commentary* [OTL; Philadelphia, PA: Westminster, 1970] 144), in discussing 11:15, argues that Ezekiel differs from the theology of Deuteronomy: "The way in which he delivers Israel to out and out damnation, and can no longer see in her anything good or pleasing to God, so that she cannot even begin to exist again except by some incomprehensible new act of grace on the part of Yahweh, is quite alien to that theology."

[43]*Ezekiel 1*, 51.

[44]Ibid., 52.

[45]Ibid.

[46]"Theological Traditions of Israel in the Prophetic Judgment of Ezekiel" (Ph.D. diss., Princeton Theological Seminary, 1979). Zimmerli hinted at that in his article "Knowledge of God according to the Book of Ezekiel" (*I am Yahweh* [Atlanta: John Knox, 1982], 146, n. 30),

ments in the prophetic accusations: breaking of covenant law, rebellion of Israel, profanation of the holy, cultic apostasy, and bloodshed. In the announcements of judgment he considers seven elements: the wrath and jealousy of Yahweh, the exile, famine and wild beasts, languishment, the face of Yahweh against Judah, judgment of Israel as an adulterous wife, and judgment on the idolatrous city, Jerusalem.

Park concludes that the similarities between Ezekiel and P "originate from Ezekiel's familiarity with the speech forms, vocabulary, and theological outlook of the Priestly tradition of the Jerusalem Temple." Similarities between Ezekiel and Deuteronomic theology are expressed in the condemnation of idolatry. The common ground for the two traditions is their common concern for centralized worship in the Jerusalem temple. Ezekiel attempted to articulate a message derived from a synthesis of those traditions. The conditional Sinai Covenant theology of Deuteronomy and the "everlasting covenant" theology of the Priestly tradition are bound together in Ezekiel.[47]

That synthesis has given rise to the problem of tradition-historical investigation in Ezekiel. Either the synthesis is ascribed to the deliberate working of Ezekiel or the Ezekiel tradition, or the synthesis is ascribed to the artificial overlaying of redactional layers by traditionists who sought to modify or even to correct Ezekiel.[48]

In its present form, however, the book of Ezekiel exhibits a unique blending of interests. As Park notes concerning the judgment speeches,

> while Ezekiel delivered judgment speeches relentlessly from the standpoint of the conditional covenant theology, at the same time he believed with Priestly theology that, in the final analysis, Yahweh's relationship with his people was not bound by the limitations and contingencies of Israel's obedience or disobedience.[49]

I would suggest, however, that the synthesis in the book of Ezekiel is not as clearly stereotyped as that. The Deuteronomistic theology is not simply

---

where he writes: "the assumption of a direct dependence of Ezekiel on the Priestly writing inadmissibly oversimplifies the problem of tradition. . . . The real tradition-critical problem as regards the Prophecy of Ezekiel and the circle following him is the combination of priestly and prophetic influence."

[47]Ibid., 201-202.

[48]Recent redaction-critical perspectives tend to highlight discontinuity between the prophet and the book of Ezekiel. So, e.g., H. Schulz, *Das Todesrecht im Alten Testament: Studien zur Rechtsform der Mot-Jumat-Sätze* (BZAW 114; Berlin: Töpelmann, 1969); J. Garscha, *Studien zum Ezechielbuch: eine redaktionskritische Untersuchung von Ez 1-39* (Europäische Hochschulschriften 23; Bern: Herbert Lang; Frankfurt: Peter Lang, 1974).

[49]"Theological Traditions," 203.

a theology of "law" and obligation, nor is the priestly theology simply a theology of grace. Ezekiel offers a synthesis, rooted in a theology of "Yahweh in community." To address the questions of tradition from the dichotomy of law and gospel, from which I think much analysis of Ezekiel derives its impetus, is to fail to read Israelite traditions from within.

As Carley notes, "both Ezekiel and Deuteronomy, as well as the Holiness Code, regarded Yahweh's statutes and judgments as standards by which all aspects of Israelite life were to be regulated."[50] Still, questions remain. Are there nuances that would enable us to distinguish between Ezekiel and the two law codes? And does Ezekiel articulate a distinctive view of the function of statutes and ordinances in the exilic community?

Wilson thinks that Ezekiel was probably influenced by the Deuteronomic movement before the exile, which in part explains the Deuteronomisms in the book. Ezekiel's message, however, does not reflect a total commitment to Deuteronomic theology. Instead, Ezekiel sought to integrate the Deuteronomistic tradition into his own material. As Wilson puts it, Ezekiel represents a "personal synthesis of Zadokite and Deuteronomistic positions."[51] In several matters Ezekiel integrates the two traditions, particularly in his theology of judgment (chaps. 6-7), his use of the adultery image (chaps 16 and 23), and punishment for past sins (chap. 20). "The theology has Deuteronomic features but is slanted toward Zadokite concerns, particularly the role of law." Wilson notes the curious Ezek 20:11-26 in which some of the laws are viewed as God's judgment for past sins.[52]

Wilson does not think that Ezekiel was a central prophet in the exilic community. "Rather, the evidence suggests that he was a peripheral prophet whose views were largely rejected by the orthodox Zadokite community." In support of that conclusion Wilson cites the occasions in the book of Ezekiel in which Ezekiel is opposed, the warnings that the prophet will not be heeded, and the emphasis on the call and the Spirit as enhancers of the prophet's authority. The prophet's support group was probably composed of "fellow Zadokites who had also been influenced by the Deuteronomic reforms."[53]

The question arises, however, as to whether he did in fact "synthesize" or whether he sided with one over against the other. And could that synthesis have been selective or unilateral? Could Ezekiel be closer to P in

---

[50]*Ezekiel among the Prophets*, 57.

[51]*Prophecy and Society*, 284.

[52]Ibid., 284. This will be explored in Chapter 6, which treats the function of law in Ezekiel.

[53]*Prophecy and Society*, 285. Wilson notes the "righteous men" in 23:45 as a likely allusion to such a group.

some matters, and on others closer to D?[54] If any of that can be argued
one way or another, then there may be no need to posit complex redactional
differences based on linguistic or ideological criteria. But that investigation
lies beyond the scope of this work.

What can then be said about Ezekiel's relationship to both theological
traditions in the light of recent work on P? Linguistic similarities do not
determine literary dependency. In this regard the comments of A. Hurvitz
are instructive. They apply both to the relationship of Ezekiel to P (which
Hurvitz discusses extensively), and to D. Hurvitz suggested:

> (1) that the *Priestly activity* in the biblical period extended over many
> centuries and expressed itself—in different generations—in different forms and
> in various measures;

> (2) that the *Priestly texts* in biblical literature are not of a monolithic nature,
> but rather reflect changes—and even contradictions—which result from histo-
> rical developments;

> (3) that the *Priestly phraseology* in BH [Biblical Hebrew] was not static, but
> that it always reflects various modifications occurring in the realm of the cult
> during the biblical period. Similarly, in spite of inherent esoteric peculiarities,
> it was not totally cut off from developments which took place in the main
> stream of BH. The dynamic character of the Priestly language is demon-
> strated above all by its two rival tendencies to preserve archaisms on the one
> hand and to adopt neologisms on the other.[55]

Clements also offers a helpful corrective that applies to Ezekiel's
relationship to both the Priestly and the Deuteronomistic traditions.[56]
Although he focuses on the Priestly tradition, it is clear that both traditions
are concerned with the Jerusalem cult tradition. That common reference
point with its focus on the temple and Zion is the matrix within which both
theological traditions can be synthesized in the book of Ezekiel.

More specifically, Clements suggests that "the measure of theological
and literary connection that can be shown to exist between them [Ezekiel
and P] is not such as to suggest any immediate community of authorship."

---

[54]For terminology from P that seldom occurs elsewhere but in Ezekiel see Driver
(*Introduction*, 146-47) for a partial list of expressions. This demonstrates that Ezekiel at least
is a product of a common school or tradition. On the divergences between Ezekiel and P see
Y. Kaufmann, *The Religion of Israel: From its Beginnings to the Babylonian Exile* (New York:
Schocken, 1960) 429, 434-35. Perhaps Kaufmann's (433) general statement that Ezekiel is
"rooted in Torah literature" is most appropriate.

[55]*The Priestly Source and the Book of Ezekiel*, 21.

[56]"The Ezekiel Tradition."

Instead, the common outlook and interest of the two ought to be understood as a sharing of a commitment to the Jerusalem cult tradition.[57] What we find in the book of Ezekiel is the integration of Ezekiel's oracles (the *traditio*) with the situation of those who were attempting to revitalize and reconstitute the Jerusalem Temple and its cultus. Clements finds continuity, therefore, between the two, especially in the fact that the Ezekiel tradition has been shaped in one specific direction.[58]

TRADITION, ETHICS, AND SOCIAL CHANGE

Working Hypothesis 1

Ezekiel 18 and the legal tradition in the book of Ezekiel belong to the Ezekiel Reconstruction Program and must be dated no later than 516 B.C.E.[59] Clements thinks that the Ezekiel tradition may have been developed during the period before the completion of the temple, perhaps as early as 538 B.C. (between 571 and 538 B.C.E.).[60] That suits the theological and ethical elements that integrate land, king/prince, temple, and new community organized around the vision of a repentant community that is obedient to the ordinances of Yahweh.

It has become impossible to make generalizations about the authorial relationship of the community responsible for the book of Ezekiel and that of the Holiness Code. In spite of the efforts of some to define that relationship, very little can be said besides this: "What is very clear is that there is an undoubted relationship between Ezekiel and H, but this is not

---

[57]Ibid., 128.

[58]Ibid., 129.

[59]This approach may not be able to account for the complexity of the compositional history of the Book of Ezekiel. But it does allow investigation of the larger document without being weighed down by the old question of determining inauthentic matter from authentic prophetic proclamation. M. Greenberg's recent article ("What are Valid Criteria for Determining Inauthentic Matter in Ezekiel?" *Ezekiel and His Book: Textual and Literary Criticism and their Interrelation* [ed. J. Lust. Leuven: Leuven University Press/Peeters, 1986] 123-35) sets out some of the difficulties in that process. Recent research on Ezekiel displays radically divergent positions on the question of redaction-history. See, e.g., Thomas Krüger (*Geschichtskonzepte im Ezekielbuch* [BZAW 180; Berlin/New York: de Gruyter, 1989]), who places Ezekiel 18 within the orbit of Ezekiel's own work. By contrast, J. Garscha (*Studien zum Ezechielbuch*) places the chapter several hundred years later than Ezekiel. I shall argue in various ways throughout the dissertation, although not always explicitly, that Ezekiel 18 ought to be read in the light of its function in the early exilic period.

[60]"The Ezekiel Tradition," 131-32.

one that can be reduced to any one simple formula."[61] Clements rejects the simplistic conclusions that Ezekiel was the author of H, or that H is later than Ezekiel across the board. "What we have in the two literary works . . . are compositions that have undoubtedly exercised a mutual influence on each other."[62]

The correspondences between the two literary traditions can be ascribed to the theological and historical situation of the Babylonian exiles, and with those who returned to Judah after 538 B.C.E.[63] According to Clements, "what we have is a form of literary commentary and adaptation of Ezekiel's prophecies particularly directed towards the hope of restoring the Jerusalem cultus."[64] For Clements it is possible to say that "virtually all the substantive material in the book belongs to the sixth century B.C." The canonical shaping of the book, therefore, has made it into a "charter" for that reconstruction.[65]

It is that commentary function of the book of Ezekiel that makes Ezekiel the quoter par excellence in the Hebrew Bible. The Ezekiel tradition is a prime example of inner-biblical exegesis. The discussion of three moral concerns in Part II below will show how Ezekiel participates in Israel's theological traditions, yet stands independently of them as a separate program for reconstitution of the community of faith.

Working Hypothesis 2

This working hypothesis functions in the dissertation more as a leading question than as an assumption. Could it be that the Ezekiel tradition functions as an interpretive corrective within Israel's *tôrâ* traditions by offering an alternative that addresses the current crisis?

The attempt to articulate the identity and aims of the Ezekiel tradents leads Clements to a further concern, the relationship between the Holiness Code and the book of Deuteronomy. Citing Alfred Cholewinski's analysis of that relationship positively, Clements suggests that "the Holiness Code

---

[61]Ibid., 130.

[62]Ibid., 130. In contrast R. Friedman (*The Exile and Biblical Narrative: The Formation of the Deuteronomistic and Priestly Works* [HSM 22; Chico, CA: Scholars Press, 1981] 63) states that "Ezekiel and P are not merely drawing on a common bank of vocabulary. One depends directly on the other." He comes to that conclusion from a comparison of common vocabulary and phraseology. Friedman (61) suggests that the Priestly idealization of the tabernacle is not a creation of the community after the destruction of the first temple, nor is it a program for a restored Second Temple.

[63]Clements, "The Ezekiel Tradition," 126.

[64]Ibid., 132.

[65]Ibid., 133.

can be seen to offer some kind of 'corrective' and reworking of cultic rulings and practices that are dealt with in the Book of Deuteronomy.[66] More specifically, Clements argues that

> the tensions and conflicts between the D-School and the P-School, if we may broadly describe these movements, would appear to have been a central and prominent framework of theological and religious reasoning which moulded the life of the post-exilic community in Jerusalem. The ultimate outcome would seem to have represented some form of compromise between the two.[67]

Further to that, Friedman suggests "that the priestly houses of Judah were each engaged in the composition of Torah literature and that the writings of each received a less-than-cordial welcome from the other."[68] Following the views of F. M. Cross, Friedman suggests that Dtr1 and P may derive from the two Priestly houses, the Mushite and Aaronid. These Priestly groups promulgated alternative *tôrôt* between the time of Josiah and the Exile.[69] Friedman understands the reference to *tôrâ* in Jer 8:8 as an attack on "other, vain Torah" promulgated by an alternative group.[70] Could Ezekiel be party to that tension? It may well be that Ezekiel finds commonality with the Priestly tradition as it seeks to define itself over against the Deuteronomistic School. According to Friedman, just as

---

[66]Ibid., 132. See A. Cholewinski, *Heiligkeitsgesetz und Deuteronomium: Eine vergleichende Studie* (AnBib 66; Rome: Biblical Institute Press, 1976). The synthesis of tradition in Ezekiel 18 seems to offer similar reworkings, but in the other direction. Ezekiel 18 seems to "correct" the retribution doctrine of the Priestly tradition. See Park, "Theological Traditions," 166-76.

[67]"The Chronology of Redaction in Ez 1-24," *Ezekiel and His Book: Textual and Literary Criticism and their Interrelation* (ed. J. Lust; Leuven: Leuven University Press /Peeters, 1986) 285.

[68]*The Exile and Biblical Narrative*, 75. I suggest that "less-than-cordial" may be saying more than we can know.

[69]See Cross, "The Priestly Houses of Early Israel," *Canaanite Myth and Hebrew Epic: Essays in the History and the Religion of Israel* (Cambridge, MA: Harvard University Press, 1973) 195-215. For discussion of the problem in Ezekiel see J. Levenson, *The Theology of the Program of Restoration of Ezekiel 40-48* (HSM 10; Missoula: Scholars Press, 1976) 129-51; and J. G. McConville, "Priests and Levites in Ezekiel: A Crux in the Interpretation of Israel's History," *TynBul* 34 [1983] 3-31). Although Levenson allows for Zadokite polemic in Ezekiel more than does McConville, both suggest that the tension between priests (Zadokites) and levites cannot be explained solely in terms of social history, that is, as a power struggle between priestly families.

[70]Friedman finds other Jeremiah texts that critique the Priestly tradition (Jer 4:19-27; 3:16-17; 7:22-23). On 7:22-23 see M. Weinfeld ("Jeremiah and the Spiritual Metamorphosis of Israel," *ZAW* 88 [1976] 52-55) who states that this text is "a slap in the face for the Priestly Code." See also Friedman, *The Exile and Biblical Narrative*, 74-75, n. 74.

"Jeremiah attacks those who ignore the Deuteronomic Torah, Ezekiel attacks priests who have done violence to the Priestly Torah and have ignored its precepts."[71]   That tension is evident in Ezek 22:26, where priests are accused of failing to distinguish between the holy and the profane (cf. Lev 10:10).[72] But Ezekiel is not bound to the Priestly tradition since we also find correspondences with the Deuteronomistic School.[73] Thus, Jeremiah and Ezekiel represent, at least in the books that bear their names, independent and alternative appeals to Israel's ancient traditions that may have been rooted in the claims of priestly houses.

If that is correct, then Ezekiel's ethics will not simply be an extension of a particular theological core tradition, but an envisioning of a new future with a view to changed social conditions and reconstructive social programs. It is my intent in what follows to show how Ezekiel's ethical concerns reflect a program for the reconstitution of peoplehood. Ezekiel's program may well be rooted in the Aaronid priesthood, but it differs significantly enough to illustrate that Ezekiel represents an independent voice in the midst of competing claims between 597 and 516.

---

[71]*The Exile and Biblical Narrative*, 75.

[72]Ibid., 75. Friedman recognizes that "both Jeremiah and Ezekiel attack priests, prophets, kings and the nation for violating fundamental commands." Ezekiel refers explicitly to Torah in 7:26; 22:26 (cf. also 43:11; 44:5, 23).

[73]Herrmann (*Die prophetische Heilserwartungen*) ascribes many of the hope oracles in Ezekiel to a Deuteronomistic redaction. Clements ("Chronology," 285) comments that Herrmann's view may be an overstatement, since the hope oracles with their distinctive vocabulary may represent a common stock of "the late exilic, and early post-exilic, periods on the part of a small community to formulate the essential agenda for Israel's future restoration."

3

FORM-CRITICAL ANALYSIS OF EZEKIEL 18

INTRODUCTION TO THE EXEGESIS

This chapter and the next explore the text of Ezekiel 18 and provide the foundation for discussions in Chapters 5, 6, and 7 of the dissertation. Through analysis of the structure, the genre and the traditional conventions, Chapters 3 and 4 seek to articulate the compositional conventions of Ezekiel 18. The exegesis shall serve as a guide for discussion of moral discourse and ethical convictions in Ezekiel 18 and the Book of Ezekiel.

TRANSLATION AND TEXTUAL COMMENTARY

1   The word of Yahweh came to me:

2   What is the matter with you[1] who recite this proverb concerning the land of Israel:[2]
"The fathers eat[3] unripe grapes,
and the children's teeth grate"?[4]

---

[1]The *lākem 'attem* here is not redundant, but reflects an emphatic use of the pronoun *'attem* (*GKC*, #135g). As Greenberg (*Ezekiel 1-20*, 327) suggests, it conveys the idea: "You of all people!"

[2]Some suggest that the line reflects a proverb recited in the land of Israel (so Zimmerli, *Ezekiel 1*, 377-78). The LXX seems to have translated freely: "Among the sons of Israel." The preposition *'al* can be understood rather as "concerning," specifying what happened to the land of Israel (R. J. Williams, *Hebrew Syntax* [2nd ed.; Toronto/Buffalo/London: University of Toronto, 1976] #289).

[3]The present tense is to be preferred in a proverbial saying (*GKC* #107g; Williams, *Syntax*, #168). Although Brownlee's (*Word Biblical Commentary. Volume 28. Ezekiel 1-19* [Waco, TX: Word, 1986] 279) conditional "If fathers eat" is possible (following GKC #159b), it is not necessary.

[4]The verb *qhh* occurs only here, in Jer 31:29-30, and in Eccl 10:10. In the latter the reference is clearly to a dull instrument of iron. Brownlee's suggestion (*Ezekiel 1-19*, 277) of "grate" is in keeping with the acidic effect of sour or unripe fruit.

3   As I live! (an oracle of Yahweh the Lord)
     You shall not cite[5] this proverb in Israel[6] again.

4   Here is why:[7]
     All persons[8] are mine, the father as well as the child.
     It is the sinner who will die.

5   Now if a man is righteous, and does what is just and right—

6   He does not eat on the mountains[9]
     nor lift up his eyes to the idols of the house of Israel,
     nor defile his neighbor's wife,
     nor approach a menstruous wife[10] for sexual relations.
7   He wrongs no one,
     he gives back his debt-pledge,[11]
     he does not practice robbery,
     he gives his food to the hungry,
     and provides clothing for the naked.

---

[5]The syntax here is difficult: *'im yihyeh lākem 'ôd mĕšōl*. The *'im* expresses a negative after the oath formula (Williams, *Syntax*, #456). The infinitive construct *mĕšōl* does not need to be repointed as a participle (Zimmerli, *Ezekiel 1*, 370), since it acts as a gerundive following the verb "to be": "This proverb will not be cited by you again" (Williams, *Syntax*, #196). The *lākem* refers therefore to the agent of the action (Williams, ibid., # 280), even though the verb is not strictly passive.

[6]Here the preposition *b* with Israel stands for Ezekiel's common "house of Israel," which refers to the entire community affected by the catastrophe.

[7]*hēn* introduces the argument against using the proverb.

[8]There is no adequate way to translate *nepeš*, as Zimmerli (*Ezekiel 1*, 370) points out. Zimmerli (ibid.), Greenberg (*Ezekiel 1-20*), and Brownlee (*Ezekiel 1-19*) consistently insert "person" wherever *nepeš* occurs in this verse. The initial *kol-nĕpāšôt lî* adequately presents the case that all *persons* are Yahweh's concern. The threefold repetition of *nepeš* in the rest of the verse emphasizes that fact. The repetition of "person" in each instance, however, violates the meaning of the Hebrew expression.

[9]Some commentators have suggested that "eating on the mountains" (*'el hehārîm*) is a corruption of "eating with the blood" (*'al haddām*). That is not necessary here because the expression is part of Ezekiel's prophetic polemic against cultic abuses. See the more detailed discussion in Chapter 6.

[10]Brownlee (*Ezekiel 1-19*, 279) notes that the imperfect *yiqrāb* implies an ongoing relationship, hence the translation "wife."

[11]18:12 reads *hăbōl lō' yāšîb*; and 18:16 *hăbōl lō' hābāl*. There is a difficulty with the word *hôb* in 18:7. Greenberg (*Ezekiel 1-20*, 329) thinks *hôb* is Aramaic "debt," replacing an older word *nsy* (2 Kgs 4:7). We find a *hapax legomenon* in *hăbōlâ*, a feminine form of *hăbōl* just as we find the parallel of *gēzel* and *gĕzēlâ* in 18:7 and 18. Greenberg emends to *habōlat hôbô* = "pledge of his debt."

8   He does not lend at interest,
     or collect with excessive increase;[12]
     He keeps himself from injustice,[13]
     and practices authentic justice in community.[14]

9   He lives[15] according to my statutes
     and keeps my ordinances by doing them;[16]
     He is righteous, he shall surely live.
                              (An Oracle of Yahweh, the Lord)

10   Now should he have a violent son—a murderer—
     and he commits any of these acts[17]

11   (now his father had not done these things)[18]—

     Instead he eats on the mountains,
     and defiles his neighbor's wife;

12   He oppresses the poor and the needy,
     practices robbery,[19]
     does not give back the debt-pledge,

---

[12]See the discussion of *nešek* and *tarbît* in Chapter 6.

[13]Literally: Keeps his hand from iniquity.

[14]Rendering *bēn 'îš lĕ'îš* as reflecting an orientation toward the community. On the use of *ben* with the preposition *lē* see *GKC*, #102h and the similar construction in 2 Kgs 10:21.

[15]Zimmerli (*Ezekiel 1*, 370-71) emends, on the basis of a possible dittography of the previous *y*, to a perfect *hālak*, which parallels the following *šāmar* and the *hālak* in v 17. Greenberg (*Ezekiel 1-19*, 330) suggests, however, that the imperfect reflects other "formal variations [that] mitigate the repetitiousness of this oracle."

[16]The LXX *auta* suggests that *'emet* was read as *'ōtām*, which is likely original since v 19 has *'otam*. Greenberg (*Ezekiel 1-20*, 330) suggests that *'emet* reflects a faulty repetition from v 8.

[17]The line is awkward: *wĕ'āśâ 'āḥ mē'aḥad mē'ēlleh*. The two *min* prepositions reflect a privative and a partitive use respectively (Williams, *Syntax*, #321, #324). The *'āḥ* poses the difficulty. Greenberg (*Ezekiel 1-20*, 331) suggests that it represents an uncorrected start of *mē'aḥad*. For a summary of commentators' opinion and a unique but unlikely solution to the problem see Israel W. Slotki, "Ezek. 18:10," *AJSL* 43 (1926/27) 63-66.

[18]This line seems to be an awkward repetition of the previous one. Zimmerli (*Ezekiel 1*, 371) thinks it is an addition, and that the *hû'* refers to the father. Greenberg (*Ezekiel 1-20*, 331) suggests that the two lines "arose as alternative solutions to the puzzle of how to negate a list containing both positive and negative statements." Brownlee (*Ezekiel 1-19*, 280) suggests that the first line reflects sins of commission and the second sins of omission. I have translated the line as an aside that contrasts the actions of the father, which is supported in part by the contrastive *kî gam* at the beginning of v 11b.

[19]Zimmerli (*Ezekiel 1*, 371) points out that *gĕzēlôt* does not occur elsewhere in the Hebrew Bible, and deviates from the normal form *gĕzēlâ* found in 18:7, 16; 33:15.

lifts his eyes to the idols,
commits abominable deeds,
13   lends at interest
and collects with excessive increase—

Shall he live?[20]

He shall not live.
He has committed all these abominable acts.
He shall certainly suffer death.[21]
He is responsible for his own death.[22]

14   Now, should he have a son who sees all the sins that his father has
committed, and having considered,[23] he does not do likewise—

15   He does not eat on the mountains,
does not lift up his eyes to the idols of the house of Israel,
does not defile his neighbor's wife,
16   does not wrong anyone,
does not take a pledge,[24]
does not commit robbery,
but gives his food to the hungry

---

[20]Zimmerli (ibid., 371) emends the *why* to *whw*, which makes this line correspond to v 28 with its infinitive absolute *hāyô*. The infinitive absolute occurs with the verb in the Hebrew Bible only in Ezek 3:21; 18:28; 33:15, 16; 2 Kgs 8:10, 14. Brownlee (*Ezekiel 1-19*, 280) suggests that the MT may simply reflect stylistic variation.

[21]The Hophal *yûmāt* here is unlike the other occurrences of the Qal verb in the chapter (vv 17, 20, 21, 24, 28). Note Zimmerli's (*Ezekiel 1*, 372) explanation of the MT as corresponding better with the following clause: "Since this formula [*dāmāw bô yihyeh*] turns away any guilt from the executioner in sentences carried out by men, the formulation [*yāmût*] cannot be presupposed here, which points to the divine carrying out of the punishment" (see also p. 384). See Lev 20:6-19, 27, where the passive form *yûmāt* always occurs with the bloodguilt formula. In Lev 20:17-21 the Qal form occurs, and there without the bloodguilt formula. I have translated the phrase passively, but without the connotation of actual capital punishment. I shall argue that Ezekiel uses the concept of death metaphorically referring both to the reality of exile and to the failure to be incorporated into the community of Yahweh.

[22]Here I translate dynamically the idiom "his blood shall be on himself."

[23]Although the LXX translates "to fear," from *yr'*, the double meaning of the verb *r'h* is more likely in the two occurrences here. Zimmerli (*Ezekiel 1*, 372) adduces the frequent use of the verb "to see" in Ezekiel, and the infrequent use of "to fear" as argument for keeping the MT reading.

[24]J. Milgrom (*Cult and Conscience: The Asham and the Priestly Doctrine of Repentance* [SJLA 18; Leiden: Brill, 1976] 95) states that because the noun is modified by its own verb, the property should not have been seized in the first place.

and provides clothing for the naked.
17   He keeps himself from injustice,[25]
       and does not take interest or excessive increase—

       He keeps my ordinances
       and lives according to my statutes.

       He shall not die for the iniquity of his father.
       He shall certainly live.

18   As for his father—because he practiced extortion, committed
       robbery,[26] and did what was not good among his people—he dies[27]
       for his own iniquity.

19   And you ask: Why should not the son bear the consequences of the
       father's guilt?

       The son has done what was just and right;
       He has observed all my statutes and kept them.
       He shall certainly live.

20   The person who sins shall die.

       A son shall not bear the consequences of a father's iniquity; nor shall
       a father bear the consequences of a son's iniquity. The righteous are
       responsible for the consequences of their own righteousness, and the
       wicked are responsible for the consequences of their own wickedness.

---

[25]The word *mē'onî* is a departure from the expected *mē'āwel*, which occurs in v 8. The LXX reflects the latter. The MT would mean to refrain from oppressing the afflicted. Given the recent mention of the *'onî*, perhaps v 17 is making a verbal connection with v 12. It is more likely that the MT v 17 reflects the combination of "poor, hungry, and naked" in Isa 58:7, and that the LXX reflects the earlier Hebrew text.

[26]The LXX does not reflect the word *'āḥ*, brother. Zimmerli (*Ezekiel 1*, 372) suggests that here, as in v 12, a scribal error has changed the ending of the noun *gēzēlâ*. Wevers (*Ezekiel* [NCB; London: Nelson, 1969; reprint ed. Grand Rapids, MI: Eerdmans; London: Marshall, Morgan & Scott, 1976] 111) thinks it was an error of hearing the wrong sounds in copying by dictation. But the reference to "his people" in the next clause may allow for the parallel "brother." The form *gezel* occurs elsewhere only in Eccl 5:7.

[27]The perfect here expressing certitude (Williams, *Syntax*, #165).

21   Now if the wicked one turns from the sins[28] that he has committed
     and observes all my statutes and does what is just and right, he shall
     certainly live. He shall not die.

22   All his rebellious actions will not be held against him. Because of his
     righteous actions he will live.

23   Do I really delight in the death of the wicked?
                         (An Oracle of Yahweh, the Lord)
     Would I not rather he turn from his ways and live?

24   But when a righteous person turns from his righteousness and does
     wrong—like all the abominable things that the wicked person has
     done—shall he behave like that and live?[29] None of his righteous
     actions[30] will stand in his favour. On account of his unfaithful and
     sinful behaviour[31] he will die.

25   Yet you say: The way of the Lord is arbitrary.[32]

     Hear now, O house of Israel: Is it my way that is not fair? Is it not
     that your ways are erratic?

---

[28]The MT has "his sins," which is redundant in English.

[29]According to Zimmerli (*Ezekiel 1*, 373) *yaʿāśeh wāḥay* breaks the flow of thought. It
is not reflected in the LXX, and therefore may be a gloss. But it may be like the question in
v 13. In that case it is best to understand *yaʿāśeh* in a modal sense, followed by the question
concerning life: "Can he behave [like this] and live?" (so Brownlee, *Ezekiel 1-19*, 279).
Eichrodt (*Ezekiel*, 234) notes the parallel with the previous case in vv 12-23, and translates:
"shall he do so and yet live?"

[30]The plural reading suggested by the *Qere* is supported by the plural verb.

[31]The nouns here are singular (*māʿal* and *ḥaṭṭāʾt*), which function as cognate accusatives.
I have translated them adverbially since the verbal action (translated as "behaviour") is stressed
by the syntax of verb and cognate noun.

[32]The translation of the verb *tkn* is a problem here. The verb is significant in the
disputation because it focuses the question of theodicy. Of what is it that Yahweh is being
accused? The verb in Qal and Piel forms means to measure (Prov 16:2; Isa 40:13). I have
chosen deliberately to translate the word (occurring five times in vv 25 and 29) in a variety of
ways in order to highlight the possible ambiguity of meaning. Outside of Ezekiel the niphal
verb occurs only in the Song of Hannah (1 Sam 2:3) where God is said to *tkn* actions. That
is parallel to the previous bicolon in which Yahweh is said to be a God of knowledge (*daʿat*).
The sense is that the Yahweh's actions are somehow not discernable, erratic, arbitrary, or
unjust. See Greenberg (*Ezekiel 1-20*, 333-34) and Brownlee (*Ezekiel 1-19*, 289-90) for further
discussion.

26   When a righteous person turns from his righteousness and does wrong, he dies on that account.[33] For the wrong that he does he shall die.

27   But when a wicked person turns from his wicked acts and does what is just and right, he preserves himself.
28   He considers and turns from his rebellious acts.
      He shall surely live; he shall not die.

29   But the house of Israel says: The way of the Lord is arbitrary.
      Are my ways not fair, O house of Israel? Is it not that your ways are erratic?

30   Therefore I will judge you, O house of Israel, each one on the basis of his actions.
                              (An Oracle of Yahweh, the Lord)
      Repent and turn away from all your rebellious acts, so that iniquity will not become your downfall.
31   Get rid of all your rebellious acts[34] and fashion for yourselves a new heart and a new spirit. Why should you die, O house of Israel?

32   For I do not delight in anyone's death.
                              (An Oracle of Yahweh, the Lord)
      So turn, and live.[35]

STRUCTURE

Introduction

Ezekiel 18 appears to move logically toward a designed conclusion, yet it bears marks of inner contradiction. I shall explore the structural elements of the text in order to clarify four facets: the extent of the basic

---

[33]The word *'ălêhem* (for them) is not reflected in the LXX and Syriac translations. Since the syntax is not awkward (the pronominal suffix referring to the previously mentioned acts), it is best to allow the word to stand.

[34]The preposition with the pronominal suffix completes the relative word *'ăšer* ("by which") and need not be omitted (even thought the LXX reflects a first person singular pronominal suffix "against me"). The plural antecedent of the pronoun is the rebellious acts.

[35]The LXX omits this line. Wevers (*Ezekiel*, 112) suggests that this may have been a marginal note that was added as a summarizing gloss. The fact that it occurs after the oracular formula cannot add support to that view, since the formula also occurs in vv 3 and 23 in the middle of a divine saying to emphasize the authority of the saying.

unit, the literary structure of its parts, the logical structure of the parts, and the compositional structure of the whole.[36]

Extent of the Basic Unit

The basic unit of the text is established by the introductory reception formula (*Wortereignisformel*) in v 1. Here, however, the formula occurs without the customary messenger formula.[37] The unit closes with the introductory *lākēn* in v 30, and a summary conclusion at the end of v 32. Two questions remain that will be considered in the following discussion. Does the conclusion provide an adequate or fitting closure to the matters presented in the introductory verses? And is internal consistency maintained throughout the chapter?

In summary, the basic unit is defined by clear introductory and concluding formulae. I shall argue below that the material within the chapter is unified by common formal, linguistic, and thematic features.

Literary Structure

The literary structure of chapter 18 is complex, either because the text is composed of disjointed smaller units that do not cohere well, or because the argument of the whole operates on several levels.[38] As Greenberg notes, "a feature of this oracle is the interweaving of its parts with an absence of clear formal boundaries."[39]

Formal boundaries are, nevertheless, discernible. After the initial reception formula in v 1, divine speech continues throughout the chapter, broken by five occurrences of the formula *nĕ'um 'ădōnāy yhwh* (vv 3, 9, 23, 30, 32). That formula is not used primarily to indicate a structural break in the text, but to emphasize a divine statement. The initial divine declaration in vv 2-3 is followed by a summary statement introduced by *hēn*, "behold." That summary statement is then developed by means of three case studies, vv 5-9, 10-13, and 14-18. Vv 5, 7, and 16 begin with

---

[36]This four-fold schema is from Perry Yoder, *From Word to Life: A Guide to the Art of Bible Study* (Scottdale, PA: Herald, 1982) 55-79.

[37]On the messenger formula see R. Rendtorff, "Botenformel und Botenspruch," *ZAW* 74 (1962) 165-77.

[38]For example, within the chapter a transition divides the text into two distinguishable parts, vv 1-20 and 21-32. The change is subtle, not marked by formal criteria, but by a change in content. In addition, repetition has led some commentators to argue that the chapter is an expanded unit.

[39]*Ezekiel 1-20*, 335.

wĕ'îš, but only the first of those introduces a smaller textual unit.[40] V 10 begins with a disjunctive *waw*, and v 14 with a disjunctive *waw* followed by *hinnēh*.

Numerous repetitions and correspondences within the chapter serve to integrate the various sub-units. The correspondences are of three basic types: lexical, grammatical, and rhetorical.[41]

Several repetitions echo the initial citation of the *māšāl* of v 2. V 19 begins with *wa'āmartem* as does v 25. V 29 then picks up the verb *'mr*, but with the subject *bêt yiśrā'ēl*, "house of Israel," instead of the second person plural of vv 19 and 25. Although the plural form of address begins in v 2, it is not picked up again until v 19. Then, in v 25, after the repetition of the verb from v 19, the vocative "house of Israel" is introduced for the first time. Surprisingly, I think, that phrase is repeated four more times in vv 29-31, as the subject of the verb at the beginning of v 29, and then again as a vocative in vv 29, 30, and 31. The repetition of v 25 in v 29 has led some to posit that vv 26-29 are an addition.[42]

The repetition of motifs is also instructive. The motif of *derek* ("way") in vv 25 and 29 illustrates finally, and in a concrete way, the accusation embedded within the *māšāl* of v 2. So also the divine declaration of having no pleasure in anyone's death is first stated in v 23, and then again in v 32. Along with that declaration in v 23 is the wish that the individual "turn and live." The motif is repeated in v 30, and in v 32 in a shorter form. "Life" and "death" are also prominent motifs in the chapter, and are related to the important motifs of "the righteous" and "the wicked."

Correspondences with vv 30-32 suggest also that the section is integral to the chapter. V 30 begins with *lākēn*, which by assonance reflects the *yittākēn* of vv 25 and 29. The next word, *'îš*, picks up the *'îš* of v 5. And the third word, *dĕrākîm*, reflects the motif of "way" in vv 23, 25, and 29. The vocative *bêt yiśrā'ēl* repeats the vocative of vv 25 and 29. The plural address is consistent with the beginning of the chapter (vv 2-3). At least the first half of v 30 seems to bring the chapter to a conclusion, and bears the greatest number of linguistic similarities with vv 25-29. The question in v 31b and the motive statement in v 32a reiterate one of the major themes of the chapter, death. The statement in v 32a makes clear what was a

---

[40]Vv 7 and 16 both begin with the prohibition of oppression (*ynh*), which may indicate that the *wĕ'îš* belongs to the formulaic use rather than a pattern corresponding to the beginning of v 5.

[41]H. Van Dyke Parunak, "Structural Studies in Ezekiel" (Ph.D. diss., Harvard University, 1978). See also Greenberg (*Ezekiel 1-20*, 334-38) who makes a great deal out of this.

[42]E.g., Fohrer, *Hauptprobleme*. Rhetorical differences, however, suggest that the repetition may be deliberate. For example, v 29 changes the singular *hădarkî*, "my way," to *haddĕrākay*, "my ways."

rhetorical question in v 23. The phrase *šûbû wĕhāšîbû*, (RSV: "repent and turn") echoes the previous vv 21, 23, 24, 26, 27, and 28 (the exact construction is found only in Ezek 14:6). The verses, therefore, bear marked similarity to vv 21-29, and ought to be read as a unit with them. The similarities make those verses a literary unity in this setting, even though 33:10-20, which parallels in large measure 18:25-30a, does not include the call to repentance that we find in 18:30b-32.

We conclude that vv 30-32 cannot be isolated as formally distinct from the rest of the chapter, and especially not from vv 21-29. The exhortation belongs to the rhetorical unity of chapter 18. That does not resolve the matter of whether vv 21-32 are a second stage in the literary development of the chapter.

The internal literary structure of chap. 18 needs clarification, for the divisions between parts and the movement of the argument are not altogether clear. What follows is a brief summary of three approaches to the structure of the chapter.[43] This is necessary in order to illustrate the various ways the chapter has been perceived, and to illustrate the complexity of the chapter's organization.

According to most commentators, vv 5-18 present three vignettes in which we find the depiction of a righteous man (vv 5-9), his wicked son (vv 10-13), and a final righteous son of the third generation (vv 14-17). V 18 provides a retrospective, harking back to the second vignette. Each of the three cases is couched as a conditional, and the protasis of each "contains not only a general statement of the righteousness or sinfulness of the man involved (18:5, 10, 14), but a detailed list of morally significant actions which he either has or has not done."[44]

Correspondences among the three sketches are, according to Parunak, "illustrative of the principle of varied repetition." In the first sketch we notice that all the elements of the commended behaviour, except *'îš lō' yôneh* in v 7a, occur in pairs.[45]

---

[43]Greenberg, *Ezekiel 1-20*, 334-38; A. Schenker, "Saure Trauben ohne stumpfe Zähne: Bedeutung und Tragweite von Ez 18 und 33:10-20 oder ein Kapitel alttestamentlicher Moraltheologie," *Mélanges Dominique Barthélemy: etudes bibliques offertes à l'occasion de son 60e anniversaire* (ed. P. Casetti, O. Keel, and A. Schenker; OBO 38; Fribourg, Suisse: Editions Universitaires; Göttingen: Vandenhoeck & Ruprecht, 1981) 449-70; and Parunak, "Structural Studies."

[44]Parunak, "Structural Studies," 276.

[45]Parunak (ibid., 276) suggests: "Thus the first two refer to idol worship, the next two to laws of purity, the third to property rights, the fourth pair to laws of lending, the fifth in a general way to just dealings with other men, and the sixth and last pair to obedience to the Lord's statutes."

Within the three descriptions we find considerable lexical correspondence, as the following chart illustrates.[46]

Lexical Correspondence	vv 5-9	10-13	14-17
'ākāl 'el-hehārîm	1	1	1
nāśā' 'ênāyîm	2	6	2
timmeh 'iššâ	3	2	3
qārab 'el 'iššâ niddâ	4		
ynh	5	3	4
ḥôb	6	5	5
gzl	7	4	6
leḥem nātan lĕrā'ēb	8		7
'êrōm kissâ beged	9		8
nešek	10	8	10
lāqaḥ tarbît	11	9	11
hēšîb yād mēXXX	12		9
'āśâ mišpāṭ	13		
hālak bĕḥuqqôtay	14		13
šāmar mišpāṭay	15		12
tô'ēbâ 'āśâ		7	

Although v 18 is a shorter summary referring back to the second case, it, too, contains a list of actions that includes *'šq, gzl,* and *lō' tôb 'āśâ.*

The sentence of life or death in the apodosis appears in each of the four sections (vv 9b, 13b, 17b, 18b).

> The first sentence is given wholly in terms of life: *hāyōh yihyeh.* The second and third use both *hāyâ* and *môt* (affirmed or denied, as is appropriate). The fourth sentence is pronounced without even the denial of life, but simply affirming, *wĕhinnēh-mēt ba'ăwōnô.* This series is a good example of rotation of correspondences.[47]

Parunak's careful analysis of correspondences within vv 5-18 provides us with ample evidence that we are dealing with what he calls an "integral structure." That is to say that the text in its present configuration displays a good measure of literary integrity.

Within vv 19-32 we notice the correspondence between the beginnings of vv 19 and 25. In both cases the audience challenges what has just been said. Since the answer to the first audience response extends to v 20, the

---

[46]Ibid., 277. The chart indicates the order of the statements using vv 5-9 as the base point.
[47]Ibid., 279.

statement of v 25 challenges vv 21-24. The answer to the challenge of v 19 concludes the discussion about inter-generational transmission of guilt. The answer to the challenge of v 25 begins with a rhetorical question that turns the challenge back to the audience, and follows with a summary statement in vv 26-28 of the principle first illustrated in vv 21-24. V 29 repeats the challenge of v 25a, along with a slightly modified rhetorical question of v 25b. V 29 picks up the verbal root *'mr*, but now with the subject *bêt yiśrā'ēl*. Finally, another indicative follows in v 30a, indicating that each person will be judged according to his own conduct.[48]

Parunak notes that a division after v 30a is indicated by two facts.

First, the parallelism between 18:25 and 18:29 leads us to expect a parallel to 18:26-28 after 18:29. 18:30a is a reasonable parallel, viewed as an abstraction of 18:26-28. However, the imperatives of 18:30b, 31 do not correspond to anything in 18:26-29. Second, when this passage is used in 33:13-20, 18:30a, but not 18:30b, is associated with 18:25-29.[49]

The section 18:21-24 is a chiasm. The repetition and correspondences can be shown by the following chart.

A   a   18:21 The repentance of the wicked
     b   18:22 Assurance of forgiveness and promise of life
B   18:23 Yahweh's rhetorical question
A'   a'   18:24a Apostasy of the righteous
     b'   18:24b Past righteous deeds will be forgotten

Parunak notes that the centre of the chiasm is Yahweh's rhetorical question. We can add that the rhetorical question is repeated in the form of an indicative statement in 18:32, where it serves as the grounding for a call to repentance.

Parunak has established the overall literary integrity of 18:5-30a. The four separate units (18:5-18, 19-20, 21-24, and 25-30a) correspond to one another rhetorically and lexically. 18:19-20 and 25-30a correspond rhetorically in that both have a question and answer pattern, and lexically in that both begin with *wa'ămartem*. 18:5-18 and 21-24 correspond in the following way:

Both begin with an *casus pendens* construction. The clause in 18:21, *wĕhārāšā' kî yāšûb* is reminiscent of the similar construction at the head of

---

[48]Ibid., 280.
[49]Ibid., 280-81. We can add that the concluding formula *nĕ'um 'ădōnāy yhwh* at the end of 18:30a indicates a break in the text there, but that is not unusual in view of how the formula is used elsewhere in chap. 18. See textual commentary on v 30.

18:5-18, *wĕ'îš kî yihyeh*. Furthermore, 18:5-18 is the presentation of the teaching which is challenged in 18:19-20, that sons and fathers are not responsible for one another's sins. Similarly, 18:21-24 presents the doctrine of repentance and apostasy which is challenged in 18:25-30a, as is confirmed by the repetition of that doctrine in the Lord's answer to his challengers in 18:26-28.[50]

Parunak notes in passing that numerous lexical and grammatical correspondences between 18:21-24 and 25-30a function "to establish a sequential, and not a balanced, structure between them." He notes also that those more intricate correspondences are the building blocks of the larger structures, and they ought not be used to define types of structures. Parunak seems to be making a distinction between what we might call macro and micro structures or correspondences.[51]

Next Parunak turns to the first and last portions of the chapter, 18:1-4, and 30b-32. Those sections are connected to the first and last halves of the chapter, respectively. 18:1-4 ends with *hannepeš hahōtē't hî' tāmût*, which is repeated in 18:20. And the indicative statement in 18:32 repeats the content of Yahweh's rhetorical question in 18:23. Parunak thinks that we may find an intentional use of rhetorical question in the first and last paragraphs of the chapter. The rhetorical question brings beginning and end together and in each section serves

> to focus on the question under discussion. In probing the people's motive for citing the proverb of the grapes in 18:2, the writer introduces his denial of one theological interpretation of that proverb. And in pleading, "Why will ye die?" in 18:31b, he urges them to take advantage of the doctrine of repentance and to turn from their sin to the Lord.[52]

A. Schenker proposes that 18:5-28 is composed of four symmetric exemplifications (of unequal length) of the principle expressed in 18:4.[53] Those four exemplifications are divided into two opposing pairs, vv 5-23 and vv 24-28. He sets out the interrelationship as follows.

---

[50]Ibid., 282.
[51]Ibid., 282, n. 63.
[52]Ibid., 284.
[53]"Saure Trauben," 460-64.

A. The first opposing pair: Two Generations.

Case 1   Case 2
vv 5-13   vv 14-23

Father------------Son   Father--------------Son
righteous   unrighteous unrighteous   righteous
A   //   B   B   //   A

B. The second opposing pair: Past and Present of Individual

Case 3   Case 4
vv 24, 26   vv 27-28

First Phase---Second Phase   First Phase---Second Phase
righteous   unrighteous   unrighteous   righteous
A   //   B   B   //   A

In the first opposing pair, the correspondence lies in the father-son relationship. Two persons are depicted whose behaviour is characterized as diametrically opposite. In the second opposing pair, the symmetry lies in the exact opposition of the two cases. In 18:24, 26 the righteous one turns from righteousness, with the result that the past righteous deeds are forgotten. In 18:27-28, a wicked one turns from wickedness, with the result that past wickedness is no hindrance to receiving the gift of life. Thus, the two phases of a person's life are set over against one another.[54]

Schenker divides the chapter into two parts on the basis of the divine saying in vv 23 and 32. Those two verses present a summary of the divine will, and a call to repentance. V 23 is in the form of a rhetorical question, and v 32 recalls the question in terms of an indicative followed by an imperative. Several points stand in Schenker's favour. The break between vv 20 and 21 is blurred because v 20b clearly spans both halves of the chapter (i.e., if a break there is accepted). Against Schenker's break at v 23, however, we recognize that the principle of v 20b is elaborated not only in vv 21-22, but also in v 24 (a dual pattern that is repeated in vv 26-28). Moreover, the correspondences between vv 21-22 are stronger with v 24 than with anything before v 21. Rather, we ought to consider vv 26-28 as an inversion of the A/A' pattern at the two extremes of the chiasm in vv 21-24. Thus, we have the following correspondences:

---

[54]Ibid., 460-64. This analysis clearly focuses only on the content of the cases rather than on the actual rhetorical shape of the text, which would have to include the argument of vv 25 and 29, which draw the individual character of these two cases into the context of the "house of Israel."

```
A     a -- v 21
      b -- v 22
B       -- v 23
A'    a' -- v 24a
      b' -- v 24b
C       -- v 25
A'      -- v 26
A       -- v 27-28
C       -- v 29
D       -- v 30a
E       -- v 30b-31
B       -- v 32
```

M. Greenberg divides the chapter into two main parts, vv 1-20 and vv 21-32.[55] The revelation formula (v 1) and the citation of the proverb (v 2) are followed by a theoretical refutation of the proverb (vv 3-20). The second section (vv 21-32) carries on the thesis of the first, "that the past does not determine the evaluation of the present," but extends the application from the relationship between generations to the life of the individual. The two sections are bound together by the conclusion of the chapter, vv 30-32, beginning with *lākēn*.

Greenberg finds the limits of the first section in the repeated statement of principle, first in v 4, and then inverted and expanded in v 20. In spite of that, he chooses to begin the section at v 3 since both vv 3 and 4 refer back to the proverb in v 2. Thus, content takes precedence over form here, for the refutation begins with v 3. So also, the closing of the section ends with v 20b[ª], since v 20b provides the bridge to the second section.

The three cases are interrelated as follows: the first case describes the righteous man, who gains life; the second case defines the wicked man, who gains death; and the third case, the righteous son of a wicked father, makes the connection with those who were fond of the proverb in v 2. They represent, in fact, the one depicted in the third case. Greenberg remarks that the first two generations (cases) are required to illustrate the "supererogatory" statement of v 20, "a father shall not die for . . . his son," but only the last two generations (cases) are necessary to counter the proverb of v 2. The citation in verse 19a (possibly a fiction) restates the issue emphatically (i.e., "the moral autonomy of the generations"). Surrounding that citation, vv 18 and 19b present a "detailed justification for the disparate fates of the last two generations." V 20 follows with a forceful reiteration of the principle stated in v 4. Together those verses (vv

---

[55]*Ezekiel 1-20*, 334-36.

18-20) present "the pith of the argument." Thus, states Greenberg, "the proverb has been refuted in principle.[56]

Throughout the first section the interplay between the generations has been the guiding structural motif. In v 20b, however, a new contrast is established: "righteous(ness)" and "wicked(ness)."[57] It is that opposition that guides the next half of the chapter. It is interesting to note in that regard that "the wicked" or "wickedness" are not mentioned in vv 1-20a. Thus, according to Greenberg, vv 3-20 deal with the principle of individual retribution, whereas vv 21-32 deal with "God's constant readiness to accept and save penitents." Following the pattern of the first section, the second section is marked off by vv 23 and 32, "a statement and a restatement of its essential doctrine."[58] How, then, are vv 21-22 connected to the second section if v 23 forms a boundary? As Greenberg argues for v 3, so also here. Vv 21-22 present the premise ("repentance expunges past sins"), and v 23 forms the conclusion, which is phrased as a rhetorical question. That conclusion is repeated and "closes the consequential part of the oracle in the form of a declaration and an exhortation."[59]

Following that first statement, a secondary (if unnecessary) proposition (v 24) asserts that "reversion from righteousness expunges past merits."[60] Then a popular criticism of the arbitrariness of divine action is quoted, which is turned back on the audience (v 25). The rule remains clearly in force, and the criticism is answered in vv 25-29 by a reiteration of the principle first cited in vv 20b, 21-22, and 24.

Greenberg's analysis of vv 21-32 is similar to mine:

B 1 Doctrine: a repentance expunges past sins
                  b God desires repentance
                  c reversion expunges past merits
B 2 Cavil and   d not God's ways but yours are perverse
   retort   c' reversion expunges merits
                  a' repentance expunges past sins
                  d' not God's ways but yours are perverse
B 3 Call to repentance

---

[56]Ibid., 335.

[57]Ibid., 335. Note also Parunak's discussion of transitional techniques in "Transitional Techniques in the Bible," *JBL* 102 (1983) 525-48.

[58]Greenberg, Ibid.

[59]Ibid.

[60]Ibid., 336. He also notes that v 24 is "a logical outcome of the doctrine and a triumph of consistency, even if it is properly irrelevant to the chief interest of the oracle in encouraging repentance." Is it, in fact, irrelevant?

The correspondences between vv 1-20 and 21-32, according to Greenberg, are typical of the "'halving' structure of Ezekiel's oracles," with a conclusion that mirrors aspects of both parts.[61]   V 20 functions rhetorically as a hinge between the two parts of the chapter. As mentioned above, v 20b introduces a new element found only in the second half of the chapter. It is thought that v 20 belongs structurally to the first half of the chapter, but if its function as a hinge between the two halves is recognized, then it stands independently, mirroring aspects of both. V 20a mirrors v 4 and the argument of vv 5-19. V 20b mirrors the argument of vv 21-32.[62]

Logical Structure

I have already noted that v 20a summarizes the argument begun in v 4 and that the latter part of v 20 provides a turning point hinging both parts of the chapter. The central thesis stated at the end of v 4 is now placed at the beginning of v 20, which is elaborated by two axioms. The first of those axioms summarizes the argument in response to the *māšāl*, whereas the second axiom is a logical extension of the central thesis, and leads the reader into the second portion of the chapter. Hence, v 21 begins with *hārāšā'*, making the connection with v 20 explicit. In fact, the parallelism or alternation between "the righteous" and "the wicked" in vv 21-32 begins in v 20. Thus, the opposition of vv 21-22 and 24, and the reversal of that parallel in vv 26 and 27-28, are examples of the axiom of v 20b^b. Both halves of the chapter are linked by v 20, and both are developments of the thesis of v 4.

---

[61]Ibid., 336.

[62]The line between "linked keyword" and "hinge" is fine. "The hinge is a transitional unit of text, independent to some degree from the larger units on either side, which has affinities with each of them and does not add significant information to that presented by its neighbors. The two larger units are joined together, not directly, but because each is joined to the hinge" ("Transitional Techniques," 540-41). The pattern in Ezekiel 18 is A/ab/B, where v 20 links the larger units A/B. Although he does not discuss Ezekiel 18, the categories presented here are from Parunak, "Transitional Techniques."

Greenberg provides a synthesis of the "halving" technique.[63]

A	B
proverb, first statement of doctrine of retribution (vss. 2-4) and its illustration (vss. 5-18)	first statement of God's good will toward penitents, within presentation of doctrine of judgment according to present state (vss. 21-24)
people's stricture (vs 19)	people's cavil and God's retort (vss. 25-29)
restatement of doctrine (vs. 20)	practical consequences of doctrines of A and B with restatement of God's good will toward penitents (vss. 30-32)

The development of the argument progresses through three phases. First, within the didactic style of vv 1-20 the tone is impersonal, with the only personal note in the "my" suffix of "my laws" and "my statutes" (vv 9, 17, 19). Second, in vv 21-29 the impersonal is interspersed with divine declarations and rhetorical questions (vv 23, 25, 29). Third, in vv 30-32 the style is entirely personal divine exhortation. As Greenberg notes, "A clear gradation of passion pervades the oracle, reaching a climax at the end."[64]

The argument can be analyzed further by considering the development of the principle regarding guilt transferred between fathers and sons. The proverb of v 2 speaks of the children's experiencing the results of the parents' action. V 20, however, goes far beyond the ordinary in denying the reverse, that parents will not experience the results of the children's actions. Thus, v 20 provides a complete refutation of the proverb. The conclusion is obvious. Each generation is responsible for its own behaviour and its effects.

What, then, is the relationship of vv 21-32 to that conclusion? If each generation is morally autonomous, then the present generation must be held accountable for the present disastrous situation. Vv 21-32 present not only an elaboration of the principle, but a necessary prelude to the exhortation of vv 30-32. The refutation of the proverb in vv 3-20 would be logically incomplete without vv 21-29, for there we find the preliminary stages of the argument that concludes in vv 30-32--the principle of repentance. Without vv 21-29, the exhortation of vv 30-32 would lack the grounds necessary for

---

[63]*Ezekiel 1-20*, 337.
[64]Ibid.

its fulfillment within the overall structure of the argument of the chapter. Not only would the exhortation be without a basis, the judgment of v 30a would be an intrusion, since nowhere in vv 1-20 do we find an explicit accusation.   The impersonal tone of those verses and the theoretical refutation do not bear the marks of a judgment speech. If chap. 18 contains an element of judgment (as v 30a suggests), then vv 21-29 are essential for the "therefore I will judge you" of v 30a. Similarly, the call to repentance in vv 30b-32 needs the argument of vv 21-29, for there we find the argument that the guilty can, in fact, turn around. The refutation of the proverb demands both the judgment and the call to repentance, for the refutation alone would lead to despair.

Compositional Structure

We turn now to a final concern, the compositional structure of the chapter. Some evidence suggests that the chapter is a composite unit.

First, the retort of v 19 seems not to follow from the proverb and its refutation in vv 2-19, nor does the audience reply in vv 25a and 29a accord with v 19a.   This problem must be resolved by appeal to the rhetorical structure of the chapter (see above), and by considering the function of the citations in the chapter.

Second, it is argued by some that the legal material in the chapter (specifically vv 4-20) indicates a time of composition later than the prophet Ezekiel.[65]

Third, vv 26-29 duplicate vv 21-25. Again, the rhetorical shape of chap. 18 has shown an inner dynamic in which the duplication contributes significantly.[66]

Fourth, portions of the chapter occur in essentially the same form in other parts of the book of Ezekiel. The closest parallel, 33:10-20, duplicates parts of 18:21-32. Greenberg notes that the integrity or aptness of the section in chap. 18 must be compared to the composite ("derivative") character of chap. 33.   The literary connections of the two halves of chap. 18 rule against origin in chap. 33.   Moreover, several elements that are repeated in chap. 33 belong more logically to the argument of chap. 18: the complaint against God's ways (18:25, 29; 33:17, 20), and the statement that God judges each according to his ways (18:30; 33:20).   Those elements do not

---

[65]Among others, H. Schulz, (*Das Todesrecht*) and J. Garscha (*Studien zum Ezechielbuch*). That conclusion is based on form-critical and religio-historical considerations that, as I shall argue, are not as convincing as the rhetorical function of the legal material in the literature of the Book of Ezekiel.

[66]That dynamic will be further illuminated in the discussion below on the genre of disputation speeches.

suit well the response to the despondency of 33:10.[67] I conclude that chap. 18 is best understood as a single compositional unit. The chapter's integrity is apparent from consideration of the literary, rhetorical, and logical structure of the text. It is not an expanded unit, nor a composite unit, although more will be said in Chapter 4 about how traditional literary conventions and forms contribute to the composition of the text.

GENRE: DISPUTATION SPEECHES

The Matter of Definition

The history of research on disputation speeches has shown that the genre has not been well defined. In fact, as Adrian Graffy notes, "the chief problem facing all the studies of the disputation speech is the lack of a clear common structure."[68] Graffy defines the genre as "the quotation of the people's opinion and the refutation which corrects this opinion."[69] D. F. Murray nuances this by suggesting a three-fold pattern: "Only where the elements thesis, counter-thesis, dispute, are present or clearly implied in the text is the use of the term appropriate."[70]

---

[67]Greenberg (*Ezekiel 1-20*, 338) concludes, as I have above, that the second portion of chap. 18 is a continuation of the first, "and its repentance theme was spun out of the principle of A by way of drawing out its consequences. In order to serve later as a retort to the saying of despair (33:10), B was recast and supplied with other ingredients of our prophecy (cf. 33:14b-15 with 18:5, 7) and of others. . . . The reuse and combination of elements of ch. 18 in the mosaic of ch. 33 is a good example of Ezekiel's practice of both mixing wines and putting old wine into new bottles."

[68]Adrian Graffy, *A Prophet Confronts His People: The Disputation Speech in the Prophets* (AnBib 104; Rome: Biblical Institute Press, 1984) 21. So also R. R. Wilson, "Form-Critical Investigation of the Prophetic Literature: The Present Situation," *Society of Biblical Literature Seminar Papers I* (ed. G. MacRae; Cambridge, Mass: Scholars Press, 1973), 100-127, especially p. 108.

[69]*A Prophet Confronts*, 105.

[70]D. F. Murray, "The Rhetoric of Disputation: Re-Examination of a Prophetic Genre," *JSOT* 38 (1987) 114.

Comments on the History of Research[71]

Gunkel was the first to make observations about prophetic disputations. His selection of representative texts ranged so widely as to include genuine as well as implicit disputations, along with texts that seek to convince in an argumentative way. The genre intends to convince an audience and to respond to their objections. Gunkel included almost anything that reflected differences of opinion between the prophet and his audience. What Gunkel presents as disputation is actually a style of prophetic speech, which may include different rhetorical devices and genres. He pays special attention to the way a disputation refutes a quotation.[72]

Recent work on disputation speeches attempts to pay disciplined attention to structure and tries to define more clearly the nature of the genre and its aim. Graffy infers from the work of Westermann that "the clear statement of an opposing viewpoint followed by its refutation is the basic structure of the disputation speech."[73] Graffy also comments on the shift in scholarship since Gunkel, who understood the disputation speech as a product of disagreement between prophet and audience. For later scholarship such speeches are "a logical process of thought passing from basis to conclusion, with no clear indication whether the listener agrees or not." This latter development, he claims, "does not merit the title 'disputation speech'."[74]

Both Graffy and Murray lament the failure of modern form-critical study to develop an acceptable definition of the genre "disputation speech." Graffy's focus is a clear delineation of the structure of the disputation speech. Murray focuses more specifically on the function of the genre. The analysis above has given credibility to the view that Ezekiel 18 is a text with both linguistically and logically coherent structural features. My discussion below, therefore, will begin with the works of Graffy and Murray who have analyzed the major difficulties with the genre of disputation.

---

[71]It is impossible to include a detailed history of research on disputation speeches here. The literature covers large portions of the Hebrew Bible. Such a survey can be found in A. Graffy, *A Prophet Confronts*, 2-23. I shall make several comments here that have a bearing on this study. I shall then focus on the recent work of Graffy and Murray.

[72]H. Gunkel, "Einleitung: Die Propheten als Schriftsteller und Dichter," in H. Schmidt, *Die Grossen Propheten* (2nd. ed.; Die Schriften des Alten Testaments II/2; Göttingen: Vandenhoeck & Ruprecht, 1923) xxxiv-lxx. These observations are also made by both Graffy (ibid., 2-5) and Murray ("The Rhetoric of Disputation," 99-100).

[73]Ibid., 10. Of central concern to Graffy is that previous research on disputation speeches have simply demonstrated "a progression of thought, so generic as to be hard to apply with rigour, and which does not show any clear structure" (13).

[74]Ibid., 14.

Along the way I shall offer several suggestions about how Ezekiel 18 might function within the overall rhetorical shape of moral discourse in Ezekiel.

The Work of Adrian Graffy

Adrian Graffy's study of disputation speeches analyses all prophetic texts that "use the device of refuting the quoted words of the people."[75] What is most helpful is his delineation of the common structure of disputation speeches, which he finds in nine Ezekiel texts.[76] Although the structure of Ezekiel 18 is complex, the chapter fits the generic categories of structure that Graffy has discovered.

It is therefore important to distinguish between the formal category of disputation speech and texts that begin with a citation. D. Clark's analysis is helpful for its description of the rhetorical function of quotations, and Graffy's study defines formal structures of the genre of disputation speeches. But quotations are not the primary marker of a disputation speech. It is always the macrostructure that marks genre. Thus, although Ezekiel 18 utilizes the rhetorical feature of citation, it has more in common with a limited number of other Ezekiel texts of the same genre.

Graffy's analysis leads to the isolation of a characteristic formal structure consisting in two parts: "the quotation of the people's opinion and the refutation which corrects this opinion." These texts he distinguishes

---

[75]Ibid., 1. On citations in the prophets see H. W. Wolff, "Das Zitat im Prophetenspruch: Eine Studie zur prophetischen Verkündigungsweise," *Gesammelte Studien zum Alten Testament*, pp. 36-129 (2nd ed.; TBü 22. Munich: Chr. Kaiser, 1973. Douglas Clark ("The Citations in the Book of Ezekiel: An Investigation into Method, Audience, and Message" [Ph.D. diss., Vanderbilt University, 1984]) has studied all the texts in Ezekiel in which the prophet cites a saying of his audience. Clark's analysis deals with five types of citations: antithetical, explanatory, supplementary, self-citations, divine self-citations. All the texts treated by Graffy fall into the antithetical category, but Graffy does not deal with all the citations that are treated antithetically in the book of Ezekiel because they do not all fit the formal criteria for disputation speeches. Although Clark deals effectively with the rhetorical function of antithetical citations in Ezekiel, he does not further the discussion of genre. Thirty-eight citations are on their own singled out for analysis within specified textual units. More generalized discussion on the identification of quotations can be found in R. Gordis, "Quotations as a Literary Usage in Biblical, Oriental, and Rabbinic Literature," *HUCA* 22 (1949) 157-219; and M. Fox, "The Identification of Quotations in Biblical Literature," *ZAW* 92 (1980) 416-31.

[76]11:2-12; 11:14-17; 12:21-25; 12:26-28; 18:1-20; 20:32-44; 33:10-20; 33:23-29; 37:11b-13. Although the extent of the units sometimes differs, those are the texts that Zimmerli (*Ezekiel 1*, 280) classified as disputations. Besides those Ezekiel texts, Graffy also analyses Isa 28:14-19; Jer 8:8-9; 31:29-30; 33:23-26; Isa 40:27-31; 49:14-25; Hag 1:2, 4-11.

from "disputations" or "dialogue disputations," which record the dispute in direct speech.[77]

In disputation speeches the prophet himself reports both sides of the dispute. The disputation speech proper contains a quotation and a refutation.[78] More precisely, the syntactical and stylistic elements include:

1) Introduction. The most common introduction is the word reception formula. "The formula of the coming of the word makes quite clear that it is Yahweh who informs the prophet of the people's words."[79]

2) Quotation. The quotations vary widely with few grammatical and syntactical correspondences.

3) Explanatory and Preparatory Remarks. In only two of the texts, Jer 33:24b and Ezek 11:4-6, do we find comments that "build up the expectation for the refutations to come."[80]

4) Refutation: This element includes a variety of ways in which a quotation can be rejected. Although sometimes a quotation may be denied explicitly, more often there are reasons provided.

> In almost every disputation speech Yahweh's coming intervention is announced, and usually in the first person. . . . In Ezek 18,1-20 it is Yahweh's rule of conduct in judgment, 'it is the person who sins that shall die' (v. 4), which provides the basis of the refutation of the quotation. . . . It can be said that the refutation either considers how Yahweh acts habitually, as in Jer 31,29-30; Ezek 18,1-20 (that he punishes individually) and Ezek 33,10-20 (that he wants the sinner to live), or announces what he plans in the future. . . . Fundamental to every refutation therefore is a consideration of

---

[77]Graffy (*A Prophet Confronts*, 22-23) outlines eight limitations on the designation "disputation speech." Not all texts, therefore, that quote the words of the people are disputation speeches. 1) Some quotations are simply illustrations; 2) In some texts the citation is only implied; 3) Argumentative tone does not alone indicate a disputation speech; 4) A logical argument within a text without stating the opinion of the audience is not a disputation speech; 5) Disputation speech does not record a dialogue in direct speech, as in Job; 6) The speeches of Malachi are structured differently, for a different purpose; 7) Speeches beginning with *hôy* challenge an opinion, but are dominated by threat; 8) Some texts that have the quotation and refutation structure may actually be part of a longer textual unit (e.g. Jer 2:23a). Not all Clark's antithetical citations fall into the disputation speech genre.

[78]Graffy, *A Prophet Confronts*, 105.

[79]Ibid., 108. The verb most often used is *'mr*, but where another verb is used, *lē'mōr* is added. So Ezek 12:22 and 18:2 use *mšl*, but add *lē'mōr*. The form of the verb varies, but in Ezekiel the participle dominates (six of the nine speeches) (ibid., 116). Usually the introduction to the quotation is a statement, but it can also be a question about the quotation (Jer 33:24; Ezek 12:22; 18:2; Jer 8:8; Isa 40:27). The subject of the principal verb can be incorporated into the verb or designated by a pronoun (Ezek 18:2; 20:32). Sometimes the speakers of the quotation are described in more detail (Ezek 11:2, 15; 12:27; 33:24) (107-109).

[80]Ibid., 110-111.

Yahweh's action, habitual or expected, the announcement of which implies the falsity of the quotation."[81]

5) Double Refutation: Several of the disputation speeches contain a double refutation (Ezek 11:2-12; 11:14-17; 33:23-29; Isa 49:14-25; Hag 1:2, 4-11). In all but Hag 1:9-11 a new argument different from the first refutation is presented, but the new argument continues as a refutation of the initial quotation. Ezek 18:5-18 presents a single refutation in three parts. Refutations in stages within a single argument are also found in 33:12-16 (two parts) and 20:34-44 (three parts).

According to Graffy, Ezek 18:21-32 does not belong to the disputation speech, and therefore cannot be considered a second refutation.[82] I suggest, however, that the addition of vv 21-32 transforms the generic disputation speech into a theological-ethical disputation. It not only seeks to refute an opinion, but to present an alternative, to prevent misunderstanding, and to motivate to action.

That Ezekiel 18 contains two refutations and follows the pattern outlined by Graffy can be demonstrated by the fact that the first refutation (vv 5-20) deals obliquely with the generational problem and the situation of the exiles (father/son). The second refutation (vv 21-30a) focuses on the situation of the exiles themselves. The first deals with the past-present tension, whereas the second addresses the present-future possibilities. Therefore the double refutation in chapter 18 meets the criteria set out by Graffy that the double refutation often shows a chronological sequence in the argument (as in Ezek 11:7-10, 11-12; 11:16, 17; 33:25-26, 27-29; Isa

---

[81]Ibid., 111. I disagree, however, with Graffy's suggestion that Ezekiel 18 deals primarily with individual punishment. Still, the comment highlights the fact that theodicy is a crucial element in disputation speeches.

According to Graffy (ibid., 111-12), "the refutation by definition represents a challenge to the people's words. It is therefore understandable that this part of the disputation speech should usually begin with the messenger formula, announcing that Yahweh thinks differently from the people." Seven of the nine disputation speeches in Ezekiel begin with the messenger formula. Two of those (20:33-44; 33:25-29) also contain the oath formula hay-'$\bar{a}n\hat{i}$. In 18:3; 20:33 and 33:11 the oath formula is supported by the formula common to Ezekiel, $n\check{e}$'um '$\check{a}d\bar{o}n\bar{a}y$ $yhwh$ (18:3 and 33:11 do not have the messenger formula). The formula also occurs throughout chapter 18 to emphasize elements of the refutation (vv 9,23, 30, 32). The oath formula is found in only one disputation speech outside Ezekiel (Isa 49:15-25).

[82]See the section on structure and my conclusions regarding unity. Consider also the correspondences between vv 1-20 and 21-32, Greenberg's argument cited there, and the fact that v 5 begins with the $\mathfrak{s}add\hat{i}q$, whereas v 21 begins with the $r\bar{a}\check{s}\bar{a}$'. Each part of the chapter refutes a different aspect or dimension of quotation. Vv 5-20 refute intergenerational retribution, whereas vv 21-29 refute a possible misunderstanding of the programmatic refutation of vv 3-4 ("the soul that sins shall die").

49:16-21, 22-23). The entire argument presents a way for a reconstitution of "house of Israel" (vv 25, 29, 30, 31) that is a development from the "land of Israel" (vv 2-3).

6) Programmatic and Concluding Refutations: This device is found in Ezek 18:3-4; 20:33; 33:11; Isa 49:15 and Hag 1:4. "This element gives a preliminary refutation of the quotation which will be explained in the detailed refutation which follows." It is found only in the texts that have the longest refutations. In the three Ezekiel texts the oath formula *ḥay-'ānî* is followed by *nĕ'um 'ădōnāy yhwh*.[83]

7) Rejoinder and Reply: According to Graffy, this element occurs in 18:19-20 and twice in 33:17-20. Since chapter 18 can be considered a literary unit, then the rejoinder and reply occurs also in 18:25-30. Thus, each part of Ezekiel 18 contains a rejoinder and reply, since each part deals with a related refutation of the quotation in v 2.[84]

Thus, the formal structure of Ezekiel 18 falls into the generic pattern established by the analysis of other disputation speeches.

Introduction	v 1-2a
Quotation	v 2b
Programmatic refutation	vv 3-4
Refutation in three parts	vv 5-9
	vv 10-13
	vv 14-18
Rejoinder and reply	vv 19-20

And if we add vv 21-32 we must see in v 19a a rejoinder that is answered not only in vv 19b-20, but in vv 19b-32. The disputation fragments after the first rejoinder in v 19a into a back and forth debate, all still narrated by the prophet but in the first person speech of Yahweh. Thus, we must add several elements to the simple structure of vv 1-20 as outlined by Graffy.

Rejoinder and reply	vv 19-24
Rejoinder and reply	vv 25-28
Rejoinder and reply	vv 29-32

In the case of the last rejoinder in v 29a, the text breaks out of the constraints of the generic and adds the specific element that makes Ezekiel 18 unique among the disputation speeches--the call to repentance in vv 30b-32. It remains a disputation speech, but the unique elements provide

---

[83]*A Prophet Confronts*, 114-115.
[84]Ibid., 115.

the nuance that allows us to articulate its intent more fully. According to Graffy, the structure alone enables us to state the intent of the text, yet if the structure never varies significantly within the genre, even though content changes, the intent must remain the same. My argument is that the basic intent may be similar, but it is the unique elements within any given text that allow for a nuanced reading that make any one text stand out as contributing something different within the generic category of disputation speech. Ezekiel 18 stands out because of its distinctive content and because it moves beyond the bounds of the generic formal structure. In doing so not only does it emphasize the refutation of an opinion, but it seeks also to change behaviour and modify the shape of the community to whom the prophet is speaking.[85]

Related to that, Graffy suggests that, "the aim of the disputation speech is quite simply to contest and refute the quotation, not to introduce the call to conversion in vv 30-32, which is quite a different issue. Nevertheless, the starkness of 18:1-20 plainly invited the addition of more auspicious words inspired principally by 33,10-20."[86] But one would have to ask whether all texts that display the structure of a disputation speech must bear the same aim or function. It is one of the weaknesses of form criticism as it is narrowly defined that it pays attention only to similarities and generic structural criteria. The point of discovering the generic, however, is to discern the uniqueness of how particular texts diverge from the characteristic conventions of the genre. Similarly, even if Ezekiel 18 is an expanded unit, the fact that 18:1-20 now belongs to a longer, self-contained unit demands that we analyze not only the shorter unit, but also its modification or extension.

The Revision of D. F. Murray

Murray observes that the two dangers of form criticism apply to the study of disputations: first, that the genres are given "so vague a definition that quite disparate material can be comprehended within its range;" and second, that we work with "so strict a definition that material with real similarities of structure and content cannot be accommodated by it."[87]

---

[85]Murray's recent work on disputations ("The Rhetoric of Disputation") confirms these observations. He states (95) that "within the commonality of situations which allows us to typify our experiences and elaborate shared forms with which to express them, there remains an element of uniqueness which demands a flexibility of expression. Forms are, or ought to be, the servants of their users."

[86]*A Prophet Confronts*, 64.

[87]"The Rhetoric of Disputation," 95.

At the root of Murray's criticism is this: "The principle of a 'pure genre' having a one-to-one relationship with a strictly definable unitary *Sitz im Leben* can no longer be held."[88] His summary critique is worth noting:

> "Not only is [*Sitz im Leben*] in any case a polyvalent term (Knight 108f.), comprehending the whole gamut of social and cultural matrices, but also for every genre it is multiform (Knight 113f.), since the constitutive settings or matrices of any given genre are plural, depending as they do on a complex interlocking of a number of intellectual and social factors. Moreover, any given text need not necessarily manifest just one genre. . . . Social reality, being complex, gives rise to complexity of forms."[89]

In addition, Murray draws on Knierim's approach which looks not so much for particular social settings as for the more universal "basic structure of an existential human situation."[90] Thus, it is reasonable to suppose that "the forms which disputation may take, and the strategies adopted to resolve it, vary quite markedly."[91] Murray therefore suggests three basic types of disputations.

First, some disputations are like the Platonic dialogues in which the "constituent elements may appropriately be termed thesis, inquiry, conclusion." In that kind of disputation the element of dispute can revolve around a counter-argument, or can present a counter-thesis.

In a second type of dispute each party attempts to persuade the opponent of the correctness of their position through presentation of thesis and counter-thesis. There is no dialectical development of one or the other position toward a new synthesis. There may, in fact, be no resolution to the debate. This kind of dispute may serve a rhetorical function in which "detached observers may be persuaded of the cogency of the one position

---

[88]Murray (ibid., 96) refers to the well known works of R. Knierim, "Old Testament Form Criticism Reconsidered," *Int* 27 (1973) 435-68; M. J. Buss, "The Idea of Sitz im Leben—History and Critique," *ZAW* 90 (1978) 157-70; and D. A. Knight, "The Understanding of 'Sitz im Leben' in Form Criticism," *Society of Biblical Literature Seminar Papers I* (ed. G. MacRae; Cambridge, MA: Scholars Press, 1973) 105-25. Buss's comments also suggest that one must be cautious about compositional history of a text on the basis of its literary conventions. He writes: "Styles and content of speaking are not determined directly by the external setting, but by the interplay of the roles of participants. . . . Since individuals play more than one role and have multiple opportunities, speech can change its character without a change in circumstances" (168). Thus, the unique features of Ezekiel 18 that are explored here and in the next chapter provide insight into the function of language in the human community as much as into the function of the setting in shaping the language of the text.

[89]"The Rhetoric of Disputation," 96.

[90]Ibid., 96, citing Knierim, "Form Criticism Reconsidered," 446.

[91]Murray, ibid., 97.

rather than the other." I would add that this is probably the rhetorical function of literary texts, to which readers are called to pay attention and make judgments. Murray suggests that the book of Job is one such example.

A third form of disputation has similar logical structure, but is slightly different. Murray's comments deserve extensive citation.

> It occurs when a person seeks to counter objections, actual or potential, to a position he maintains, or to counter views which are explicitly or implicitly contrary to that position, without engaging in an actual debate with an opponent. In this type of disputation, the opponent is given the minimum of scope: there are neither interchanges of question and answer, nor set-piece speeches. At best the opponent's position is merely reported, often in the form of ostensible verbatim quotation.[92]

Ezekiel 18 is that third type of disputation. The opposing position is quoted and reiterated by means of rhetorical devices that anticipate objections by the audience/reader.

> Since the maintenance of the one view over against possible objections or contrary views is the rationale of this kind of disputation, its very heart consists of a refutation of these objections or contrary views, and the emphatic statement or re-statement of the espoused view by way of conclusion. Again, since there is no actual debate, the refutation, though it may avail itself of a wide range of rhetorical devices to give liveliness and cogency to its arguments, allows of no response, and thus of no dialectical development. Indeed, in some cases refutation and emphatic (re-)statement may be collapsed together, the simple (re)assertion of the espoused view being regarded as refutation enough."[93]

Our structural analysis of Ezekiel 18 has shown that that is exactly what happens in the chapter. Although Murray does not analyze the chapter, his observations can be brought to bear not only on the determination of genre, but on the discovery of meaning and function in the moral discourse of Ezekiel 18 (and perhaps in Ezekiel generally). According to Murray, there are three elements that constitute disputation: thesis, counter-thesis, and dispute. What is especially appropriate, and supportive of my conclusion that Ezekiel 18 is a coherent textual unit, is Murray's observation that

---

[92]Ibid., 98.
[93]Ibid., 99.

both thesis and counter-thesis may well consist of more than one proposition. However, since each constitutes one argument, the singular is appropriate and convenient. Further, although it is logically possible that there might be n counter-theses to the one thesis, formally these would be resolvable into a series of separate disputations."[94]

Ezekiel 18, then, contains an argument that functions on several levels, as I have argued above in the section on logical structure (as well as in my response to Graffy's limitation of the disputation to Ezek 18:1-20). What is especially important, therefore, is to recognize that the "rhetorical surface structure" need not be representational of the three-fold pattern of thesis, counter-thesis, and dispute. Similarly, the order of the three elements may vary from text to text, depending on "the rhetorical strategy in each instance." Murray therefore does not identify one rhetorical pattern as descriptive or definitive for the genre.[95]

Murray's analysis differs from Graffy's on one major point. For Graffy the structure of the disputation speech contains two major elements: quotation and refutation. Murray, on the other hand, finds three elements: thesis, counter-thesis, and dispute. Murray suggests that the binary structure is inadequate because it allows for only one way of relating the dispute and counter-thesis elements, and because thesis and counter-thesis are not given formal status. Counter-thesis is not simply part of the refutation (or a second refutation), but intrinsic to the genre of disputation.[96]

Since Murray does not analyze Ezekiel 18, a related example will make clear how the structure is recognized. The three-fold structure of Ezek 33:23-29 is clear. V 24 presents the thesis, which is quoted verbatim. Vv 25-26, the dispute in which the thesis is refuted, are marked by the introductory *lākēn*, the call to speak and the oracle formula, along with rhetorical questions. The counter-thesis in vv 27-29 begins with new introductory formulae and is reinforced by the divine oath formula. In contrast, Graffy's approach uncovers the following pattern in the same text. After the introduction of vv 23-24, the quotation in v 24, he defines all of vv 25-29 as the refutation, but in two parts. The first refutation (vv 25-26) takes on the claim of v 24 directly. It contains two lists of three misdemeanors, each concluding with a rhetorical question. The second refutation (vv 27-29) announces punishment.[97] According to Murray, that second refutation ought to be labelled the counter-thesis, for it is the main point of the oracle.

---

[94]Ibid., 116-17, n. 11.
[95]Ibid., 99.
[96]Ibid., 102, 117-18, n. 21.
[97]*A Prophet Confronts*, 78-82.

With regard to Ezek 33:23-29 it is important to recognize the mode of argumentation used by the prophet. The thesis, dispute, and counter-thesis pattern is significant in this demonstration oracle of judgment.

> The people who were the objects of that word of judgment held, in the prophet's view, a firm conviction which was such an obstacle in the way of proper reception of the prophetic word, that he sought to remove it by disputation. Hence he combined with the demonstration oracle the disputation oracle form. But in so doing he fully integrated both forms, in a way which left the rhetorical structure of each intact and patent. That it is a question of the combination of independent forms is shown by the fact that there are demonstration oracles in *Ezekiel* which are not also disputations, as there are disputations which are not also demonstration oracles.[98]

That being so, we are in a better position to appreciate the uniqueness of Ezekiel 18 as a rhetorical unit. And given those possibilities for how Ezekiel utilizes disputation speeches in a variety of formats, it is possible to confirm that Ezekiel 18 falls within the disputation speech genre.

SYNTHESIS AND SUMMARY

How, then, is Murray's three-fold pattern evident in the specific rhetorical strategy of Ezekiel 18? The dispute is in the form of a theological-ethical argument that includes rejoinders from the audience.

The text begins with the reception formula, characteristic of many Ezekielian texts. Verse 2 introduces the citation of the *māšāl* by asking the audience a question, and then by citing the *māšāl* in the form of a quotation. In that rhetorical device of quoting the audience's opinion, also common to Ezekiel, the prophet states the thesis that will form the centre of the disputation to follow. In this instance v 2 addresses the prophet with the plural pronoun *lākem*, as though speaking directly to the listeners or readers.

Thus, the question is raised immediately as to the identity of the audience. Do we find ourselves listening in on a discourse to the exiles in Babylon, or ought we posit a rhetorical audience/reader more generally defined? Is Ezekiel 18 addressed to the "house of Israel" at large, including those remaining in the land, or to his fellow exiles alone? In either case the obstacle between the opinion stated in the citation and accepting the

---

[98]Murray, "The Rhetoric of Disputation," 104. Examples of the combination include 11:2-12; 37:11-14; examples of demonstration oracles that are not disputations are 25:1-5, 6-7, 8-11, 12-14, 15-17; and disputations that are not demonstration oracles include 11:14-21 (combined with a proclamation of salvation); 12:21-25, 26-28 (pure disputation); and 18:1-32 (theological disputation motivating a call to repentance) (ibid., 118, nn. 29, 30, 31).

prophet's counter-thesis might be different.[99] I suggest that the intention of the text is evident in the plural address and in the expression "house of Israel." The audience are exiles who are distraught concerning the invasion of the land.

Following the thesis of the audience the prophet states the counter-thesis.[100] Ezek 18:3 begins with the divine oath formula and the oracle formula. In v 3b the use of the *māšāl* is rejected. It is not clear whether the rejection is because the *māšāl* is invalid as an authentic reflection on life, or because it will be unnecessary. The imperfect form of the verb *hyh* with the infinitive construct of the verb *mšl* (used as the accusative introducing an object clause) suggests that the counter-thesis presents an expectation of a time when such observations about life will not be necessary. Thus, the counter-thesis introduces in v 3 a proleptic glimpse toward a new possibility, a new construction of reality not yet imagined. Verse 4a states a theological basis to which certainly both audience and prophet can agree. It forms part of the counter-thesis in that it provides a hinge from the thesis to the counter thesis. That hinge is necessary because both thesis and counter-thesis depend on a model of divine involvement in the affairs of the human community. After presenting that basis, the prophet succinctly presents the counter-thesis "the person that sins shall die." With vv 3-4, however, the text has not exhausted the counter-thesis element. But the rhetorical strategy shifts to another element before the full counter-thesis can be restated and rephrased. The rhetorical strategy in vv 3-4 is to reject the use of the *māšāl* and all that it represents, to state a theological basis to which both disputants can agree, and to present a counter-thesis that presents an alternative to the *māšāl* of v 2b.

The dispute proper begins in v 5. The reader has now been presented with both thesis and counter-thesis. The rhetorical strategy is deliberate in that one anticipates that the tension between the opposing theses will be the creative factor that moves the text along. One already knows the trajectory of movement—the counter-thesis will be confirmed. But one does not know how that resolution will be reached. In fact, the reader may well be predisposed to agree with the thesis (v 2b), and wonder at the credibility of the counter-thesis, given the experience of exile through which the theological problem of the relationship of actions and consequences has been filtered.

Verse 5 introduces the three-generational pattern that extends to v 18. Verse 5 begins with the formulaic introduction that is characteristic of casuistic legal material (*'îš kî*). Verses 10 and 14 continue the casuistic

---

[99]See Murray (ibid., 118, n. 28) for the suggestion that opponents and rhetorical opponents are significantly different. Hence it is clear that one's decision about the identity of the opponents may alter one's reading of the text.

[100]The order of the generic elements is therefore different from the order in, for example, Ezek 33:23-29.

structure with a disjunctive *waw* and the verb *yld* (except v 14 begins with *hinnēh*). Thus, the three cases extend from v 5 to v 18 and serve to present the grounds for the counter-thesis of vv 3-4 on the basis of Israel's legal tradition. Each of the three cases also concludes with a formal statement indicating the outcome of "life" or "death."[101]

The text now returns to a citation of the audience in v 19a by reiterating the thesis in other words. What may have been read as a complaint in v 2 is now clearly to be read as an assertion of a theological position that has grounded the world view of the audience. The citation serves to pose an argument against the counter-thesis by appealing to the common assumption that actions carry intergenerational consequences. The rhetorical question of v 19a is answered by a reiteration of the counter-thesis in vv 19b-20. Verse 20 serves as the "hinge" between the two sections of the disputation speech in that it looks back to the intergenerational cases in vv 5-18, and at the same time it introduces a new element in v 20b that looks ahead to the case of the individual having changed within one lifetime.

The dispute continues in v 21 in the case style again with a disjunctive *waw* before the noun, which is followed by a *kî*. The contrast is set between the wicked person (*rāšā'*, vv 21-23) and the righteous person (*saddîq*, v 24). Characteristically in the dispute section we find a rhetorical question in v 23, which partially introduces the motives of the disputant, Yahweh. Yahweh does not delight (*ḥps*) in the death of anyone. On that note v 24 introduces the case of the righteous person who does, in fact, become wicked. Thus, the reiteration of thesis and counter-thesis in vv 19-20 make possible the introduction of a new element inherent in the original thesis. That is to say, given the possibility that intergenerational consequences will not prevail, what prospects are there for those who recognize their complicity in evil in the present generation? That, of course, is the movement that the discourse seeks to foster. The trajectory of the dispute has shifted away from the initial thesis and counter-thesis to a probing beneath the surface for other implications of the counter-thesis should it be accepted as valid.

Remarkably, however, after moving more deeply into those possibilities for transformation in vv 21-24, the audience is cited again, but this time providing another angle of vision. Given the counter-thesis, and the fact that no one had substantially disputed the thesis (v 2) before in Israelite theological circles, could it not be argued that this God is fickle, or does not govern the universe according to consistent principles? Thus the argument that the way of Yahweh is not just, or is not consistent. What is

---

[101]Technically v 17 ends the third case, and v 18 serves to contrast the third and the second cases.

being challenged in the citation here is Yahweh's integrity, or his moral character.[102] The response to this accusation is terse, with hardly any new data presented. Immediately Yahweh accuses the house of Israel in v 25b with failing on the same count as it is accusing Yahweh. That, we know, is one of the central interests of the first part of the book of Ezekiel—establishing the guilt of the house of Israel. The argument of vv 25b-29 reiterates exactly what had been said in vv 21-24, including the formula statements of life/death. The conclusion of the response in v 29 repeats the accusation cited in v 25a along with a repetition of the terse response of v 25b. There is no dialectical development, but straightforward repetition. The contrast is explicit and unbending. The dispute revolves around the integrity of the house of Israel over against the integrity of Yahweh. Thus, the question of theodicy/anthropodicy brings the dispute full circle.

Unique to this disputation speech is the call to repentance in vv 30-32. Here the trajectory of the dispute presents itself most clearly. Verse 30a reiterates the counter-thesis in other words, and v 30b states the succinct call to repentance, a totally new element in the disputation. Verses 31 and 32 bolster the call to repentance with theological and moral arguments that mirror other elements of the text as well as other motifs from the book of Ezekiel. Verses 30-32 appeal to the audience outside the framework of the disputation speech. In fact, it is no longer the validity of the thesis or counter-thesis that is in question.

It is the assumption of judgment that presents itself as the central reality for the house of Israel in v 30a. That for Ezekiel is beyond dispute, both here and in the rest of the book of Ezekiel. Judgment had not been part of the disputation speech until v 30, and thus an new twist enters the dispute. No longer is the question theoretical as to whether or not transference of guilt would apply to their situation. The theological affirmation of judgment, terrible though it may be, impinges on the dispute and provides a context within which the audience must find itself coping. On the other hand, the call to repentance in vv 30b-31 seems to suggest that the audience has the potential, by an act of repentance, to engage in new possibilities that make for life. That element introduced here is indeed the scandal that marked the disputation all along. Inherent in the thesis and its reiteration in v 19a is the comfortable assumption that things do not change. Reality is structured so that it can be counted on.

But these final verses posit two new assumptions that were not considered in the disputation thus far. First, that the human community can engage in responsible moral discernment and transformation. They have the

---

[102]It is this fact that leads me to argue later in the dissertation that Yahweh is perceived by Ezekiel as a moral agent, one who has a significant role in history, whose acts can be evaluated according to a standard.

power to grasp that possibility that leads to life. They can get for themselves a new heart. Second, reiterating the rhetorical question from v 23 in the form of a statement, Yahweh is presented finally as the moral agent whose pathos engages in the situation of the audience yet allows them to make their own movement toward life. Of course that pathos is restless, and pushes the trajectory even further in other Ezekiel texts so that it becomes Yahweh who initiates the giving of the new heart. But for this disputation speech the prophet calls for action within the human community. He calls for the people to recognize the power of life and death inherent in their actions, and he invites them to move toward life.

That invitation is framed not only by the disputation speech itself, but also by the traditional conventions with which this particular disputation has been shaped. The next chapter explores the elements of the text that colour the rhetorical strategy and suasive potential of this moral discourse.

4
TRADITIONAL CONVENTIONS IN EZEKIEL 18

THE PROBLEM

In the last chapter I discussed the structure and genre of the text and made some suggestions about the intent and function of the discourse in the exilic setting. I turn now to an investigation of the traditional elements or conventions that give the text its particular rhetorical shape. The text in its present configuration contains numerous individual units, some as short as a formula, and others longer, self-contained genres in themselves. It is my task here to investigate those elements in chap. 18, and at the same time to understand them within the overall genre, intention, and function of the chapter.[1] These various facets of the text provide clues to understanding the specific shape of moral discourse in the Book of Ezekiel.

FORMULAIC MATERIAL

The Reception Formula:
wayhî dĕbar yhwh 'ēlay lē'mōr (v 1)[2]

The reception formula occurs fifty times in the Book of Ezekiel.[3] The formula is consistently used in the first person, a significant factor in the autobiographical stylization of the Book of Ezekiel.[4] Although direct address by Yahweh usually follows the formula, it occurs here alone.[5] The

---

[1]The following three chapters will discuss more extensively the implications of the rhetorical shape of chap. 18.

[2]See F. Hossfeld, *Untersuchungen*, 26-30; Zimmerli, *Ezekiel 1*, 25-26, 144-45; P. K. D. Neumann, "Das Wort, das geschehen ist," *VT* 23 (1973) 171-217.

[3]So K. von Rabenau, "Die Entstehung des Buches Ezechiel in formgeschichtlicher Sicht," *Wissenschaftliche Zeitschrift* (Halle) 5 (1955/56) 685, n. 67; Hossfeld, *Untersuchungen*, 26, n. 35; J. W. Miller, *Das Verhältnis*, 80 (48 times); L. Rost, "Gesetz und Propheten," *Studien zum Alten Testament* (BWANT 101; Stuttgart: Kohlhammer, 1974) 30-31 (53 times). The number of occurrences is also detailed in Zimmerli, *Ezekiel 1*, 144.

[4]Hossfeld, *Untersuchungen*, 26.

[5]Also 17:11; ibid., 65.

primary structural function of the formula is to mark off the beginning of a text, but several factors indicate that its significance is more comprehensive. First, the formula occurs more often in Ezekiel than in any other book. Second, the personal *'ēlay* occurs seldom in earlier literature. It occurs more than 83 times in Ezekiel, whereas only 8 times in Isaiah, 3 times in Amos, and once in Hosea.[6]

The suggestion arises whether that combination signifies a special characteristic of the Book of Ezekiel. The Book is shaped in the "I-style," but throughout we find that the prophet is simply the vehicle for the divine word. Formally that is emphasized by the overlay of three major formulae on the entire Book of Ezekiel. According to von Rabenau, the *Visionsformel*, the *Wortempfang*, and the *Anrede* "liegen wie ein dichtes Netz über dem ganzen Buch."[7] Thus, even without an analysis of the prophetic call in Ezekiel, we can posit that the reception formula serves to support the authority of the prophetic word. Zimmerli comments that "this formula . . . delineates the introduction of a new speech unit, which is thereby marked out as possessing the character of an event."[8] The concept of "word of Yahweh" in conjunction with the reception of that word by the prophet followed by an oracle such as we have in chap. 18 may suggest something about the relationship between the prophetic oracle, the prophetic vocation, and the intention or function of chap. 18. Rost suggests that "das neue Verständnis prophetischen Wortempfangs enthält eine Weiterentwicklung theologischer Reflexion, die sich gegenüber älteren Anschauungen durchsetzt."[9] That assertion, however, needs to be explored further and with more substantiation before we can draw conclusions about the prophetic vocation as it is depicted in the Book of Ezekiel.[10]

---

[6]Miller, *Das Verhältnis*, 80.

[7]von Rabenau, "Die Entstehung," 681.

[8]Zimmerli, *Ezekiel 1*, 25.

[9]Rost, "Gesetz und Propheten," 30-31.

[10]Note Zimmerli's comments (*Ezekiel 1*, 39) about the relationship between the proof-saying and the prophetic word. Often conclusions about social role are drawn from form-critical observations without sufficient support (so, e.g., Reventlow, *Wächter über Israel*). Zimmerli (*Ezekiel 1*, 144-45) discusses the traditio-historical background of the formula, and the meaning of the phrase "word of Yahweh."

The Formula for a Divine Saying (Oracle Formula)
ně'um 'ădōnāy yhwh (vv 3, 9, 23, 30, 32)

The formula occurs 85 times in Ezekiel either as a conclusion of a unit, or within the context of an oracle.[11] According to von Rabenau, the use of the formula for a divine saying occurs in Ezekiel 18 in three different types of locations: 1) at the end of a sentence, here, a cultic declaration (vv 9, 30, 32; cf. 44:15; 45:15); 2) in the middle of a sentence with special content, in this case to underscore the divine "I" of a cultic declaration (v 23; cf. 36:32), and 3) after specific formulae, here, after an oath formula at the beginning of a sentence (v 3). In itself the formula is supplemental and rhetorical, strengthening the sense of the utterance to which it is attached.

Hossfeld offers a different estimation. The formula can stand at the end of a text (often followed by the reception formula), or at the end of a sentence (*Satz*) within a text. In v 9 the formula, followed by a conjunction, marks a break within a text. Its significance can only be determined by an analysis of the context. In vv 23, 30, and 32 the formula functions within a context: "Sie unterstreicht den Vorgängersatz und hebt ihn als bedeutend heraus."[12] Hossfeld cautions, however, that because of the heavy prose style of Ezekiel the end placement and the context placement may be interchangeable, and the differentiation can only be determined by the context.[13]

My observations on the structure of the text corroborate Hossfeld's suggestion, especially at vv 30 and 32, where I read the formula in v 30 as an end formula. Following Rendtorff's study of Jeremiah, Hossfeld suggests that "ein wichtiges Kriterium für Kontextstellung nämlich entfällt, die Position zwischen den beiden Gliedern eines Parallelismus membrorum und seiner nicht metrischen Nachahmungen; diese Position macht beim Jeremiabuch eine Entscheidung möglich."[14] In that regard we note the correspondence between vv 23, 30, and 32. In vv 23 and 32 the same pat-

---

[11]Zimmerli, *Ezekiel 1*, 26. Von Rabenau ("Die Entstehung," 678) calls this the *Bekräftigungsformel* "weil sie immer einer anderen Formel, einem Satze oder einem ganzen Spruche nachgestellt wird." He notes that a simplified form of the formula (*ně'um yhwh*) occurs in the mouths of the false prophets in 13:6-7, which form occurs elsewhere in Ezekiel only in 16:58 and 37:14 (692, n. 259). For a summary of the uses of the *Bekräftigungsformel* see pp. 678-79. See also R. Rendtorff, "Zum Gebrauch der Formel *ně'um jahwe* im Jeremiabuch," *ZAW* 66 (1954) 27-37; F. Baumgärtel, "Die Formel *ně'um jahwe*," *ZAW* 73 (1961) 277-90; D. Vetter, *Seherspruch und Segensschilderung* (Calwer Theologische Monographien 4; Stuttgart: Calwer, 1974), 29.

[12]*Untersuchungen*, 38. Other such uses of the formula in Ezekiel are 16:8, 23, 30, 43; 20:36, 40; 30:6; 32:8, 14; 36:14, 23, 32; 38:18, 21; 39:8, 13; 43:19; 44:12, 15; 45:15.

[13]Ibid., 39-40.

[14]Ibid., 39. See R. Rendtorff, "Zum Gebrauch der Formel," 36-37.

tern is repeated: the statement concerning the divine displeasure at anyone's death, followed by the oracle formula and a word concerning repentance and life. In v 23 the pattern is expressed as a rhetorical question, whereas in v 32 an indicative is followed by an imperative. That in those two verses the formula stands within a context rather than at the end of a sentence is confirmed by the continuation of the rhetorical question by *hălô'* in v 23, and by the conjunctive *waw* in v 32.[15] Verse 30, on the other hand, places the formula at the centre, followed by a call to repent. The beginning of the verse, however, states the divine sentence: "Therefore I will judge you." One might think that the judgment clause here functions to provide a motive for repentance, which appears to be the dominant theme.[16] Thus, Hossfeld's suggestion that vv 23, 30, and 32 have the formula in the context of a sentence is confirmed, and the proposal that we find a strong break between 30a and 30b is tempered by the parallelism found in vv 23 and 32, and which is modified in v 30.[17]

The third use of the formula is in conjunction with other formulae.[18] In particular, the oracle formula occurs often with the oath formula, as we find it in 18:3.[19] "In Verbindung mit anderen Formeln spielt die Gottesspruchformel textlinguistisch die Rolle, die den Formeln zukommt, mit denen sie verwachsen ist."[20]

Summarizing the use of the oracle formula in Ezekiel, Hossfeld notes the following:

> Sie funktioniert als Endsyntagma eines Textes; sie markiert das Ende eines Abschnittes, unter Umständen das Ende eines in sich abgeschlossenen

---

[15]Hossfeld (ibid., 38) writes: "Wenn der Gottesspruchformel Sätze folgen, die durch eine Partikel oder eine Konjugation oder einen Themawechsel einen neuen Satz bzw. eine Satzkette anzeigen, dann markiert die Gottesspruchformel eine Zäsur, deren Gewicht erst bei genauer Kontextanalyse bestimmt werden kann."

[16]The interplay between the two, judgment and repentance, needs consideration especially in the light of A. Vanlier Hunter's proposal (*Seek the Lord! A Study of the Meaning and Function of the Exhortations in Amos, Hosea, Isaiah, Micah, and Zephaniah* [Baltimore: St. Mary's Seminary and University, 1982]) that repentance functions merely to confirm or strengthen the reason for judgment.

[17]*Untersuchungen*, 37-38.

[18]See the summary in Hossfeld, ibid., 39. It may be illustrative to note the formulae that do not appear in this chapter. For example, von Rabenau ("Die Entstehung," 679-80) notes that the messenger formula (*Botenformel*) regularly is missing before "sakralrechtlichen Entscheidungen" (18:3; 20:3, 31; 33:11).

[19]In Ezekiel: 5:11; 14:16, 18, 20; 16:48; 17:16; 18:3; 20:3, 31, 33; 33:11; 34:8; 35:6, 11. The oracle formula probably gave way before the messenger formula (*Botenformel*) in 17:19 and 33:27 (Hossfeld, *Untersuchungen*, 39, n. 59).

[20]Ibid.

Mikrotextes. Als Kontextformel unterstreicht sie den Vorgängersatz und in fester Verbindung mit bestimmten Formeln unterstutzt sie deren Emphase und textlinguistische Aufgabe.[21]

The Oath Formula

The asseveration *ḥay 'ānî* occurs numerous times in Ezekiel.[22] Formally, the oath seems often to introduce the divine legal decision, which was probably closely related to the context of request for an oracle.[23] Functionally, the oath emphasizes that Yahweh wishes to empower and guarantee the word that is spoken.[24] Like the oracle formula, the oath formula also heightens the rhetorical function of the divine presence in the prophetic voice and in the text. Thus, Yahweh is already present to the exilic community by means of the rhetorical features of the text.

The Declaratory Formulae

Several formulae appear in various guises following each of the series of laws in 18:5-9, 10-13 and 14-17. First, in v 9 the formula *ṣaddîq hû'*, "he is righteous," concludes the list.[25] Second, the formula *ḥayoh yiḥyeh*, "he shall surely live," summarizes the fate of the righteous one (cf. v 17). In like manner, an alternative formula summarizes the fate of the wicked son in v 13b, *môt yûmāt*, "he shall surely die." Then, concluding v 13 the formula "his blood shall be upon himself" summarizes the thesis of vv 4b, and 20a, and is reiterated in modified form in v 20b. Notice also the related

---

[21]Ibid., 39-40.

[22]5:11; 14:16, 18, 20; 16:48; 17:16, 19; 18:3; 20:3, 31, 33; 33:11, 27; 34:8; 35:6, 11. Only in 17:19; 20:3; 33:27 does the formula occur without *nĕ'um 'ădōnāy yhwh*. See M. Greenberg, "The Hebrew Oath Particle *ḥay/ḥê*," *JBL* 76 (1957) 34-39.

[23]See 18:3; 20:3, 31; 33:11. Von Rabenau ("Die Entstehung," 679) also notes the connection with the *Rechtsentscheid* in those texts as well as 14:16, 18, 20.

[24]Ibid. On this form see Zeph 2:9; Jer 22:24; 46:18; Isa 49:18; and also Num 14:21, 28 (P).

[25]According to Zimmerli ("Form- and Traditio-Historical Character," 523), this formula is "completely superfluous." That can now be debated with the data from the Egyptian inscriptions. In fact, the entire entrance liturgy model may be misleading. Instead I will refer to the "entrance *tôrâ*" form that has been integrated into this text. See Weinfeld ("Instructions for Temple Visitors in the Bible and in Ancient Egypt," *Egyptological Studies* [ed. S. Israel-Groll; Scripta Hierosolymitana 28; Jerusalem: Magnes, 1982], 224-50) and the discussion of legal forms later in this chapter.

statements in v 18: "he shall die for his iniquity" and in v 17 "he shall not die for his father's iniquity."

Rodney R. Hutton's work on declaratory formulae is concerned with a sociological reconstruction of Israel's institutions by means of studying "the formulaic forms that are relatively resistant to redactional manipulation." Specifically he is interested in the "institutional forms of authoritative address."[26] According to Hutton,

> Declaratory formulae manifest the societal need to designate status to the members of society, to their actions and material surroundings. . . . Declaratory formulae are those formulaic statements which are made by a person authorized to do so in a given situation which declare a certain action, person or object to be in a specified status with regard to the community as a whole.[27]

In addition, the formulae are significant in that they provide clues about the intent or function of the lists of laws in the discourse.

"He is Righteous," ṣaddîq hû'

According to R. Rendtorff and G. von Rad, "he is righteous" is a declaratory formula. The formula "is particularly characteristic in priestly terminology," notes Zimmerli, for "it probably has its *Sitz im Leben* in the priestly declaration at the temple gate. By means of this formula, the priest expresses his decision at the threshhold [sic] of the temple whether a temple visitor will be allowed to enter the sanctuary or not."[28] Similarly, Zimmerli notes that the formula "he shall surely live" (18:7) reflects a Priestly declaration rooted in the temple, "for whoever enters into the temple enters into the spere [sic] of life." He concludes, "We are therefore within the tradition which is reflected by the entrance Torah, best known to us from Ps xv and xxiv. Thus Ezekiel develops what he has to say about the new life in the language of the temple liturgy."[29] Zimmerli thinks, there-fore, that the formulae *môt yûmāt*, "he shall surely die," depicts the

---

[26]"Declaratory Formulae," 2-3.

[27]Ibid., 38.

[28]Zimmerli, "Form- and Traditio-Historical Character," 523. See G. von Rad, "Faith Reckoned as Righteousness," *The Problem of the Hexateuch and Other Essays* (New York: McGraw Hill, 1966) 125-30; idem, "'Righteousness' and 'Life' in the Cultic Language of the Psalms," *The Problem of the Hexateuch*, 243-66; R. Rendtorff, *Die Gesetze in der Priesterschrift. Eine gattungsgeschichtliche Untersuchung* (FRLANT 62; Göttingen: Vandenhoeck & Ruprecht, 1954).

[29]"Form- and Traditio-Historical Character," 523.

exclusion from the temple, outside of which existence is "death." The issue for Zimmerli is inclusion or exclusion from the sacral community.[30] He does not make it clear how that conclusion suits either a time of anticipated judgment in Judah, or a context in exile. Moreover, the contrast that he suggests between the two formulae needs to be reconsidered.[31]

Although the data presented by Weinfeld[32] on the Egyptian inscriptions would lead us to question the idea of a liturgy at the temple gate, nevertheless, the intention of the declaration is similar: entrance as a member of the sacral community into the sphere of the holy. The worshiper is challenged to conform to the virtues that characterize the true Israelite. The fact that the explicit parallels with the legal formulae are found in Ezekiel 18 does not necessitate the conclusions that H. Schulz reaches, namely, that similarity between the two legal forms and the proposed combination of those forms in Ezek 18:5-9 means that we are dealing with a later historical development.[33] Two points argue against that. First, the general formal similarity with the Egyptian texts and other biblical texts (a threefold pattern of general introduction, list, and summary conclusion) may be a closer parallel than the hypothetical reconstruction of the merging of two independent forms. Second, it is not surprising that the Priestly formulae should be used here in view of the Priestly heritage of the prophet and the overall intention of the text.

Wevers presents a different view of the formula "he is righteous."[34] He thinks that its original setting is not an entrance liturgy, but the recitation of apodictic law at "a feast of covenant renewal in which the demands of the covenant were recited and vocally accepted by the participants." This formula may have been a declaration of one's qualification for participation,

---

[30]Zimmerli, "Die Eigenart der prophetischen Rede des Ezechiel: ein Beitrag zum Problem an Hand von Ezech. xiv 1-11," *ZAW* 66 (1954) 23-24.

[31]This has a bearing on Zimmerli's view of the nature of the community and individual retribution. In "Die Eigenart" (22) he writes, "Ist es nicht viel eher so, dass auch hier wieder eine uralte, spezifische Eigenart des sakralen Rechtes unversehens eine scharfe prophetische Radikalisierung und Gültigmachung in der Predigt über Gesamtisrael erfährt?" For all his concern for the individual, Ezekiel always returns to the fate of the community, the "house of Israel." H. H. Schmid suggested in conversation (March 26, 1984) that the interplay between individual and "house of Israel" in chap. 18 may be similar to the phenomenon in Deuteronomy where, when all Israel is addressed, each Israelite understood him- or herself to be addressed. Schmid also suggested that Ezekiel 18 may be a reaction to Deuteronomic theology.

[32]"Instructions for Temple Visitors." See the discussion on legal forms below.

[33]*Das Todesrecht.* See also the critique of Schulz's proposal in W. Zimmerli's review of *Das Todesrecht* in *TLZ* 95 (1970) 891-97 and in "Deutero-Ezechiel?" *ZAW* 84 (1972) 501-16.

[34]Wevers, *Ezekiel,* 140.

which could have been followed by a declaration of cultic life. Wevers's proposal for its setting is unnecessarily hypothetical.

Wevers also suggests that the formula is not necessarily of Priestly provenance. His argument is that the Priestly formula deals with purification (clean or unclean) whereas Ezekiel is dealing with sin and individual responsibility for sinful behaviour. That difference, however, may well be explained by the deliberate reapplication of the formula, along with an intentional reinterpretation (or radicalization) of the Priestly concept of purification. Could it be that according to Ezekiel 18 sanctification is being defined in a new way?[35]

That last suggestion by Wevers needs further investigation. The data presented by Rendtorff indicates that the formula *XXX hû'* occurs in two distinct contexts. First, it is found with almost all offertory terms as a concluding declaration: "it is the 'X offering'" (e.g. Exod 29:14).[36] Second, it is found with terms denoting cultic cleanness, uncleanness, and holiness (e.g. *thwr*, Lev 13:13; *ṭm'*, Lev 11:35a; 13:15, 36); *qdš*, Lev 6:18, 22; 14:13; *šqṣ*, Lev 11:13a, 41). Concerning the second context Rendtorff suggests that "sie stellt die Diagnose des priesterlichen Arztes dar auf Grund der angeordneten Untersuchungs- und Beobachtungsmethoden. Aber diese Diagnose hat Konsequenzen: sie ist zugleich eine Entscheidung über rein und unrein."[37]

The question remains, however, as to whether the specific formula "he is righteous" is to be understood as a Priestly formula in the same way. Is it possible that Ezekiel may have adapted or deliberately reapplied the formula? Evidence in support of that suggestion must come either from specific occurrences of *ṣaddîq hû'* outside Ezekiel, or from other adaptations of the *hû'* or *ṣaddîq* formula within Ezekiel. Nowhere else in the book of Ezekiel, however, does *ṣaddîq hû'*, or any form of the formula *XXX hû'*, occur. In contrast, the exact phrase occurs only once in the Hebrew Bible,

---

[35]The priest's task is to decide between clean and unclean. Consider the lack of uses of the holiness concept that are similar to P. Two texts refer to Yahweh's making the people holy (Ezek 20:12; 37:28; cf. Lev 20:7-8). But even within the Lev text a dual action is evident: be holy, and I sanctify you. That duality is also present in the Ezekielian motif of the new heart. Holiness is still defined in terms of separation, but the ethical dimension is stronger in Ezekiel. In Ezekiel the concept of defilement of holiness takes a larger place in providing warrants for judgment. In the salvation oracles the restoration is depicted as a renewed presence of Yahweh with people, and a renewed relationship resulting in a new kind of people—a people that keeps Yahweh's law. Holiness had not been observed or enacted by the people. It is still part of Ezekiel's concept of peoplehood in relationship to Yahweh, but it seems to have been replaced by different concepts.

[36]R. Rendtorff, *Die Gesetze in der Priesterschrift*. For other texts see p. 74, n. 51.

[37]Ibid., 75. Greenberg (*Ezekiel 1-20*, 346) adds another example, the declaration of the murderer in the legislation concerning levitical cities (Num 35:15b-21).

in Lam 1:18. There, however, the full form occurs in the context of a confession in the mouth of Jerusalem: "The Lord is in the right (*ṣaddîq hû' yhwh*), for I have rebelled against his word" (RSV). The *hû'* may, however, be emphatic, and may not be part of the specific *ṣaddîq hû'* formula. Two other instances of *ṣaddîq hû'* occur, but the formula is expanded by another adjective.[38] Again, both texts are acknowledgments of Yahweh's character. In only three declarations of righteousness are human beings the object of the declaration, and all are direct address with a second person pronoun following the *ṣaddîq* (*ṣaddîq 'āttâ*, Prov 24:24; *ṣaddîq 'āttâ mimmenni*, 1 Sam 24:18); and a plural *ṣaddîqîm 'attem*, 2 Kgs 10:9).[39]

Greenberg's conclusion bears noting: "For the definition of the righteous man he [Ezekiel] chose the casuistic form widely used in priestly definitions."[40] The remarkable similarity, for example, of the definition of a murderer in Num 35:15b-21 parallels the formula in Ezek 18:9 where the form has been infused with new content. Instead of a formula like *rōṣēaḥ hû' môt yûmāt harōṣēaḥ*, "he is a murderer; that murderer shall be put to death" (Greenberg), Ezekiel has substituted *ṣaddîq hû' ḥāyōh yiḥyeh*. In the conclusions of the next two cases (in vv 13 and 17), however, the declaratory formula is changed while preserving the formal elements of the old Priestly declaration. The new content in v 9, however—the declaration of righteousness and the certainty of life, as opposed to the older declaration of death (*môt yûmāt*)—provides a rhetorical centre for the chapter. The emphatic assertion of life and righteousness takes over the formal elements from the Priestly sphere, where ordinarily declarations of death, cleanliness, uncleanliness, etc., comprised the primary content.

It seems to me that there is little formal difference between the *ṣaddîq hû'* and the general *ṣaddîq* + Pronoun forms. Either of the forms, with the second person pronoun (singular or plural), or with third person pronouns, can have a declaratory or confessional character. It is interesting to note, however, that three of the uses of *ṣaddîq/îm* have the character of confessions of guilt. In Exod 9:27 Pharaoh confesses his guilt, along with that of his people, and in so doing announces that Yahweh is *ṣaddîq*. In Lam 1:18, Jerusalem confesses the guilt of her inhabitants, and declares

---

[38]Zech 9:9, *ṣaddîq wěnôšā' hû'*; Deut 32:4, *ṣaddîq wěyāšār hû'*. See also Ps 112:4; 116:5.

[39]Note also the declaration by Judah, "she is more righteous than I" (*ṣādĕqâ mimmenni*) in Gen 38:26. All other occurrences of *ṣaddîq XXX* are either descriptive of Yahweh in the third person (*ṣaddîq yhwh*, Dan 9:14; 2 Chron 12:6; cf. Ps 11:7; 145:17; but consider the reversed *yhwh ṣaddîq*, Ps 129:4; Zeph 3:5; cf. Exod 9:27), or in vocative direct address (*ṣaddîq 'āttâ*, Ezra 9:15; Neh 9:8, 33; *ṣaddîq 'āttâ yhwh*, Ps 119:137; Jer 12:1; cf. vocative *ṣaddîq* without *hû'*, Isa 41:26).

[40]*Ezekiel 1-20*, 346.

Yahweh to be ṣaddîq. Finally, in 2 Kgs 10:9 Jehu announces that he is responsible for the atrocity, and the people are ṣaddîq.[41]

We can conclude that the above occurrences of the formula suggest that we are not dealing with a fixed "Priestly formula." In that respect, Wevers is correct. But his hypothesis of a setting in a covenant renewal feast is unlikely simply because we have no supporting textual evidence. Instead, the formula ṣaddîq hû' in Ezekiel 18:9 must be read as a singular creative transformation and reapplication of the Priestly declaration (XXX hû'). That is especially significant in the light of the overwhelming use of the ṣaddîq declaration to refer to Yahweh.[42]   In Ezekiel 18 both the proverb of v 2 and the altercation depicted in vv 25-29 challenge the fairness or rightness of Yahweh's ways. Although the word ṣaddîq is not used in the criticism of Yahweh's ways, the connotation is clear.[43] Yahweh's ways are not ṣaddîq (cf. Gen 18:19). But in Ezekiel 18 the implication (and critique) is that no one has said of Yahweh, ṣaddîq 'āttâ. The chapter, therefore, plays on the ambiguity inherent between the declaratory ṣaddîq hû' and the absent confessional ṣaddîq 'āttâ or ṣaddîq yhwh.

Instead, the synonym tkn is used to elicit the response of the hearers. To acknowledge that "Yahweh is righteous" would dilute the demand for the repentant person to make that acknowledgment. Thus, the prophet can conclude concerning the ideal righteous person, ṣaddîq hû', but for the prophet to declare that Yahweh is righteous would be to minimize the rhetorical thrust of the call to repentance, which the chapter seeks to elicit.

Thus, the chapter seeks a dual response: the person's alignment with the divine order embodied in tôrâ, and the acknowledgment that Yahweh's actions accord with that order (i.e. ṣaddîq hû'/'āttâ). The second response can be supported by considering the uses of the formulae "Yahweh is righteous" and "You are righteous, O Yahweh." Several of the instances occur as part of confessions of guilt on the part of the speaker. That is why the word ṣaddîq does not appear in the criticism of Yahweh (see Lam 1:18 where Jerusalem confesses; Exod 9:27, where Pharaoh confesses; cf. 2 Kgs 10:9). It is such a confession of Yahweh's righteousness or innocence that Ezekiel seeks to elicit from his hearers. Thus, theodicy is a motivating factor in the rhetorical thrust of the chapter, but the author seeks at the same time to explore the potential for human transformation.

---

[41]Gen 38:26 seems to belong here as well.

[42]Consider especially the possible connection with the texts in Daniel, Ezra, Chronicles, Psalms (as noted above).

[43]Only Jer 12:1 uses the formula alongside a critique of Yahweh.

"He Shall Surely Die," môt yûmāt

One can hardly understand Ezekiel, let alone this text, apart from the concepts of "life" and "death."[44] The *môt yûmāt* formula appears to have been subordinated to the thematic focus of the text. By that I mean that the formula has lost its original sense in this context because the conceptual opposition of life and death has become the dominant factor. Two reasons support that suggestion. First, the formula *ḥāyōh yiḥyeh*, "he shall surely live," is artificially modeled after this one, thereby creating a tension between the two declarations. Second, the frequency of the terms "life" and "death" in the chapter indicates that the "death sentence" is not the operative function of the formula. The juxtaposition of the two concepts throughout the chapter indicates that the text presents a call for choice. If death means the loss of national and religious identity, the chapter presents a program for restitution that the people can grasp, and in which they can become partners with Yahweh. That possibility does not remove the necessity or inevitability of judgment, but it does imply that judgment is not the last word. Judgment does not rule out the prophetic ideal of transformation of the social order.

The formula *môt yûmāt*, "he shall surely die," stands at the heart of the form-critical problem of vv 5-9.[45] As I have already mentioned, the formal elements of the declaration "he shall surely live" (*ḥāyōh yiḥyeh*) may well be formally derived from the Priestly legal declaration *môt yûmāt*. Along with discussion of the formal characteristics, development, and legal setting of the phrase *môt yûmāt*, I shall note how the phrase relates to the legal list in vv 5-9 and how the declaration contributes to the rhetorical development and thrust of the chapter.

The phrase "he shall surely die" (*môt yûmāt*) occurs in chap. 18 only in v 13. This Qal infinitive absolute and Hophal imperfect construction occurs numerous times in other texts, but in Ezekiel only once. The variety of other expressions concerning death in chap. 18 is important, for it tempers the central position often given to the phrase in 18:13. Before discussing the phrase *môt yûmāt* the following paragraphs describe other expressions for death in Ezekiel 18.

---

[44]See, for example, W. Zimmerli, "'Leben' und 'Tod' im Buche des Propheten Ezechiel," *TZ* 13 (1957) 494-508; L. Wächter, *Der Tod im Alten Testament* (Arbeiten zur Theologie II/8; Stuttgart: Calwer, 1967); G. Wagner, "Umfang und Inhalt der *môt-jûmāt*-Reihe," *OLZ* 63 (1968) 325-28; Marie-Louise Henry, "'Tod' und 'Leben': Unheil und Heil als Funktionen des rechtenden und rettenden Gottes im Alten Testament," *Leben angesichts des Todes: Beiträge zum theologischen Problem des Todes (FS. H. Thielicke)* (Tübingen: Mohr-Siebeck, 1968) 1-26.

[45]Schulz, *Das Todesrecht*.

18:18. wĕhinnēh mēt. The idiom occurs in 2 Sam 4:10; 1 Kgs 3:21; and 2 Kgs 4:32 and expresses a "recognition of the fact of death."[46] Here, as in v 17, the cause of death is given as *ba'ăwōnô,* "because of his iniquity."

18:17-18. The cause of death given in 18:17-18 is "iniquity" (*'āwōn* prefixed by the preposition *b*). The preposition expresses either the reason for death, or the way of death. The phrases that predominate in Ezekiel are formulaic expressions describing the causes of death in terms of sin. Illman discusses these terms in two groups: the cause of sin as *ba'ăwōn(ô)/bĕ'awlô,* and as *bĕhet'ô/bĕhatta'to.*

The verb "to die" (*mwt,* Qal) occurs with *'āwōn* in Ezek 3:18//33:8; 3:19//33:9; 18:17, 18; 7:16; Jer 31:30. The differences in Ezek 18:17-18 are the negative in v 17 and the perfect form in v 18. The other occurrences have *ba'ăwōnô yāmût.*

Ezekiel alone combines the words *'āwel* and *mwt* in 18:26; 33:13; 18:26 ("for the wrong that he does he shall die"); 33:18 (Illman translates: ". . . and takes to evil ways and dies because of them."). The first two of those are similarly constructed with a relative clause, and like the constructions with *'ăwōn(ô)* these have the preposition *b* and the verb *yāmût.* The second two are identical "paratactical forms without the relative clause." Priestly legal formulations are again said to be the source of the language.[47] One wonders, however, why the formulae are not found in the so-called Priestly literature.

The verb "to die" (*mwt*) occurs also with the substantives *hēt'/hattā't,* along with the preposition *b*. The concrete example in Num 27:3 (perf.) depicts Zelophehad who died because of his sin. The other formulaic examples cite a principle (Deut 24:16; 2 Kgs 14:6; 2 Chron 25:4; Ezek 3:20; 18:24, all imperf.) Only Ezekiel uses the substantive *hattā't.* In Ezek 18:4 and 20 we find a restatement of the principle, "the person that sins shall die" (cf. Amos 9:10). Illman thinks that these are all variations of one formula, and it appears that Deut 24:16 is the earliest of the group.[48]

18:31//33:11. "Why should you die?" (death of individual: Eccl 7:17; 1 Sam 20:32; death of group: Gen 47:15, 19; Deut 5:22; Jer 27:13). In each of those texts, a cause of death is cited or implied by the context. That is especially clear in 1 Sam 20:32 where Jonathan asks concerning Saul's intention to kill David, "Why should he be killed, what has he done?" In the Jeremiah text, the reason for death is given as submission to the king of Babylon. In Ezekiel, however, the "house of Israel" is threatened with death on account of sin. That entity is depicted in Ezekiel 18 in terms of

---

[46]Karl-Johan Illman, *Old Testament Formulas about Death* (Meddelanden Från Stiftelsens för Åbo Akademi Forskningsinstitut 48; Åbo: Åbo Akademi, 1979) 35; see also pp. 27-28.
[47]Ibid., 84-85.
[48]Ibid., 85-86.

the generations in vv 1-20. The rhetorical question is therefore a variation of a formula "with the function of pointing to a danger which would inevitably lead to death unless it were removed."[49] In this respect, the question is directly related to the call to repentance. A deliberate act is called for, and a real alternative is envisioned. As Illman notes, "sins, then, are misdeeds of the past, which are considered to be the cause of deportation and exile. This again would have fatal consequences for the national survival of the people, if they did not repent."[50]

Knierim thinks that these texts that deal with causes of death have their original *Sitz im Leben* in civil law (cf. Deut 21:22; 22:26).[51] Illman suggests, however, that Num 18:22 and 27:3 (both P) have begun to shift from the civil to the sacral realm. In all other cases (including Amos 9:10) "it is a question of legal formulations, not within a legal procedure but transferred to preaching (Deut 24,16; 2 Kings 14,6; 2 Chron 25:4; Ez 18,4.20; 3,20)."[52]

All the phrases discussed above deal with the reason for death, prefixed by the preposition *b*. Illman summarizes:

> Although most of the phrases seem to have originated from civil or sacral law, they have been transferred from this *Sitz im Leben* to another, namely Deuteronomistic and prophetic preaching about the law. Their common theme was that a man dies because of his own sin, provided of course that he has committed a sin that required punishment.[53]

A final observation by Illman deserves noting. Other uses of the verb "to die" with *b* indicate ways of death: battle, sword, pestilence, thirst, and famine. Those "represent a special kind of evil death, and not ways of death in general" (cf. Ezek 5:12; 6:12; 7:15; and without *mwt* in 6:11;

---

[49]Ibid, 83.

[50]Ibid. He notes that it is not clear in Ezekiel 18 and 33 whether an individual or a collective is threatened with death, but that the context indicates the latter.

[51]Knierim, *Die Hauptbegriffe für Sünde im Alten Testament* (Gütersloh: Gerd Mohn, 1965) 49.

[52]*Formulas about Death*, 88. Illman refers to Knierim (*Hauptbegriffe*, 49), who considers the combination *mwt-ht'* formulaic, except that the texts with slight variations are considered "bedingt formelhaft." Illman thinks this applies also to Num 18:22; 27:3 as well as Deut 21:22; 22:26. Amos 9:10 is not considered formulaic. In 2 Sam 12:13, however, another non-formulaic text does present *hattā't* as a cause of death, which is avoided because "The Lord has removed your sin, you shall not die."

[53]Ibid., 97.

12:16).[54] In all expressions giving the causes of death—either a reason for death, or the way of death—premature death is implied, and is

> considered not only as an 'evil,' but as a punishment by God. [In 1 Sam 20:32] . . . the reason and way of death come together: when reasons are given they point to the guilt of men, and when extinctions of collective groups are threatened, these too are thought of as punishments for sins.[55]

Death in Ezekiel 18 must certainly, therefore, refer to the premature extinction of the people, Israel.

In the light of those observations, the concept of death in Ezekiel 18 as discussed thus far has these characteristics: the chapter depicts a sufficient reason for death; the subject is the premature death of a community, the House of Israel; and the rhetorical use of the concept of death along with a didactic use of *tôrâ* implies an alternative of some kind that would allay or prevent the final consequences.

That hypothesis is further confirmed by considering the remaining uses of the verb "to die," and especially its connection with the verb "to live."

In Ezek 18:21, 28; 33:15, the negated Qal imperfect form implies that "death is the outcome of guilt and can be avoided through repentance." That observation is in keeping with the majority of the fifteen uses of the negated form of *yāmût*, which "express a conditional avoidance of death."[56]

The formula *môt yûmāt* in 18:13 is one of three occurrences of the formula (of a total of 28) outside legal texts (Gen 26:11; Judg 21:5). Otherwise, the phrase is found primarily in the legal texts in the Pentateuch.[57] The laws in the Book of the Covenant are consistent in having a participle at the beginning and the *môt yûmāt* formula at the end. Two middle elements may vary: an object, and a consequence. The

---

[54]Ibid., 88. He suggests, following L. Wächter (*Der Tod im Alten Testament* [Arbeiten zur Theologie, II, 8; Stuttgart: Calwer, 1967] 138-39) that Ezekiel borrowed the formula from Jeremiah and altered it, indicated by its relatively free use in Ezekiel. See also G. Fohrer and K. Galling, *Ezechiel*, 40.

[55]Illman, *Formulas about Death*, 97.

[56]Ibid., 111.

[57]Book of the Covenant: Exod 21:12, 15-17; 22:18; Holiness Code: Leviticus 20; and other places, Exod 31:14, 15; Lev 24:16, 17; 27:29; Num 15:35; 35:16, 17, 18, 21, 31. Illman (ibid., 126) notes that *yûmāt* in Deuteronomy has the same meaning as *môt yûmāt* elsewhere, i.e., for capital punishment. The Qal form *môt yāmût* is also peculiar to Dtr. Ezekiel uses *môt tāmût* three times (3:18; 33:8, 14). G. Liedke (*Gestalt und Bezeichnung alttestamentlichen Rechtssätze: Eine formgeschichtlich-terminologische Studie* [WMANT 39; Neukirchen-Vluyn: Neukirchener Verlag, 1971] 127, n. 1) does not think the meaning of the two expressions can be distinguished.

structure of the laws in Leviticus 20 follow the pattern *'îš 'îš / wĕ'îš 'ăšer,* "anyone who," a Qal imperfect verb, and the *môt yûmāt* formula. Added to the end of the formula is the bloodguilt formula *dām-bô* or *dĕmēhem bām,* "his/their blood be upon him/them." The pattern in Leviticus 20 is said to be a later development of the formula found in the Book of the Covenant.[58] Other legal texts represent a breaking up of the strict casuistic legal formulation. It is presumed by many that Ezek 18:13 represents such a late development as well.[59] Illman concludes:

> We therefore have to take into account a distant development from the strict form and restrictive use of the formula in the old legal codes through a long period of adaptation and more extensive use in later legal formulations and then, parallel to this, its influence on narrative texts, etc.[60]

Since the stems *mwt* and *hyh* occur juxtaposed over 100 times in the Hebrew Bible, the fact that the terms are used together in Ezekiel 18 may have a bearing on their meaning.

First, in the expression "live and not die" in Ezek 18:21, 28 the negated form of the verb "to die" complements the positive "to live." "The function of the negated forms is quite clearly to emphasize the positive opposite."[61] In the Ezekiel texts, the phrase is a promise of life to "the wicked person who repents . . . and does what is just and right" (18:21); "because s/he took heed and turned back from all the transgressions that s/he had committed" (18:28); and "if the wicked person restores a pledge, makes good what s/he has taken by robbery, follows the laws of life, and does not commit iniquity" (33:15 NJV, adapted). Illman considers the phrase to be formulaic (in form and function), calling it a "save-your-life" formula. Except for Deut 33:6 and Ps 118:17, the "formula underscores in all cases an exhortation to do or not to do something."[62] In that case, the motifs in Ezek 18 do not function primarily as references to capital punishment but belong to the persuasive rhetoric of moral discourse.

In other texts the verbs "live" and "die" express opposites, but are not in formulaic phrases. The phrases in Ezek 18:23, 32 deny the possibility that Yahweh should wish the death of the wicked (also Ezek 33:11). In each of those the emphasis is that the person should repent, change

---

[58]Illman, *Formulas about Death*, 123-24. See Schulz, *Das Todesrecht*, 46-47.
[59]Illman, *Formulas about Death*, 125-26.
[60]Ibid., 127.
[61]Ibid., 155. Cf. Gen 42:2; 43:8; 47:19; Num 4:19; Deut 33:6; 2 Kgs 18:32; Ezek 33:15; Ps 118:17.
[62]Ibid., 155.

behaviour, and live.[63] These are the only occurrences of the phrase in the Hebrew Bible, although two other texts with God as subject state that Yahweh does not wish or wishes to kill (Judg 13:23; 1 Sam 2:25). All five texts have the verb *hps*, "to wish, intend," but only the Ezekiel texts add the alternative of life. As Illman notes, these are to be considered repeated phrases peculiar to Ezekiel.[64] Illman discusses other texts that present the opposition "live" or "die."[65] The only formal feature that those texts share is the opposition of *mwt* and *hyh*. Two of the texts are not true alternatives, for the negative merely repeats the other term (Gen 42:20 negates *mwt*; Exod 19:13 negates *hyh*). In all the other texts the opposites "live" or "die" represent alternatives. In those texts,

> one common feature lies in the contexts: choosing the right alternative, either avoiding death and choosing life, or being liable to capital punishment, always presupposes that something is done or left undone.[66]

What is done or undone, however, can be different, as can the alternatives. Thus, Illman does not consider these to have a common function. Nevertheless, in Ezekiel 18 the rhetorical opposition has a positive function of stressing the consequence of choice, and presenting the option of "life" or "death."[67]

It is interesting to note, also, that Exod 19:12-13 exhibits a structure similar to Ezek 18:13, where the opposition entails the juxtaposition of *môt yûmāt* and *lō' yihyeh*. Concerning the Exodus text, Illman remarks: "Perhaps v. 13a is to be regarded as a variant of v. 12b, which would explain the discrepancy between what looks like a death sentence (*môt yûmāt*) and a deadly consequence of touching the mountain (*lō' yihyeh*)."[68] We should regard the juxtaposition of the two terms in both texts as a rhetorical opposition, which supports my conclusions about the rhetorical intention of Ezekiel 18, to call for an alternative.

---

[63]The language of Deuteronomy 30 similarly focuses on choosing life over death. Cf. also Deuteronomy 28.

[64]*Formulas about Death*, 130, 158.

[65]2 Kgs 8:10; Gen 19:19-20; 20:7; 42:18, 20; Deut 5:24-26; Jer 27:12-13; Num 14:35-38; Jer 21:9 [text ?]; 38:2 [text ?]; Exod 19:12-13.

[66]Illman, *Formulas about Death*, 159.

[67]We should note that the choice presented in our text is not between "life" and "death," but between the consequences of certain actions that lead to life, and the consequences of certain actions that lead to death. This observation is significant because the Deuteronomic phraseology does not appear in Ezekiel 18. For the Deuteronomic phraseology, see Illman, ibid., 168-69, 206, nn. 275-76.

[68]Ibid., 204, n. 263.

Within the book of Ezekiel, only Ezek 18:13 has the formula *môt yûmāt*. In other verses where death is mentioned within chapter 18 (vv 4, 18, 23, 24, 26), the reason for death (on account of sin) is the factor that is stressed. In v 30 transgression and iniquity are depicted as a stumbling block—a hindrance to repentance. Death in vv 31-32 is portrayed as a last resort, an extreme consequence from which all can turn. It is offered as the *wrong* alternative. Death, therefore, is not a death sentence, but the rhetorical opposite of life or blessing. Presumably the death sentence has already been passed, and experienced. Similarly, the alternatives of life and death do not pertain to avoiding judgment, but avoiding extinction as a people. Ezekiel assumes the survival of a remnant, but judges those who remain as wicked. Thus, whether Ezekiel 18 addresses those who experienced the first deportation, or those who have just returned from exile, the judgment on the behaviour remains until the choice is made to repent.

"His blood shall be on himself:" dāmāyw bô yihyeh (v 13)

This expression is bound up with other terms that focus the issue of responsible action in Ezekiel 18.[69] H. G. Reventlow argued that the formula had virtually the same meaning as the expressions "he shall bear his own iniquity" (*nś' 'wn*: Lev 20:17, 19, 20) and "to be cut off from the people" (*krt*: Lev 17:9, 10, 14; 20:18). He suggested that the formula indicated a cultic-legal disqualification from the covenant community.[70] By comparing Ezekiel 18:10 and 13 with the expressions in Ezekiel 22:6, 9, 12, Reventlow noted the parallel of *šōpek dam* (18:10) and *dāmāyw bô* (18:13). He suggested that the reference to blood indicated a stereotypical description of an arch-sinner (*Erzsünder*) and not that of capital crimes *per se*. Thus he translates the phrase "Seine Verschuldung komme über ihn"[71]

---

[69]On this formula see debate between H. G. Reventlow, ("Sein Blut komme über sein Haupt," *Um das Prinzip der Vergeltung in Religion und Recht des Alten Testaments*, 412-31 [ed. K. Koch; Darmstadt: Wissenschaftliche Buchgesellschaft, 1972]; originally in *VT* 10 [1960] 311-27) and K. Koch ("Der Spruch 'Sein Blut bleibe auf seinem Haupt' und die Israelitische Auffassung vom vergossenen Blut," *Um das Prinzip der Vergeltung*, 432-56; originally in *VT* 12 [1962] 396-416). The discussion was initiated by Koch's article "Is there a Doctrine of Retribution in the Old Testament?" *Theodicy in the Old Testament* (ed. J. L. Crenshaw; Issues in Religion and Theology 4; Philadelphia, PA: Fortress; London: SPCK, 1983) 57-87; originally in *ZThK* 52 (1955) 1-42. See also H. Kosmala, "His Blood on Us and on Our Children," *ASTI* 7 (1970) 94-127.

[70]"Sein Blut komme über sein Haupt," 420-21.

[71]Ibid., 422. My translation "he is responsible for his own death," although not literal, is more in keeping with the interest of the text, and corresponds to the use of the expression in 33:4-5.

as a statement of legal judgment but not as a declaration of capital punishment.

K. Koch, however, argued that Reventlow's explanation is too juridical. The formula is, rather, a *Schätzformel*, spoken to ensure that the consequences of the action remain on the offender rather than fall on anyone else. Koch reiterates his thesis that the expression refers to the fate-engendering deed (*Schicksalwirkende Tat*) and therefore that the emphasis is not on the blood coming upon the offender but remaining on the person.[72]

Without drawing conclusions about the matter of retribution,[73] it is possible to discover the rhetorical function of the formula in Ezekiel 18. Its use in v 13 follows the pattern of Leviticus 20, but it has become part of a rhetorical juxtaposition in a new context. The one who is a *šōpek dām*, a shedder of blood (v 10), now finds his own blood on himself. This is an exaggerated description of the wicked person who must be held responsible for his own actions and their consequences. It is not capital punishment that is the issue here; the language has been borrowed from that realm of discourse. But with Koch, is it not "cultic law" that is being promulgated here, but virtues that have their roots in the life of the family and the clan. The blood-guilt formula serves here, therefore, to emphasize the responsibility of the moral agent, the one who sins.

But more, the formula also functions as part of the theodicy motif in chap. 18. In v 4 the statement is made that all persons belong to Yahweh; the person who sins (*ht'*) will die. That is repeated and spelled out in more detail in v 20. Although the speaker in chap. 18 alternates between prophet and Yahweh, it is clearly Yahweh's voice that dominates the disputation. Following Koch's suggestion, the blood-guilt formula serves to absolve Yahweh of responsibility for the consequences of the sinner's actions. Thus, the statement that the person will be responsible is especially significant in light of Ezekiel's theocentric interests.   Since Ezekiel conceives of Yahweh as being victimized by the people, the use of the blood-guilt formula in the argument places the responsibility clearly on the offender rather than on Yahweh.[74]   That point is only implicit in the rhetoric of vv 10-13, but as the argument gains momentum the theodicy question in relation to human responsibility also becomes more explicit.

---

[72]"Die Israelitische Auffassung vom vergossenen Blut," 437-38.

[73]On this matter see Chapters 5 and 6.

[74]On the idea that God is the victim in cases of *ḥaṭṭā't* and *peša'* see K. Koch, *"ḥāṭā'*," *TDOT* 4 (1980) 311.

THE PROVERB (*māšāl*)

What becomes explicit as the argument gains momentum begins only implicitly in the citation of a proverb. The *māšāl* of v 3 poses several problems. The *māšāl* is not well defined according to form-critical criteria. J. W. Wevers gives it the meaning "simile." Those can be short sayings as we have here in v 3, but they can also be of various types, including "animal and plant stories, fables, allegories, but all are in some way applied to the contemporary situation."[75] Bentzen describes the *mĕšālîm* as "sentences," "popular proverbs," as well as other types of literature.[76] Bertholet, citing Ezek 12:22; 16:44; and Lam 5:7, states that the *māšāl* is a "landläufige Redeweise, die in möglichst kurzer und knapper Form fest geprägt ist."[77] The commonly used meanings of the term are "sovereign saying," "word of power," or "likeness."[78] According to W. McKane,

> the effectiveness of a *māšāl* derives from its concreteness and from the circumstance that a model of general truth stimulates the imagination and clamours for attention, as a matter-of-fact statement would not. It may even offer some resistance in the first place to understanding, but this works to its advantage in the long run, because once the representative character of the model is grasped and the relationship of resemblance invited, the initial effort expended adds to the impressiveness of the discovery.[79]

In a recent article on the *māšāl* in the Bible, T. Polk surveys the current research on the *māšāl* and pays close attention to the use of the term in the Book of Ezekiel.[80] Much of the research to date has dealt with the *māšāl* as a genre. G. M. Landes's work on the Book of Jonah focuses on

---

[75]*Ezekiel*, 20.

[76]The taunt song is one example: Isa 14:4ff.; Mic 2:4; Ezek 12:22ff. The words of seers and poets are also called *mĕšālîm*, for example the oracles of Balaam. A. Bentzen, *Introduction to the Old Testament* (Copenhagen: Gad, 1958). 1. 167-68.

[77]A. Bertholet and K. Galling, *Hesekiel* (HAT 13; Tübingen: Mohr-Siebeck, 1936) 68.

[78]Wm. McKane, *Proverbs: A New Approach* (OTL; Philadelphia: Westminster, 1970) 24. An early study of the *māšāl* is by O. Eissfeldt, *Der Maschal im Alten Testament* (BZAW 24; Giessen: Töpelmann, 1913). For a survey of the lexical data see J. A. Soggin, "*māšāl*," *THAT* 1 (1971) 930-33.

[79]*Proverbs*, 28.

[80]T. Polk, "Paradigms, Parables, and *Mĕšālîm*: On Reading the *Māšāl* in Scripture," *CBQ* 45 (1983) 564-83. A more comprehensive survey of scholarly opinion can be found in Carole Fontaine, *Traditional Sayings in the Old Testament* (Bible and Literature Series 5; Sheffield: Almond, 1982).

the content and function of the *māšāl*.[81]   And D. Suter attempts to deal with both function and form, and speaks therefore of "family resemblances" among the variety of types of *mĕšālîm*.[82]   Polk, on the other hand, wishes more to discover what the *māšāl* does than what it is.[83]   That is important in light of the diversity of literary types that are called *mĕšālîm* in the Hebrew Bible.

Landes and Suter allow for diversity in the literary shape of the *māšāl*, and therefore are not bound by strictly formal criteria.[84]   According to Landes, *mĕšālîm* partake of a "basic meaning" that can be summarized as "a comparison or analogy for the purpose of conveying a model, exemplar, or paradigm."[85]

Suter points out, however, that to posit an "essential meaning" of the *māšāl* appears on the surface to unite the diverse *mĕšālîm*, but in fact blurs the matter of form.[86]   Rather than relying on a basic meaning, Suter considers a criss-crossing network of resemblances among various literary types that can include formal features, functions, and contents.[87]   Thus, although comparison is usually an element of the *māšāl*, that is not always explicit. As Polk notes,

> in one instance, the comparison may be an explicit and integral part of the genre so that we would say that that particular speech form *is* a comparison, model, or paradigm, whereas another instance may have a speech form that does not always and of necessity entail a comparison but is nevertheless employed so as to *effect* one.[88]

---

[81]G. M. Landes, "Jonah: A *Māšāl*?" *Israelite Wisdom Theological and Literary Essays in Honor of Samuel Terrien* (ed. J. G. Gammie, W. A. Brueggemann, W. L. Humphreys, and J. M. Ward; New York: Scholars Press/Union Theological Seminary, 1978) 137-58.

[82]D. Suter, "*Māšāl* in the Similitudes of Enoch," *JBL* 100 (1981) 193-212. See also A. S. Herbert, "The 'Parable' [*Māšāl*] in the Old Testament," *SJT* 7 (1954) 180-96.

[83]Polk, "The *Māšāl*," 564.

[84]Landes ("Jonah," 140-46) classified the *mĕšālîm* according to four types: popular proverb, satirical taunt poem of weal or woe, didactic poem, and allegorizing parabolic fable. Fontaine (*Traditional Saying*, 231) lists seven literary types designated as *māšāl* (those in brackets are not designated as *māšāl* by the text): similitudes (Ezek 16:44; [Gen 10:9]; 1 Sam 10:11); popular sayings ([Jer 23:20; 31:29; 1 Sam 24:13; Isa 32:6; 1 Kgs 20:11]); literary aphorisms (Prov 10:1-22:16; 25-29; Eccl 9:17-10:20); taunts (Isa 14:4; Mic 2:4; Hab 2:6-8; Ezek 12:22-23; 18:2-3); bywords (Deut 28:37; 1 Kgs 9:7; Jer 24:9; Ezek 14:8); allegories (Ezek 17:1-10; 20:45-49; 24:3-14); Discourses (Num 23:7, 18; 24:3-24; Job 27:1; 29:1; Ps 49:4; 78:2).

[85]Both Landes (ibid., 140) and McKane (*Proverbs*) come to that definition by beginning with the popular proverb as the earliest form of the *māšāl*.

[86]Suter, "*Māšāl*," 197-98.

[87]Ibid., 197, n. 22.

[88]"The *Māšāl*," 567. See also Suter, "*Māšāl*," 197-98.

Thus, Polk emphasizes the affective dimension of the *māšāl* as discourse. He suggests that the issue is an hermeneutical one, namely, "that when used in and as *religious* discourse, the *māšāl* wants to do something to, with, or for its hearers/readers." His thesis is that "speech-acts designated *mĕšālîm* are aptly suited for religious discourse (and Scripture) by virtue of a heightened performative and reader-involving quality. This quality [he calls] . . . paradigmatic-parabolic."[89]

Polk criticizes Landes and McKane for beginning their discussions of the *māšāl* with the popular proverb. One understands the tendency to begin there, "since several of the key features in the web of resemblances among the *māšāl* family are so strikingly exhibited there."[90]   Among those features the aspect of comparison (cf. the root *mšl*, "to be like"), "is often *not* there at all as a formal feature, but only comes into play implicitly as the effect of certain features that *are* present formally."[91]   Ezek 18:3 provides an example.   There, according to Polk, one finds the formal features of concrete and specific imagery (McKane's observation regarding characteristics of the popular proverb).   McKane views that imagery as lending the proverb a "hermeneutical openness" that demands application or comparison.   In this case, however, even though the imagery highlights the paradigmatic aspect of the proverb, "the *reader* makes the comparison; it is not that the proverb *is* one."[92]   Hence, to focus on function rather than form is more truly descriptive, for, as Polk suggests, "a paradigmatic quality does, in fact, seem to extend across the many different forms of biblical *mĕšālîm*."[93]

To defend his view of *māšāl* as paradigm, Polk makes two comments.[94]   First, he argues that "paradigms typically serve *both* a normative and a noetic function."   By that he means that a paradigm has two functions: it provides "standard cases by which students learn the prevailing theories and methods of the field" as well as providing some way to describe reality.   In addition, Polk notes that the "normative" may often include the "noetic."   Thus, "admonishing, prescribing principles, and setting standards of procedure [the normative] do not exist apart from beliefs about matters of fact [the noetic]."

---

[89]Polk, ibid., 564-65. It is unnecessary to suggest a special "religious" rhetoric, but Polk's observations are instructive.

[90]Ibid., 568.

[91]Ibid.

[92]Ibid., 568-69.

[93]Ibid., 569. Suter ("*Māšāl*," 197, n. 21) however, questions that description, contending that "'model,' 'exemplar,' and 'paradigm' are probably too narrow since they suggest a normative function, while a comparison at times may serve a noetic function."

[94]Ibid.

Second, he suggests that in a religious context the *māšāl*-paradigm would not be expected to have a strictly noetic function, for in that context "it is the extra-informational, behaviour-affecting function of the *māšāl* that bears the greater weight." He proposes that "paradigm" is not too limiting a description, but too broad and needs filling out by a qualified use of the term "parable." Thus,

> if we keep to family resemblances, . . . we can see that there are fictive, figurative, or otherwise imaginative dimensions to the *māšāl* that may well warrant attributing to it a parabolic *quality*, if not the full designation 'parable.' Relatedly, like the parable the *māšāl* has the marked ability to involve its addressee, or target, in a self-judgment.[95]

Polk understands the *māšāl*, therefore, as both paradigm and parable. As paradigm it functions noetically and normatively; as parable it includes the readers/hearers

> by requesting their assent and a decision about their life-relation to the subject. Put another way, telling a parable is a matter of presenting to others an imaginatively shaped paradigm (a model of reality, a description of experience) and asking that they recognize it as somehow true. From the point of view of the parable, the readers' determination toward it, whatever their responses, identifies their place in the parable's world, and hence their relation to its truth.[96]

We turn now to Ezekiel, and to our text in particular. Since sixteen of the fifty-seven occurrences of the root *mšl*[1] in the Old Testament are found in the Book of Ezekiel, the matter gains importance for the study of Ezekiel 18.[97] Several types of *mēšālîm* are found, including popular proverb and allegorical tale (12:22-23; 14:7-8; 16:44; 17; 18:2-3; 21:5; 24:3). The use of the *māšāl* in the Book of Ezekiel is consistent, and may illuminate the function of the proverb in 18:2 within the chapter.

In the seven different texts within Ezekiel, the root *mšl* occurs in both verbal and nominal forms. Of all the occurrences in the Hebrew Bible, only in Ezekiel does the noun function as a cognate accusative along with the verb.[98] Two occurrences of the root in 16:44, a Qal plural participle and a Qal imperfect, seem to be a similar construction, but with the nominative

[95]Ibid., 570.

[96]Ibid., 573.

[97]G. Lisowsky, *Konkordanz zum Hebräischen Alten Testament* (2nd ed.; Stuttgart: Würtembergische Bibelanstalt, 1958) 874-75.

[98]Cf. Ps 49:5, 13, 21; Isa 14:4, 10; where the noun and verb play on one another, but are not in the same syntactical relationship as in the Ezekiel texts.

participial form taking the place of the accusative noun as the second element in the line (cf. 18:2; Num 21.27). In Ezek 14:8 the noun stands parallel to *'ôt*, "sign."[99] That parallel may inform our reading of 18:2, for it highlights an aspect of the *māšāl* that remains for the most part implicit in Ezekiel—that the people as a whole become a *māšāl*.

In Polk's survey of the *māšāl* in Ezekiel he attempts to demonstrate the "paradigmatic-parabolic" factor that serves "the prophetic task of summoning from a reluctant audience a response to the call and claim of God."[100] As C. Fontaine notes, that call and claim in every instance (except for 16:44) contrast with the situation and perspective of the audience. That makes the *māšāl* perform an evaluative or affective function. Thus, "the proverb performances work to emphasize the difference between God's vision and that of the covenant community, and in every case, God's actions or assertions in the Context Situation are *not* what the community expects."[101]

In 12:22-23 the citation of the people's *māšāl* provides a stereotypical portrait of the popular opinion and focuses on the matter of the people's attitude toward the prophets. The proverb implies that Ezekiel's prophecies are inconsequential. Ezekiel does not assent to their judgment of the prophetic task, but answers with a reversal of their statement, with another *māšāl* in fact. Every vision will be brought to reality. The prophet's challenge is interpreted as a declaration that Yahweh will indeed act, and the prophetic word will be vindicated. The second *māšāl* asserts that the judgment that the prophet levels at the people is accurate, and it challenges them to reconsider their stance.

The *māšāl* of Ezek 16:44 pictures the moral heritage of the people and calls for recognition of guilt, care for the poor and the needy (16:49).

In 14:7-8 the people are depicted as a *māšāl*:

> They have become a paradigm—archetypes of a bad fate and, in that bad fate was understood as the consequence of moral turpitude, a bad life. Being labelled a *māšāl*, they are intended to reach a self-judgment. . . . It is expected that they should assess the course of their lives and recognize the connection between their deeds and the inevitable consequences.[102]

---

[99]Cf. the parallels with *šĕnînâ*, "taunt, byword" in Deut 28:37; 1 Kgs 9:7; Jer 24:9; 2 Chron 7:20).

[100]"The *Māšāl*," 573. What follows depends largely on Polk, 573-83.

[101]*Traditional Sayings*, 249-250. In Appendix C, "Proverb Performance in the Old Testament Prophetic Books" (242-52), Fontaine presents a brief illustration of proverb performance in conflict situations in order to generate evaluative or affective communication. In Ezekiel, 33:10 and 37:11 are affective, 9:9; 12:22; 18:2, 25 are evaluative, and 16:44 is both evaluative and affective.

[102]"The *Māšāl*," 577.

Besides the self-judgment that is called for, the people are to become paradigmatic for others: "They are to be the living testimony to [Yahweh's] sovereign lordship and the text in which other potential apostates can read their fate."[103]

Concerning chapter 17 Polk states that the parallel designations ḥîdâ, "riddle," and māšāl emphasize the "reader-involving dimensions" of the text:

> Ḥîdâ suggests that the chapter ultimately poses a paradox and mystery which are constitutive of reality and incumbent upon the readers to discern. Māšāl characterizes the chapter as a paradigm of divine activity, modeling the structure of reality and the ways of God with human beings in such a way as to invite or compel the readers to define their own place within that picture.[104]

Polk then suggests that the comparisons within the chapter illustrate its māšāl-like character:

> first, between the fable and the application; second, between Israel's status as a loyal and then a treasonous vassal (within just the application); and third, between Israel judged and condemned and the Israel redeemed (across the two parts of the compound judgment-salvation oracle).[105]

The various levels of comparison allow the chapter to be appropriated by the people as a whole, and do not restrict the meaning of the allegory to the historical level of apostate kings. In the māšāl the specificity of Israel's history as judgment and salvation takes on a paradigmatic character. The allegory depicts "Israel's death and life and destiny."[106]

Finally, 18:2-3. "The fathers eat unripe grapes, and the children's teeth grate." Polk again draws attention to the affective dimension of the proverb. On the surface the saying is paradoxical in that the content is not an observable fact of day to day existence. Agreeing with McKane, Polk states the obvious: the maxim models "the general truth that later generations always end up paying for the errors of earlier ones."[107] And he adds:

> The affective component of the māšāl could be, variously, resentment toward the fathers, resignation in the face of the unavoidable, consolation that the

---

[103]Ibid., 578.

[104]Ibid., 578-79.

[105]Ibid., 582.

[106]Ibid., 583.

[107]Ibid., 575; See McKane, *Proverbs*, 29.

fault is not one's own, or a resolve to rectify historical and systemic wrongs.[108]

But he rejects those options. Rather,

what is being modeled is not so much a general truth as a particular religious dogma, viz., that the sins of the fathers shall be visited upon the sons (Exod 20:5; 34:7; and Num 14:18), a dogma which the *māšāl* wants to express "in such a form as to expose it to ridicule and condemnation."[109]

The *māšāl* functions to point up the absurdity of the dogma. "The existential point is that whoever decreed the ordinance ought to recognize his own caprice, or be rejected as unjust."[110] That observation is supported by the paraphrase in v 25: "Yet you say, 'The way of Yahweh is arbitrary.'" In response, Yahweh reverses the accusation and points it at the people (cf. 12:22-25). The counter-accusation carries with it its own affective dimension, as does the original proverb. As Polk continues,

both the premise and the point of the people's *māšāl* are spurned; meanwhile a counter-paradigm is being propounded in a different form, though it too has its affective component. That is to say, the chapter's legal material, couched in priestly casuistic style and presenting God's norms for human action, serves both to vindicate Yahweh and motivate his accusers to take responsibility for their own lives instead of hiding behind glib and self-serving aphorisms.[111]

That sounds harsh, and may be tempered by recognizing the function of the *māšāl* in a slightly broader way, as I have suggested above. Perhaps the people as a whole become a *māšāl*/sign/parable. In the new reality that is called for in the recognition that the *māšāl* evokes, there is also a recognition of Yahweh's point of view (hence the ubiquitous occurrences of the recognition formula in Ezekiel?). Ezekiel 18 depicts the people/individual ("all souls are mine") of 18:4 as the new *māšāl* that God gives after the initial one of the people. That new *māšāl* in v 4 is explained

---

[108]Ibid., 575.

[109]Ibid., 575, citing A. S. Herbert, "The Parable," 186. Fontaine (*Traditional Saying*, 249), commenting on Jer 31:29, states that the intent of the traditional saying there is affective. It contrasts the proverb situation and the context situation: "Israel and Judah must not act as if the 'old rules' embodied in the saying are still in operation." The intent of the proverb use is 18:2, however, is evaluative. Although Polk uses the term "affective," he means "evaluative" according to Fontaine's terminology.

[110]Polk, ibid., 575.

[111]Ibid., 576.

by the legal cases throughout the chapter. The statement-response pattern (reversal) begun in vv 3-4 also continues.

We turn next, therefore, to consider the contribution of the legal forms in articulating the character of that new reality.

LEGAL FORMS

The legal material in Ezekiel 18 is often assumed to be the most significant factor contributing to our understanding of the chapter's setting and intention, as well as its compositional or redactional setting in the Book of Ezekiel. The investigation of the legal dimension within the chapter has focused mainly on form-critical and traditio-historical concerns. Those two areas of research are not easily separated in the study of legal literature. The traditio-historical task is generally considered to deal with the pre-history or the pre-literary level, whereas the form-critical task focuses on the structure, genre, setting, and intention of the literary level of the text. Naturally, that latter task involves the study of the history of a literary form or type, and the former examines the oral history and social location of the tradition that influenced the composition. Thus, considerable overlap occurs, for the boundaries between the oral and the literary stages of legal texts are not always clear. That is especially of concern for understanding Ezekiel 18 because of its supposed close proximity to the Holiness Code and the Priestly tradition. I shall in this section, therefore, examine the aspects of Ezekiel 18 that share common conventions of structure, style, and content with the legal literature in the Hebrew Bible. In Chapter 6 I shall consider the more specific question of the distinctive literary-theological tradition within which the chapter finds a home.

Series of laws reminiscent of the Decalogue occur seldom in the prophetic literature, although the prophets are certainly familiar with the legal traditions.[112] Hos 4:1 and Jer 7:9 are instances of such lists, used in judgment speeches to indict the people for wrongs that they have committed. Similar lists in the Book of Ezekiel do not bear as striking a resemblance to the content of the decalogue as do those in Hosea and Jeremiah, but are analogous to the laws found in the Holiness Code (cf. Ezek 22:6ff.; 33:15). Ezekiel 18 contains three such lists: vv 5-9 and 14-17 depict the ideal righteous person, and vv 10-13 the image of the wicked person. Those laws are framed in the casuistic style typical of *tôrâ* literature. The three generations depicted reflect Priestly genealogical lists. And two formulae

---

[112]See W. Zimmerli, *The Law and the Prophets* (Oxford: Blackwell, 1965; reprint ed., New York, NY: Harper & Row, 1967); R. V. Bergren, *The Prophets and the Law* (Monographs of the Hebrew Union College 4; Cincinnati: Hebrew Union College, 1974).

(discussed above) strengthen the legal flavour of the chapter: the series of laws is concluded by the "declaratory formula" *saddîq hû'*, and the declaration of life (*ḥyh yḥyh*) or death (*môt yûmāt*).[113]

The Generational Pattern

The question arises whether the three generations in Ezek 18 represent an historical analogy. For example, G. Hölscher suggests that the three-fold schema refers to: 1) Josiah; 2) his wicked sons, Jehoahaz, Jehoiakim, and Zedekiah; 3) Zedekiah.[114] Such explicit historical referents, however, cannot be sustained even though the redactional placement of chap. 18 does lend itself to that kind of speculation. The rulers are not clear patterns for the argument of the chapter, for the schema righteous-wicked-righteous is too contrived to do justice to the reality of the situation. The reigns of the four kings after Josiah do not fit the pattern well. It appears as though the threefold schema serves the purpose of the argument, and that the generations are a cipher for the past.

Zimmerli suggests that the historical figures are irrelevant since "the entire sketch is not drawn from history, but from case law." He points out the genealogical lists in the Priestly tradition, which here serve to bolster the legal case style. That leads him to the conclusion that "in Ezekiel 18 a legal case is worked out which is concerned with the problem of the divine justice through several generations, in the framework of a list."[115] The question remains open, however, since the application to a specific historical context (or persons) is not excluded by the formal legal elements in the text. The generational schema is subordinate to the intention of the larger unit of which it is a part. But one can also make the case that the larger unit is informed by the import and impact of the generational schema.

---

[113]Zimmerli, "Form- and Traditio-Historical Character," 523-24; idem, *Ezekiel 1*, 375.

[114]*Hesekiel, der Dichter und das Buch.* So also V. Herntrich, *Ezechielprobleme* (BZAW 61; Giessen: Töpelmann, 1932) 103. G. A. Cooke (*A Critical and Exegetical Commentary on the Book of Ezekiel* [ICC; New York: Scribner's, 1937] 198) also finds a parallel in Hezekiah, Manasseh, and Josiah. R. Smend (*Der Prophet Ezechiel* [2nd. ed.; Kurzgefasstes exegetisches Handbuch zum Alten Testament 8; Leipzig: S. Hirzel, 1880] 114) understands the generations to begin with Manasseh, and those who receive the punishment according to the old formula (cf. Ezek 18:19), are the third and fourth generations, Josiah and his sons, the nephews and great-nephews of Manasseh. Herntrich (ibid., 103) does not think Manasseh is the referent, since that was sixty years earlier. Instead, he derives from Ezekiel 18 itself the clue that vv 14-20 are an allusion to the time of Zedekiah, whom the prophet assures that sons do not inherit guilt, and from whom he seeks a decision to repent. Thus, vv 10-13 would refer to the time of Jehoiakim and vv 5-9 to Josiah's time.

[115]Zimmerli, *Ezekiel 1*, 375.

To understand the gist of the three generational pattern, we must consider the way in which the portrait of a righteous or a wicked person is painted: by a series of laws.[116]

Legal Lists

In Chapter 3 I noted the verbal correspondences between the three lists of laws in Ezekiel 18. In what follows I shall look more closely at the shape of those lists. I shall then evaluate suggestions concerning the function and origin or social context in which the legal list form was used. I shall note the similarities and differences that mark this text, and make several suggestions regarding the function of the lists as they are incorporated into the chapter.

The first concern is to explore the legal lists in Ezekiel 18. To make the matter clearer for purposes of this discussion, the following paragraphs present several representative divisions of the list of laws.

J. W. WEVERS:[117]   vv 5-9   vv 10-13   14-17

		vv 5-9	vv 10-13	14-17
1.	does not eat upon the mountains		1	1
2.	or lift up his eyes to the idols of the house of Israel		6	2
3.	does not defile his neighbor's wife		2	3
4.	or approach a woman in her time of impurity			
5.	does not oppress anyone		3	4
6.	restores to the debtor his pledge		5	5
7.	commits no robbery		4	6
8.	gives his bread to the hungry			7
9.	and covers the naked with a garment			8
10.	does not lend at interest		8	10
11.	or take any increase		9	11
12.	withholds his hand from iniquity			9
13.	executes true justice between man and man			
14.	walks in my statutes			13
15.	and is careful to observe my ordinances			12

Whereas the third list follows the order of the first until no. 11, and then modifies the order slightly for the last three, the second list appears to

---

[116]See further the discussion on kinship terminology in Chapter 5.

[117] *Ezekiel*, 108. Note: In vv 10-13, nos. 4, 8, 9, 12, 13, 14, 15 are missing. In vv 14-17, nos. 4, 13 are missing.

follow no order at all. In fact, an additional clause is added as the seventh, "commits abomination." In the first list, nos. 1 and 2 are parallel. Only no. 1 is repeated in vv 10-13, whereas both are repeated in vv 14-17. Nos. 3 and 4 from the first are parallel, yet only no. 3 is repeated in the next two lists. Nos. 8/9, and 10/11 are also parallel. If we combine the parallel laws, we discover a list with 10 parts: 1/2, 3/4, 5, 6, 7, 8/9, 10/11, 12, 13, 14/15.

W. HARRELSON[118]

1. One who does not eat upon the mountains
2. Does not lift up his eyes to idols
3. Does not defile his neighbor's wife
4. Does not approach a woman in her time of impurity
5. Does not oppress anyone, but restores to the debtor his pledge
6. Does not commit robbery
7. Does give bread to the hungry
8. Does cover the naked with a garment
9. Does not lend at interest
10. Does not take an increase
11. Does withhold hand from iniquity
12. Does execute true justice between man and man
13. Does walk in God's statutes and observe his ordinances

Harrelson thinks that Ezekiel is probably listing requirements and prohibitions that number approximately ten. Harrelson suggests that numbers 9 and 10 ought to be placed together, and that number 11 may be the original ending of the list of ten that Ezekiel had available to him. Implied is the possibility that numbers 12 and 13 were his own summary conclusions.

S. MOWINCKEL[119]

[Gesegnet der Mann,]
1. der gerecht ist und Gerechtigkeit tut,–
2. der nicht auf den Bergen isst,–der seine Augen nicht zu den Götzen des Hauses Israel erhebt,–
3. der nicht das Weib seines Nächsten schandet,–
4. der nicht zu einem Weib geht, wenn es unrein ist,–
5. der niemanden bedruckt,–

---

[118]*The Ten Commandments and Human Rights* (OBT; Philadelphia: Fortress, 1980) 37.
[119]His reconstruction in *Psalmenstudien V: Segen und Fluch in Israels Kult und Psalmendichtung* (Amsterdam: P. Schippers, 1924) 117.

6. der das, was er gepfandet hat, wiedergibt,–
7. der nichts mit Gewalt an sich bringt,–
8. der sein Brot dem Hungrigen gibt und den Nackten mit seinem Kleide bedeckt,–
9. der nichts auf Wucher hingibt und keine Zinsen nimmt,–
10. der seine Hand von Unredlichkeit fernhalt,–
11. der einen ehrlichen Spruch tut zwischen den Leuten,–
12. der in meinen Geboten wandelt und meine Gesetze beachtet, sei ehrlich erfullen!

J. HERRMANN (10 laws)[120]

18:5-9
1. nicht auf dem Bergen essen
2. nicht Götzendienst treiben
3. nicht Unzucht treiben [Secondary: sich nicht mit dem Weibe eines Volksgenossen verunreinigen]
4. nicht Bedruckung üben
5. Pfand zurückgeben
6. keinen Raub begehen
7. Barmherzigkeit üben
8. nicht auf Wucher geben und keinen Zins nehmen
9. keine Unredlichkeit begehen
10. ehrlich als Schiedsrichter urteilen

Similarly, Herrmann finds ten laws in Ezek 22:7-9, 12a (vv 10-11 are omitted, perhaps as interpretive additions to the last clause in v 9. So also v 12b is omitted).[121]

22:7-12

1. Vater und Mutter gering achten
2. mit dem *gēr* gewalttätig umgehen
3. Waise und Witwe bedrücken
4. die *qdšym* Jahwes verachten
5. die Sabbate Jahwes entweihen
6. Verleumdung üben (in mörderischer Absicht)
7. auf den Bergen essen
8. Unzucht treiben (mehrere Fälle werden aufgezahlt)

---

[120]*Ezechielstudien* (Beiträge zur Wissenschaft vom Alten Testament 2; Leipzig: Hinrichs, 1908) 132.
[121]Ibid.

9.   Bestechung nehmen (wo es sich um Leben und Tod jemandes handelt,
      wie 6)
10. Wucher und Zins nehmen

By comparing the two lists we find several parallels, but differences
are clear. Herrmann sees four corresponding clauses: in his chap. 18 list,
nos. 1, 3, 4, 8, and 10 correspond respectively to nos. 7, 8, 4, 10, and 9 in
his chap. 22 list. It is of interest that the nos. 4/4 parallel depends on
emendation, the nos. 10/9 parallel is a correspondence of sense, and not a
strictly verbal parallel, and the nos. 3/8 parallel is indirect in that 22:10-11
catalogue five possible acts of lewdness (*zimmâ*, v 9c).

K. KOCH[122]

1.   Auf den Bergen hat er nicht gegessen.
2.   Seine Augen hat er nicht zu den Götzen . . . erhoben.
3.   Die Frau seines Gefahrten hat er nicht entehrt.
4.   Einer Frau hat er sich während ihrer Unreinheit nicht genähert.
5.   Arme und Elende hat er nicht bedrückt.[123]
6.   Ein Pfand hat er nicht gepfändet.[124]
7.   Einen Raub hat er nicht mit Gewalt an sich gerissen.[125]
8.   Um Zins hat er nicht (Geld) geliehen.
9.   Wucherischen Aufschlag hat er nicht genommen.[126]

It is obvious that Koch derives this list by moving the sentences about, and
not from the natural order within the text. The artificial reconstruction
assumes rigid formal criteria that are not necessary. Also assumed is that
Ezekiel must have had a preexistent list that he adapted to suit his purposes
here.

---

[122]"Tempeleinlassliturgien und Dekaloge," *Studien zur Theologie der alttestamentlichen
Überlieferungen* (ed. R. Rendtorff and K. Koch; FS von Rad; Neukirchen: Neukirchener
Verlag, 1961) 56-57.
[123]The words of v 12.
[124]The words of v 16.
[125]Here Koch notes that vv 7 and 16 add two positive rules regarding care for the naked
and the hungry, probably added by the prophet himself.
[126]Koch suggests that a tenth member may be hiding at the end of v 12: "Abscheuliches
hat er (nicht) getan." That statement may be positively restated in v 8: "withholds his hand
from iniquity."

The Setting and Intention of Legal Lists

How then ought we make sense of Ezekiel's use of the legal list form? G. von Rad was among the first to illustrate that the legal list form has significant similarities in ancient Near Eastern literature. The conclusions that we may draw from the correspondences, however, ought to be kept in perspective. As von Rad notes in his study of confessional lists, "the bearing of such [Egyptian and Babylonian] lists upon Israelite forms is altogether too problematical."[127]   Because of the diversity of settings in which such lists were used, it is likely that the legal list form was highly adaptable, capable of being incorporated into a variety of literary and oral settings.[128]   It is not the place here to dispute the origin of the laws, or the original setting of those laws.[129]   My main concern is to survey possible social and religious contexts within which such lists were used, and then to suggest how the lists in Ezekiel 18 function within the chapter and perhaps also within the book of Ezekiel.[130]

Several models have been proposed for the setting in life and intention of the legal lists. Each model illuminates elements of the tacit dimension inherent in the rhetorical strategy of Ezekiel 18. But it is exactly here that setting in life proves to be a tenuous concept because the rhetorical function of the text depends on a bundle of tacit conventions that may not have anything to do with oral or literary performance in specific social settings.

Decalogue/Instruction

Wevers suggests that because of the differences in the three lists of Ezekiel 18 "the list of laws is not a well-known one such as the Decalogue."[131]   Nevertheless, others have recognized in those lists a decalogue-like form that is not necessarily literarily dependent on the decalogue of Exodus 20 or Deuteronomy 5. Mowinckel states that one may have used a decalogical form in Israel in specific contexts to highlight the

---

[127]"The Early History of the Form-Category of 1 Corinthians xiii.4-7," *The Problem of the Hexateuch and Other Essays* (New York: McGraw Hill, 1966) 316, n. 25.

[128]I argue below, therefore, that as M. Weinfeld ("Instructions for Temple Visitors") suggests, temple entrance inscriptions do provide appropriate analogies for understanding Ezekiel's use of legal lists.

[129]For a succinct summary of the issue see W. Harrelson, *The Ten Commandments and Human Rights*, chap. 2, pp. 19-48.

[130]As I shall argue in Chapter 6, Ezekiel uses laws in three main ways: in judgment speeches or allegories of judgment, in providing a hope and a shape for the future, and in instruction that provides a "way" to move from judgment to hope.

[131]*Ezekiel*, 140.

obligations of God. As he writes: "So hat der Verfasser des Ezechielbuches in Kap. 18 die wichtigsten Merkmale eines Gerechten in 12 Punkten zusammengestellt."[132] And Harrelson remarks that the Decalogue served as a paradigm for most of the lists.[133] Like the Decalogue, the lists functioned as "statements about the character of life in community."[134]

In another study, Mowinckel suggests that Deut 27:14-26 may reflect a series of blessings of the sort that we find in Psalms 15 and 24, or a moral catechism such as is found in Ezekiel 18. In those lists "die Zusammenstellungen der wichtigsten religiösen und moralischen Gebote zu kurzen 'Dekalogen' oder 'Dodekalogen' auf solche moralisch gefärbten kultischen Segens- und Fluchworte zurückgehen." Thus he concludes that short aggregations of divine laws and prohibitions originate from cultic *Segensformeln*. And those lists of laws (such as Pss 15; 24; Isa 33:14ff.; Mic 6:6-8), just as the "Segens- und Fluchformeln, im Zusammenhang mit dem Kulte des Herbst- und Neujahrs-, d.h. des Bundeserneuerungsfestes, und sind dabei öffentlich vorgetragen worden."[135] Thus, Mowinckel thinks that Ezekiel must have had an arrangement of religious and moral laws in mind (like a decalogue or dodecalogue) when he formulated his "catechism."[136]

If Mowinckel is correct about the cultic setting of the short catechism, what connection might that have to Ezekiel's concepts of covenant and repentance? Perhaps Ezekiel uses the form in order to call to mind the renewal of the covenant in which such formal language may have been used.

---

[132]"Zur Geschichte der Dekaloge," *ZAW* 55 (1937) 234-35. Mowinckel claims that the decalogues (especially the two decalogues that he uncovers in Leviticus 19) and the entrance liturgies of Psalms 15 and 24 (as well as others: Lev 20:9-27; Deut 27; Ezek 18) are unrelated to the Sinai covenant tradition. Because the decalogues or law lists vary and are used creatively he concludes that they are secondary to the Sinai tradition.

[133]*The Ten Commandments and Human Rights*, 39.

[134]Ibid., 13.

[135]*Psalmenstudien V*, 107.

[136]Ibid., 116. In fact, if one placed *bārûk hā'îš* before the list, one would have a parallel to Deut 27:14ff. "Er zählt hier die Handlungen und Unterlassungen auf, die einen Menschen zu einem Gerechten *saddîq* machen, deren Nichtbeachtung aber ihn zu einem gottlosen Frevler . . . macht, und knupft daran die Verheissung des göttlichen Lohnes, bezw. die Bedrohung mit der göttlichen Strafe" (116-17).

Entrance/Tôrâ Liturgy

H. Gunkel and J. Begrich suggested that the legal list form derives from a *tôrâ*-liturgy or gate/entrance liturgy that reflects the interaction between priest and worshippers at the entrance to the temple.[137]

Klaus Koch developed that thesis further (concerning Ps 15) in response to A. Alt's analysis of participial apodictic law lists. According to Koch, "Alt hat den Sinn solcher partizipialer apodiktischer Reihen darin gesehen, dass sie unbedingt todeswürdige Verbrechen herausstellen und Störungen der Gemeinschaft abwehren wollen." But according to Koch, that is only indirectly the purpose of Psalm 15. He suggests instead that "der unmittelbare Blickpunkt ist auf anderes gerichtet, nämlich darauf, den weiteren 'Bestand' des einzelnen Israeliten und damit der gesamten Kultgemeinschaft zu sichern."[138]

Koch continues his argument by drawing an analogy between the Egyptian Book of the Dead (chap. 125) and Ps 15:3-5a, and proposes that the Psalm text is part of an *Unschuldsbeteuerung des Laien* as in the Egyptian text. Deut 26:13-15 is the only Old Testament text that clearly depicts such a statement of innocence, and since that text may not originate from Jerusalem, he looks elsewhere for further evidence to support the thesis concerning Psalm 15. First, he refers to the Decalogue where the imperfect, which looks ahead, is compared with the perfect in Psalm 15, which looks back on one's life path (perhaps influenced by Deuteronomy 26).[139] Second, he appeals to the role of the priests as depicted in Lev 10:10-11 and Ezek 22:26; 44:23. "Die Priesterantwort in der Tempeltorliturgie ist zweifellos *Toraerteilung*, die zur Belehrung des Laien über heilig und profan, rein und unrein . . . gehört." Koch then states that

---

[137]H. Gunkel and J. Begrich, *Einleitung in die Psalmen* (2nd. ed.; Göttingen: Vandenhoeck & Ruprecht, 1966) 408-409, 327-29. See also J. Begrich, "Das priesterliche Heilsorakel," *ZAW* 52 (1934) 81-92; idem, "Die priesterliche Tora," *Werden und Wesen des Alten Testaments* (ed. P. Volz, F. Stummer, and J. Hempel; BZAW 66; Berlin: Töpelmann, 1936) 63-88.

[138]"Tempeleinlassliturgien und Dekaloge," 48. See A. Alt, "The Origins of Israelite Law," *Essays in Old Testament History and Religion* (New York: Doubleday, 1967) 101-171. Koch (ibid., 60) says that once these forms become part of literary books, they serve a different purpose in the life of Israel: "Sie dienen nun der Selbstprüfung der frommen Gemeinde und verwandeln sich damit in eine andere Gattung, die man wohl *Beichtspiegel* nennen könnte." Koch also claims that the entrance liturgy was not practiced after the exile, and in spite of similarities, the setting in life of other texts like Job 31, Test Iss 7, 1QS X, 17ff. must be found elsewhere. It appears to lie between the oral use (setting in the temple), and the purely literary use. Nevertheless, the literary setting of the form within Ezekiel 18 must take precedence over the history of the form. Yet it is that very history that informs the meaning of its adapted placement within Ezekiel 18.

[139]Ibid., 50.

if his thesis is correct, "dann gehörte in Jerusalem das apodiktische Recht zum (grösseren) Bereich der priesterlichen Tora."[140]   Third, Koch considers the term "clean hands" of Ps 24:4 to be a Priestly concept that does not mean mere ethical cleanness. Following Mowinckel he argues that the expression has to do with the levitical concept of uncleanness, yet in that, all behavior is included: "in sie ist aber das gesamte Verhalten einbegriffen."[141]

Koch suggests a development of the form "entrance-liturgy" in two stages: 1) simple, positive entrance requirements in a series of three (Ps 15:2, 5b; Mic 6:6-8); 2) enlarged by adding negatively formulated laws (Ps 15:35a; 24:3-6; Isa 33:14-16; Ezekiel 18). Koch claims that the second stage was already completed during the period of the monarchy. Ezekiel 18 expresses the expanding importance of or need for specific laws. Simple positive statements no longer suffice. The development of the form into the time of Ezekiel shows how "die Frage nach der *rechten Beschaffenheit der Kultgenossen* ein immer grösseres Gewicht erhalt. Die alten positiven und allgemeinen Hinweise auf die Rechtschaffenheit im Leben und Handeln genügen nicht mehr." So the responsible priests endeavor not merely to state "eine möglichst vielseitige Schilderung" of right human behavior, but they choose "*einzelne ganz bestimmte Gottesgebote*" to incorporate into their entrance requirements.[142]

In spite of the development of the form, according to Koch, all the individual expressions have a common element.   "Doch geht *eine* Gemeinsamkeit durch die aufgenommenen Sätze, es wird überall *gegen ein unrechtmässiges Gewinnstreben* und damit gegen wirtschaftliches und soziales unrecht Stellung genommen."[143] Koch underlines his assertion by showing that of the six perfects in Psalm 15, at least three belong to this group; of the concrete regulations in Isa 33:14-16, the first two (v 15b); and of the ten negative laws of Ezekiel 18, five belong to this group.

> Das *wirtschaftliche und soziale Leben* spielt also bei den Überlegungen, welche die Priester über die Torliturgie anstellen, eine entscheidende Rolle. Man wird nicht fehlgehen, wenn man den Anlass dazu in den sozialen

---

[140]Ibid., 50, n. 14.

[141]Ibid., 52, n. 20. Also behind other texts such as Mic 6:6-8 and Isa 33:14-16 lie independent expressions of the Gattung, *Einlasstorot*. From the Micah text he argues that the ethical demands derive not *de novo* from the prophetic consciousness, but "von der kultischen Praxis herkommen." The earliest of these short entrance liturgies, he thinks, had only three clauses (*Bestimmungen*). Ibid., 54-56.

[142]Ibid., 58. That conclusion, however, is suspect. Ezekiel 18 must be understood according to the specific setting and intention of the chapter, not a hypothetical history of forms that presupposes the movement from simple to complex, short to long.

[143]Ibid., 59.

Umwälzungen der späteren Königzeit sieht, die *Alt* einmal ausführlich behandelt hat.[144]

Bentzen also suggests that our text reflects a "liturgical torah." The approach, however, is slightly different. He states that in ancient Israel many people may have "asked for divine guidance concerning conditions excluding them from the service in the temple." They were asked questions concerning problems of race (Deut 23:4; Ezra 2:63), health or disease (Deut 23:2; cf. leprosy in Leviticus 13-14), and sexual uncleanness (Leviticus 12; 15; cf. 1 Sam 20:26; 21:4ff.). Other moral problems could also be set before the priests, who were like "spiritual guides." They "had a large corpus of traditions as foundation for answering questions of this kind." Laws were developed over time to define those proceedings. When cases arose that presented new problems, new answers had to be given.[145] Ezekiel may reflect just such a situation. Exile forced exclusion from land, temple, kingship, and presence of God, according to Ezekiel's interpretation. What, then, is Ezekiel attempting to do? Is not the priest, in his role as literateur-instructor, attempting to restore inclusion? Ezekiel has a new case, and needs a new answer.

Family/Clan Instruction

E. Gerstenberger proposes the name *Tugendkataloge* (list of virtues) for the lists in chap. 18.

> Sie verallgemeinern die Fragestellung nach dem Allgemeinmenschlichen hin. Nicht darauf kommt es an, wie König, Priester, Richter beschaffen sein müssen oder sich zu verhalten haben, sondern darauf, wie der *Gerechte* zu leben habe. Der Gerechte ist dabei als Glied einer nach aussen abgeschlossenen Gruppe gedacht. Ez 18:5-9, 14-18 (vgl. Jes 33:15; Ps 15:2-5; Ps 24:4) sind Beispiele für diese Art von Katalogen.[146]

Gerstenberger argues against the view that the lists originate with Entrance-*tôrâ* or Decalogue lists.[147]   Instead, Gerstenberger attempts to

---

[144]Ibid., 59.

[145]*Introduction.* 1. 189.

[146]*Wesen und Herkunft des "Apodiktischen Rechts"* (WMANT 20; Neukirchen-Vluyn: Neukirchener Verlag, 1965) 69.

[147]Mowinckel states that "the whole 'decalogical tradition' is attached to the cultic festival." *Psalmenstudien V*, 116. See also *Le decalogue* (Paris: Alcan, 1927) 114ff., 141ff.; idem, "Zur Geschichte der Dekaloge," *ZAW* 55 (1937) 218-35; idem, *The Psalms in Israel's Worship* (2 vols.; New York/Nashville: Abingdon, 1962). 2. 69.

show in his analysis of the *Prohibitivrecht* that the laws originate in the family/clan setting, and only secondarily came to be taken over by the cult and by literary expressions such as the lists in Ezekiel 18.

The *Tugendkataloge*, just as the *Amtsspiegeln* or *Standeskataloge* like Lev 21:17ff. and Deut 23:1ff., derive from the same impetus. Gerstenberger thinks that whether the lists of laws were formed to define the responsibilities of an office, or to present a list of virtues of the righteous individual, the function is the same, to isolate a group of qualifications for inclusion or exclusion.[148]

Thus, Gerstenberger may well be correct in his assertion that the lists formulated in the third person are secondary and later than the individual *Prohibitivrecht*. What makes that likely is his suggestion that the larger "catalogues" of laws were formulated for a variety of practical reasons.[149] Gerstenberger does not, therefore, allow a great distance between the clan and the cultic setting or use of the *Prohibitivrecht*. If that is the case, then there is reason to think that those responsible for the cult collected and taught those norms.[150]

Although the laws may have a home in the family/clan as well as in the cult (mediated by the priests), it is likely that the prophets proclaimed a "prophetic *tôrâ*" as well. Like the priests, the prophets "use the form of proclaiming the commandments of Yahweh." Just as the priests developed the *tôrâ* liturgy, the prophets developed the "prophetic *tôrâ*," which "has affinities with the style of the laws," including the hypothetical and the categorical forms of law.[151]

Confession of Integrity

Kurt Galling agrees with Mowinckel's estimation of the early provenance of the temple *tôrâ* (entrance liturgy), and with the institutional setting of the form.[152] The cultic situation of the entrance *tôrâ* depicts a

---

[148]*Wesen und Herkunft*, 69-70.

[149]"In erster Linie gibt wohl die Jugenderziehung dazu den Anstoss, aber auch die juristische Praxis und schriftstellerische, gelehrte Behandlung des Materials werden eine Rolle gespielt haben. Tugendkataloge, Bekenntnisformulare, prophetische Anklagereden geben Zeugnis davon, dass solche grösseren Sammlungen bestanden oder ad hoc hergestellt wurden." Gerstenberger cites Ezek 22:6-12; 18:5-9, and compares Job 31 along with earlier prophetic literature, Hos 4:2; Amos 2:6-8; 5:10-12; 8:4-6; Mic 6:10-12. Ibid., 87.

[150]Ibid, 143.

[151]Bentzen, *Introduction*, 1. 201-201. Hypothetical: Hag 2:12f.; Jer 3:1; cf. Ezek 18; Isa 58:6ff.; 66:3. Categorical (in imperative form or infinitive absolute: Amos 5:23; Isa 1:17; 56:1; Jer 7:21; Zech 8:16; 8:19; Isa 58:7.

[152]"Der Beichtspiegel: Eine gattungsgeschichtliche Studie," *ZAW* 47 (1929) 125-30.

dialogue between the priest and the worshiper, or more specifically, between the worshiper and the deity. God is asked concerning the requirements for entry into the holy place, and God provides the answer. Galling appeals to the oracular character of Psalm 24 to begin his argument.

Galling's contribution is to ask whether the ritual is complete with the question of the worshiper and the answer of the priest. He proposes that a third element must follow: the response of the worshiper affirming that the requirements have been fulfilled. Only following that response can one enter the sanctuary.[153]

Galling thinks that that hypothesis explains why the entrance *tôrâ* in Psalm 24 consists primarily in negative statements. "In der Negation wird das ethische Programm wirklich konkret umschrieben, wie auch die negative Aussage eines Unschuldsbekenntnisses fassbar ist." In support of his thesis he points out other Old Testament texts, but affirms that the pattern "verschiedene Ausdrucksformen haben konnte."[154] In Deut 26:12-14 the function is similar but the setting is not, as in the *tôrâ* liturgy, the entrance to the temple, but that of a pilgrim seeking entrance to the festival. In a second person form in Psalm 50:16-20 Galling finds close parallels to the decalogue of Exodus 20. He sees in Ps 50:7c a reflection of "I am Yahweh, your God" of the introduction to the decalogue. In that he suggests how the decalogue became incorporated into the cultic setting. The original first person declaration is the original form of the list.[155]

Galling suggests that one would expect the final words of the entrance liturgy to be "Wer so handelt, darf zum Heiligtum eintreten."[156] But the formula that one actually finds in the texts that gives away the fact that a removal from the original cultic setting has taken place, proposes a different question: "wer darf der Segnungen der Gottesgemeinschaft gewiss sein."[157] The answer to that question is provided in various ways in each of the texts in Psalm 15; 24; and Isaiah 33.[158] Although Galling does not claim proof for his reconstruction of the temple entrance liturgy, he claims that analogies in the Old Testament make it probable that a complete form once existed.

---

[153]Ibid., 126.

[154]Ibid., 126.

[155]Ibid., 127-28. Other examples of the same form removed from its cultic setting are Mic 6:8; Ps 119:101102; 101:3. Exceptions are the declarations of innocence in the psalms and prayers of lament (Ps 26; cf. Deut 21:6; Ps 73:1) where Galling thinks the washing of hands is an additional element of the "In-Beziehung-Tretens zur Tempelthora, der dritte Akt zu Frage und Antwort." Ibid., 128.

[156]Ibid., 128.

[157]Ibid., 129.

[158]Galling concludes that in Ps 24 one finds that the priest's speech ends at v 5, and v 6 is the expression of the layperson who seeks entry, the *Beichtspiegel*. V 6 reflects either a portion of an *Unschuldsbekenntnis*, or a shortening of it in order not to repeat the list twice.

That is all the more probable, he thinks, because of the proposed confession of the dead in chap. 125 of the Egyptian Book of the Dead, which probably reflects a ritual used at the entrance to the temple. "Das Unschuldsbekenntnis öffnet die Pforten des Tempels wie die der Gerichtshalle des Osiris. Solcher Art war das in Worte gekleidete Waschen der Hände in Unschuld."[159]

Based on Galling's "confessional mirror," Harrelson helpfully suggests that the list in Ezekiel 18 holds "before the community and its individual members the qualities of life that Yahweh approves and insists upon within the community that approaches him as Lord."[160]   But that conclusion is not based on the assumption that forms and contexts are inseparable.   The diversity of literary expressions of the confessional list suggests again that the setting in the literature can evoke the cultic context, but cannot determine the particular meaning and function of the list in its literary setting.

Instructions for Temple Visitors

The form-critical models described above help us to understand possible settings and functions of the legal lists, but all are in some measure inadequate, not because they do not each present an appropriate hypothesis, but because they are constructed on the basis of incomplete data.   Until now, the only way to make sense of the proposals has been to say that they each highlight an aspect of the literature that surely has foundation in reality.   That is to say, entrance liturgies, instructional genres, and confessions of integrity probably existed in some form or other in ancient Israel.   Blankly to assert that Ezekiel 18 is a development of all three is claiming too much, especially when the evidence for the existence of any one of the three is hypothetically reconstructed from fragments of texts, or conjectured situations in the social and institutional life of the people.

A recent article by Moshe Weinfeld opens a new avenue with concrete evidence from Egyptian inscriptions.[161]   Weinfeld begins where others begin, by comparing the structure of three similar texts: Psalm 15; 24:3-6; Isa 33:1416. Each of those, he notes, follows the pattern: question (Who may dwell/ascend?), answer (in the form of a list of conditions for entrance), and promise (statement of stability, blessing, or security).   In

---

[159]Ibid., 130.

[160]*The Ten Commandments and Human Rights*, 39. In chap. 2 he discusses the origin, structure, and setting of the Ten Commandments, to which he relates all the lists of laws in the OT (he pays attention to Exod 20:2-17; Deut 6:6-21; Deut 27:15-26; Exod 34:14-26; Lev 18:6-18; 20:2-16; Ps 15).

[161]"Instructions for Temple Visitors."

addition Weinfeld notes that Ps 5:3-8 contains the same elements as in the previous three texts, but without the list of conditions.

> In all these passages, the ideal behavior of the one who is granted admission to the holy place is described both in the positive manner and in the negative. The positive formulation is mainly of a general definitive character whereas the negative enumerates the deeds in detail.[162]

Each text begins with a general positive statement, which is followed by a catalogue or list of concrete details.

Weinfeld then compares the list in Ezekiel 18:5-9. The pattern is similar. A general positively formulated casuistic definition stands at the head of the catalogue: "If a man is righteous and does what is just and right" (v 5). A list defining negatively the characteristics of the righteous follows the general introduction. Near the end the characteristics are summarized in a positive statement: "he deals with true justice between man and man, he walks in my laws and observes my commands." The list concludes with a promise, just as in the other texts: "Such a man is righteous, he shall certainly live, says the Lord God." Weinfeld proposes concerning the Ezekiel text that "although nothing is said here about the temple, the language of the list, as well as the character of the prophet Ezekiel make us believe that the provenance of the list is priestly and was crystallized in temple circles."[163]

---

[162]Ibid., 226-27.

[163]Ibid., 228. Weinfeld points out another type of list, which presents an affirmation of the king's intention to walk uprightly in his house (Ps 101). "The king assures that he will walk with perfection in his house. In consequence of this he will keep away from his house crooks, liars, perverts and slanderers; only the one who walks in perfection will serve him" (228). The king promises to "destroy the wicked of the land and will rid the Lord's city of all evildoers" (229). In contrast to the Psalmic lists, this is a negative confession and is couched in the first person. "The king declares that he will not violate justice and will fulfill his functions as a just king" (229). Following the LXX and M. Dahood (*Psalms III: 101-150* [AB 17A; Garden City, NY: Doubleday, 1970]), Weinfeld suggests that the psalm reflects a royal confession, of which parallels are found in Egyptian and Mesopotamian literature.

A text in Ezekiel parallels Psalm 101. In Ezek 22:6ff., in an oracle about "the city," "the princes of Israel" are judged as those responsible for moral order in the city (cf. Ps 101:8). Weinfeld proposes that because the temple is in the city of God, the city itself must be free from wickedness (Ps 46:5; Isa 1:26; cf. Zech 8:3; Jer 31:22). In a hymn to Enlil from the city of Nippur, we find a similar perspective: "Hypocrisy, distortion, abuse . . . enmity, oppression . . . arrogance—all these evils the city cannot tolerate . . . the city endowed with truth where righteousness and justice are perpetuated" (230; *ANET* 573-574). So also the city of Barsip is described as "the city of truth and justice." Cited in Weinfeld, "Instructions for Temple Visitors," 250, n. 6a; W. G. Lambert, "Literary Style in First Millennium Mesopotamia," *JAOS* 88 (1968) 128, Col. Ib, line 16.

After presenting the textual data, Weinfeld discusses the *Sitz im Leben* of the lists of virtues. He asks, "Are these rhetorical questions aimed to inculcate moral values and therefore are to be seen as literary-didactic creations, or do they come out of a reality that is a ceremonial act?"[164]

Weinfeld argues against the existence of an entrance liturgy. He argues first that the biblical literature provides no evidence for such a ceremony.[165] The second level of argument is more instructive. Weinfeld cites "injunctions, addressed to the priests, inscribed on the doorposts and lintels of the temples in Egypt of the Hellenistic period"[166] He notes that similar injunctions were also used in the Ramesside period, and were therefore rooted in Old Egyptian tradition.[167] Of particular importance is the inscription

> on the lintel of the southwest door in the forecourt of the temple of Edfu [where] we find a speech uttered by Seshat the mistress of writing and addressed to Horus:
>
> "I have come to you...that I may set down in writing before you the doer of good and the doer of evil, to wit:
>
> he who initiates wrongfully
> he [who enters] when unclean
> he who speaks falsehood in your house
> he who knows [to discern] right from wrong
> he who is pure
> he who is upright and walks in righteousness . . .

Perhaps one can make a connection between the ideals and responsibilities of the king and the list of virtues in Ezekiel 18. That way the two motifs of Jerusalem as holy city and king as guardian of virtue in the city/land can be conjoined. Perhaps the close relationship between chapter 17 and 19 is to be explained not by the hypothesis that chapter 18 separated the two in the redactional stages, but that chapter 18 ties the two together.

[164]"Instructions for Temple Visitors," 230.

[165]Weinfeld (ibid., 231) argues thus: first, "if such an institution had been in existence we would expect the priest instructing the pilgrims about ritual, purity, etc. (as, for example, in Hag. 2:11f) and not only about moral integrity." Second, evidence from the Sinai narrative about procedures before the event (purification and sanctification: Exod 19:10, 15; instructions to remain at a distance: Exod 19:12, 13), and from Gen 35:2 where instructions include putting away alien gods, purification, and changing clothes, indicate no such pre-entrance liturgy. Third, legal material in the Pentateuch contain both ritual and moral injunctions (cf. Lev 19).

[166]Ibid., 232. On p. 245-46, n. 14, Weinfeld cites M. Alliot, *Le Culte d'Horus à Edfou au temps des Ptolémées*, 1949, pp. 181ff. This work was unavailable to me.

[167]He cites R. Merkelbach, who refers to private communication with E. Otto, in "Ein ägyptischer Priestereid," *Zeitschrift für Papyrologie und Epigraphik* 2 (1968), 29, n. 32.

he who loves your attendants exceedingly
he who receives bribes . . .
he who covets the property of your temple
he who is careful . . .
he who does not take rewards or the share of any man.

I write down good for the doer of good in your city, I reject the character of
the evil doer . . . [he who does righteousness] in your house [is] enduring for
ever, but the sinner perishes everlastingly."[168]

The similarities with the Psalm and Isaiah texts are striking except that
the list is not arranged in order. Positive and negative are mixed. "The
positive exhortations include: purity, integrity, and respect for God's
servants. The negative ones include: dealing wrongfully, speaking lies,
accepting bribes and gifts and coveting property."[169] Both the negative
and the positive characteristics are either paralleled or implied in the lists
from Psalms 15, 24, and Isaiah 33. Weinfeld finds verbal similarities with
the Hebrew lists in two of the positive expressions in the Egyptian text: "he
who is upright and walks in righteousness" and "he who loves your attendants exceedingly" (cf. Isa 33:15; Ps 15:2a, 4). Another similarity is found
in the conclusions. The Egyptian text reads "he who does righteousness in
your house endures for ever." Each of the Hebrew texts contains a similar
declaration, although we find no exact parallels. In Ezekiel 18 the
declaration that the righteous will certainly live is a variant on the same
theme (cf. Ps 15:5; 24:5; Isa 33:16).[170]
     Another Egyptian text cited by Weinfeld was found on a side door of
a temple and is addressed to priests.

O, you priests . . . who enter to the gods . . . who are in the temple. Do not
deal wrongfully, do not enter when unclean, do not utter falsehood in his
house, do not covet the property [of his temple]; do not tell lies; do not

---

[168]Ibid., 232-233; citing from H. W. Fairman, "A Scene of the Offering of Truth in the
Temple of Edfu," *Mitteilungen des deutschen Archaeologischen Instititut Abteilung Kairo* 16/II
(1958) 86-92.
     [169]Ibid., 233.
     [170]In fact, the structure of Ezek 18:5-9 compares so closely with the three-fold pattern of
the Psalm texts and the Egyptian text cited above, including the general positive statement,
followed by the list, and then the assurance of security or blessing, that we can hardly any
longer affirm Schulz's thesis that the Ezekiel 18 text is a late development from the *môt-yûmāt*
laws. What is similar is the Priestly casuistic introduction to Ezek 18:5, and the Priestly
declaration of life or death, but the overall structure of Ezekiel 18:5-9 follows the pattern of
the Egyptian temple inscription and the other Hebrew texts.

receive bribes; do not discriminate between a poor man and a great; do not add to the weight or the measuring cord . . . (etc.)[171]

The conclusion of that text reads: "He who is loyal to you is not troubled." According to Weinfeld, most of these "inscriptions were destined to inculcate the priests with virtue and devotion"[172]

Parallels to the commands to the priests and Priestly oaths in the Egyptian texts can be found in Ezekiel.

> Most of the sins found in the Egyptian texts occur in the lists of Ezekiel: abstaining from forbidden meals, sexual aberrations, and social sins like oppressing the poor, taking bribes, stealing, etc., are all represented in Ezek. 18:5ff, 22:6ff, 33:14f. The catalogs of Ezekiel are coined in priestly language, and it seems therefore that the origin of these lists has to be sought in the Temple amongst the priests.[173]

Finally, Weinfeld summarizes in four points what he thinks can be learned from these parallels.

1) Although there is no material evidence supporting this possibility, it may be that moral injunctions like those in Egypt were inscribed on temple entrances in Israel. Following the clues of Deut 6:9 and 11:20 Weinfeld thinks that because the *Shěma'* (and possibly also the Decalogue) was inscribed on the doorposts of homes and on city gates, it is likely that more stringent regulations may have been written on temple gates. That, he thinks, is more plausible than "the suggestion about a priest or priests standing at the Temple door and interrogating, for which no evidence can be presented at all."[174] In addition, Weinfeld mentions the exhortations that are proclaimed at the temple gates by the prophets (Jer 7:2; 22:2).[175]

2) The Egyptian lists of virtues always contain ritual admonitions, whereas the Israelite Psalmic lists do not.[176]

---

[171]Weinfeld, "Instructions for Temple Visitors," 234-35.

[172]Ibid., 235. Besides the temple inscriptions, similar contents are found in oath texts that install the priest to the Priestly task. The oath includes the denial of murder and fornication, after which we read: "I will not drink the things that are not lawful . . . nor will I put my finger [for theft]; I will not measure on the threshing floor . . . I will not lift a balance in my hand . . . I will not visit an impure place."

[173]Ibid., 235-36.

[174]Ibid., 238. On the possibility of including the decalogue on the writing on doorposts of homes, see M. Weinfeld, "The Loyalty Oath in the Ancient Near East," *UF* 8 (1976) 409, n. 267.

[175]"Instructions for Temple Visitors," 238.

[176]Weinfeld (ibid., 239) suggests that "keeping the ritual and abstaining from crime belong to the normal code of behavior, whereas the postulates brought up in these Psalms characterize

3) The Egyptian data help to clarify the problem of the relationship between the Decalogue and the lists of virtues. Mowinckel attempted to find in Psalms 15 and 24 a "decalogical tradition" that would provide the original setting for the decalogue. In contrast, Weinfeld states that

> the decalogue constitutes . . . a minimal list of basic postulates for the Israelite who is bound by national religious covenant to observe them, whereas the lists of virtues are addressed especially to the pious, the *ṣdyq*, who seeks nearness to God. In Egypt these lists were especially designated for priests and prophets. In Israel, everybody can achieve nearness to God by virtue. It seems that the lists in Ezekiel, Chapters 18, 22, can be put somewhere between the Decalogue—with its religious national postulates on the one hand—and the Psalmodic lists with their ethic-personal [sic] demands on the other. Ezekiel combines both of them.[177]

Allowing for the correctness of Weinfeld's suggestion, why does Ezekiel combine the two lists? One possible explanation is that the virtues of the *ṣaddîq* shape the identity of the moral community. Thus, Ezekiel's list is not "between" the two types of list, but purposefully integrative.

4) The lists in the psalmic texts appear to function as requirements for entrance to the temple, as in the Egyptian texts, but a distinction must be made because in the Psalms those lists "actually constitute a model for ideal behavior," and are once removed from their original setting. "The dwelling of God in the Psalms has been spiritualized. It is not the physical Temple which gives security and shelter. Everybody can feel God's presence if he deserves it through his behavior. God's shelter is conceived in the Psalms in a spiritual manner."[178]

---

the *ṣdyq*, which is of a higher moral-religious level than the average man. Observing ritual purity could be controlled by the public, as was the case in the Second temple period, where the Levites were responsible for not admitting into the Temple the unclean, unlike moral integrity, which is a matter of inner conscience only." He also notes the distinction between the cultic negative confession in Deuteronomy 26 and the moral one in Job 31. Weinfeld notes the paucity of ritual and cultic acts confessed in the Job 31 text, and emphasizes the predominance of moral integrity in the biblical lists. Only one religious transgression is noted in Job 31:26-28, adoring the luminaries.

[177]Ibid., 240. Weinfeld thinks the lists of virtues "represent general principles of piety which are idealistic and even utopian. *To walk in perfection, to do what is right and to speak the truth from the heart* is not an easy task. No one will boast to say that he fulfills these demands" (240-41).

[178]Ibid., 241. I suggest, however, that integrating the moral character of the community with the cultic concept divine presence in Pss 15, 24 and Ezekiel is a radical reinterpretation of the mythic rather than a spiritualizing. It is the physical reality of moral peoplehood that Ezekiel wishes to recreate.

Summarizing the function of lists of virtue, Weinfeld states:

> Moral instructions for Temple visitors were common in Israel as well as in
> the Ancient Near East; however, in Israel these were more refined—they do
> not include ritual at all; they were conceived not only as postulates for those
> entering the Temple but for everyone wishing to enter into the domain of the
> Lord.[179]

Weinfeld may be drawing the lines too finely here, for, even as he notes, a
sense of physical security may be associated with God's house.[180]

I return now to Weinfeld's assertion that the lists in Ezekiel stand
between the decalogue and the lists of virtue. If the lists in Ezekiel are a
step removed from the original provenance of the lists, as are the Psalm
texts, but they contain both ritual and moral injunctions, does that mean that
they are intended to inform concerning the demands of the national religious
covenant, and to instruct concerning the ideal behavior of the pious? Could
it be that Ezekiel is actually modelling his list after the decalogue with its
"first table" of laws relating to God, especially the first two
commandments? He would thereby be calling for public recognition of the
continuing validity of the covenant to which both the people and Yahweh
were committed, as well as a renewal of piety expressed in a transformation
of behavior befitting one who wishes to worship that God? Loyalty to
Yahweh (cultically and ethically) will bring the reward of "life." Thus, the
legal lists enable the chapter to function as a sermon exhorting the people
against all appearances to trust the sovereignty of Yahweh, to act
responsibly, and to take part (in spite of judgment) in the reconstitution of
the people of Israel.

Thus, the legal lists in Ezekiel 18 have been drawn into the unique
focus of the disputation—to call forth the new reality of a peoplehood
committed to its covenant Lord. It is that goal to which the final traditional
convention beckons—the call to conversion.

THE CALL TO CONVERSION (vv 30-32)

We have already considered the place of vv 30-32 in the structural
unity of Ezekiel 18. Several additional concerns need to be addressed.
First, is there a tradition of exhortation to which these verses belong?
Second, how are we to understand the call to conversion in the light of the
larger purpose of the chapter as a disputation? Is there a tension or is there

---

[179]Ibid., 242.
[180]Ibid., 250, n. 30.

continuity between the theological and ethical understandings of these final verses and the rest of the chapter?[181]

Do Exhortations Display a Formal Structure?

Is there a formal structure, or are exhortations identified simply from their content? According to A. Vanlier Hunter, exhortations are "utterances using imperatives (or jussives or sometimes declarative statements) that when taken in isolation or at face value seem to call seriously for decision and action on the part of the audience addressed."[182] There are, therefore, no structural elements that characterize the exhortations as independent units in preexilic prophetic literature.

According to T. Raitt, however, the prophetic summons to repentance contains an appeal and a motivation. The appeal may include the messenger formula, a vocative address and an admonition. The motivation may include promise, accusation and threat.[183]

A Tradition of Exhortation?

According to popular opinion, these verses are to be understood as one of the many prophetic "exhortations." Hunter's survey of scholarship on the exhortations suggests two basic positions.[184] The majority view, as he calls it, is that "the exhortations reveal the true purpose of prophecy, namely, to call the people to repentance in order that Yahweh's announced judgment need not happen and that salvation may come."[185] The minority view, and that of Hunter, is that "the exhortations serve to bolster the

---

[181]On conversion/repentance in Ezekiel see J. Delorme, "Conversion et pardon selon le prophète Ezéchiel," *Mémorial J. Chaine* (Bibliothèque de la Faculté catholique de Lyon 5. Lyon: Facultés Catholiques, 1950) 115-44; H. Gross, "Umkehr im Alten Testament: In der Sicht der Propheten Jeremia und Ezechiel," *Zeichen des Glaubens. Studien zu Taufe und Firmung. Balthasar Fischer zum 60. Geburtstag*, (ed. H. auf der Maur and B. Kleinheyer; Zürich: Benziger; Freiburg: Herder, 1972) 19-28. On the root *šwb* see W. L. Holladay, *The Root Šûbh in the Old Testament with Particular Reference to its Usages in Covenantal Contexts* (Leiden: Brill, 1958).

[182]*Seek the Lord!*, 4-5.

[183]"The Prophetic Summons to Repentance," *ZAW* 83 (1971) 35. Raitt suggests the following order in Ezek 18:30-32: threat, vocative, messenger formula, admonition, accusation, admonition, accusation, admonition, accusation, promise, messenger formula, admonition, promise.

[184]*Seek the Lord!*, 7-38.

[185]This view is reflected, for example, in T. Raitt, "The Prophetic Summons to Repentance."

announcement of either judgment or salvation but do not place a condition on either."[186]

The issue at stake concerns "the basic intention of the prophetic message."[187] That is related fundamentally to whether there exists an independent exhortation genre. According to the majority view, "the intention of the exhortation takes precedence over the other genres." The import of that view for understanding Ezekiel 18 would be that the disputation speech genre has been absorbed into the intention of the exhortation. Hunter outlines the logic of this position.

> The first step is to see the exhortation as a call for a change in attitude and behavior, . . . *so that* Yahweh may send salvation and not the threatened judgment. In the next step, it is surmised that the real purpose of the *reproach* is likewise to prompt a reversal in the people by denouncing their sin. The final step in reasoning is achieved when the *threat* is thought to be only a device whereby the prophet can move the people to a new stance vis-a-vis Yahweh by threatening disaster if they do not repent. In other words, . . . the occasional appearance of an exhortation makes the oft-repeated announced judgment conditional and reveals that the true purpose of prophecy is to call Israel to repentance in order to avert the judgment.[188]

Methodologically, Hunter's central interest is to discover the "*original intention* of the passages with exhortatory features in the life situation of the prophets themselves."[189] He concludes that the exhortations are not serious attempts to avert judgment by last minute obedience.[190] He discovers, for example, that in eight texts in Hosea and Isaiah exhortation is a subordinate element within a judgment speech.[191] "These exhortatory elements are *summaries* of earlier options when the future was still thought to be open for Israel."[192]

Hunter therefore seeks to provide evidence for "whether the prophetic utterances presuppose that the future is unalterable or whether the

---

[186]*Seek the Lord!*, 38. Scholars whose work contributes to this position are: H. W. Wolff, "Das Thema 'Umkehr' in der alttestamentliche Prophetie," *Gesammelte Studien zum Alten Testament* (TBü 22; Munich: Chr. Kaiser, 1964); C. Westermann, *Basic Forms of Prophetic Speech* (Philadelphia: Westminster, 1967); K. Koch, *The Growth of the Biblical Tradition* (New York: Scribner's, 1969); and W. H. Schmidt, *Zukunftsgewissheit und Gegenwartskritik. Grundzüge prophetischer Verkündigung* (BibS[N] 64; Neukirchen-Vluyn: Neukirchener Verlag, 1973).

[187]Hunter, *Seek the Lord!*, 35.

[188]Ibid., 16-17.

[189]Ibid., 5.

[190]Ibid., 276.

[191]Hos 2:4-15; 4:15-19; 10:9-15; 12:1-15; Isa 1:18-20; 28:7-13; 28:14-22; 30:15-17.

[192]*Seek the Lord!*, 275.

announcements of judgment are really meant to offer a last minute opportunity in the present for repentance that would alter the future."[193] That is an especially significant concern for Ezekiel 18 because v 30a is an explicit statement of judgment that is followed by an exhortation.

For Ezekiel, however, judgment had already fallen. That fact alone makes exilic prophecy different from eighth century prophecy. The announcement of judgment in v 30a and the call to repentance in v 30b, therefore, are restatements of the prophetic world view that Ezekiel is seeking to reestablish in the face of the catastrophe of judgment. Repentance will not avert a judgment, since that judgment has already been set in motion. Repentance, for Ezekiel, must have a specific and different connotation from earlier prophecy.

In order to resolve that tension it is important to note that a fundamental weakness in much study of the prophets is the strict delineation of judgment and salvation as two independent spheres of divine activity. The assumption is often made that the call to repentance must have the intention of averting impending disaster.   That dichotomy is unnecessary.[194] It is possible to announce judgment without thinking that repentance will avert judgment. Similarly, a call to repentance need not imply the guarantee of salvation. Hunter makes that point in a paragraph in his conclusion. "The exhortations can be viewed as summonses to repentance, if it is understood that such calls did not imply a necessary link between obedience and canceling the judgment."[195]

Hunter goes on to suggest that even though for the classical prophets a word of judgment is the final word for the future, the exhortation serves to set forth the divine will, even in the midst of judgment.   The Deuteronomistic tradition interpreted all earlier prophetic exhortations as summons to avert disaster. This re-interpretation, according to Hunter, has been absorbed into the majority position that has interpreted the primary function of Israelite prophecy as calling for repentance and the subsequent deliverance from judgment. Instead, states Hunter, the classical prophets, as it were, placed a moratorium "on the ordinary functioning of repentance as a condition for eluding trouble and thereby leading to salvation."[196]

I shall argue, however, that the call to repentance is a fundamental facet of Hebrew moral discourse.[197]   The prophet exhorts the people not

---

[193]Ibid., 1.

[194]This view is developed by T. M. Raitt, *A Theology of Exile: Judgment/Deliverance in Jeremiah and Ezekiel* (Philadelphia, PA: Fortress, 1977).

[195]*Seek the Lord!*, 278.

[196]Ibid., 280.

[197]B. Lang (*Kein Aufstand in Jerusalem: Die Politik des Propheten Ezechiel* [SBB; Stuttgart: Katholisches Bibelwerk, 1978] 167-68) suggests that even the symbolic actions are homiletical enactments whose intention is to invite repentance. Thus, the intention of prophetic

simply because he is interested in averting judgment, nor simply to guarantee salvation. Rather, the exhortation serves as the basic statement of human responsibility in a cosmos that is characterized by order. The human and the divine are inextricably linked to that order. The actions of human beings and of the human community of Israel have a bearing on the future. Submitting oneself and the community to the cosmic order will have repercussions for life or for death. And Ezekiel, in this case, is arguing for life. Ezekiel 18, however, suggests that repentance and turning from transgression will avert ruin (not judgment), and that getting a new heart and a new spirit will avert death.

To make sense of that we need to understand the traditions of human and divine responsibility within which Ezekiel is working. To rely only on the two options presented by Hunter is to limit ourselves to a reductionistic approach to the prophetic view of the future. Since Hunter studies only prophecy before the seventh century, we have to account for the massive dissonance produced by the exile. As Hunter himself notes, "the outlook of this time signaled a basic shift in the interpretation of prophecy."[198]

Yet even in Ezekiel, contrary to Hunter's perspective on the eighth-century prophets, the exhortations do not soften the judgment or set up the conditions for a last minute staving off of judgment.[199] Judgment is an experienced reality. Ezekiel, however, articulates the view that judgment continues to operate in the present and that the moral life ordered according to the divine way is the only path by which the human being (and the Israelite community) can find a secure way into an uncertain future.

Thus, whether or not the eighth-century prophets saw a future for Israel, the call to conversion in Ezekiel must be evaluated differently. For Ezekiel the call to repentance is a vibrant call—a call to life.[200] And that is not incompatible with the notion of divine action, since keeping *tôrâ* is based ultimately on the prior act of God in deliverance. So for Ezekiel, keeping *tôrâ* is a proleptic act, in the hope of a new act of God.[201]

---

discourse that Hunter seeks must be found in a wider matrix than simply the formal call to repentance. As Lang suggests, Ezekiel is calling for a political alternative—what I have called the reconstitution of a people of character.

[198]*Seek the Lord!*, 4.

[199]Ibid., 277.

[200]R. W. Klein (*Ezekiel: The Prophet and His Message* [Studies on Personalities of the Old Testament; Columbia, SC: University of South Carolina Press, 1988] 108) states that "chapter 18 calls them to do what they can in fact do: to turn and live." For Ezekiel the option for life is not simply a rhetorical flourish with which to lash out at a despondent people for whom no hope lies except in an act of God. It is the possibility of action that makes the divine action comprehensible, as I shall argue in Chapter 7.

[201]On the function of law in Ezekiel see further Chapter 6. Such a view of law as envisioning and enabling a future has been suggested by W. Harrelson, *The Ten Com-*

Theological and Ethical Impact
of the Exhortation

The exhortations in Ezekiel stand in continuity with the Deuteronomistic and Jeremianic exhortations in terms of historical context. Whatever we say about the original function of exhortations in the speeches of the eighth-century prophets, we must admit that the exile made clear what for earlier prophets was at best ambiguous. That is to say, the earlier prophets did not fully comprehend the import of their messages of judgment. An eighth-century exhortation may well have served as a basis or support for an inevitable judgment. We ought not, however, rule out the possibility of ambiguity. Perhaps the exhortations highlighted the recalcitrance of the prophets' audiences, and at the same time bore within themselves the seeds of transformation and vision of a larger reality.

After the exile, however, the hope for transformation of reality takes a different shape. One can scarcely imagine the revolution in thinking that must have been necessary for exilic Israel to envision a hope for the future and a peaceful existence in the world of the nations. We bandy about the contemporary expression "paradigm shift" with ease, without being aware of the anguish that accompanies such all-encompassing changes. The nearest examples in our day are the holocausts and genocidal acts of the twentieth century. But the world view that shapes Ezekiel's vision is based on an awareness of cosmic and moral order. Ezekiel cannot fail to take seriously the impact of the exile's devastation. Ezekiel 18 and the ethical and exhortatory texts in Ezekiel find their place in the imagined world between judgment and reordering.

For Ezekiel the judgment is a result of disorder in the moral world of Israel. Salvation is conversely viewed as a reordering. Just how that reordering is to be experienced is not altogether clear to the twentieth-century reader.

The place of human responsibility is equally ambiguous. It seems as though Ezekiel finds the individual righteous person incapable of effecting social change (chap. 14). Ezekiel does not, therefore, affirm a simple individual responsibility and a concomitant individual salvation. The devastation of the community and its undergirding and supporting institutional structures has forced him to articulate a theology that is compatible with the reality that he knows. That is not to make Ezekiel a "materialist." Ezekiel continues to affirm the correspondence between act and destiny on a personal and corporate level. He also continues to affirm the involvement of Israel's God in that process or movement into the future. The task of moral suasion, therefore, is both critical and constructive—a task

---

mandments and Human Rights, chap. 8.

that has been shaped uniquely by means of numerous traditional conventions that have shaped this unique disputation speech.

We turn now to a discussion of the traditional moral problems and concerns that Ezekiel 18 seeks to address.

5

INDIVIDUAL RESPONSIBILITY
IN COMMUNITY

INTRODUCTION

In this chapter I shall deal with the matter of the individual's responsibility within the orbit of the community. A number of questions will be addressed in the following discussion. How are we to describe the identity of the moral agent, and the context in which the moral agent operates? Related to that, are the notions of "life" and "death" ultimate ontological categories as they are connected with the act-consequence relationship? Or are they moral categories that apply to individual human beings? Or further, are they communal categories within which individuals find orientation? In addition, what factors lead to the emerging possibilities for solidarity as a reconstituted Israel after the exile? Perhaps, as before the monarchy, a mixture of factors conspire to give shape to a new community. Hutton suggests that the community is shaped by "an attachment to the same life style, values, norms and cultural propensities."[1]

Rehearsing the scholarship and the biblical data has been done many times elsewhere.[2] I shall highlight aspects of the scholarly tradition in

---

[1]"Declaratory Formulae," 327.

[2]J. R. Slater, "Individualism and Solidarity as Developed by Jeremiah and Ezekiel," *The Biblical World* 14 (1899) 172-83; M. Löhr, *Sozialismus und Individualismus im Alten Testament: Ein Beitrag zur alttestamentlichen Religionsgeschichte* (BZAW 10; Giessen: Töpelmann, 1906); J. B. Mozley, "Visitation of the Sins of the Fathers Upon the Children," *Ruling Ideas in Early Ages and Their Relation to Old Testament Faith* (London: Longmans, Green, and Co., 1906) 104-125; S. R. Driver, "The Worth of the Individual: Ezekiel xviii.2-4," *The Ideals of the Prophets* (Edinburgh: T. & T. Clark, 1915) 62-72; J. Cales, "Retribution individuelle, vie des justes et mort des pecheurs d'apres le livre d'Ezechiel," *RSR* 11 (1921) 363-371; J. Pedersen, *Israel: Its Life and Culture* (2 vols.; London: Oxford University Press; Copenhagen: Brannerog Korch, 1926); H. Bueckers, "Kollektiv- und Individual-vergeltung im Alten Testament," *TGl* 25 (1933) 273-87; H. W. Robinson, "The Hebrew Conception of Corporate Personality," *Werden und Wesen des Alten Testaments* (eds. P Volz, F. Stummer, J. Hempel; BZAW 66; Berlin: Töpelmann, 1936) 49-62; M. J. Gruenthaner, "The Old Testament and Retribution in this Life," *CBQ* 4 (1942) 101-110; A. R. Johnson, *The One and the Many*

---

order to focus on suggested angles of vision by which the various perspectives in Ezekiel and the Hebrew Bible can be understood. I shall first suggest a typology of opinion on the question of the relationship between the individual and the community. Second, I shall survey the relevant narrative and legal texts that raise the issue to the forefront. Then I shall survey the data in the book of Ezekiel that give rise to apparently diverse perspectives within the book. Finally, I shall offer several ways of looking at the book of Ezekiel that provide a coherent synthetic reading

---

in the Israelite Conception of God (Cardiff: University of Wales Press, 1942); idem, *The Vitality of the Individual in the Thought of Ancient Israel* (Cardiff: University of Wales Press, 1949); D. Daube, "Communal Responsibility," *Studies in Biblical Law* (Cambridge: Cambridge University Press, 1947) 154-59; V. Korosec, "Die Kollektivhaftung im hethitischen Recht," *Archiv Orientalni* (Praha) 18/3 (1950) 187-209; J. de Fraine, "Individu et Société dans la religion de l'Ancien Testament," *Bib* 33 (1952) 324-55, 445-75; F. Spadafora, *Collettivismo e Individualismo nel Vecchio Testamento* (Quaderni Esegetici 2; Rovigo: Istituto Padano di Arti Grafiche, 1953); J. Harvey, "Collectivisme et individualisme: Ez. 18, 1-32 et Jér. 31,29," *ScEccl* 10 (1958) 167-202; J. Scharbert, "Unsere Sünden und die Sünden unserer Väter," *BZ* 2 (1958) 14-26; idem, *Solidarität in Segen und Fluch im Alten Testament und in seiner Umwelt, Band I: Väterfluch und Vätersegen* (BBB 14; Bonn: Peter Hanstein, 1958); H. G. Reventlow, "Sein Blut komme über sein Haupt;" G. E. Mendenhall, "The Relation of the Individual to Political Society in Ancient Israel," *Biblical Studies in Memory of H. C. Alleman* (eds. J. M. Myers, O. Reimherr, H. N. Bream; Locust Valley, NY: Augustin, 1960) 89-108; K. Koch, "Is there a Doctrine of Retribution in the Old Testament?"; A. H. van Zyl, "Solidarity and Individualism in Ezekiel," *Studies on the Book of Ezekiel* (Pretoria: Die Ou Testamentiese Werkgemeenskap in Suid-Afrika, 1961) 38-52; H. G. May, "Individual Responsibility and Retribution," *HUCA* 32 (1961) 107-120; B. Lindars, "Ezekiel and Individual Responsibility," *VT* 15 (1965) 452-67; J. R. Porter, "The Legal Aspects of the Concept of Corporate Personality in the Old Testament," *VT* 15 (1965) 361-80; J. W. Rogerson, "The Hebrew Conception of Corporate Personality: A Re-Examination," *JTS* 21 (1970) 1-16; H. Kosmala, "His Blood on Us and on Our Children"; J. Gammie, "The Theology of Retribution in the Book of Deuteronomy," *CBQ* 23 (1970) 1-12; L. Rost, "Die Schuld der Väter," *Studien zum Alten Testament* (BWANT 101; Stuttgart: Kohlhammer, 1974) 66-71; P. Joyce, "Individual Responsibility in Ezekiel 18?" *Studia Biblica 1978: Papers on Old Testament and Related Themes* (ed. E. A. Livingstone; JSOTSup 11. Sheffield: JSOT, 1979) 185-96; idem, *Divine Initiative and Human Response in Ezekiel* (JSOTSup 51; Sheffield: JSOT, 1989); idem, "The Individual and the Community," *Beginning Old Testament Study* (ed. John Rogerson; Philadelphia, PA: Westminster, 1983) 74-89; idem, "Ezekiel and Individual Responsibility," *Ezekiel and His Book: Textual and Literary Criticism and their Interrelation* (ed. J. Lust; Leuven: Leuven University Press/Peeters, 1986) 317-21; B. L. Ross, "The Individual in the Community: Personal Identification in Ancient Israel" (Ph.D. diss., Drew University, 1979); P. D. Miller, *Sin and Judgment in the Prophets: A Stylistic and Theological Analysis* (SBLMS 27; Chico, CA: Scholars Press, 1982); T. Frymer-Kensky, "TIT for TAT: The Principle of Equal Retribution in Near Eastern and Biblical Law," *BA* 43 (1980) 230-34; R. L. Hubbard, "Is the 'Tatsphäre' Always a Sphere?" *JETS* 25 (1982) 257-62.

without discounting the possibility of diachronic literary development of the book of Ezekiel. My point of orientation will always be Ezekiel 18, which will provide a vantage point from which to view the entire book.

THE SCHOLARLY DEBATE: A TYPOLOGY OF OPINION

One can no longer scan Introductions to the Old Testament and find statements declaring that Ezekiel was the prophet who championed a new development in Israelite religion, the notion of individual responsibility or moral individualism. Yet in 1939, commenting specifically on Ezekiel 18, I. G. Matthews stated that this chapter "is the classic expression of the dogma of individualism."[3] Phrasing the question another way, G. von Rad posited that Ezekiel "disputes the popular thesis of a yawning gulf between act and effect."[4] Thus the question is framed in terms of individual or corporate responsibility, individual or corporate retribution, or a tension between actions and consequences. In what follows I shall not present a comprehensive survey but highlight representatives of a changing interpretive tradition.

Developmentalism

Matthews, in the introduction to his Ezekiel commentary, reflects a representative developmental view:

> To the field of ethics, belongs his [Ezekiel's] contribution on individualism, which some have considered his chief message. While national solidarity had been the preaching of the earlier prophets, the query must often have arisen as to the justice of the saint suffering with the sinner. That the sins of the fathers should be visited on the children, to the fourth generation, was questionable justice. In national practice individuals, not families, had been condemned (cf. 2 Kings 14:5, 6); and this had been written into the code of Deuteronomy as something new (Deut. 24:16). But it was the destruction of the city that shattered group life, thereby shattering national solidarity that furnished an incentive for the new philosophy, individualism. . . . In the light of this, instead of being bound up in the bundle of life, the individual who sins dies. Individual responsibility for individual acts puts a cutting edge on justice.[5]

---

[3]*Ezekiel* (An American Commentary on the Old Testament; Philadelphia: The American Baptist Publication Society, 1939) 63.

[4]*Old Testament Theology.* 1. 393.

[5]*Ezekiel*, xxiii-xxiv. Matthews refers here to Ezek 14:14; 18:1-24; 33:10-20.

Matthews' developmental approach to Israelite religion is characteristic of this period of Ezekiel study. He breaks that development down into roughly six time periods or categories: first, the period of tribal law (Exod 20:5); second, occasions in which some individuals stood out (e.g. heroes in 1 Sam 14:45; 17:31-54; judges in 2 Sam 16:23; innovators 1 Kgs 4:26; 6:2); third, the beginning of the ninth century B.C.E. (2 Kgs 14:6); fourth, the legislation of Deut 24:16 in the seventh century B.C.E.; fifth, the time of Jeremiah (31:29); and sixth, the time of Ezekiel.[6]

The Legacy of "Corporate Personality"

The argument from primitive mentality and corporate personality is a refined form of developmentalism.

---

[6]Ibid., 63. Others also take a developmental approach to individualism in Israelite religion. R. H. Pfeiffer (*Introduction to the Old Testament* [rev. ed.; New York: Harper & Brothers, 1948] 551), for example, thinks personal religion developed after 621. He compares wisdom's focus on the individual's success, and wisdom's later identification with the law (550).

D. M. G. Stalker (*Ezekiel: Introduction and Commentary* [London: SCM, 1968] 34) similarly favors a beginning of individualism around 621 in the Deuteronomistic movement reflected in Deut 24:16. The view is developed first in Jer 12:1; 31:29-30, and then further in Ezek 14:12-20; 18. Of particular interest is Stalker's critique of the individualism in Ezekiel. First, it is not consistently applied by the prophet. Second, merit is not a highlight of Ezekiel, since it is for Yahweh's sake that he acts (36:22). And third, it is theoretic and atomistic (35-36). Stalker suggests that increasing individualism and the old idea of solidarity created a tension that led to the question of theodicy and a "mood of moral paralysis and feelings of fatalism."

F. Spadafora argues for a collective retribution before the fall of Jerusalem in 587, and a concept of individual retribution after the catastrophe (*Collectivismo e individualismo*, 363-98; see the critique by Scharbert, *Solidarität*, 227, n. 377).

J. Skinner (*The Book of Ezekiel* [The Expositor's Bible; New York: Armstrong, 1895] 143) explains the tension between the national retribution of chap. 16 ("moral unity") and the individual responsibility of chap. 18 by recourse to "dispensations." Ezekiel does not reconcile the two, since during the era of the state the solidarity principle applied, and with no state, individual responsibility applied.

A. Bertholet (*Das Buch Hesekiel* [Kurzer Hand-Kommentar zum Alten Testament 12; Freiburg/Leipzig/Tübingen: Mohr-Siebeck, 1897] 69) states that one observes how little Ezekiel is interested in resolving the tension between the individualistic and collective views. This unexplained tension Bertholet ascribes to an incomplete theology (a kind of developmentalism within the prophet's own thinking)–"eine Unvollkommenheit einer Theologie, die noch in ihren Anfängen stecke."

In 1911 H. Wheeler Robinson first proposed the idea of corporate personality.[7] According to Robinson, in primitive religion human beings were perceived

> not on the basis of the single life which consciousness binds together for each of us, but as members of a tribe, a clan, or a family: hence the familiar practice of blood-revenge, or the idea that the sin of one (e.g. Achan) can properly be visited on the group to which he belongs, and into which his own personality, so to speak, extends.[8]

Robinson appealed particularly to legal aspects of corporate personality in support of his argument. Specifically he used the following examples: the story of Achan (Josh 7); the Gibeonites and the descendants of Saul (2 Sam 21); Levirate marriage (Deut 25:5-10); the law of undetected murder and the responsibility of the city (Deut 21:1-9); the motive clause in the second commandment (Exod 20:5; Deut 5:9); and the law of blood revenge (e.g. Gen 4:15, 24).

Robinson made a distinction with regard to ancient Israel, where he discerned a shift: "from the emphasis on corporate personality we move forwards to the recognition of moral individuality." In the Old Testament we discover a specific contribution of ancient Israel, a "moral and spiritual individualism," which Robinson contrasted with other primitive religions.[9] In that respect, Robinson's view is connected to the simpler developmentalist view, but with significant differences.

"Corporate personality" meant that "the individual person was conceived and treated as merged in the larger group of family or clan or nation."[10] Within this way of viewing social reality the group experiences the consequences of an individual's actions. According to Robinson, the proverb in Ezek 18:2 "faithfully expressed the earlier doctrine of corporate personality"[11] The prophet challenged that assumption by asserting that "the good man finds his present reward, the bad man his present punishment, in accordance with the strictest individual equity, and quite unaffected by the solidarity of the family or race, and by the continuity of personality itself."[12]

In his 1936 essay "The Hebrew Conception of Corporate Personality," Robinson suggested four specifics of that concept:

---

[7]*The Christian Doctrine of Man* (Edinburgh: T. & T. Clark, 1911) 8.

[8]Ibid.

[9]Ibid., 11.

[10]Ibid., 27.

[11]Ibid., 33. Robinson does not suggest that Ezekiel is the first to express such a view, which he thinks is already seen in Elijah's critique of Ahab.

[12]Ibid., 34. That is what Robinson meant by "moral individualism."

(1) the unity of its extension both into the past and into the future; (2) the characteristic "realism" of the conception, which distinguishes it from "personification," and makes the group a real entity actualized in its members; (3) the fluidity of reference, facilitating rapid and unmarked transitions from the one to the many, and from the many to the one; (4) the maintenance of the corporate idea even after the development of a new individualistic emphasis within it.[13]

Concerning Ezekiel, however, Robinson was critical. He asserted that Ezekiel's counter-proposal in 18:4 "is untrue to the facts of life." From the perspective of common sense Robinson concluded that the only way to be true to life would be that corporate personality and moral individualism "must in some form be combined."[14] He suggested, therefore, that "the corporate idea remained even after the new individualistic emphasis had developed"[15] For example, in Jeremiah and Ezekiel: "The group conception remained dominant, notwithstanding the extreme consequences as to moral and religious responsibility which Ezekiel draws from his individualistic emphasis; we only have to think of his restored and regenerated community to see this."[16] I shall argue below that Ezekiel does, in fact, combine the corporate and individual dimensions, but in a way that does not leave Ezek 18:4 being "untrue to the facts."[17]

Aubrey Johnson started with Robinson's work but suggested that instead of corporate personality being a function of the nation, it ought to be viewed as part of the kinship complex. He posited that each kinship group was characterized by its own *nepeš*, which was "not something conceived as but one (albeit the superior) part of man's being, but the complete personality as a unified manifestation of vital power."[18] Johnson's refined concept of *nepeš* found expression in several areas: first, a human being could affect the community for good or for ill, for blessing or for curse; second, a man lived on through his "name" after his death;

---

[13]In *Werden und Wesen des Alten Testaments* (eds. P. Volz, F. Stummer, and J. Hempel; BZAW 66; Berlin: Töpelmann, 1936) 50.

[14]*Christian Doctrine*, 34.

[15]"Corporate Personality," 50.

[16]Ibid., 54.

[17]A. B. Davidson (*The Book of the Prophet Ezekiel* [The Cambridge Bible; Cambridge: The University Press, 1896] 131, 133) stated the matter somewhat differently. He suggested that Ezekiel's views on individualism run against the prevailing notions of the age, and against much of human experience. He claims that the Israelite had not yet learned to draw a distinction "between the spiritual relation of the mind to God and the external history of the individual. Therefore Ezekiel's expression is an ideal, an eschatological hope of spiritual relationship to God perfectly expressed.

[18]*The One and the Many*, 2.

third, his personality extended through his "house" or extended family; and fourth, one's property was an extension of the personality.[19]   *Nepeš*, became for Johnson the equivalent of the "personality:"   "In Israelite thought the individual as a *nepeš* or centre of power capable of indefinite extension, is never a mere isolated unit: he lives in constant reaction . . . [with] the social unit as his extended or larger 'self'."   The flip-side of that is that "the social unit or kin-group . . . is a single *nepeš* or 'person'."[20]

Critique and Refinement of "Corporate Personality"

A number of scholars have commented specifically on the idea of corporate personality and have in turn modified and presented critiques of it. The critiques will be especially helpful for recognizing the problems that have arisen in Ezekiel research.

David Daube studied some of the cases that Robinson used to develop the idea of corporate personality (Abraham's intercession in Genesis 18; David's census of Israel and its consequences; David's murder of Uriah; David's adultery with Bathsheba, etc.). Daube showed that in the Genesis 18 text communal merit was the issue rather than communal responsibility. In the cases in which a king was involved, Daube introduced the concept of "ruler punishment," which is "the case where the wrong committed by a ruler is repaid to him by a move against those under his rule, by taking away or damaging his subjects."[21]   By distinguishing between corporate responsibility and ruler punishment, Daube introduced a new possibility for biblical interpretation.[22]

H. G. May presented a brief analysis of the relevant texts in Jeremiah (31:29-30) and Ezekiel (3:17-21; 14:12-23; 18:1-32; 33:1-20), and paid special attention to Deut 24:16. At the beginning of his article he cautions against the developmental view of individualism and states that "Israelite thought always gave a large place to the individual and to the importance, value, and responsibility of the person."[23]   For Ezekiel 18 in particular, May notes that the critique of the proverb of v 2 is addressed to "the house of Israel" (vv 25, 29, 30, 31; 33:10, 17). Therefore "one of the motives of this form of individualism is to solve the problem of the relationship of the

---

[19]Ibid., 2-6.

[20]Ibid., 7-8.

[21]*Studies in Biblical Law*, 163.

[22]E.g., with respect to Ezekiel in particular, could chap. 18 include allusions to Israelite kings through its kinship terminology? Or is Ezekiel creating new options for responsibility now that the continuation of kingship is in question? If Yahweh will be Israel's shepherd (king), perhaps it is his merit that will reestablish the merit of the people.

[23]"Individual Responsibility and Retribution," 107.

post exilic *community* to the pre-Exilic *community*, the interest not being exclusively individualistic."[24]

J. R. Porter's interest in examining the concept of "corporate personality" is to curb misuse of the idea and to suggest ways that its use be limited appropriately.[25] Porter focuses primarily on the legal aspects of the idea, where it is most clearly applied. Porter makes several important observations. First, with regard to the Jonathan incident in 1 Sam 14, "verdict and penalty rest on an individual basis and involve only the individual," even though the people do suffer consequences. Second, "the basis of all Israelite law-codes is the responsibility of the individual, and it may be questioned whether the principle of communal responsibility really appears in them at all."[26]

Porter suggests that in some cases "group responsibility" or "communal guilt" are recognized, but they do not fit the normal categories of legal operation. First, there are cases involving breaking a religious prohibition or taboo (the sin of Achan, Saul's descendants and the Gibeonites, and David's census). Second, sins like murder, adultery, and apostasy were sins "with which the Old Testament Law provided no machinery, for they were sins of a 'high hand' and so outside the regular operation of the law that gave concrete expression to the covenant."[27]

Porter considers each of the texts that Robinson used in his argument to show that the matter of ascribing corporate personality to the situation is more complex than it seems. For example, Porter determines from the Achan story that the crime is an offence against holiness.

> For the basis of law in Israel is the nation's covenant with Yahweh. As long as a person is within that covenant relationship, his offenses can be coped with by society and dealt with by a regular judicial procedure, but if he puts himself outside the covenant relationship, he can have no place in society.[28]

Thus, Porter thinks that cases within the legal sphere are better explained by other aspects of Hebrew thinking.[29]

---

[24]Ibid., 109.

[25]"The Concept of 'Corporate Personality.'"

[26]Ibid., 364-65.

[27]Ibid., 367.

[28]Ibid., 371. Porter (379) writes that "as far as the whole Hebrew legal system is concerned, there seems little reason to depart from the picture suggested by the Book of the Covenant that the law operated on the basis of the individual rather than the group, and was concerned to fix individual guilt and inflict individual punishment."

[29]In other cases Porter (ibid., 378) suggests that concepts like "blood" and "sin" may better explain the circumstances than the notion of corporate personality.

Outside the legal situations, corporate personality may be a more useful category. Individuals were responsible for their actions, but sometimes there is correspondence or continuity of punishment because of "the notion that a man can possess persons in much the same way that he possesses property and by religious beliefs about the contagious nature of blood, holiness, sin and uncleanness."[30]

J. W. Rogerson examines those instances of so-called corporate personality that were based on non-legal texts. He also evaluated the theory of primitive mentality on which Robinson's thesis was based.[31] Above all he shows that corporate personality is an ambiguous term that is based on the inadequate cross-cultural anthropological assumptions of Levy-Bruhl and others. Rogerson suggests that we "drop the term corporate personality completely, and . . . abandon any attempt to explain Old Testament phenomena in terms of primitive mentality." At the same time Rogerson acknowledges that "there are certain parts of the Old Testament where there is a tension between the collective and the individual that has to be explained."[32]

George E. Mendenhall approaches the problem from the point of view of the individual's relationship to political society. According to Mendenhall, "the individual never identified himself with the state because his real citizenship was in the smaller community of which he was a real part," the kinship group.[33] He describes the status of the individual as a connection primarily with the covenant community which was "directly in relationship to Yahweh, to whom alone he swore allegiance, and from whom he received protection."[34] The introduction of state, or particularly the monarchy, he thinks, marked a decisive shift away from the individual's connection to the God of covenant structures. "It seems far more appropriate to speak of the submergence of individuals, rather than the emergence of individual personality in the course of ancient Israelite history,

---

[30]Ibid., 380.

[31]"The Hebrew Conception of Corporate Personality."

[32]Ibid., 14, 16. See also Rogerson's, *Anthropology and the Old Testament* (Atlanta, GA: John Knox, 1978) 55-65.

[33]"The Relation of the Individual to Political Society," 97.

[34]Ibid., 100. Speaking in broad theological terms, E. Jacob (*Theology of the Old Testament* [New York/Evanston: Harper & Row, 1958] 154) suggests a "blending of individualism and socialism, both of them thoroughgoing." Explaining that further he writes: "The best solution is probably of this kind, yet it must never be forgotten that, although the individual incarnates in himself the group, he is also personally responsible and that the Old Testament never thinks of the people as a neutral entity but as the assembly of individuals, each of whom has a personal link with God" (155). See also Vriezen, *An Outline of Old Testament Theology* (2nd ed.; Oxford: Blackwell, 1970) 382-87.

until the destruction of the state."[35] His thesis is therefore that the state must be regarded "as the outermost of concentric circles, which incorporates a number of pre-existent socio-political units, themselves usually both religious as well as political in nature."[36]

Next, Mendenhall considers the obligations of individuals in relation to society, and particularly in relation to the role of law. If the gods became "agents of the state," as Mendenhall puts it, it is likely that Ezekiel attempts to root responsibility in the structures of community that would most foster responsible reconstruction. Mendenhall's comments help to place Ezekiel's emphasis on *tôrâ* in a larger context. A fundamental aspect of *tôrâ* in Israelite community is that violation of stipulations was not only a sin against God, but against the community.[37] Therefore "justice is not so much a *right* of the individual as a religious obligation of the entire community and of each individual, from the point of view of OT law." Thus the "rights" of the oppressed is not the ultimate issue, but the obligations of covenant rooted in commitment to Yahweh. There are, therefore, no distinctions between secular and sacred law. It is the religious community under Yahweh that produces the legal traditions of the OT.[38] It is in the village, therefore, that law is administered. And there the individual has a primary role. "The elders, not priests, were the legal administrators and arbitrators."[39]

It may be helpful to place Ezekiel in the context of Mendenhall's discussion of the DtrH. Mendenhall writes: "The Deuteronomist is attempting to place the individual again under divine authority."[40] The question arises whether Ezekiel's view of the individual is at all related to the reconstitution of a religious covenant community for which the law would function to locate the primary relationship between *people* and Yahweh. The difference between the Deuteronomist and Ezekiel is that although the historian emphasizes the generational (individual?) responsibility (Deut 24:16), he does not address clearly enough the failure of *tôrâ*'s promise (Deut 30:11-14). Ezekiel more clearly presents Israel and Yahweh as co-active partners. That is particularly evident in the emphasis on divine enablement in Ezekiel which appears to be missing in the "return" theme of Deuteronomy 30.[41] It is also partially evident in the duality of

---

[35]Mendenhall, "The Relation of the Individual to Political Society," 91.

[36]Ibid., 93.

[37]Ibid., 104.

[38]Ibid., 105.

[39]Ibid., 106. Cf. Gerstenberger's discussion (*Wesen und Herkunft*) of the setting of legal instruction. It is not surprising, then, that the role of elders in Ezekiel is connected with legal concerns in chaps. 14 and 20.

[40]"The Relation of the Individual to Political Society," 107.

[41]See the discussion in Chapters 6 and 7, which return to these concerns.

the kingship theme in Ezekiel, in which we find both a view of a restored Davidic kingship and the restorative kingship of Yahweh.

Toward a Reconciliation

Both/And

Although Robinson suggested that corporate personality did not disintegrate after the development of moral individualism, it was considerably later that scholars responded by recognizing that even in the earlier periods of Israelite existence individualism and corporateness were not separate categories, nor were they essentially developmentally related.[42]

N. K. Gottwald represents the view that Ezekiel is not arguing one or the other, but both ways of viewing the same problem.

> The catastrophe is not the result of the sins of the few or even of the king alone, yet all the guilty will receive their punishment and the righteous few will somehow be spared (cf. 9:4-6). The seeming unrealism of this view of a collective guilt compounded of innumerable individual guilts, each to be requited, is, nevertheless, thoroughly understandable as a serious effort by the prophet to combine the predominant collective guilt theory with a sharp re-emphasis and heightening of an equally ancient belief in individual responsibility. It is not that Ezekiel first introduces 'individualism' but rather that he reasserts individual guilt in company with collective guilt as two ways of seeing the same truth[43]

---

[42]J. Hempel's comments (*Das Ethos des Alten Testaments* [2nd ed.; BZAW 67; Berlin: Töpelmann, 1964] 40-41) may serve as a starting point: "Was man den 'Individualismus' im AT nennen mag, ist mindestens zunächst eine Selbstständigkeit im Rahmen einer Gemeinschaft, aber nicht ohne oder etwa gar gegen die Gemeinschaft.... Kollektivismus und Individualismus sind im AT keine sich zu einem bestimmten Zeitpunkt ablösende Welten."

[43]*All the Kingdoms of the Earth* (New York: Harper & Row, 1964) 309. J. S. Park ("Theological Traditions," 171-72) suggests that "the term 'individual responsibility' applied to Ezek. 18 is quite misleading if taken as advocating individualism in Yahwistic faith, or as denying the concept of corporate responsibility. It is also far from the intention of Ezekiel to reduce the covenant relationship between Yahweh and Israel to a relationship between Yahweh and the individual. In Ezekiel, the consciousness of Israel as a believing *community* and of the corporate nature of the existence of Israel is stronger than in any other prophet.... Rather, he teaches that the punishment for sin of one generation will not be extended to another."

Paul Joyce has written the most extensive study of the problem.[44] He contends that Ezekiel 18 asserts the moral independence of the generations, not of individuals. The author is not concerned about "the *unit* of responsibility, . . . but rather the urgent need for his audience to accept responsibility as such."[45] Joyce also argues that the legal case language in Ezekiel 18 functions to justify the punishment of the present generation, not some hypothetical past generation, since the call to national repentance would only be possible after responsibility is acknowledged.[46]

Although elements of individual responsibility surface in chaps. 9 and 14, it is with the principle of "communal merit" that those chapters are concerned.[47] And although the individual wicked will be expelled according to 20:38, they "are excluded from the community in order that the *community* may be pure, the holy people of Yahweh." Joyce goes beyond a both/and position by suggesting that the issue does not revolve around the individual or the collective. As Joyce sees it, "the overwhelming emphasis in Ezekiel 1-37 (and the rest of the book too) is rather on the *People* of God as the unit which Yahweh saves."[48]

A Larger Orientation

The focus on the individual in Ezekiel 18, therefore, is in the service of a larger goal—the reconstitution of Israel as the people of God. According to Haag, the prophet is interested in the creation of a holy people on the basis of individual choice. He sees the relationship between individual and community in this way: "Jede Seele steht persönlich ihrem Gott gegenüber, und doch hat jede ihre Verantwortung und Aufgabe um die Heilsgeschichte des Gesamtvolkes"[49] In other words, perhaps we should see here that the individual is the means through which the social-religious order might be saved.

Similarly, Zimmerli's view focuses on the prophet's intention, which was to call for a return to God. Ezekiel spoke into a situation of oppression

---

[44]*Divine Initiative and Human Response in Ezekiel.* See also his "Individual Responsibility in Ezekiel?"; and "The Individual and the Community."

[45]"Individual Responsibility?" 187.

[46]*Divine Initiative and Human Response*, 42-55.

[47]Joyce, "Individual Responsibility," 193. Joyce refers to Daube's (*Studies in Biblical Law*, 155-58) "communal merit" here.

[48]"Individual Responsibility," 194. Joyce notes the contrast between Ezekiel 14 and 21:8-9 (3-4), which tension is resolved by noting that the common theme is the sin of the nation, not the individuals.

[49]He speaks of "eine eigenartige Verbindung von Individualismus und Kollektivismus." (*Was lehrt?*, 83). Herzog (*Die ethischen Anschauungen*, 72-73) holds a similar view.

and assured the exiles that a future was possible, even for each person. "Their past guilt need not oppress their present life. They must therefore return to God."[50]

But that return has been shaped by the ultimate vision of the book of Ezekiel, which is the formation of a new community with which Yahweh can again be present. The freedom and responsibility of the individual that Ezekiel argues for ought to be interpreted in the light of that larger goal.[51]

According to B. A. Pareira, the question Ezekiel deals with is inclusion or exclusion from the community. Inclusion in the community of the faithful in exile is important because the community "will be the bearer of the future of Israel. To be excluded from the community means to be excluded from participation in the salvific gifts which Yahweh will bestow on the new Israel."[52]

Before carrying the argument further, we turn to consider the biblical data that might help to shed light on the problem in Ezekiel 18.

INDIVIDUAL AND COMMUNITY IN PENTATEUCHAL TRADITIONS

The question of the relationship between the individual and the community, and the correlative relationship between guilt and punishment, or actions and consequences, reverberates throughout the Hebrew Bible. The debate within the Ezekiel tradition has always been discussed in the context of that larger inner-Biblical debate. The texts that I shall consider touch primarily on the question of the correspondences of sin and consequences between the generations. The purpose of this overview is to place the question as it is focused in Ezekiel within the larger dialogue in ancient Israelite traditions.

One begins almost as a matter of course with Gen 18:25, where Abraham chides Yahweh: "Far be it from thee to do such a thing, to slay the righteous with the wicked, so that the righteous fare as the wicked! Far be that from thee! Shall not the Judge of all the earth do right?"[53] That

---

[50]*The Law and the Prophets*, 85.

[51]So Cooke, *Ezekiel*, xxv. For Sakenfeld ("Ez 18:25-32," *Int* 32 [1978] 296) the larger questions focus on the need for and efficacy of repentance. "Is it ever too late to repent? Is it indeed any use to repent? What does it mean to repent? The call to repentance is addressed to the community *as a whole*, and it is the restoration of the whole people to life before God for which Ezekiel presses."

[52]I disagree, however, when Pareira (*The Call to Conversion in Ezekiel: Exegesis and Biblical Theology* [Rome: Pontificia Universitas Gregoriana, 1975] 41) continues by stating that "the new salvific act of God is not based, however, on the conversion of the people." See my discussion in Chapter 7 on the relationship between human and divine agency.

[53]On this text see C. S. Rodd, "Shall not the judge of all the earth do what is just? (Gen.

critique of divine justice comes after Yahweh thinks that he will not withhold anything from Abraham: "I have chosen him, that he may charge his children and his household after him to keep the way of the Lord by doing righteousness and justice; so that the Lord may bring to Abraham what he has promised him" (18:19). Daube suggests that the issue here is not individual responsibility, nor, I would add, the one and the many, but communal merit. Abraham assumed the communal principle, but "he substituted communal merit for communal responsibility."[54] The text gives as the basis for the communal merit of Lot's family the fact that Abraham contrasts them, as righteous, with the wicked people of Sodom. One surmises, however, that the deeper issue is that grace is predicated on the intercession of Abraham.

In the Decalogue the question is especially focused in the second commandment. There the motive clause reads: "for I the Lord your God am a jealous God, visiting the iniquity of the fathers upon the children to the third and the fourth generation of those who hate me, but showing steadfast love to thousands of those who love me and keep my commandments" (Exod 20:5b-6). At the giving of the second set of tablets in Exodus 34, the famous statement by Yahweh echoes the second commandment. Again, the Lord "will by no means clear the guilty, visiting the iniquity of the fathers upon the children and the children's children, to the third and fourth generation" (Exod 34:7). Here the expression is elaborated as part of a divine self-assertion in the third person, whereas in Exod 20:5-6 it is a motive clause of a single legal statement.[55]

A plausible explanation of the generational pattern in Exod 34:6-7 has been suggested by R. Mosis. The mention of four generations does not assume that God will punish the fourth generation with the sin of the first. Rather, four generations is the largest possible number of successive generations that can live together in an extended family, "so dass gerade noch die vierte Generation mit der Sünde der Väter wirklich selbst etwas zu tun haben kann."[56]

In Numbers 14:18 Moses uses the divine statement of Exod 34:6-7 to intercede for the people.[57] The result is that Yahweh pardons the people

---

18:25)," *ExpTim* 83 (1972) 137-39.

[54]*Studies in Biblical Law*, 157.

[55]J. Scharbert ("Formgeschichte und Exegese von Ex. 34,6f und seiner Parallelen," *Bib* 38 [1957] 131) argues that Exod 34:6-7 is the older formulation. See also M. Fishbane, *Biblical Interpretation in Ancient Israel* (Oxford: Clarendon, 1985) 335, n. 52.

[56]*Das Buch Ezechiel. Teil I. Kap. 1:1-20:44* (Geistliche Schriftlesung 8/1; Düsseldorf: Patmos, 1978) 212-213. See also idem, "Ez 14,1-11—ein Ruf zur Umkehr." *BZ* 19 (1975) 161-94.

[57]On source-critical distinctions in Numbers 13-14 see Driver, *Introduction*, 62; P. J. Budd, *Word Biblical Commentary. Volume 5: Numbers* (Waco, TX: Word, 1984) 140-64.

after having accused them in 14:10b-12. The Lord appears as "the glory of the Lord" (v 10b), and after the intercession of Moses he vows: "As I live" and "as all the earth shall be filled with the glory of the Lord" (v 21). In a concluding statement in v 33 Yahweh asserts that the children will suffer for the faithlessness of the present wilderness generation.

The rebellion of Korah in Numbers 16 follows after cultic regulations regarding sacrifices in chap. 15. Most interesting is the mention of atonement for unwitting sin by the whole congregation and by an individual. By contrast, the action "with a high hand" deserves the consequence of being cut off from the people (Num 15:30-31). The example that follows in 15:32-41 is of a man caught gathering sticks on the sabbath who is executed for breaking the commandment. To be cut off is decisively interpreted as capital punishment here. So also in the Korah episode, only there it is Yahweh who carries out the consequence rather than the congregation.

Numbers 16 is especially important in the way the distinction is made between those in the congregation who willfully sin and those who do not participate in the act. Moses and Aaron fall to the ground and cry out "O God, the God of the spirits of all flesh, shall one man sin, and wilt thou be angry with all the congregation?" (16:22). Yahweh responds to their plea, which is not unlike that of Abraham in Genesis 18, with the separation of the innocent from the guilty.

Clearly within the space of three chapters we find a theological question raised. In both chapters, however, transgenerational consequences are anticipated. The larger question that emerges in the episodes is that of part and whole. Shall the entire congregation experience the consequences of part of the congregation's action? In Numbers 14 the answer is yes, and in Numbers 16, no. Numbers 15 presents a mediating position that depends on whether transgression is willingly done or not.[58]

Another text is worth noticing in Numbers. The brief comment in Num 27:3 by the daughters of Zelophehad is insightful: "Our father died in the wilderness; he was not among the company of those who gathered themselves together against the Lord in the company of Korah, but died for his own sin." The connection of the daughters of Zelophehad and the inheritance of land is significant for understanding the relationship between the priestly understanding of the act-consequence relationship and the notion of inheriting the land. Further, the Priestly concepts of life and death belong to the theological vision of acquiring land.[59]

---

[58]Park ("Theological Traditions," 174) suggests that in Numbers 16 the question is one of "the punishment of many because of the sin of a few" whereas in Genesis 18 the problem is the opposite. I think rather, it is a part and whole problem, not one and many. In all cases the real issue is that it is only the guilty who are punished, as Daube suggests.

[59]See Haag, *Was lehrt?*, 92, 95.

We turn now to Leviticus 26. The chapter has often been compared to the ideas in Ezekiel.[60] Here, in a listing of rewards for obedience ("walking in my statutes and observing my commandments") and punishments for disobedience ("to walk contrary to me"), the Priestly tradition makes it clear that exile is a result of the congregation's iniquity and the iniquity of their fathers: "And those of you that are left shall pine away because of their iniquity; and also because of the iniquities of their fathers they shall pine away like them" (26:39). V 40 continues, however, with a hope of confessing both their and their fathers' iniquity. Confession and making amends open the way for Yahweh's covenantal action on their behalf. V 45 makes it clear that it is "for their sake," which is different from what we find in Ezekiel, "for my sake."

One question remains. Does Lev 26:39 and its explanation of exile differ from the land acquisition theology of the Priestly tradition in Numbers 14-16? According to Haag, the sins of others do not hinder the new generation from entering the land.[61] I suggest that it is that tension that Ezekiel seeks to clarify by siding with Deuteronomistic tradition on the matter of the relationship between actions and consequences, but by siding with the Priestly tradition in connecting the presence of Yahweh with a holy people in the land. Thus, retribution and hope are resolved in a dynamic symbiosis in which Yahweh and people are co-agents in a transformational process that is both eschatological and contains present possibility for change.

In the Deuteronomistic tradition we find the central text in Deut 24:16. The law states clearly that "The fathers shall not be put to death for the children, nor shall the children be put to death for the fathers; every man shall be put to death for his own sin." Many suggest that this law modifies an older tradition that the group was affected by the sinful act. That tradition, they think, is reflected in texts like the Korah narrative (Numbers 16), the Achan story (Josh 7:24-25), and the death of Saul's sons (2 Sam 21:1-9). But even the book of Deuteronomy acknowledges the possibility of a community suffering the consequences of action. In Deut 21:1-9 an unresolved murder case is brought forward. A heifer is to be killed to bear the consequences of the murder. In Deut 13:12-18 the case is presented of "certain base fellows" who entice the inhabitants of the city to serve other gods. In such a case the entire city is to be destroyed, not only the instigators. Daube notes that in Deuteronomy communal responsibility is applied in the case of apostasy (Deut 13:12-18), but not in the case of the undiscovered murderer (Deut 21:1-9).[62] Moreover, the Decalogue

---

[60]I discuss some of the correspondences with Ezekiel 18 Chapter 6.

[61]*Was lehrt?*, 95.

[62]*Studies in Biblical Law*, 184. Communal responsibility does not apply in the latter case because "the bonds holding together the individual citizens are loosened." Communal

provision of Deut 5:9-10 repeats the notion of consequences falling on the third and fourth generation.

In the DtrH other texts refer to the consequences falling on others (for example, the house of Ahab in 1 Kgs 21:21). Perhaps 2 Kgs 24:1-4 belongs in that category, which places the blame for the incursion of armies on the sins of Manasseh.[63] The only text in the DtrH, however, that explicitly applies Deut 24:16 is 2 Kgs 14:6. After killing the murderers of his father, Amaziah "did not put to death the children of the murderers; according to what is written in the book of the law of Moses." At that point the text quotes Deut 24:16 in full.

That legislation seems to contradict the affirmation in the Deuteronomic Decalogue (Deut 5:9). So also, as May remarks, it does not suit 1 Kgs 11:12 where punishment for Solomon's sins is postponed to his son.[64] Daube raises the question whether Deut 24:16 ought to be understood as applying to communal responsibility or ruler punishment. He asks also:

> Which idea had the prophets in mind when they prophesied Israel's downfall to its wicked kings? Did they mean that the kings would be punished for their sins by their people's ruin (ruler punishment)? Or that the whole people would have to answer for the sins committed by its rulers (communal responsibility)? Or both?[65]

In the story of David's rise to power, Yahweh avenges the wrongs, and leaves David free of guilt. Notice 1 Sam 26:10, where David suggests several possibilities for the fate of Saul. Later in the chapter David makes the principle clear: "The Lord rewards every man for his righteousness and his faithfulness" (v 23). This motif forms part of the defense of David, which is also reflected in the repeated use of the refrain "your blood be on your head" (2 Sam 1:16; etc.).[66]

The theme of the sin of Jeroboam is another major theological device in DtrH.[67] According to the historian, by his actions Jeroboam "drove Israel from following the Lord and made them commit great sin." But the historian makes it clear that the sins of each generation participated in

---

responsibility persists, suggests Daube, where the group is bonded together, and the contagiousness of sin is a prominent idea. Ibid., 181-82.

[63]According to Stalker (*Ezekiel*, 34), that is repudiated by Ezekiel.

[64]Cf. also 2 Kgs 20:16-19; May, "Individual Responsibility," 116.

[65]*Studies in Biblical Law*, 184.

[66]See K. W. Whitelam, *The Just King: Monarchical Judicial Authority in Ancient Israel* (JSOTSup 12; Sheffield: JSOT, 1979) 91-121.

[67]See 1 Kgs 15:34; 16:2, 7, 19, 26, 31; etc.; F. M. Cross, *Canaanite Myth and Hebrew Epic*, 274-89.

Jeroboam's sin in that "they did not depart from them." It is not likely that the historian is trying to demonstrate that the fate of the people was sealed with Jeroboam.[68]

What I have presented thus far suggests that we do not find in those texts a way of resolving the tension within the Hebrew Bible as such. Israel's theologians must have recognized two foci, both of which were valid, and both of which could be validated from human experience. There were cases in which consequences were clearly understood to be more than personal, which affected the group to which the offender belonged, be that family, clan, city, or nation. The range of the group or groups involved was probably commensurate with the status of the person(s) and the nature of the action. There were other cases in which expected consequences were to be prevented by certain cultic measures. And there were also cases in which consequences did not follow from actions, and ought not to follow to the group, especially within the family nexus. Those latter cases seem not to have been dominant, although they probably reflect the agenda of certain groups at specific times in Israel.[69]

We turn now to a reevaluation of the texts in the Book of Ezekiel that address this problem.

THE PROBLEM IN EZEKIEL

Introduction

As is evident in many discussions of Ezekiel, the prophet is often thought to be inconsistent. J. W. Wevers, for example, suggests that Ezekiel favours individual responsibility in chaps. 18 and 33, and emphasizes corporate responsibility in the often repeated phrase "rebellious house" (17:12). In chapter 18, according to Wevers, Ezekiel's greatest contribution is "that man is not bound by laws of generation to a fate; rather each man individually faces God and is judged on his own merits."[70] Koch states the matter even more strongly when he writes concerning Jeremiah and Ezekiel: "Yahweh's direct relationship to the individual Israelite is felt so strongly that the collective component is already attacked as failure to understand

---

[68]See Park, "Theological Traditions," 175.

[69]A more complete survey would include other texts. For example, in Pss 79:8 the psalmist calls on God, in the face of the ruin of Jerusalem, not to remember the iniquity of the forefathers. In Ps 106:23 Moses stands in the breach for the community (cf. the references in Ezekiel 14 to Noah, Job, and Daniel). Note Ps 62:13, and especially the ethical tone of vv 10-11. See also Lam 5:7; Jer 5:1-8; 13:14; 11:22-23; 15:4; 16:1-4, 10-18; 32:18 Jer 31:29-31; Isa 65:7; Job 21:19; Ecclesiastes.

[70]*Ezekiel*, 108.

God's order and justice."[71]   Koch judges Ezekiel's contribution: "the solution is not convincing."[72]

In this section I shall survey the relevant texts to see how the connection between the individual and the community is portrayed in the book of Ezekiel.   I shall follow Boadt and Greenberg, who favour a synchronic analysis, while recognizing the possiblity of diachronic development.[73]   After surveying the material in the Book of Ezekiel, I shall consider chap. 18 more closely by describing how the chapter interprets the problem.   Finally, I shall suggest a synthesis that integrates three facets of the chapter: the self and the community, actions and consequences, and the function of kinship terminology.

M. Fishbane identifies the process in which chap. 18 participates as "inner-Biblical exegesis," more particularly as aggadic exegesis.[74] According to Fishbane, *aggadah* refers to "that category and range of inner-biblical exegesis which is strictly speaking neither scribal nor legal, on the one hand, nor concerned with prophecies or futuristic oracles, on the other."   Fishbane notes two contrasts to inner-biblical legal exegesis.   First, in contrast to legal exegesis, which reinterprets pre-existing legal texts within new contexts, "aggadic exegesis utilizes pre-existing legal materials, but it also makes broad and detailed use of moral dicta, official or popular *theologoumena*, themes, motifs, and historical facts."   Second, in contrast to legal exegesis which prescribes specific action in the new context, "aggadic exegesis is primarily concerned with utilizing the full range of the inherited *traditum* for the sake of new theological insights, attitudes, and speculations."   Third, unlike legal exegesis, which fills in perceived gaps in the *traditum*, "aggadic exegesis . . . characteristically draws forth latent and unsuspected meanings from it."   In other words, it emphasizes "potential meanings and applications."   Thus, legal exegesis "shows how a particular law can be clarified and reinterpreted *qua* law," and aggadic exegesis "shows how a particular law (or topos, or *theologoumenon*) can transcend its original focus, and become the basis of a new configuration of meaning."[75]

In Ezekiel 18 "an exegetical revision occurs" which includes an explicit rejection and "an elaborate aggadic reworking" of the *traditum*.[76]

---

[71]*The Prophets. Volume 2. The Babylonian and Persian Periods* (Philadelphia, PA: Fortress, 1982) 195.

[72]Ibid., 203.

[73]L. Boadt, "Rhetorical Strategies in Ezekiel's Oracles of Judgment," *Ezekiel and His Book: Textual and Literary Criticism and their Interrelation* (ed. J. Lust; Leuven: Leuven University Press/Peeters, 1986) 182-200. Greenberg, *Ezekiel, 1-20.*

[74]*Biblical Interpretation*, 281.

[75]Ibid., 281-83.

[76]Ibid., 284.

Although the chapter provides an example of explicit citation, Fishbane notes that most cases of aggadic exegesis are implicit. "In these cases, it is not by virtue of objective criteria that one may identify aggadic exegesis, but rather by a close comparison of the language of a given text with other, earlier Scriptural dicta or topoi."[77] It is the revisionist approach of Ezekiel that I wish to explore below.[78]

The Texts in Ezekiel

Ezekiel 7

"I will judge you according to your ways and will punish you for all your abominations" (Ezek 7:3). The line is found in a judgment speech that reflects Amos 8:2. Like Amos, Ezekiel calls for "an end" for the land of Israel. Ezek 18:30 repeats part of the statement: "Therefore I will judge you, O house of Israel, every one according to his ways." In both Ezek 7:3 and 18:30 the pronominal suffixes are singular (in 7:3 feminine, with *'eres* as the antecedent; in 18:30 masculine, with *'îš* making explicit the specificity of the individual, but turning immediately to the plural form of address in v 30b). In Ezek 22:31 the same expression is used, with a plural referent of the princes, priests, and prophets. In an interesting aside Yahweh comments that he looked for a person (*'îš*) "to stand in the breach before me for the land, that I should not destroy it; but I found none" (22:30).[79] In 24:14 Yahweh speaks out of inner desperation. Having recognized that the bloody city refused to be cleansed, he resolves not to change his mind: "I will not go back, I will not spare, I will not repent; according to your ways and your doings I will judge you."

It is clear from these texts that Ezekiel perceives Yahweh to be involved in the punishment, and it is a punishment not of the past generations but of the present generation. The prophet consciously rests his case on the current situation. So also, the texts do not depict Yahweh as dispassionate but as an involved participant in the process.

According to Greenberg that is characteristic also of Ezekiel's careful working out of a theology of divine retribution. The prophet takes pains to articulate the reality of correspondence between sin and punishment. "Time

---

[77]Ibid., 285.

[78]Fishbane (ibid., 293-94) does not think a reinterpretation occurs in Ezek 22; 33:25-26; 44:21-25, 31. Note also that he connects Ezekiel 18 with Exod 22:10, 24-26 and its reworking in Deut 24:10-18. And Ezek 22:10-11 parallels more closely Lev 20:10-18 (as in his article "Sin and Judgment in the Prophecies of Ezekiel," *Int* 38 (1984) 131-50).

[79]That is an interesting point considering the statements in chap. 14 about Noah, Job, and Daniel.

and again the principle of measure for measure is invoked: Israel has committed unheard-of crimes, God will deal out to them an unheard-of fate (5:5-10; 9:9-10; 20:24-25). . . . He must make it plain that 'not for nothing' (6:10) will this happen"[80] Even survivors will recognize the validity of Yahweh's action (12:16; 14:22-23).

Ezekiel 9

In chap. 9 Yahweh tells a man clothed in linen, who has a writing case at his side, to "go through the city, through Jerusalem, and put a mark upon the foreheads of the men who sigh and groan over all the abominations that are committed in it" (v 4). In v 5 others are told to go through the city and slay everyone except those who have the mark. The text has an individualistic flavour. By considering the context and purpose of the text, however, we discover that the main concern is the punishment of the wicked. Joyce comments that the list of victims in v 6 highlights the inclusiveness of imminent punishment, including old men, little children, and women. Ezekiel intercedes in v 8 by asking, "Wilt thou destroy all that remains of Israel? But the answer in vv 9-10 indicates that "blood" and "injustice" have reached their limit. Yahweh "will requite their deeds upon their heads." The man simply reports that he has done what was asked, but no mention is made of the righteous who were marked (v 11).[81]

Ezekiel recognizes the importance of the righteous in chap. 9, but realizes also that the righteous will suffer along with the wicked because of the Babylonian incursion (21:3-4). That raises the inevitable question of how he can take an interest in the righteous and then recognize that they must also perish. What then is the purpose of holding up the righteous as an ideal in chapter 18? We can suggest tentatively that for Ezekiel, the righteous, or the community of ṣaddîqîm, do not escape participation in the judgment. The identity and character of the ṣaddîqîm do not imply that they are not also implicated in the crimes for which Ezekiel criticizes the house of Israel. What is important is not that the ṣaddîqîm are "not guilty" and therefore exempt from the judgment, but that they are repentant. That, more

---

[80]"Prolegomenon," *Pseudo-Ezekiel and the Original Prophecy*, by C. C. Torrey (Library of Biblical Studies; ed. H. M. Orlinsky; New York: KTAV, 1970) xxvii.

[81]"Individual Responsibility," 318. Joyce suggests that in this chapter we find "a rather more collective notion of responsibility" as in Josh 7:24 and Num 16:32. Joyce (ibid., 319) cites Y. Kaufmann who wrote: "collective and individual responsibility are spoken of in the same breath" (*The Religion of Israel: From Its Beginnings to the Babylonian Exile* [Chicago, IL: University of Chicago Press, 1960; reprint ed., New York: Schocken, 1972] 439).

than anything, seems to be the crux around which the tension between Ezekiel 9 and 21 can be resolved.[82]

Ezekiel 14:1-11

The first part of chap. 14 is set in a narrative context in which the elders of the house of Israel appear before Ezekiel. The narrative context gives way, however, to divine speeches beginning in v 3. Vv 3-5 are explanatory, yet allow the prophet a glimpse into the divine "heart" as Yahweh asks whether he should allow himself to be inquired of at all (v 3b). The decision seems clear enough. Idols (*gillûlîm*) have been taken "into the hearts" of the elders. Inquiry of Yahweh and idols in the heart are incompatible. But Yahweh's refusal to answer is motivated by the clause, "that I may lay hold of the hearts of the house of Israel, who are all estranged from me through their idols" (v 5). In the instruction to the prophet that follows in v 6, the prophet is given a call to repentance. The second person plural address of v 6 changes in vv 7-9 to the impersonal third person singular speech of vv 4-5. In the case sequence of vv 7-9, only v 8b returns to the second person plural in citing the recognition formula. Vv 10-11 change again from the singular to third person plural. The entire text is therefore framed by the plural at key points (vv 3-4a, 5, 6, 8b, 10-11). The only singular statements are found in the explanations that are given in terms of case style (vv 4, 7). Thus, the case descriptions in vv 4 and 7-9 serve as legal explications of the larger public concern. The issue is not primarily the individual in the case, but the public actions of the "house of Israel."

That observation is confirmed in two ways. First, the punishment in v 8 is reminiscent of Priestly terminology. The threat of being "cut off" is of special interest to Ezekiel.[83] Second, the ultimate motivation of Yahweh is reiterated throughout the text: first, in v 5 where Yahweh wishes to regain the hearts of the house of Israel; second, in v 8b where the recognition formula expresses a common Ezekielian concern; and third, in v 11 where reconstitution of Israel is expressed in terms of the Priestly dictum "that they may be my people and I may be their God." Ultimately they will no longer go astray or be defiled by their transgressions. Thus, the idolatry in their hearts and the stumbling block of iniquity of v 3 is resolved in v 11. In the entire text the relationship of the community to Yahweh is at issue.

---

[82]Note the interesting verbal parallel between 9:4 and 21:6 in the verb "to sigh" (*'nh*).

[83]The other expressions are also important: "I will set my face against" and "sign and byword."

Ezekiel 14:12-20

Fishbane suggests that the lack of a call to repentance in Ezek 14:12-20 is significant. Vv 12-20 "seems more designed to provide theological doctrine to the exiles than a teaching of hope to the citizens of Jerusalem. One may therefore suppose that 14:12-20 is another prophetic piece attempting to quash false confidence in Jerusalem's salvation among the exiles." Vv 21-23 reinforce that, but as Fishbane sees it, vv 21-23 contradict the fact that in vv 12-20 the sinful survivors are saved in spite of their sins. The purpose of that is to teach the exiles that they are not saved by their own righteousness.[84]

These verses are similar to Priestly case law in that they work out a problem posed at the beginning: "When a land sins against me by acting faithlessly." The rest of the chapter argues that Yahweh's judgment will inevitably come on the land. In each of the four judgments three "righteous men," are brought into the hypothetical argument. If Noah, Daniel, and Job were there, they would not be able to save the lives of others; only their own lives would be spared. They are paradigmatic righteous ones, the kind who would have been marked according to chap. 9. Vv 21-22, however, assume that all will be subject to punishment. The text acknowledges the possibility that righteous persons might be saved, but that is hardly likely here. Individualism, as Joyce again asserts, is not a new element. Could it be that Ezekiel is simply assuming that none will be found righteous? Joyce states: "The concern of Ezekiel 14:12ff is to stress the absolute certainty of imminent and thorough judgment." Joyce stresses the hypothetical nature of the case discussion, which is characterized by hyperbole and rhetoric. The test-case format is used "as a teaching technique rather than to any systematizing concern." The text assumes the ideal of individual responsibility, but at the same time articulates an imminent and total judgment. Given the fact that there may be survivors, the text adds, do not assume that it is because they are righteous. They, too, will be found wicked, which will further serve to justify the judgment that has fallen.[85]

Ezekiel 16 and 17

Chapters 16 and 17 are linked by the theme of covenantal unfaithfulness. Both 16:59 and 17:19 speak of despising the oath in breaking the covenant. Chapter 17 focuses on the sin of the king of Judah,

---

[84]"Sin and Judgment," 137.
[85]"Ezekiel and Individual Responsibility," 320.

which is a breaking of the covenant with the king of Babylon and in v 19 is redefined as a covenant with God. Chapter 16 only focuses on national sin. In chapter 17, however, the nation suffers for the actions of the king, perhaps in the sense of "ruler responsibility" (cf. vv 16, 19 with 21).

Ezekiel 20

In chap. 20 Ezekiel surveys the history of Israel in terms of four eras. First, Israel rebelled against Yahweh while still in Egypt.[86] They did not turn from the idols of Egypt, but for the sake of his own name Yahweh brought them out of Egypt into the wilderness (vv 5-10). Second, the first generation in the wilderness were given good commandments that made for life, but Israel rebelled against Yahweh. Yet for the sake of his name Yahweh spared them (vv 11-17). Third, to the children in the wilderness Yahweh counselled, "Do not walk in the statutes of your fathers, nor observe their ordinances, nor defile yourselves with their idols." But the children rebelled and Yahweh again acted for the sake of his name and prevented judgment, but promised exile throughout the nations. In fact, Yahweh gave them "statutes that were not good and ordinances by which they could not have life" (vv 18-26). The prophet then speaks to the exiles and reflects on the generation before the exile and ties them in with that earlier generation, their fathers (vv 27-29). Finally, the prophet speaks to "the house of Israel," the generation of the exile (vv 30-44). Contrary to the actions of the people, Yahweh will intervene as king over them and judge them in the wilderness (note the exodus theme with Yahweh as warrior/king against his own people), after which the people will be restored to the covenant blessings. They will be brought from the nations of exile and Yahweh's holiness will again be made known. This future work is one in which Yahweh will act for the sake of his name, a work of grace not based on the merit of actions nor according to the consequences deserved.

The rhetorical thrust of the chapter leads the reader from the generations of the fathers to the present in the fourth scene beginning in v 30. In v 31b Yahweh makes the same decision as in v 14. He will not be inquired of by Israel. Yet even as Israel became "like the nations" throughout its history, Yahweh refuses to allow that to be an option for the

---

[86]Liwak ("Überlieferungsgeschichtliche Probleme," 156) thinks that in Ezek 20:4 the present generation is judged according to "the abominations of their fathers" (tô'ăbōt 'ăbôtām), which he thinks is foreign to Ezekiel's thought in chap. 18. On that basis Liwak comes to the conclusion that chap. 18 is from Ezekiel and the Deuteronomistic ideas from later redaction. Chap. 20, however, never implies that the fathers' sins are the basis of present judgment. The past is depicted analogously in order to show that the present is exactly like the past, and that Yahweh is about to make an abrupt end to the cycle of apostasy.

present (v 32). The scene of the present generation moves directly into the scene of the coming kingly rule of Yahweh (vv 33-44). There the judgment of the wilderness generation and the promises to the fathers are the source for hope in the present situation of exile. Yahweh's action will result in bringing Israel out from the peoples and in restoring worship and authentic service of Yahweh in the land.

Ezekiel 33

The people are quoted in 33:10 as saying: "Our transgressions and our sins are upon us, and we waste away because of them; how then can we live?" Here the prophet uses the verb *mqq*, "to waste away." The verb also appears in Ezek 4:17 and 24:23. Ezek 4:17 is part of a judgment speech in which Yahweh declares what the people will do "in their punishment" (*nāmaqqû baʿăwônām*). In a similar text in 24:23 Yahweh explains the meaning of the death of Ezekiel's wife: "You shall pine away in your iniquities." It is interesting to note that in Lev 26:39 (the only occurrence in Leviticus) the judgment of *mqq* is for their sins (also *ʿwn*) and sins of the fathers. As Park comments, "in great contrast, in Ezekiel, in all three occurrences of *mqq*, the judgment of Yahweh is directed to the sins of the present generation. The idea of bearing judgment because of the sins of the fathers is consistently absent in Ezekiel."[87] On this point Ezekiel is charting an independent course from the Priestly tradition. In the Priestly perspective the transgenerational consequences of sinful actions is not challenged.[88]   Priestly   theology   is   clearly   different   from   the Deuteronomistic on this point. Whether or not P is generally a reaction to D (as Friedman asserts), we can conclude that Ezekiel is not siding with the Priestly tradition.[89]

Ezekiel 18 and Transgenerational Retribution

In Ezekiel 18 the prophet disputes a proverb that reflects popular opinion. The proverb offers the observation that punishment is transferrable.

---

[87]"Theological Traditions," 168.

[88]So also Park, ibid., 174.

[89]See R. Friedman, *The Exile and Biblical Narrative*. In fact, Ezekiel describes the history of Israel as a history of continuous sin. In chaps. 16, 20, and 23 Ezekiel depicts Israel from the Exodus experience as rebelling against Yahweh. The present generation is not blamed for the sins of the fathers, but is accused of being like them. Further, Ezekiel does not separate individual from collective retribution in texts regarding enemies and foreign nations (cf. Isa 14:20-21; Jer 49:8-10; Ezek 26:6-8). See J. Scharbert, *Solidarität*, 216.

In the chapter, however, "only gradually is the prophet's theological strategy and logic made clear."[90] In what follows I shall discuss the rhetorical strategy of the disputation with regard to the problem of actions and their consequences. I shall be particularly interested in Ezekiel's interaction with Israelite tradition and how the chapter states its case in view of that tradition.

It is often said that Ezek 18:4 cites Deut 24:16. But the language is different. Deut 24:16 reads "The fathers shall not be put to death for the children, nor shall the children be put to death for the fathers; every man shall be put to death for his own sin (*'îš běhet'ô yûmātû*)." Ezek 18:4, instead of citing the text itself, reads: "All *hannĕpāšôt* belong to me; the *nepeš* of the father and the *nepeš* of the son are both mine. The *nepeš* of the one who sins will die." Ezekiel emphasizes the *nepeš* instead of the *'îš*. That may be because the legal context in Deuteronomy favours *'îš*, just as the cases in Ezekiel 18 do not avoid using *'îš*. The use of *nepeš* in Ezek 18:4 is consistent with other occurrences in Ezekiel where *nepeš* simply refers to the person or the life of the person.[91]

The argument has been captured well by Greenberg:

> Since I, as the dispenser of life, own everybody; since, therefore, I have an equal stake in fathers and sons (or: therefore fathers and sons are alike to me); hence sinners appear to me not as fathers and sons but simply as sinful individuals, and as such each takes the consequences only for his own conduct. This denies that any person is morally an extension of another.[92]

We can phrase the issue slightly differently. Yahweh states: "I have a stake in or obligation for all persons. It is 'encumbent upon' me to preserve life.[93]   Father and son without discrimination are alike in my care. Therefore the one who sins abrogates/I release from my care." In either formulation of the problem, the response of v 4 reverses the mechanistic correspondence alluded to in the proverb.

Vv 5-32 develop a theological argument couched in legal form. The chapter touches on two interrelated issues: the matter of intergenerational transfer of merit or guilt, and the matter of personal change, repentance, and act-determinism within one person's lifetime. The argument is summarized and elaborated both in vv 20 and 30. In v 20, as Greenberg points out, the

---

[90]Fishbane, "Sin and Judgment," 140. Greenberg (*Ezekiel, 1-20*, 328) likewise states that in the syllogism "the meaning of the premises and their relation to the conclusion are not perfectly clear."

[91]3:19, 21; 13:18, 19, 20; 14:14, 20; 17:17; 22:25, 27; 27:13; 32:10; 33:5, 6, 9.

[92]*Ezekiel, 1-20*, 328.

[93]On this use of the preposition *lĕ* see Williams, *Hebrew Syntax*, #284.

structure is clearly dependent on Deut 24:16 by means of inversion.[94] Ezekiel summarizes his critique again in v 30 by saying that every one will be judged according to his ways.

M. Fishbane presents another way of looking at the argument. His comments deserve a lengthy quotation, since I shall be interacting with his reading of Ezekiel:

> In order to reject the notion of vicarious punishment and assert the principle of individual responsibility—a theological necessity if the people in exile were to assume religious responsibility for their lives—the prophet had first to stress the uniqueness of each person (and so each generation) before the law, and this he did via the apodictic legal formulation in v 4 (and v 20) and the casuistic legal formulations found in vv 5-18. He was still left with a religious problem, however, for while the first argument emphasized that there was no transfer of guilt from one generation (person) to another, nothing was said about the sinner and his own lifetime. Was a (repentant) person to be considered guilty in later years for sins committed earlier, and vice versa? Surely not, says the prophet: The Lord wants repentance and so the life of the sinner. Thus, implies the prophet, those in exile are there for their own sins and not those of their parents, and since their relationship with God is not an intractable or inherited fate they can take responsibility for it and return to YHWH. In presenting this teaching, the prophet Ezekiel wished to rebut any notion of religious fatalism or self-satisfied piety; more positively, he wished to generate a new spiritual realism in the nation and enliven the religiously passive and self-satisfied with the ever renewed challenge of righteousness.[95]

This kind of emphasis on the individual, however, will do nothing to stave off judgment on Jerusalem, since chap. 14 already asserted that fact. Repentance will not prevent judgment. It will, however, give life and prevent ruin for the present generation. Thus, by recognizing the central focus of the chapter as "the house of Israel," it is possible to understand the place of the individual as a rhetorical device that serves the cause of the larger unit. Chapter 18 stresses "the responsibility of the whole contemporary house of Israel rather than the responsibility of the individual."[96]

But Fishbane raises an interesting tension. He suggests that chaps. 18 and 20 are explicitly contradictory, for in chap. 20 "the themes of repentance and individual responsibility are not so much ignored as radically flouted."[97] The contrast is most seen in the way individual responsibility

---

[94]"The 'normal' sequence 'fathers—sons' appears in initial position in Deuteronomy; this suggests that Ezekiel was the borrower." *Ezekiel, 1-20*, 333.

[95]"Sin and Judgment," 141-42.

[96]Joyce, "Ezekiel and Individual Responsibility," 320-21.

[97]"Sin and Judgment," 142.

is treated. In the first and the fourth periods of Ezekiel's scheme the matter of punishment is resolved by recourse to the promises to the patriarchs (vv 5-6, 42). But it is not, as Fishbane suggests, on the basis of the ancestors' merits that they are delivered. Nor does the text contradict 14:12-20.[98] In the second and third periods of the scheme the responsibility of the individual generations is highlighted. The first wilderness generation profaned Yahweh's name and were judged but not destroyed. The children in the second wilderness generation were addressed independently and exhorted to follow Yahweh's commandments. They refused and were accused of setting their eyes on their fathers' idols (v 24). They were to be scattered among the nations, as Ezekiel's exiles now found themselves.

Fishbane's critique here is worth noting. It is possible that Ezekiel assumes that each generation since the second wilderness generation is found culpable, and therefore each generation receives its own punishment. If that is what Ezekiel is saying in chap. 20, then a problem arises because the second wilderness generation did not experience the scattering through the nations. Their sins were deferred to the future, which is exactly what 18:2 complains about. Moreover, in 20:25 Yahweh confounds the intent of the law, giving them "ordinances by which they could not have life." Therefore "the theological core of Ezekiel 20 is diametrically opposed to the teaching of chapter 18." In fact, claims Fishbane, "the people do not live in religious freedom—free from their father's sins and with a chance for repentance—but rather live out the consequences of earlier sins."[99]

Fishbane therefore sees an irreconcilable conflict among chapters 14, 18, 20, and 21. The tension is simply this:

> Is he [Ezekiel] the champion of repentance and individual responsibility, or is he the theologian of historical fate and indiscriminate doom? Or is he all of these things and perhaps more, speaking the divine word as it came to him at different times and with different emphases?[100]

Fishbane suggests that a demand for consistency may be inappropriate. He leans toward acknowledging no clear continuity in the thought of Ezekiel. He finds a tentative answer in Ezekiel's major concern: "the religious psychology of the Judeans in exile. It was their false confidence, their sense of divine justice, and their sense of religious freedom that concerned him most."[101]

Since the argument in Ezekiel 18 depends in part on a larger issue that goes beyond the interplay with Deut 24:16, the relationship with Exod

---

[98]Ibid., 143.
[99]Ibid., 143, 144.
[100]Ibid., 148.
[101]Ibid., 148.

34:6-7 and other Pentateuchal traditions is important for understanding Ezekiel's concerns.[102]   In Exod 34:6-7 the divine attributes are listed: "merciful and gracious, slow to anger, and abounding in steadfast love and faithfulness, keeping steadfast love for thousands,[103] forgiving iniquity and transgression and sin."   The point of tension with which the Ezekiel tradition struggles is the last part of v 7: "but who will by no means clear the guilty, visiting the iniquity of the fathers upon the children and the children's children, to the third and the fourth generation."[104]

Fishbane suggests, in commenting on Exod 34:6-7 and its exegetical transformations, that here

> vicarious punishment clearly refers to divine punishments, as against the penal sanctions of human jurisprudence. . . It may be concluded that a double standard of justice was prevalent in ancient Israel from early times—a theological standard, applicable to God alone, which envisaged transgenerational effects for actions committed, and a human standard, applicable in human jurisprudence, which held the transgressor to be culpable and punished for his own delict.[105]

Neat as this interpretation is, Fishbane offers several caveats. Some laws like Exod 21:31 were designed to prevent inappropriate carrying out of vicarious punishment of family members. The fact of the explicit statement in Deut 24:16 suggests a deliberate attempt to control or curb the practice of vicarious punishment. So it was not a matter simply of divine *or* human judgment, but of human judgment that was in the process of being mitigated.[106]

In the face of exile, Jeremiah and Ezekiel attempt "to qualify the ambiguities and injustices which were felt to obtain in the juridical notion of transgenerational or deferred punishment."[107] Both are responding to the ambiguity in the Exodus text itself. Both Jeremiah and Ezekiel attempt to provide a response to the situation of exile in which "there was little motivation for the sons to practice proper behaviour, or to take responsibility for their actions, if they believed themselves subject to the delayed or extended punishments due to their fathers."[108] By quoting a version of Deut 24:16, Jeremiah rejects the older *traditum* by focusing on the hope for

---

[102]See J. Scharbert, "Formgeschichte und Exegese von Ex. 34,6f," 130-50.

[103]Or "to the thousandth [generation]."

[104]Fishbane (*Biblical Interpretation*, 335) translates: "But he will not acquit guilt forever; but will requite the iniquity of the fathers."

[105]Ibid., 336.

[106]Ibid., 336.

[107]Ibid., 337.

[108]Ibid., 337.

the postexilic age. In the new age it will not be like that. Ezekiel's citation, however, focuses rather on the present possibilities for the exilic
community.

In doing so, Ezekiel goes beyond Jeremiah and beyond a simple
rejection of the proverb and the issue of transgenerational responsibility.
According to Fishbane, Ezekiel expands the meaning of Deut 24:16. The
legislation in Deuteronomy does not comment on its particular application
to civil cases, nor do the legal statements that Ezekiel cites from
Pentateuchal law prescribe a penalty. They are, thinks Fishbane, "addressed
to the moral will of the person." In Ezekiel 18, however, those same legal
statements are cited with the specific sanction of capital punishment.
Fishbane writes: "Since such penalties are unthinkable in actual biblical law,
one may conclude that Ezekiel's hyperbolic rhetoric was designed to rebut
thoroughly the prevailing notions of vicarious guilt, and to emphasize the
unilateral application of the standard of individual responsibility."[109]

Ezekiel expands Deut 24:16 in another way by stressing the
significance and potential of an individual's present actions over the
consequences of past actions. Fishbane suggests two reasons for that.[110]
First, Ezekiel wishes "to counteract motivational indifference;" and second
"he is concerned to inspire the courage for repentance and thus show the
exiles a way of religious renewal." It is hard to imagine, however, that the
pastoral problems Ezekiel addresses are those cited by Fishbane.[111] So
also, it is unthinkable that Ezekiel is "narrowing the scope of individual
responsibility to each and every separate action." Ezekiel is not dealing
with the question of divine acceptance, which is dependent on the current
status of an individual's actions, as Fishbane states. Rather, Ezekiel is
seeking to reconstitute a devastated congregation in exile. They are not
"intransigent" in their questioning, "Why does the son not bear the guilt of
the father?" (18:19), nor in their criticism "The Lord acts without principle"
(18:25, 29; 33:17, 20).[112] They are exhibiting the normal responses to
disaster that leave a community shattered and without a will to act one way
or another. That is the real issue, not theological dogma.[113]

---

[109]Ibid., 338. In Chapter 6 I argue that the function of law in Ezekiel 18 is not simply to
serve as a foil for the doctrinal disputation, but as a guide to shaping the character of the new
community that is taking shape through the experience of judgment. I argue, moreover, that
capital punishment is metaphorical in Ezekiel in two ways: first, in that exile is a form of
death; and second, that the alternatives of life/death are ciphers for possiblity that Ezekiel sees
emerging after the wilderness of exile has come to an end.

[110]Ibid., 338.

[111]Fishbane (ibid.) suggests that some presumptuously thought that one could be guilty
forever because of transgression, or that righteousness would allow one to act without principle.

[112]Fishbane's translation (ibid., 338).

[113]See Chapter 7 for a discussion of the function of theodicy in Ezekiel 18.

Although I disagree with Fishbane's insistence on Ezekiel's reason for being concerned for the individual, and with his depiction of the audience's motivations for citing the proverb and criticizing Yahweh's actions, I agree that Ezekiel uses Pentateuchal civil legislation along with Deut 24:16 to create a unique reinterpretation of *tôrâ* for his own purposes. The "exegetical analogy" that Ezekiel creates is that "all cases, theological and civil, are alike. There is thus no double standard of justice."[114]

How precisely does the citation of Deut 24:16 function in relation to the specific laws cited in Ezekiel 18? Fishbane suggests, continuing his explanation of aggadic discourse, that Ezekiel cites Deut 24:16 for two reasons. First, some of the laws cited in Ezekiel 18 bear resemblances to laws in Deuteronomy, which are found in the same context as 24:16 (Deut 23:20-21; 24:6, 10-15, 17). That cannot be allowed to carry much weight because as I show in Chapters 4 and 6, resemblances to Priestly laws are at least as strong, if not stronger, than to Deuteronomic laws. Second, Fishbane suggests that Ezekiel may have chosen Deut 24:16 because it was itself an exegetical development based on Exod 34:6-7.[115]

Since the prohibitions that are cited in Ezekiel 18, which correspond to similar laws in Deuteronomy 23 and 24, do not have any penalties stipulated in the Deuteronomic context, Fishbane proposes that Deut 24:16 was included in its Deuteronomic context "in order to counter tendencies to exact vicarious retributions in cases of economic collapse. . . . Each person is rather to be regarded as a self-contained economic unit."[116] That suggestion is supported by lack of children mentioned in Deut 15:12-17, a distinct difference from the slave laws of Exod 21:2-6 where the wife and children of the slave must continue to serve the master. Fishbane suggests that the reason for the odd juxtaposition of a law rejecting vicarious punishment with laws concerning economic liability in Deuteronomy 24 is because the Deuteronomic Code is limited by the *traditum* from which it was derived, namely, the apodictic laws of economic justice in Exod 22:20-23:12.[117] In the correspondences between Exod 22:20-21 and Deut 24:14-15 Fishbane finds the reason for the existence of Deut 24:16 in Deuteronomy 24.

> After the exhortation not to oppress the weak in Exod 22:20-1 the legal draftsman-teacher has included this divine sanction: 'For if you do in fact oppress him [viz., the weak], I shall truly heed his cry if he appeals to me;

---

[114]*Biblical Interpretation*, 339.

[115]Ibid.

[116]Ibid., 339.

[117](1) Deut 24:10-11 // Exod 22:24; (2) Deut 24:12-13, 17b // Exod 22:25-26; (3) Deut 24:14-15 // Exod 22:20-21; (4) Deut 24:17a // Exod 23:6; (5) Deut 24:19-21 // Exod 23:11-12; (6) Deut 25:1 // Exod 23:7. Ibid., 340.

and my anger will be aroused and I shall kill you by the sword, so that your wives shall become widows and your sons orphans.'[118]

The law in Deut 24:14-15 is considerably different from that of Exod 22:20-21. It contains no mention of oppressing strangers, widows, or orphans, but it does mention the cry to the Lord for help.

Deut 24:16, therefore, functions in Deuteronomy 24 to transform and mitigate the divine punishment of death in Exod 22:23-24. The punishment now becomes a "sin" before God (Deut 24:15), and the oppression is expanded to include a prohibition against transgenerational economic exploitation. But Deut 24:16 seems not to suit its context.[119] Fishbane comments that the original use of Deut 24:16 (before its incorporation into chap. 24?) was "to prohibit vicarious substitutions in capital cases, or their gross extension to blood relatives" (as in 2 Kgs 14:5-6). But in its present context in chap. 24,

> the draftsman . . . intended Deut 24:16 to be *contextually construed* as a hyperbolic legal exhortation stressing that a lender may not seek vicarious satisfaction of any kind for defaulted debts. Conceivably, Ezekiel, who was concerned to emphasize individual responsibility for theological as for civil transgressions, was aware that Deut. 24:16, his key text, was itself an exhortation rejecting earlier notions of vicarious punishment for economic crimes. If not, he remarkably arrived at a similar aggadic application of it by other means.[120]

The traditional formulation of Exod 34:6-7 and the matter of retribution was, as Fishbane points out, clearly in tension in the biblical traditions. Jeremiah harmonizes the divine attribute formulary with the sentiments of Deut 24:16.[121] But in Jer 32:18-19 the attribute formulary is demonstrably altered by the exegetical addition in v 19b that Yahweh "rewards every person according to his ways and according to the fruit of his actions." The significance of this reversal is, in part, that it denies the element of mercy inherent in the original context in Exodus 32-24 and focuses on the question of justice.[122] There the attribute formulary in 34:6-7 is a response to 32:32-34, so that the verb *pqd* in 32:34 is interpreted in 34:7.[123] Fishbane notes that Isaiah's encounter with Hezekiah in 2 Kgs

---

[118]Ibid., 340.

[119]Perhaps the legist may not have been free to alter the original formulation.

[120]*Biblical Interpretation*, 341.

[121]In Jer 31:28-30 and Ezekiel 18 the formulary is not cited.

[122]*Biblical Interpretation*, 342.

[123]But note that even in Exod 34:33 Yahweh makes a silent reckoning of the ones who have sinned. Still it is not clear there whether individuals or the congregation will suffer the

20 reflects the positive aspect of the mercy of postponing punishment (see Hezekiah's response in v 19). But Jeremiah and Ezekiel do not respond the same way. For them, "the true expression of divine mercy and kindness lies in his immediate punishment of the actual perpetrators of the delict."[124]

Deut 7:9-10 also reflects a revision of the divine attribute formulary that is found in the Decalogue (which contains the words "lovers" and "haters" in Deut 5:9-10 and Exod 20:5-6, and thus is different from Exod 34:6-7). Besides the inversion of its main clauses for contextual reasons, Deut 7:9-10 clearly replaces "to the third and fourth generation" with "requites to their face those who hate him, by destroying them."[125]

Ezekiel participates in the inner-Biblical dialogue, although he never actually cites the divine attribute formulary. He clearly identifies with the tradition that sides with Deut 24:16 against transgenerational retribution. But unlike the Deuteronomic theology, Ezekiel is not particularly favouring individual responsibility, but generational responsibility. The Priestly tradition similarly debated the question, which dominates the agenda in Numbers 14-16. There, in Num 14:18 a citation of the attribute formulary occurs in a liturgical context in which Moses pleads for mercy. If Numbers 15 and 16:22 belong to the Priestly tradition, then P may be interpreting 14:18 (JE?) in such a way as to clarify the ambiguity in that citation. On this both the Deuteronomistic and Priestly traditions seek clarification.

Moreover, as Haag suggests, 18:21-23 demonstrates that Ezekiel does not promote a general principle of retribution, but utilizes it in relation to his interest in restoration to the land. This he demonstrates by arguing that even for Ezekiel evil deeds do not automatically result in death. Ezekiel 18 assumes that a sinner can live a long time before dying, and that such a person has time to repent. Even the righteous must die. For Ezekiel it is also not a matter of life after or in place of physical death. Rather, the exiles are being called to return to the land of the ancestors, and thereby to participate in the salvific life. The sinner, however, will not experience that life, but like the rebellious ones in the wilderness they will die before that (Ezek 20:35-38; cf. Numbers 16). For Ezekiel, repentance leads to life, which means return to the land.[126] Ezekiel reflects the Priestly theology

---

consequences of the action.

[124]*Biblical Interpretation*, 343.

[125]Ibid., 343-44. Fishbane provides reasons for the transformations in the Decalogue. The verbal parallel between Deut 5:11 and Exod 34:6-7 helps to explain that the two commandments in Deut 5:9-10 and 5:11 draw on Exod 34:6-7. Thus, the Decalogue itself contains the ambiguity expressed in the tension between transgenerational retributive justice (Deut 5:9-10) and individual punishment (Deut 5:11). Fishbane goes on to describe further revisions in Joel 2, Jonah 4, the Psalms, and Micah 7:18-20, all of which emphasize mercy over justice (except Nahum 1:2-3).

[126]*Was lehrt?*, 92.

that defines life in terms of entering the land. In that he corresponds to the old tradition.

Can it be said, then, that Ezekiel walks between the Priestly and the Deuteronomistic traditions? Could the previous suggestions characterize how Ezekiel maps out his own path? Ezekiel rejects the Priestly theology of intergenerational transference of punishment, and sides with the Deuteronomistic theology. Ezekiel acknowledges the Deuteronomistic sense of responsibility, but as I shall point out in Chapter 6 perhaps not with its *tôrâ*. Ezekiel acknowledges the Deuteronomistic commitment to the possibility of faithfulness, but sides with the Priestly theocentric view of divine presence and enablement over against Deuteronomistic "humanism." But he affirms the linking of life with repentance, and he defines both in terms of his ultimate concern—the shaping and creation of a moral community in the land (as in Deut 4:1; 5:33; 8:1; 16:20; 30:15-16, 19-20; cf. Lev 18:5). Still, like the Priestly theology, land is the organizing space while a holy community is the organizing principle (Ezek 20:11-12, 38, 41-42). The matter of retribution in Ezekiel must be interpreted in those terms.[127]

TOWARD A NEW SYNTHESIS

Although it is helpful to hypothesize about how Ezekiel participates in the dialogue of traditions in ancient Israel—in terms of the relationship between corporate and personal responsibility—I shall attempt here to provide a new angle of vision on Ezekiel's conception of the relationship between the individual and society. I shall describe Ezekiel's own synthesis

---

[127]Mosis' (*Das Buch Ezechiel*, 267, n. 210) position bears noting here. He sees no contradiction between chap. 18 and the judgment against Israel's history in chaps. 16, 20, and 23. "Denn in diesen Kapiteln begründet gerade nicht die mechanische Weitergabe der Schuld von Generation zu Generation das Gericht über die gesamte Abfolge der Geschlechter, sondern das verantwortliche Eintreten jeder neuen Generation in die Schuld der vorausgehenden. Eine Generation wird nicht deswegen verurteilt, weil die vorausgehende gefehlt hat. Sondern es wird festgestellt, dass jede neue Generation in den Weg der vorausgehenden eingetreten und darum demselben Urteil unterworfen ist (vgl. 20:30)." That is what Ezekiel is trying to prevent. He is trying to swing a new generation away from the way of the past generations and to make a new start. Ezek 18:20 does not answer all the questions. It assumes one is going to be righteous and another wicked. It does not deal with the case where father and son are wicked, as for example in Jer 16:10-18.

Davidson (*Ezekiel*, 133) says that the text does not deny that evil consequences do not pass from father to son, or from one's past. Rather, it is the consequence of "life" or "death" that is not passed on. The moral freedom of the individual makes it possible to be freed from the consequences of another's actions, or even of one's own past actions.

in terms of the moral self and the moral community. I shall borrow Stanley Hauerwas's concept "community of character" to redefine or at least to redescribe what I perceive to be happening in the book of Ezekiel.[128] This redescription will begin here, and will continue through the next two chapters. I shall suggest that Ezekiel is attempting to shape a new peoplehood through his use of ancient tradition. Calling on the formative memory of Israel, Ezekiel seeks to envision and enable a "story-formed community," or, as I shall put it, a *tôrâ*-formed community.[129]

A Revised Understanding
of Self and Community in Ezekiel[130]

For Ezekiel the exiles are a paradigm of the community Israel. They are castigated as the whole of Israel past has been. And they are envisioned as the whole of Israel re-formed in the future. They are the moral community *in nuce* (Ezek 2:3).

We are dealing in Ezekiel, as perhaps in no other book in the Hebrew Bible, with the problem of a community's self-definition. The Book of Ezekiel stands at a liminal stage in that process. It is from within that liminal stage that the tension between the individual and the community ought to be viewed. From within, the issue is not part of an irreconcilable tension, but part of a dialogue of a becoming community, a new

---

[128]This concept is articulated in a variety of essays in the collection *A Community of Character*. Hauerwas's work depends on the insight of Alisair MacIntyre, which is developed in *After Virtue* (Notre Dame, IN: University of Notre Dame Press, 1971). The more recent book by Hauerwas (*The Peaceable Kingdom*) is a more comprehensive statement on the intersection of narrative, virtue, and character as the building blocks of a moral community.

[129]Hauerwas (*A Community of Character*, 14) suggests that "the truthfulness of a tradition is tested in its ability to form people who are ready to put the tradition into question, or at least to recognize when it is being put into question by a rival tradition."

[130]G. E. Mendenhall ("The Conflict Between Value Systems and Social Control," *Unity and Diversity: Essays in the History, Literature, and Religion of the Ancient Near East* [ed. H. Goedicke and J. J. M. Roberts; The Johns Hopkins Near Eastern Studies; Baltimore/London: Johns Hopkins University Press, 1975] 175) describes the relationship between the individual and society in these terms: "Obligations [are] individual, but consequences (blessings and curses) are of necessity social, since they are 'acts of God'—drought, epidemic, defeat in war, etc. [This] powerfully reinforces individual responsibility to society, and social responsibility to refrain from protection of the guilty." We cannot, therefore, divorce the individual from the society either in terms of responsibility, or for discerning consequences of actions. We must articulate a refined view of the self and the community in Ezekiel.

peoplehood. We must, therefore, speak of a "social self," a new entity or moral agent, since a self and a community cannot be fully independent.[131]

To use another image, from Stanley Fish, Ezekiel is at work shaping the identity of an "interpretive community." From within such a community the traditions of Israel will again take root and shape a community of character. Within that task, Ezekiel 18 can be seen as more than a disputation speech; it is an exercise in persuasion.[132]   According to R. B. Gill, "Fish's concept of interpretive communities allows us to see that one's experience and accounts of experience are not merely passive reactions to an objective reality but an active process of shaping experience according to the community's sense of purpose"[133]

In fact, Gill continues, "interpretive communities . . . mediate between individuals and a meaningless world by giving them the patterned and purposive categories and slots into which they can place their experience." Ezekiel's audience had lost those categories. The task of the prophet in exile, therefore, was to work at constructing the foundation and to mediate that foundation to the members of the fragmented community. Gill also states that "an interpretive community . . . is basically theological because it imposes purpose on the experiences of its members, a sense of that for which an event occurs, a direction or goal which give meaningfulness and value to their lives."[134]   Ezekiel's community is in danger of accepting alternate conventions by which to interpret experience, which Ezekiel routinely calls idolatry. For Ezekiel the ancient tradition of Israel serves as the foundation around which communal experiences may be reconstructed and shaped into a meaningful whole.

The question of how the self is constituted in Ezekiel is also open to review. We have assumed a modern understanding of self, or of the individual. Without again reverting to the argument of primitive mentality or corporate personality, it is possible to say that for Ezekiel the self and the community "exist" in an interactive process in which neither is the determinant factor. Building on Fish's categories, the individual is not the "free agent," nor is the individual bound solely by social conventions. One is "a member of a community whose assumptions" about almost anything

---

[131]The term "social self" is from Jürgen Habermas, *Communication and the Evolution of Society* (Boston: Beacon, 1979).

[132]*Is There a Text in This Class: The Authority of Interpretive Communities* (Cambridge: Harvard University Press, 1980) 171. See pp. 15-17 for a definition and discussion of persuasion.

[133]"The Moral Implications of Interpretive Communities," *Christianity & Literature* 33/1 (1983) 55-56. On the teleological dimension of narrative and virtue see Hauerwas, *Peaceable Kingdom*, 19-22, 116-21. I shall develop this further in Chapter 6 in relation to the function of law in Ezekiel 18.

[134]"The Moral Implications," 57.

"determine the kind of attention [one] pays" and thus the kinds of meanings one makes. Individual decisions about ethics and community are bound up in a total package based on "a collective decision as to what will count" as constituting a moral community.[135]

In that way the individual and the community can be understood as interdependent. As Fish writes,

> if the self is conceived of not as an independent entity but as a social construct whose operations are delimited by the systems of intelligibility that inform it, then the meanings it confers on texts [or in our case, the social reality that it construes] are not its own but have their source in the interpretive community (or communities) of which it is a function.[136]

And Ezekiel is saying, I think, that there is no self apart from the moral community, just as there is no community apart from moral selves. The part and the whole are not separable.[137]

Another way of looking at the relation of self and community in Ezekiel is to think of Ezekiel's rhetoric as a form of social imagination. Ezekiel is creating space for a "value-based movement" that is defined over against a "social control system."[138] According to Mendenhall, the ancient Israelite vision of social change is based "in the internal motivation of large numbers of persons."[139] Mendenhall is arguing for recognizing a unique factor in biblical religion—that social and religious structures are never equated with the rule of God, which finds expression in community, that is to say, in human beings with moral convictions based on a vision of transcendent reality.

With regard to the relation between structures and values Mary Douglas states that "any culture is a series of related structures which comprise social forms, values, cosmology, the whole of knowledge and

---

[135]Fish speaks here specifically about reading "literature." My comments are adapted from *Is There a Text?*, 11. There is always a danger of adapting an argument from one setting and using it in another, as Roger Lindsay ("Rules as a Bridge between Speech and Action," *Social Rules and Social Behaviour* [ed. Peter Collett; Oxford: Blackwell, 1977] 151) puts it: "The drawback of interdisciplinary borrowing of this type is that too often the borrowed explanatory device, much like the rabbit introduced to Australia, succeeds too well and threatens the indigenous fauna."

[136]*Is There a Text?*, 335.

[137]Looking at a field of grain in late summer one can observe that the field is ripening. On closer inspection, it becomes clear that the field is turning yellow because the stalks of grain are ripening independently of one another. Together, however, the stalks turn the field yellow.

[138]I am borrowing the terminology from Mendenhall, "The Conflict between Value Systems and Social Control," 170.

[139]Ibid., 169.

through which all experience is mediated."[140]   Mendenhall is arguing, however, that values and social structures come into conflict except where the social structures co-opt the values and turn them into forms of social control. I am suggesting that for Ezekiel there is a strong sense that social control has run its course.[141]   All those with power—kings, priests, prophets, etc.—have brought Israel to an end. Ezekiel seeks to reconstruct the "house of Israel" using the old traditions, but is calling for commitment to a new orientation within the old traditions. In dialogue with the past, Ezekiel seeks to imagine a new reality. That is the function of his individual-community motif. It is not to place religion on a new foundation of individualism, but to create a new interdependence that will create a community of character again.

A Redescription of Actions and Consequences

Redescribing the relationship of actions and consequences in Ezekiel, along with the concept of retribution, will help further to clarify Ezekiel's idea of the relationship between the individual and the community. In attempting to reshape a moral community, Ezekiel works with the conviction that actions have certain consequences. The traditional approach to the problem has been to speak of the interrelationship of crime, guilt, and punishment.[142]

But if a major concern for Ezekiel was to deal with the exiles' understanding of divine justice, then to focus simply on interpreting Ezekiel's view of actions and consequences as the major issue is inadequate. For Ezekiel Yahweh is actively involved; "the punishment to come is the personal justice of Israel's covenantal God, not simply the working out of some impersonal principle of divine justice."[143]   And the working out of that justice is expressed variously in the Book of Ezekiel. In fact, Fishbane notes that "there is no focused attempt in the Book of Ezekiel to correlate specific sins with specific judgments."[144]   Although that may be stating

---

[140]*Purity and Danger: An Analysis of the Concepts of Pollution and Taboo* (London/Boston/Henley: Routledge & Kegan Paul, 1966) 128.

[141]According to B. Lang, *Kein Aufstand in Jerusalem: Die Politik des Propheten Ezechiel* (SBB; Stuttgart: Katholisches Bibelwerk, 1978).

[142]Note especially the proposals of K. Koch ("Is there a Doctrine of Retribution?") that actions inherently contained spheres of influence (discussed above in Chapter 4).

[143]Fishbane, "Sin and Judgment," 148. So also P. D. Miller, Jr., *Sin and Judgment in the Prophets*. Although Miller does not deal with Ezekiel, he does present a critique and modification of Koch's views.

[144]Ibid., 148.

the matter too forcefully, the observation focuses another matter—that Israel's experience of exile is not simple retribution.

Fishbane illustrates the variety of ways divine judgment is expressed in Ezekiel. (1) Many of the sins that form the basis for judgment in Ezekiel are stated in general and stereotyped terms, as for example in rebellion against laws and defilement of the sanctuary (chaps. 4-5).   (2) "Abominations" are frequently generalized references to idolatry and violence, as in chaps. 6-7. Thus, there is not consistent correlation between specific sins with specific judgments. (3) Actions portrayed in chaps. 8-9 may reflect more the time of Manasseh than Jerusalem of the exilic era. As Fishbane suggests, "the sin-judgment nexus found in chapters 8-9 may teach us more about the struggle to produce a viable theodicy in early sixth century Babylon than about the actual practices in and around the Temple of Jerusalem at that time."[145] (4) Sometimes the relationship between sin and judgment has more to do with the metaphor being developed than with a precise relationship (as in chaps. 16 and 23). (5) The talionic expressions like "I shall recompense their ways upon them" (as in 7:3-4; 9:8; 11:21; 16:43) are probably more a "rhetorical strategy . . . designed to demonstrate *the reality of divine providence* and *the logic of sin-judgment* than any strict principle of legal retribution or equivalence;" (6) the talionic judgments often connect sin and punishment in poetic and generalized ways. That can be seen, for example, in the expressions that the people have acted evilly, so the Lord will do evil to them (cf. 6:7); or since the people have rejected Yahweh's *mišpāṭîm*, so the Lord will judge (*šāpaṭ*) them (cf. 5:7-8; 11:11-12).[146]

Instead of viewing the Ezekiel tradition complex from the perspective of a crime-guilt-punishment nexus, I suggest with R. Hutton that moral categories are better viewed from the perspective of act-status-response. Hutton notes that the emphasis on "crime-guilt-punishment" and "crime-verdict-sentence" help to qualify the relationship as "one event."[147] But more significantly, according to Hutton's work on declaratory formulae,

---

[145]Ibid., 135. Fishbane reads chaps. 8-9 as a "propaganda document."

[146]Ibid., 148-49. The greatest problem perceived by Fishbane is that Ezekiel 18 and 20 reflect "diametrically opposed" teachings (143). I have discussed that tension in Chapter 4. Fishbane concludes that chap. 20 teaches that the exilic generation has inherited the consequences of the second exodus generation (20:18-26). V 30, however, makes it clear that "after the manner of your fathers" is the criterion for judgment. It is simply too much to say: "Dark, indeed, must have been the mood of the prophet who produced, and a nation which accepted, such a theodicy, deprived as it is of all hope, and filled altogether with the despair of fate and divine doom. So viewed, the final prophecy of an unrequited redemption is nothing more than the hope of hopelessness. To say that Ezekiel's divine prophecies are riven with intense contradictions is an understatement" (144).

[147]"Declaratory Formulae," 43.

certain actions effect a certain status in the community. . . . Furthermore, anytime a status is introduced which alters or endangers the wholeness (*šālôm*) of the society, measures must be taken to restore the wholeness and the balance of the community. A response is called for which is appropriate to the status which has been introduced. . . . What appears in the legal sphere as a continuum of crime-guilt-punishment is, in reality, but a manifestation of a much broader phenomenon based upon and anchored in this primary societal concern. At this basic level it is more appropriate to speak of a continuum of act-status-response. An act may result in a change of societal status from the normal *šālôm*, and a response is called for to reestablish the status.[148]

"Shalom-disturbing" acts affect the shape of the community and need to be dealt with.[149] Hutton's work is most helpful in showing that Ezekiel 18 participates in a sociological nexus, not simply a sin-guilt-punishment nexus.

That puts Ezekiel's discourses in a new light. Ezekiel is speaking of actions, status, and necessary responses, whereas the people are arguing in the *māšāl* of 18:2 from the perspective of actions, guilt, and punishment. The shalom-disturbing actions listed in chap. 18 must be integrated into Ezekiel's convictional pattern as a whole, in which holiness (itself a complex concept) becomes the cipher for *šālôm* as the symbolic centre of his world view.

To anticipate the discussion in Chapter 6 I suggest here that Ezekiel's case laws function distinctly as hortatory rather than forensic laws, and as such they address the community and the individual. Hutton distinguishes syntactically three types of "if" form laws: forensic, reflecting actual legal practice by judges or elders; hortatory, reflecting what the community must do in response to the call of *tôrâ*; and ritual instruction, concerned for ritual purity.[150] "Forensic law is concerned with the question of justice. Hortatory law is concerned with the question of communal obedience and solidarity."[151] Ezekiel's appeal to law is ultimately an address to the community in exile.

The most important aspect of Hutton's analysis of declaratory formulae for understanding Ezekiel is that Priestly law as well as narrative descriptions of judicial activity are shown to be rooted not in official circles, but in the life of the clan. "Disputes were settled by the kin group and resolved by the elders."[152] It is not surprising that Ezekiel has to deal with the elders of the house of Israel on more than one occasion. It is

---

[148]Ibid., 44.
[149]"Shalom-disturbing" is Hutton's term (ibid., 51).
[150]Ibid., 211-21.
[151]Ibid., 216.
[152]Ibid., 286; see also 258.

important, therefore, to reconsider the function of kinship terminology in Ezekiel, and in Ezekiel 18 in particular.

The Function of Kinship Terminology/Family Images

Family images dominate the disputation in Ezekiel 18: fathers and children in the *māšāl* of v 2; a sequence of fathers and sons in vv 5-20; and the house of Israel as the context for the entire disputation, which culminates in divine pathos (vv 23, 32) and calls on the family of God to make a move toward the resources tentatively offered by its household master, Yahweh. The importance of the family image is evident more widely in the book of Ezekiel, from the judgment for adultery to the reestablishment of the new community according to the tribes of Israel. Thus, Ezekiel 18 participates in a larger conceptual world in which *tôrâ* is both at home, and serves a formative function. The community is addressed through the metaphor of the family, and the community that is built as a community of *ṣaddîqîm* is reconstructed out of the ruins of the present. Ezekiel calls the generation in exile to become the eschatological *tôrâ* community.[153] Ezekiel 18 states that movement toward that end is possible, even in the midst of judgment.

It is clear that family images are the dominant model in the Hebrew Bible for describing the origin and character of Israel. According to Dale Patrick, these images range from genealogies to corporate personality: "Being an Israelite meant belonging to a community forged together by family links."[154] Although Ezekiel uses the terms father and son several times (chap. 18; 5:10), other terms such as brother, sister, mother, clan, and people also occur.[155] In those cases and others we see that Ezekiel does not wish to preserve or foster a simple concept of individual punishment. Over against that, however, he does wish to develop the notion of responsibility of the present generation, be they fathers, sons, mothers, or daughters. And he does that by using a variety of familial metaphors, including the sins of the fathers and the abominations of the adulterous wife.

---

[153]W. Harrelson's insight (*The Ten Commandments and Human Rights*, 179) corresponds to the teleological emphasis of Hauerwas, when he suggests that "it is a sense of kinship, of family ties, of life intertwined with life, of a kind of destiny that awaits and is running its course toward a goal being realized."

[154]"Political Exegesis," *Encounter with the Text* (Semeia Supplements; ed. Martin Buss; Missoula, MT: Scholars Press, 1979) 147.

[155]Scharbert (*Solidarität*, 217, 225) notes that Ezekiel speaks of old men, young men, young women, little children and women (9:6); mothers and daughters (16:44-52); sons and daughters (23:47; 24:21).

Several observations about the occurrence of kinship terms in Ezekiel will help to clarify Ezekiel's use of familial images. H. Van Dyke Parunak's analysis of density of word usage in Ezekiel demonstrates that kinship terms are found most often in chaps. 16-23. The word "father" ('āb, 27 times) occurs most frequently in chaps. 18, 20, and 22. The word "sister" ('āhôt, 24 times) dominates chaps. 16 and 23. The word "mother" ('ēm, 10 times) occurs predominantly in chaps. 16, 19, 21-23, with only one occurrence outside those chapters (chap. 44).[156]

Other kinship terms are also significant in Ezekiel, although they do not occur with as much frequency in so few texts. "Brother" ('āh) occurs ten times and randomly throughout the book.[157] The specific word bēn, which is used most often in the "son of man" formula and nine times in the expression "children of Israel," is found numerous other times.[158] Ezekiel is explicitly instructed that he is being sent to the "children of Israel."[159] The words "son" and "daughter" are used together to emphasize the generational connection in the current experience. In chap. 14 sons and daughters are not delivered by the ṣaddîqîm (14:16, 18, 20, 22). In chaps. 23 and 24 sons and daughters suffer in the midst of the parents' sinful actions (23:4, 10, 25, 47; 24:21, 25; see also 44:25). Fathers and sons are juxtaposed in one text (5:10), but that could as well be simply a reference to children. In the context of a judgment text Israel is once called "my son" (21:15 [10]). And in the restoration vision of 37:25 the specific "children's children" refers the promise of land to the ancestor Jacob conjoined with the Davidic promise and sanctuary: "They shall dwell in the land where your fathers dwelt that I gave to my servant Jacob; they and their children and their children's children shall dwell there for ever; and David my servant shall be their prince for ever."[160]

The words for clan and tribe occur seldom in Ezekiel as kinship terms. Mišpāḥâ occurs only once in 20:32, and there it refers to Israel's desire to be like the nations (gôyîm), the mišpāḥâ of the lands. Three other times gôy is used of Israel, once as a "rebellious nation" (2:3), once referring to the hope of becoming "one nation" (37:22), and once in the mouth of another group speaking about Israel and Judah (35:10). "Tribe" (šēbeṭ) is used

---

[156]Linguistic Density Plots in Ezekiel (The Computer Bible, Vol. XXVII-A; Wooster, OH: Biblical Research Associates, 1984) 15.

[157]Parunak (ibid., 34) notes the contrast between this word and the previously mentioned kinship terms, noting that the uniform distribution of "brother" over against the strength of the other terms "provides significant clues to the structure of Ezekiel."

[158]"Children of Israel" only occurs three times in Isaiah, and six times in Jeremiah.

[159]In 2:3; see also 4:13; 6:5; 35:5; 37:16, 21; 43:7; 47:22; 48:11; "my children" 16:21. "Children" (pl.) occurs also the expression "children of your people" (3:11; 33:2, 12, 17, 30; 37:18).

[160]"My servant Jacob" occurs also in 28:25 in reference to dwelling in the land.

strictly in relation to the restoration (37:19; 45:8; 47:13, 21, 22, 23; 48:1, 19, 23, 29, 31). "Congregation" (*'ēdâ*), a term that occurs throughout the books of Leviticus and Numbers, is not used in Ezekiel. Predominantly "house of Israel" occurs as the chief designation of Ezekiel's audience, and of "Israel" past, present, and future.[161]   Only in 20:5 is that "house" explained as "house of Jacob" in relation to the promise of relationship with Yahweh and promise of land. The combination of "house of Israel/Jacob" and "children of Israel" supports the suggestion that Ezekiel's image of Israel is interpreted in terms of a family metaphor, and particularly, the family of Yahweh. Ezekiel's conception of Israel seems to be a paradigm constructed after the model of the kinship group, the *bêt 'āb*.[162]

Although Parunak does not interpret those data concerning familial terminology in his concordance, it cannot be missed that those kinship terms are found in Ezekiel 16-23 more prominently than anywhere else in the book. Parunak states:

> In a text, even more than in a radioisotope scan, clusters of data invite interpretation as meaningful constructs. Texts are written by perceiving people, for other people to perceive. We are interested in clusters of target words because of their perceptual effects on people. We want to plot a text in a way that will model and explain the effect of a text on a reader, and perhaps uncover how its author or authors perceived it.[163]

I am suggesting that the familial terminology would have had a rhetorical function of stimulating the audience perception of its relationship with Yahweh and its rootedness in early Israelite tradition. Understanding its early history as a family story, the "house of Israel" in exile hears a call that interprets exile as judgment and as a necessary purifying experience leading to reconstitution of that "house of Israel" in the land. Ezekiel is attempting to reforge that familial identity in the face of the loss of a political identity. And he is attempting to recapture the kinship images in order to exploit their affective capacity for reshaping a community of character. Ezekiel is redrawing the boundaries of clan and peoplehood both in terms of the moral character of the community and the hope for a transformation of Israel's physical reality in the land.[164]

---

[161]Another use of "house" referring to the temple, "the Lord's house," occurs frequently in Ezekiel. Note especially the parallels between 8:14, 16; 10:19; 11:1 and 44:4, 5.

[162]See Daniel I. Block, "Israel's House: Reflections on the Use of *byt ysr'l* in the Old Testament in the Light of its Ancient Near Eastern Environment," *JETS* 28 (1985) 257-75.

[163]*Linguistic Density Plots*, 24.

[164]Could it be that Ezekiel is articulating the notion of the clan as faithful cultic community? (See Hutton, "Declaratory Formulae," 139). For the idea that the plural *'ammîm* is the clan as cultic community, see Zimmerli, "Die Eigenart," 17.

R. Hutton's analysis of societal matrices of authoritative language helps to place Ezekiel's conceptual world more concretely. Community in ancient Israel was conceived as kin group, national group, or as worship group.[165] Although worship is an important element of Ezekiel's world, most of Ezekiel's community language derives from kinship language. Ezekiel's concern with the basic "extended family" (*bêt 'āb*), is expressed primarily in his use of the extended metaphor "house of Israel."

In one important respect Ezekiel moves beyond metaphorical kinship language. Although Israel is viewed as a *bêt 'āb*, and it is there that the moral authority derives and to which it is addressed, in matters of life and death the king has a more prominent role. It has often been noted, however, that Ezekiel uses *melek* seldom to refer to Israelite kings (1:2; 17:12, 16; 37:22, 24; 43:7, 9), and uses *śar*, "prince" even less often (11:1; 17:12; 22:27). The more common word in Ezekiel is *nāśî'*, "prince." Ezekiel does not avoid *melek*, which carries special significance in the discussion of David's kingship in chap. 37. Ezekiel 34, however, equates the future David's rule with that of Yahweh, in that both are called "shepherds" (especially 34:15, 33-34). The verb "to rule" (*mlk*) is used only once in Ezekiel, and that of Yahweh's judging and delivering action against and on behalf of his people Israel. Thus, it is Yahweh's prerogative to name a king, but more, it is Yahweh's nature to be the king of his people. Israel is, therefore, primarily the *bêt 'āb* over which Yahweh rules. That rule is expressed through the prophetic announcement of the possiblities of life or death in Ezekiel 18. The verdict is not cast, but it stands as an option.

Hutton's research corroborates that suggestion. The king has a responsibility in capital cases. Hutton writes:

> What is singularly striking when considering the cases in which a king hands down a verdict or sentence is the number of times they concern capital offenses.[166] . . . The particular involvement of the king in capital cases is also evident in the fact that most of the royal edicts which the OT preserves stand under the sanction of death.[167] . . . In four instances the king offers a personal judgment about the persons in question deserving death.[168]

Hutton suggests that the king's statement is not always an official sentence, since "in none of these cases is the person summarily executed. The phrase

---

[165]"Declaratory Formulae," 307. Hutton (ibid., 310) acknowledges the interchangeability of some kinship terminology.

[166]Hutton cites 1 Sam 14:44; 20:2; 22:16; 2 Sam 11:15; 19:24; 1 Kgs 2:24; 21:10; Esther 5:14; 7:9; 9:13, 25).

[167]Gen 26:11; Exod 19:12; 35:2; Num 1:51; 3:10; 18:7; Judg 6:31; 1 Sam 11:13; 1 Sam 14:39; 1 Kgs 1:52; 2:37, 42; Gen 42:20; Exod 10:28; Jer 38:24.

[168]1 Sam 20:31; 26:16; 2 Sam 12:5; 1 Kgs 2:26. "Declaratory Formulae," 335-36.

is clearly a figure of speech. The fact, however, that it is only found on the lips of the king attests to his special involvement in capital cases."[169]

SUMMARY AND CONCLUSIONS

I conclude that the prophet in the book of Ezekiel is construed as Yahweh's agent of life and death. Yahweh as king is also head of the *bêt 'āb*. As such, the *tôrâ* of the community is communicated to the house of Israel, the community within which *tôrâ*-keeping is actualized. The options for life and death are presented in Ezekiel through the role of the prophet, Yahweh's agent, as a rhetorical motivating factor in the explanation for judgment and the recreation of a community of character.

In those ways Ezekiel uses family images as metaphors or symbols of society. Ezekiel's frequent references to pollution and uncleanliness in terms of the harlotry/ adultery metaphor, therefore, reflect a social pollution that is generally classified as "abomination" (*tô'ēbâ*). That also belongs to the kinship imagery, since the protection of the family entity figures prominently in the list of sexual sins in Leviticus.[170]

Mary Douglas's concept of internal/external danger is also applicable here. Ezekiel's situation is a product of external action: Babylonian invasion and exile. At issue in the book of Ezekiel is the attempt to deal with both that external attack, which has disrupted the *šālôm* of the community, and the attack from within. External danger fosters internal solidarity, but internal danger must be dealt with to preserve the coherence of the community. Douglas says that internal danger must be punished to preserve the structure; but for Ezekiel that punishment has already occurred. In Ezekiel we find an attempt to deal with disruptive forces (Douglas's "danger") from within and without. The unifying factor is Yahweh's holiness and presence in a community of character.

Thus, Ezekiel introduces a new configuration of concepts, not a new concept of individual responsibility. For the prophet the matrix of community and individual, interpretive moral community, and social moral self was not essentially different from earlier Israelite tradition. The new configuration, however, introduced a new rhetorical presentation which made possible a necessary social adaptation that was needed for survival. His thinking was not progressive but adaptive.[171]

---

[169]Ibid., 336.

[170]For the idea of the body as symbol of society, and four kinds of social pollution see Mary Douglas, *Purity and Danger*, 115, 122.

[171]See T. Overholt, "Prophecy: the Problem of Cross-Cultural Comparison," *Semeia* 21 (1981) 72.

The function of law, the individual and the community, and the notions of life and death begin to form an integrative convictional and rhetorical framework around which a community of character can be reconstructed (a holy community in covenant with Yahweh). Life and death are inclusion/exclusion from that community in formation. Here we also find the connection between Ezekiel's concept of judgement on Israel, individual responsibility, and corporate restoration. Ezekiel is attempting to forge a new community, but the entire fabric that holds things together has come undone. As he sees it, the house of Israel as a whole has abdicated the covenant by its abominable deeds. That left Yahweh no choice but to abandon the people. Ezekiel understands that the concept of holiness demands complete purging, and so he articulates the corporate guilt and judgment. But he recognizes that the basis for experience of Yahweh's saving presence is the faithfulness of the individual Israelite. The focus on law, and hence on the individual, is to begin the work of reconstituting a covenant community. That focus at the same time suggests that the essence or goal of *tôrâ* is the *tôrâ* formed community.

Ezekiel is engaged in imagining a new world. His discourse presents a mode of perceiving reality. He appeals to old conventions in order to engender or evoke new possibilities. He appeals to an interpretive community by means of the central metaphor of sacred space profaned. His goal, although not stated in these terms, is to enable the next generation to regain a coherent perception of their experience within the structure of reality with Yahweh. His task is what anthropologists call revitalization. His hope is rooted in a reinterpretation of the sacred space metaphor in which the presence of Yahweh is a living reality among a holy people.

We turn now to a fuller exploration of Ezekiel's understanding of the function of law.

6

THE HUMAN MORAL AGENT
AND THE FUNCTION OF LAW

INTRODUCTION

Understanding the relationship between human beings and moral obligations and rules within a religious community has long been a problem.[1] The modern juxtaposition of "law" and "gospel" has created artificial barriers to understanding books like Ezekiel in which law figures prominently in the theological and ethical program for the exiled "house of Israel." That marginalization of law has also blurred the distinctive function of law as an agent of transformation and as a catalyst in creating and sustaining a community of faith. As I have explored in the previous chapter, the community is the context in which the individual finds orientation and moral identity. And as Hauerwas suggests,

> Community joins us with others to further the growth of a tradition whose manifold storylines are meant to help individuals identify and navigate the path to the good. The self is subordinate to the community rather than vice versa, for we discover the self through a community's narrated tradition.[2]

The community's narrated tradition is Israel's *tôrâ*, Israel's story of covenant commitment and communal character. Therefore to understand the legal tradition in Ezekiel as an integral part of the synthesis of tradition will enable us to build a positive model for the place of legal ethics in Ezekiel, and perhaps also in ancient Israel.[3] R. Friedman's suggestion that the Priestly and the Deuteronomistic traditions are in tension during the exilic

---

[1]See the discussion of rules and obligations in Hauerwas, *Peaceable Kingdom*, 19-22. He suggests that "the concentration on obligations and rules as morally primary ignores the fact that action descriptions gain their intelligibility from the role they play in a community's history and therefore for individuals in that community" (21).

[2]Ibid., 28.

[3]What is remarkable about Ezekiel's ethics in relation to the legal tradition is that the word *tôrâ* is rarely used (see Ezek 7:26; 22:26; 43:11-12; 44:5, 24). That scarcity may well be linked to a polemic against some aspects of legal interpretation that used the term frequently.

period may provide a starting point,[4] a working hypothesis, which raises the question about how Ezekiel uses Israel's legal traditions. Does Ezekiel chart a course that avoids the clichés of the Deuteronomistic movement? Does he offer a distinctive or unique place for law in his overall program?

In this chapter I shall present an exploration of the function of the legal tradition in the moral discourse of Ezekiel as follows: (1) I shall investigate the individual laws within Ezekiel 18. As part of that analysis I shall note the occurrences of those laws in the Priestly and Deuteronomistic traditions, as well as in other texts in the book of Ezekiel. (2) Alongside that analysis I shall also explore the use of terms for observing the law in Ezekiel 18 and compare those with terms used elsewhere in Ezekiel and in the Priestly and Deuteronomistic traditions. (3) Finally, I shall draw conclusions, based on observations made here and in Chapter 4, about the function of law in the moral discourse of the Ezekiel tradition.

THE INDIVIDUAL LAWS IN EZEKIEL 18

Ezekiel 18 contains explicit citation of laws, some of which have parallels in legal codes in the Pentateuch. In this section I shall explore that relationship. Of course, we are faced immediately again with the question of the history of literature, and in this case, with the historical development of the specific laws. Certain assumptions about the validity of that enterprise need to be evaluated. H. Schulz, for example, has argued that the specific legal formula *môt yûmāt* and other formulae in Ezekiel are to be ascribed to an independent redactional layer.[5] So also, it has been argued that there is a relationship between the laws in Ezekiel 18 and the Holiness Code, the Priestly tradition generally, and the Deuteronomistic tradition.[6]

I am concerned here, however, with discovering the function of the laws and legal formulations in the chapter. In relation to that, four sets of questions need to be answered. (1) What are the relationships between these laws and other legal texts? Is there a literary or a tradition-bound relationship? (2) Is there a discernible reason why certain laws are cited and not others? Related to that, are the specific laws determinative of the historical setting of the text? (3) Can the individual laws be discussed if they are separated from the lists that have been incorporated into the chapter? Why do the three lists in 18:1-20 not correspond exactly with one another? Are the specific laws incidental to the chapter as a whole? (4)

---

[4]*The Exile and Biblical Narrative*, 70-75.
[5]*Das Todesrecht.*
[6]These matters have been addressed briefly in Chapter 3.

From the laws cited, are there clues from which we can discern how laws were understood to contribute to moral discourse and to the shaping of a moral community?

I shall begin by analyzing the correspondences between the laws in Ezekiel 18 and other legal codes. The subject has been explored before, but usually with the question of literary dependence and priority in view.[7] Although I am interested in that, my concern is to come to an understanding of how laws function within discourse rather than to develop a theory of genetic or historical relationship.

The question may be asked, in that case, what role a study of the relationship or correspondences might play. It is my working hypothesis that literary discourse is rooted in social reality. That is not to say the same thing as traditional form criticism, which would seek a specific locus (*Sitz im Leben*) from which the literary form emerges. I am assuming a broader definition of "setting" as the milieu, the social situation of the community, and the various options for social change within which that community envisions itself and its future. The text of Ezekiel 18 can be located within such a setting, but that endeavour must not be marked at the outset by the assumption that a history of forms will provide the clue to historical location. When we speak of social location and historical location, therefore, we may well be speaking of two different, but not necessarily mutually exclusive, categories. Moreover, historical situation and social function may be related, but need not be. Ezekiel 18, and the book of Ezekiel for that matter, may reflect a social function that can be fairly carefully described without rooting the historical situation concretely in this or that decade.

With regard to the "situation" presupposed by the laws in Ezekiel 18, M. Fishbane makes a comment that needs to be tested further. In the discussion of the genre of the chapter and the place of the legal lists I agreed with him that the lists "served a pedagogical and hortatory function." Fishbane notes that the form-critical conclusions about the law list force us not to use the specific laws for socio-historical reconstruction. They are, rather, used "as typifying instances of covenantal disobedience."[8] That raises a related question: if specific laws are used simply to *typify* covenantal disobedience, what specific shape would covenantal obedience take? Or, alternately, does moral discourse that includes laws function constructively in the book of Ezekiel? I shall argue that moral discourse

---

[7]Among many others: G. Hölscher, *Hesekiel*; S. R. Driver, *Introduction*; M. Burrows, *Literary Relations*; A. Hurvitz, *The Priestly Source and the Book of Ezekiel*; R. E. Friedman, *The Exile and Biblical Narrative*.

[8]"Sin and Judgment," 146.

and the formation of community go hand in hand. Law is one of the central cohesive factors that gives shape to the community's character.[9]

To approach the question of legal correspondences that way will help us to transcend the limitations of approaches that seek dependence of one text on another, or that find origin the defining criterion of function.[10]

As I try to show in my analysis, the laws in Ezekiel 18 are not in fact "quoted," but terminology, phraseology, and traditional concepts are incorporated. There may be connections between the laws and other textual units in the Hebrew Bible, but literary (i.e. genetic) relationship cannot always be proved. If specific relationships can be determined, it will probably not be uniform. Rather, we may find a mixture of relationships in Ezekiel 18 (and the Book of Ezekiel) that illustrate a mingling of allusions from the Deuteronomistic and Priestly traditions. We do well to begin with the assumption that legal traditions are essentially conservative and adaptive, and that a uniform or unilinear history of that adaptation and change may not be discoverable. We might also assume that an admixture of traditional relationships need not imply levels of composition. There may be a compositional history, but that should not be the starting point of the investigation. A danger, however, is that one may be left with an ahistorical reading of the text, or a discourse analysis that is unable to speak meaningfully of a time of composition, or of a history of composition.[11]

---

[9]For Israel, of course, law and narrative are not separate entities. Thus, what the laws in Ezekiel 18 may offer is a way into the narrative of a particular community; and in so doing, the chapter may provide us with clues to the specific vision for community identity formation and individual moral agency within that community.

[10]I am concerned also to avoid the pejorative assumptions associated with much form criticism that deals with legal material. I acknowledge that legal codification (a literary phenomenon) and the use of law (the social phenomenon) may not be historically coterminous. Still, the notion that law is a late phenomenon, at least literarily, is a conclusion that runs through much biblical scholarship. This is evident, for example, in the views of H. Schulz (*Das Todesrecht*) and J. Garscha (*Studien zum Ezechielbuch*) on the place of legal material in the literary history of the book of Ezekiel.

[11]Hauerwas (*Peaceable Kingdom*, 45) suggests that "at least one of the conditions of a truthful tradition is its own recognition that it is not final, that it needs to grow and change if it is to adequately shape our futures in a faithful manner." It is this creative openness to tradition in Ezekiel that I think demonstrates the "truthfulness" of the Ezekielian transposition of tradition. And it is that power to shape and to be shaped by tradition that makes Ezekiel's appeal to law dynamic and community forming. Hauerwas goes on to cite A. MacIntyre (*After Virtue*, 207), whose comments deserve a place here as well: "A living tradition . . . is an historically extended, socially embodied argument, and an argument precisely in part about the goods that constitute that tradition. Within a tradition the pursuit of goods extends through generations, sometimes through many generations. Hence the individual's search for his or her good is generally and characteristically conducted within a context defined by those traditions of which the individual's life is a part."

I shall also show that the complex of allusions in Ezekiel, and in Ezekiel 18 in particular, does not allow the conclusion that the author consciously followed one, or even two, literary traditions. The allusions are more multiplex than we are able to trace to one source or influence.[12]

Does not eat on the mountains
'el hehārîm lō' 'ākāl (18:6, 11, 15; 22:9)

This law does not occur in the legal codes. A similar law in Lev 19:26 reads "You (pl.) shall not eat with the blood" ('al-haddām). Ezek 33:25 reflects the Leviticus tradition with 'al-haddām. The interesting aspect of Ezek 33:25 is that it parallels Ezek 18:6a by following that with "and lift up your eyes to your idols (gillûlêkem)."[13] The LXX version of Lev 19:26, however, replaces 'al-haddām with epi tōn oreōn, as in Ezek 18:6, 11, 15, and 22:9, which have 'el-hehārîm. Although 18:6, 11 use the preposition 'el, 18:15 uses 'al.

The matter is complicated by the association of dām with gillûlîm in Ezek 33:25 and 22:3. In 22:3-4 shedding of blood and idolatry are associated, whereas in 33:25 eating blood, lifting eyes to idols, and shedding blood are associated.[14] Lev 17:10-16 presents an extended discussion of the meaning of blood, including the prohibition of eating blood (17:10, 12, 14). There, however, the word dām is not preceded by the preposition, as in Ezekiel 18 and 22:9. Only Ezek 33:25 and Lev 19:26 prefix 'al before the word dām. Otherwise all laws regarding eating blood have dām as the direct object of the verb (as in Deut 12:16 and Lev 17:10-16). One wonders whether the Lev 19:26 and Ezek 33:25 texts have been corrupted, and that the LXX reading of Lev 19:26 ought to be considered the correct reading. 1 Sam 14:32-33, however, reads 'al-haddām. Because there is no legislation paralleling Ezek 18:6, some commentators have suggested that "eating on the mountains" is a corruption of "eating with the blood."[15]

Zimmerli understands eating on the mountains to be part of the prophetic polemic against sacrifices on Canaanite cultic sites (Hos 4:13; Deut 12:2; Isa 65:7; cf. Ezek 6:13; 20:28; 34:6). It is connected in Ezekiel

---

[12]Fishbane ("Sin and Judgment," 146) considers the list in 22:10-11 to be drawn from Lev 20:10-18, and chap. 18 from Deut 24.

[13]Brownlee (Ezekiel 1-19, 279) suggests that in 33:25 the meaning is "by bloodshed you shall eat."

[14]Note the prospects of inheriting the land in 33:23-29.

[15]C. H. Cornill (Das Buch des Propheten Ezechiel [Leipzig: Hinrichs, 1886]), R. Kraetzschmar, (Das Buch Ezechiel [HKAT; Göttingen: Vandenhoeck & Ruprecht, 1900]), and Fohrer and Galling (Ezechiel) read hhrym in Ezek 33:25. Zimmerli (Ezekiel 2, 199) states that there is no support for that decision.

with the polemic against idolatry. Since "to eat on the mountains" is unique to Ezekiel we cannot make explicit connections with legal literature. Zimmerli concludes only that the phrase depicts a Palestinian context for the original formula, which meshes with Ezekiel's debate with "those in the land of Israel."[16]

We can conclude that textual emendation is not necessary because several attestations rule against it. The Ezekiel text probably stems from the common polemic against idolatry and the sacrificial meals accompanying it. The language belongs to an inner-Ezekielian concern and is expressed in terms independent of Israel's legal traditions. It bears closest resemblance to the judgment oracles in Ezekiel 1-24 which castigate prevailing idolatrous practices.

Does not lift up his eyes
to the idols of the house of Israel
wĕʿênāyw lōʾ nāśāʾ ʾel gillûlê bêt yiśrāʾēl (18:6, 15)

Again, there are no laws that bear marked linguistic similarities. The closest expression is the prohibitive in Lev 19:4, "Do not turn (*tipnû*) to idols (*hāʾĕlîlîm*) or make for yourselves molten gods." As Zimmerli notes, the entire expression in Ezek 18:6, 15 "is formulated wholly in Ezekiel's terminology."[17] The expression *gillûlê bêt yiśrāʾēl* occurs in 18:6, 15 and 8:10. *nāśāʾ ʾênîm ʾel* occurs in 18:6, 12, 15; 23:27; and 33:25. The operative expression is *gillûlîm*, which occurs in the book of Ezekiel thirty-nine times (out of a total of forty-eight occurrences in the Hebrew Bible). The expression "to lift up the eyes" is an expression signifying looking for help (cf. Ezek 23:27; Ps 123:1).

That mountains and idols are associated in 18:6a is not surprising, given their juxtaposition in other Ezekiel texts (6:1-4). Zimmerli notes that *gillûlîm* "always refers in a hostile way to heathen cult objects." Thus, Lev 26:30 "leads us to think of human or animal-shaped images."[18] In the book of Ezekiel, moreover, the *gillûlîm* are associated with cultic uncleanness, as in 16:36 (*gillûlê tôʿăbôtayik*).[19] In 20:7 the "idols of Egypt" are a source of defilement (*ṭmʾ*) (see also 23:7). Idolatry and harlotry are clearly related to one another in the symbolic world of Ezekiel (23:7, 27). There seems to be little to distinguish between alliance with

---

[16]*Ezekiel 1*, 380. Greenberg (*Ezekiel 1-20*, 328) adds, citing private conversation with D. N. Freedman, that there may be a parallel in the worship/feasting sequence in the Golden Calf story (Exod 32:6).

[17]Zimmerli, *Ezekiel 1*, 380.

[18]Ibid., 187.

[19]Note the list of offenses there.

Assyria and Egypt as described in sexual terms, and the same actions described in terms of idolatry. In 23:27 we find the statement that Israel will no longer lift up eyes to the Egyptians or remember them any more. Could 18:6 be a cryptic political polemic? One wonders whether Ezekiel is as interested in citing laws as he is in conjuring up allusions. Greenberg suggests, in addition, that the proximity of "mountains" and "lifting one's eyes" may evoke the pious gesture of Ps 121:1, only here the context is reversed and apostasy is the subject.[20] Or can apostasy and politics be that easily distinguished?

Zimmerli finds *gillûlîm* to be derived from *gēl*, found in 4:12, 15 ("dung"). Since Isaiah and Jeremiah use different terminology for idols, Zimmerli thinks that the term may have been coined during the reform.[21] The term is not specifically Priestly, although it occurs once in the curses of Leviticus. Weinfeld lists it as a characteristic Deuteronomistic expression occurring once in Deuteronomy and in the narratives of DtrH.[22] But it seems to be one among many terms used in the Deuteronomistic polemic against idolatry. In Ezekiel, however, the term dominates as though it had become a cipher within the Ezekiel tradition.

He does not defile his neighbor's wife
'et-'ēšet rē'ēhû lō' ṭimmēh (18:6, 11, 15)

Prohibitions against adultery occur in the Decalogue (Exod 20:14; Deut 5:18), in the Holiness Code, and in the Deuteronomic Code. The prohibition in Ezekiel 18 seems to reflect legislation in Leviticus because of the association with ritual uncleanness, but not because of strict formal similarity. Both Deut 22:22 and Lev 20:10 prescribe the death penalty, but they use different vocabulary for the act of adultery. Deut 22:22 reads "If a man is found lying with the wife of another man" and Lev 20:10 reads "If a man commits adultery (*n'p*) with the wife of his neighbor."

Only in Lev 18:20 is a similar law linked to ritual uncleanness: "You shall not lie carnally (*lō tittēn šĕkobtĕkā*) with your neighbor's (*'ămîtĕkā*) wife, and defile yourself with her." The reference there falls among a list of sexual offenses by which defilement and uncleanness are encountered.[23] The last phrase, *lĕṭāmĕ'â-bāh* (Qal inf. cs.) is difficult because of the sense of the preposition *bāh*. Is it "with her" or "by her?" Since the Qal infini-

---

[20]*Ezekiel 1-20*, 329.

[21]*Ezekiel 1*, 187. The term occurs otherwise only in Lev 26:30; Deut 29:16; 1 Kgs 15:12; 21:26; 2 Kgs 17:12; 21:11, 21; 23:24; and Jer 50:2.

[22]*Deuteronomy and the Deuteronomic School* (Oxford: Clarendon, 1972) 323.

[23]Zimmerli (*Ezekiel 1*, 380) thinks the prohibition in Ezekiel 18 is deliberately set in the context of ritual uncleanness.

tive construct is used, the sense is that the man will become defiled. It may also be, as in Ezek 22:3, that "defilement" arises upon her. But there we find the preposition '*ālêhā*. Ezekiel uses the Piel perfect, which is used elsewhere in Ezekiel for both violation of chastity (22:11; 33:26) and metaphorically in relation to idolatry (5:11; 23:32; 36:18), as well as defilement of Yahweh's name (43:8).[24]

Perhaps more interesting than the correspondence with the Priestly concept of uncleanness is the mention of the consequences of such actions. The list of offenses among which Lev 18:20 falls concludes with "For whoever shall do any of these abominations, the persons that do them shall be cut off from among their people." The expression "to be cut off" (Niphal/Hiphil) occurs only twice in Deuteronomy (Hiphil; 12:29; 19:1), both with reference to "nations." By contrast, the expression occurs often in Leviticus and Ezekiel.[25]

Formal linguistic similarity cannot be demonstrated, especially since there are more allusions and correspondences within Ezekiel's own linguistic usage than with other legal texts. Clearly Ezekiel reflects a legal tradition like H, but it is not a textually based dependence. Ezekiel's conception of uncleanness is connected primarily with his polemic against apostasy, which is partially how it functions in Ezekiel 18. But read against the larger Priestly sanction of being cut off from the community, the law against violation of relational sanctity causing defilement in Ezek 18:6 alludes to the threat to community that disobedience of this commandment entails.[26]

*Does not approach a menstruous wife for sexual relations
'el-'iššâ niddâ lō' yiqrāb (18:6)*

The similarity to Lev 18:19 is striking not only because of the linguistic connections, but also because the previous ordinance in Ezek 18:6 reflects the sense of Lev 18:20 (thus a chiastic relationship). Lev 18:19

---

[24]Other occurrences of *ṭm'* in Ezekiel are: 4:14; 9:7; 14:11; 20:7, 18, 26, 30, 31, 43; 22:3-4; 23:7, 13, 17, 30; 36:17; 37:23; 43:7; 44:25 cf. Gen 34:5; Num 5:14, 27ff.). The verb occurs numerous times in Priestly literature, but only twice in Deuteronomy (21:23; 24:4). The adjective, however, occurs eight times in Deuteronomy (12:15, 22; 14:7, 8, 10, 19; 15:22; 26:14) and five times in Ezekiel (4:13; 22:5, 10, 26; 44:23).

[25]Only using the Hiphil form in Ezek 14:8, 13, 17, 19, 21; 17:17; 21:8, 9; 25:7, 13, 16; 29:8; 30:15; 35:7. As I have suggested in Chapter 4 regarding *môt yûmāt*, the death penalty and the "cutting off" in Ezekiel are treated as synonyms. Ezekiel has given his characteristic expression of the death penalty the same force as the sanction of exclusion from the community.

[26]For fuller discussion of prohibitions of adultery see H. McKeating, "Sanctions against Adultery."

uses the verb *qrb* but has a longer prepositional phrase describing the woman: *'el-'iššâ bĕniddat ṭum'ātāh*. *niddâ* occurs twelve times in Leviticus, referring to menstruation or ritual uncleanness derived from menstruation. Once it occurs in Lev 20:21 as a general declaratory statement of an unclean act (in a declaratory formula). It is used in that general sense twice in Ezekiel (7:19, 20). In Ezek 22:10 and 36:17 we find a closer resemblance to Lev 18:19. In Ezek 22:10 we find *ṭĕmē'at hannidâ*, and in 36:17, *ṭum'at hannidâ*. Both have construct chains with alternate forms of *ṭm'*. Ezek 18:6 is more concise in that *'iššâ* is in construct with *niddâ*, which functions syntactically as an attributive genitive.[27]

The ordinance is cited only in Priestly texts, not in the Book of the Covenant or in the Deuteronomic Code. And it is only included in the first grouping of laws in Ezek 18:5-9, whereas the previous command occurs again in 18:11 and 15. This confirms the connection with the list of prohibitions in Leviticus 18. The laws there are cited as reasons for why "the land vomited out its inhabitants" (Lev 18:25). Lev 18:26 presents the alternative: "But you shall keep my statutes and my ordinances and do none of these abominations." Refraining from these actions will prevent defilement/uncleanness of the land, and will prevent being separated from the holy congregation.

He wrongs no one: 'îš lō' yôneh (18:7, 12, 16)

Of the fourteen times the Hiphil verb *ynh* occurs in the Hebrew Bible, seven are found in Ezekiel.[28] In Ezek 22:7 the fatherless and widow are cited as being wronged/oppressed. In 22:29 the poor and the needy are the objects of oppression. In Ezek 45:8 and 46:18 the prince is instructed regarding not dispossessing people from their land, here referred to as an act of oppression (*ynh*). The simple statement in Ezek 18:7 is modified slightly in vv 12 and 16. In v 12 we find *'onî wĕ'ebyôn hônâ*, "oppresses the poor and the needy." V 16 follows the formulation of v 7, but with the perfect verb form instead of the imperfect.

When we consider the legal material we find that Exod 22:20 (21) instructs not to wrong a stranger (used in parallel with *lḥṣ*). Lev 19:33 again has the *gēr* as the object of concern. In both texts the fact that Israel was a stranger in Egypt serves as motive. Lev 25:14, 17 are placed in the context of the jubilee legislation, and instruct Israelites not to wrong one another in buying and selling land. Deut 23:17 instructs not to oppress a

---

[27]Williams, *Hebrew Syntax*, #41.
[28]Ezek 18:7, 12, 16; 22:7, 29; 45:8; 46:18. Other occurrences are Exod 22:20; Lev 19:33; 25:14, 17; Deut 23:17; Isa 49:26; Jer 22:3.

runaway slave. Isa 49:26 reflects a general judgment on oppressors, but Jer 22:3 mirrors the legislation more closely in connecting *ynh* with the parallel verb *ḥms*, and the objects alien, fatherless and widow.

Of special interest is that in Ezek 45:8; 46:18; and Jer 22:3 the concern is with a royal figure. All three texts have land and inheritance as the major concern. So also the legislation in Leviticus 25 has jubilee and land as a concern. Greenberg suggests that the term *ynh* "denotes specifically doing a (usually helpless) person out of his property."[29]

The law in Ezek 18:7 seems, therefore, to evoke echoes of royal responsibility democratized. The previous two laws (in 18:6) are linked with defilement of the land for inappropriate sexual acts (acts that threaten the integrity of the community). So also the prohibition that begins v 7 alludes to actions in the sphere of the economy.

It is clear that Ezekiel is not quoting Pentateuchal legislation, but lives in the general ethos of legal concerns for the poor and the disenfranchised.[30]

He gives back his debt-pledge
ḥăbōlātô ḥôb yāšîb (18:7, 12, 16; 33:15)

Commentators agree that the prohibition involves some form of pledge.[31] Israel's legal traditions speak clearly to the matter. The most explicit legislation is in Exod 22:25: "If ever you take your neighbor's garment in pledge, you shall restore (*šwb*) it to him before the sun goes down." There we find the cognate accusative construction *ḥābōl taḥbōl* and, as in Ezek 18:7, the verb *šwb*. In Deut 24:6 the taking of a millstone in pledge is prohibited, and in Deut 24:17 one is prohibited from taking a widow's garment in pledge.[32] Neither of those Deuteronomic references has to do with returning a pledge.

That there is no Priestly legislation on the pledge may be instructive. Only Ezekiel uses a nominal form of the word. All other uses are with the

[29]*Ezekiel 1-20*, 329.

[30]See F. C. Fensham, "Widow, Orphan, and the Poor in Ancient Near Eastern Legal and Wisdom Literature," *JNES* 21 (1962) 129-39; H. K. Havice, "The Concern for the Widow and the Fatherless in the Ancient Near East: A Case Study in Old Testament Ethics" (Ph.D. diss., Yale University, 1978).

[31]J. Milgrom's helpful analysis (*Cult and Conscience: The Asham and the Priestly Doctrine of Repentance* [SJLA 18; Leiden: Brill, 1976] 95-98) suggests that *ḥbl* refers to the goods a creditor may seize after the loan has defaulted. But those goods must be returned after the loan has been repaid.

[32]Other occurrences of *ḥbl*: Amos 2:8; Job 22:6; 24:3, 9; Prov 20:16; 27:13.

verb. Legal and wisdom texts are equally represented.[33] This may help us to reconsider the eclectic development of legal material within different settings. A basic law like this from the Book of the Covenant finds expression in all Israelite traditions except the Priestly. Yet Ezekiel reflects that law, while alluding to other Priestly legislation that is not found in the other law codes. The prohibition against taking pledges happens to occur twice in Deuteronomy 24, which is precisely the chapter Ezekiel seems to reflect in the response to the *māšāl* in 18:3-4.

Commits no robbery
gĕzēlâ lō' yigzōl (18:7, 12, 16, 18; 22:29; cf. 33:15)

Five of the six occurrences in Ezekiel are constructed with a verb form (*gzl*) followed by a cognate accusative, although the noun form varies. Of all other occurrences of the verb, only Ezekiel uses the cognate accusative noun along with the verb.[34]

This law concerning robbery reflects the legislation of the Holiness Code (Lev 19:13), "You shall not oppress (*'šq*) your neighbor or rob him (*gzl*)" (cf. Lev 5:21, 23; Isa 3:14). According to Milgrom, "*gzl* refers to robbery and *gnb* to theft, the difference being that robbery is committed by open force whereas theft is by stealth."[35] The Holiness Code prohibits robbery as an act incompatible with the holiness of God.[36]

The juxtaposition of *'šq*, to oppress, and *gzl*, to rob, is characteristic of Ezekiel and Leviticus.[37] Of the three occurrences of the verb *'šq* in Deuteronomy, only 28:29 uses the combination of the two terms in the catalogue of curses. Of related interest is Lev 19:13, which, after the mention of oppression and robbery, prohibits the keeping of a hired worker's wages until morning (the reverse order in Ezek 18:7). Similarly, Lev 5:23 counsels the restoration (*šwb*) of what was taken by robbery, oppression, or deposit.

The robbery clauses of Ezekiel 18 resonate most closely with those of Leviticus 5 and the legislation of Leviticus 19. The juxtaposition of *'šq* and *gzl* is especially indicative of that relationship.

---

[33]See H. A. Hoffner, "*hābāl*," *TDOT* 4 (1980) 179-84.

[34]Lev 5:23 has a relative clause *haggĕzēlâ 'ăšer gāzāl*.

[35]*Cult and Conscience*, 89.

[36]J. Schüpphaus, "*gāzal*," *TDOT* 2 (1975) 458.

[37]Ezek 18:18 places the two expressions together, as do Ezek 22:29; Lev 5:21, 23; and 19:13. Note that those are the only occurrences of both terms in Leviticus.

Gives his food to the hungry
and provides clothing for the naked
laḥmô lĕrā'ēb yittēn wĕ'ērōm yĕkasseh bāged (18:7b, 16b)

The line is repeated in v 16, but is omitted in the second case (vv 10-13). V 16 differs only in using the perfect verb forms instead of the imperfect.

The legislation is not reflected explicitly in the legal codes. The sentiment is certainly found in laws encouraging care for the poor (Deut 15:7-11; cp. Deut 14:29; 24:19-22; Lev 19:9-10; 23:22). Isa 58:7 is the most explicit parallel to Ezek 18:7b, referring both to feeding and to clothing the needy. Job's defence in Job 31 similarly includes mention of food (v 17) and clothing (v 19) for the needy. A most interesting parallel is Eliphaz's accusation in Job 22:6-7, which refers to withholding pledges, taking clothing from the naked, and withholding bread from the hungry. Job's response in 24:9-10, falling in the middle of a description of people who are oppressed by the wicked, states: "There are those [the wicked] who snatch the fatherless child from the breast, and take in pledge the infant of the poor. They [the poor] go about naked, without clothing; hungry, they carry the sheaves." The sequence of robbery (*gzl*) and pledges in v 9, followed by the naked and the hungry in v 19, bears striking similarity to the pledges, robbery, bread to the hungry, and covering the naked of Ezek 18:7.[38]

It appears that Ezekiel is citing a common axiom whose provenance crosses all traditions.[39] Ezek 18:7 finds a home primarily in the moral discourse of wisdom literature. That fact suggests that the connection between legal material and traditional morality is rather fluid.[40]

---

[38]Greenberg (*Ezekiel 1-20*, 329) points out the connection between the naked, the hungry, and the pledge in the two Job passages, but does not note the fourth word, *gzl*, in Job 24:9. The giving of bread/food to the hungry also occurs in Prov 25:21, with the verbal form instead of the adjective as in Ezek 18:7.

[39]Greenberg (ibid., 330) cites the Egyptian official Harkhuf, from the end of the third millennium B.C.E., who boasts: "I gave bread to the hungry, clothing to the naked." See M. Lichtheim, *Ancient Egyptian Literature* (3 vols.; Berkeley: University of California Press, 1973, 1976, 1980). 1. 24.

[40]Zimmerli's comment (*Ezekiel 1*, 380) that the positive statement in v 7b "points to a late presentation of the demand within the legal tradition" is an unfounded conclusion if the command is never found in the legal codes that we have.

Does not lend at interest
or collect with excessive increase
banneŝek lō'-yittēn wĕtarbît lō' yiqqāḥ
(18:8, 13, 17; 22:12)

The formulation is identical in v 13 except for the change to perfect verb forms. V 17 shortens the expression by coordinating the two nouns under one verb *lqḥ*, as does 22:12.

The same legislation is found in Lev 25:36-37. The context concerns behaviour toward an Israelite who becomes poor. "Take no interest (*neŝek*) from him or increase (*tarbît*), but fear your God; that your brother may live beside you. You shall not lend him your money at interest (*neŝek*), nor give him your food for profit (*marbît*)." In Exod 22:24 we find a similar law: "If you lend money to any of my people with you who is poor, you shall not be to him as a creditor, and you shall not exact interest from him." That law is followed in v 25 with a prohibition against keeping a neighbor's pledge overnight. Deut 23:20 reads: "You shall not lend upon interest to your brother, interest on money, interest on victuals, interest on anything that is lent for interest."

Only the Leviticus and Ezekiel texts contain both terms *neŝek* and *tarbît*, as well as both verbs, *ntn* and *lqḥ*. The combination of *neŝek* and *tarbît* occurs also in Prov 28:8, where the one who increases wealth in that way gathers it for the one who is kind to the poor. Ps 15:5a reflects the wording of Lev 25:37a. And Ezek 22:12 connects bribery and interest/increase as does Ps 15:5. Since Ps 15 clearly belongs in the realm of the cult and provides a paradigm of virtue for the worshipper, it is likely that Ezek 18:12a belongs closely within that milieu as well. But again, the law is not exclusive to the legal code or the cultic descriptions, but belongs also to the broader traditional morality reflected in Israelite proverbial wisdom.[41]

---

[41]See further E. Neufeld, "The Prohibitions against Loans at Interest in Ancient Hebrew Laws," *HUCA* 26 (1955) 355-412; R. North, *Sociology of the Biblical Jubilee* (AnBib 4; Rome: Pontifical Biblical Institute, 1954) 176-79; H. Gamoran, "The Biblical Law against Loans on Interest," *JNES* 30 (1971) 127-34; R. Maloney, "Usury and Restrictions on Interest-Taking in the Ancient Near East," *CBQ* 36 (1974) 1-20; I. L. Seeligmann, "Lending, Pledge and Interest in Biblical Law and Biblical Thought," *Studies in Bible and the Ancient Near East Presented to S. E. Loewenstaam on His Seventieth Birthday* (2 vols.; ed. Y. Avishur and J. Blau; Jerusalem: Rubenstein, 1978). 2. 183-205 (Hebrew); English summary, 1. 209-10.

Keeps himself from injustice
mē'āwel yāšîb yādô (18:8, 17)

The line does not occur in the second case (vv 10-13). In v 17 the word *'āwel* is replaced by *'onî*, "the poor." LXX reads *apo adikias*. Zimmerli suggests that we read *'āwel* as in v 8.

To "withhold one's hand from" occurs elsewhere, but not with the word *'āwel*, "iniquity."[42] The more common construction links *'āwel* with the verb *'āśâ*, "to do" (Ezek 3:20; 18:24, 26; 33:13, 15, 18). In Ps 7:4 (3) the petitioner protests innocence by offering: "If there is wrong in my hands."

The word *'āwel* occurs twice in Deuteronomy. In 32:4 we find a description of Israel's God as one who is *'ĕmûnâ*, faithful, and without *'āwel*. Deut 25:16 describes the one who has unjust weights as one who acts *'āwel*, which the RSV translates as "to act dishonestly." The word occurs twice in Leviticus. Lev 19:15 and 35 refer to not doing *'āwel bamišpāṭ*. In v 15 the reference is to being partial to the poor or deferring to the rich. V 35 again refers to measures and just balances. Zimmerli thinks that the court of law is the context behind the prohibition in Ezek 18:8 as it is in Leviticus.[43] That the context of trading relationships is involved is suggested by Ezek 28:18.[44]

The next part of the line clarifies the sense of *'āwel* by means of synonymous parallelism. The linguistic parallel of *'āwel*, *'āśâ*, and *mišpāṭ* ties the entire verse to Lev 19:35. Withholding one's hand from *'āwel* refers to refraining from harmful action in the social or economic sphere.

We turn now to explore several expressions in Ezekiel 18 that seem to be catch-all expressions for observing or keeping *tôrâ*.

---

[42]The word *'āwel* occurs ten times in Ezekiel and eleven times elsewhere in the Hebrew Bible. That expression with the verb *šwb* Hiphil occurs elsewhere in Lam 2:3, 8; Ezek 20:22; Amos 1:8; Zech 13:7; Pss 74:11; 81:15 (14); Isa 1:25. It refers in those texts to harmful action performed by Yahweh in judgment, or the withholding of protection. Cf. also Jer 6:9.

[43]*Ezekiel 1*, 380-81. The word *'āwel* occurs ten times in Ezekiel (only in 28:18 outside chaps. 18 and 33), and twice each in Deuteronomy and Leviticus. The other references are Jer 2:5; Job 34:10, 34; Prov 29:27; Ps 7:4; 53:2; 82:2.

[44]But there *'āwōn* (a favorite of Ezekiel) and *'āwel* appear to be synonyms.

He practices authentic justice in community:
mišpaṭ 'emet ya'ăśeh bên 'îš lĕ'îš (18:8b)

He does what is just and right
'āśâ mišpaṭ ûṣĕdāqâ (18:5b).

Within Ezekiel 18 the line (v 8b) occurs only here. Since Lev 19:35 combines *'āwel* and *mišpāṭ*, it could be that the two parts of Ezekiel 18:8 find correlation with the two parts of that verse. Ezek 18:8 may be a paraphrase or an exegesis of Lev 19:35, but with a broader base of application. But in Lev 19:15 and 35 we find *lō' tā'ăśû 'āwel bammišpāṭ,* "you shall do no wrong in judgment." The phraseology is different.

The expression *mišpaṭ 'emet* is found only in Zech 7:9 (cf. Zech 8:16). Zimmerli points out other phrases in which *'emet* functions syntactically in the same way.[45] The particular expression here in Ezek 18:8b is unique in the Hebrew Bible. Although it reflects the sentiment of much of the legal material, the expression is not dependent on any legal text or tradition.

What does the expression contribute to the list of laws in Ezekiel 18? It follows on a series of economic injunctions in vv 7-8a. It also serves to balance v 5b, where the *saddîq* is described as one who "does what is just and right" (*'āśâ mišpāṭ ûṣĕdāqâ*). The call to "do justice and righteousness" is ubiquitous in prophetic discourse. But Ezekiel 18 does not simply "hurl the word out . . . as though it were self-evident what it means," as Mays suggests many of the prophets do.[46] Rather, Ezekiel 18 understands clearly that "doing justice" encompasses the practice of relational obligations to fellow Israelites. Those obligations lie primarily in the socio-economic sphere. V 5 suggests more broadly, however, that justice and righteousness encompass relational obligations both with God and within the human community. By widening the base of moral obligation to include Yahweh, Ezekiel emphasizes his interest in integrating the re-creation of authentic community with maintaining the integrity of Yahweh. Ethics and theodicy belong together.[47]

The list of laws serves, then, to exegete the introductory and concluding statements about doing justice and righteousness, or practicing authentic justice in community. V 10 makes that inference explicit by articulating the principle that doing justice (v 8b) is defined by the norm of the *tôrâ* tradition by which the community shapes its identity.

---

[45]Jer 2:21; 14:13; 42:5; Mal 2:6. *Ezekiel 1*, 381. In those cases *'emet* functions as an attributive genitive. Williams, *Hebrew Syntax*, #41.

[46]On "doing justice" see J. L. Mays, "Justice: Perspectives from the Prophetic Tradition," *Int* 37 (1983) 6.

[47]On this theme see Chapter 7.

Excursus on 'āśâ mišpaṭ ûṣĕdāqâ:
"to do justice and righteousness"
(18:5, 19, 21, 27; 33:14, 16, 19; 45:9).

Aside from the eight occurrences in Ezekiel, the formula occurs relatively few times in the Hebrew Bible.[48]
Practicing justice and righteousness embodies both a royal ideal and the moral ideal of imitation of God.

It is first of all descriptive of Israel's central affirmation of Yahweh's character. Gen 18:19 affirms that the "way of Yahweh" is expressed in doing righteousness and justice (*la'ăśôt ṣĕdāqâ ûmišpāṭ*). Jer 9:23 affirms that it is Yahweh's habit to "practice steadfast love, justice, and righeousness in the earth; for in these things I delight." Similarly, Ps 99:4 affirms the rule of Yahweh as one who "has executed justice and righteousness in Jacob"[49] Deut 10:18 recalls that Yahweh is the one who "does justice" (*'ōśeh mišpāṭ*) on behalf of the disenfranchised.

Second, the ideal of justice and righteousness was to be embodied in Israel's king (e.g. Jer 22:3, 15-17; 23:5; 33:15). Greenberg notes that "peculiar to Israel is the democratization of the ideal; both Gen 18:19 and Amos 5:24 require the entire community—not merely the king—to 'do what is just and right'; each individual was expected to conform to the royal standard."[50]

In Ezekiel the only occurrence of the formula outside chaps. 18 and 33 is 45:9. Listed among the "laws of the temple" is an injunction regarding Israel's "princes." They are to "put away violence and oppression, and execute justice and righteousness." Given the ambiguity of the "fathers" and "sons" in chap. 18, it is likely that Ezekiel is playing on the ideal of kingly justice and righteousness both in his oracles against the "princes," and in his judgment speeches and admonitions to individual Israelites.

The only other reference to *mišpāṭ* in Ezekiel that sheds light on our text is 22:29. There it is "the people of the land" who "have practiced extortion and committed robbery; they have oppressed the poor and needy, and have extorted from the sojourner without redress (*mišpāṭ*)." It is certainly socio-economic crimes that are referred to both there and in Ezek 18:8.

---

[48]Gen 18:19; 2 Sam 8:15 = 1 Chron 18:14; 1 Kgs 10:9 = 2 Chron 9:8; Jer 9:23; 22:3, 15; 23:5; 33:15.

[49]Cf. Ps 146:5-9 and note the reference to "Jacob" in both Psalms. Cf. also Ezek 20:5; 28:25; 37:25; 39:25.

[50]*Ezekiel 1-20*, p. 344. See also H. H. Schmid, *Gerechtigkeit als Weltordnung: Hintergrund und Geschichte des alttestamentlichen Gerechtigkeitsbegriffes* (BHT 40; Tübingen: Mohr-Siebeck, 1968) 127-28.

It is interesting that *sĕdāqâ* occurs in Ezekiel only in texts that bear similarity to chap. 18.[51] The alternate form *ṣedeq* occurs twice (3:20; 45:10), and in the same texts. The substantive *ṣaddîq*, however, occurs fifteen times, ten of those outside chap. 18.[52] Again, the expression occurs primarily in texts that bear resemblances to chap. 18. Although 13:22 belongs to a judgment speech against false women prophets, the judgment is for disheartening the righteous and encouraging the wicked. The terms righteous, wicked, way, turn, and life all correspond to similar expressions in chap. 18. So also the occurrences in chap. 21 deal with the "cutting off" of both righteous and wicked. In most of the texts, the contrast between the righteous and the wicked is also contrasted with prospects for "life" and "death."[53]

Ṣaddîq occurs repeatedly in the Psalms and often in Isaiah, but rarely in the other prophets. Ezekiel's concern for the juxtaposition of "the righteous" over against "the wicked," therefore, most certainly springs from his familiarity with the Jerusalem cult tradition. In fact, the coincidence of terminology in texts that contrast the righteous and the wicked, along with the emphasis on practicing justice and righteousness, provides a clue to linguistic usage and function in the book of Ezekiel. Although the concern for righteousness and justice is common to the prophetic tradition, in the book of Ezekiel that prophetic ideal merges with the moral ideal of the cult. "The righteous" and "the wicked" are ciphers for the moral individual in Israel. Although many "righteous" will suffer in the judgment of exile, it is they who will constitute the new community that God reconstitutes in the end. Those who gain "life" are those who are part of that reconstituted house of Israel, and who make a habit of practicing "justice and righteousness."

Although I have stressed the connection of the term *ṣaddîq* with the Jerusalem cult tradition, Schmid notes that the sphere of meaning of the root *sdq* finds affinity with royal ideology, wisdom thinking, and cultic-legal ideas.[54] What Ezekiel does, therefore, is to bring those together in a new synthesis that is evident above all in chap. 18.

---

[51]3:20; 14:14, 20; 33:12, 13, 14, 16, 18, 19; 45:9.

[52]In 3:20, 21; 13:22; 21:8 (3x), 9 (4x); 23:45; 33:12 (2x), 13, 18.

[53]Even the apparently unrelated 23:45 corresponds in that the sentence for Israel's metaphorical adultery is death.

[54]*Gerechtigkeit*, 128.

Walks in my statutes
and is careful to observe my ordinances (18:9, 17)

The expression occurs in v 9, and is reversed in v 17. The vocabulary differs, however. V 9 reads *běḥuqqôtay yěhallēk ûmišpāṭay šāmar la'ăśôt 'emet* (or reading *'ōtām* for *'emet*), whereas v 17 reads *mišpāṭ 'āśâ běḥuqqôtay hālāk*. We ought to understand such differences as stylistic variations to temper excessive repetition.[55]

According to Greenberg this "formulaic expression of obedience . . . sums up the preceding actions in terms of a canon of divine laws that enjoin them."[56] That raises several important questions. First, is there in fact a canon of laws or a "canonical tradition" to which Ezekiel is referring? Second, if so, what constitutes that canon? Third, what is the relationship of the "statutes and ordinances" to the specific situation that the text addresses? And fourth, can we draw any conclusions as to the function of these "statutes and ordinances" in the discourses of the Book of Ezekiel?

The two key words, *ḥuqqôt* and *mišpāṭîm*, are common in all biblical legal material. The specific expressions "to walk in my statutes" and "to do/keep my ordinances" find a parallel in Lev 18:3-4; 25:18; 26:3. Those texts vary the verb and the object. The closest parallel is 26:3: "If you walk in my statutes and observe my commandments and do them." (cf. Lev 26:15).[57] In Lev 18:3-4 we find both verbs "walk" (*hlk*) and "keep" (*šmr*) associated with *ḥuqqôt*. In Lev 25:18 the word *ḥuqqôt* has the verb "to do" (*'śh*). It is clear that stylistic variations within the Holiness Code do not allow us to posit quotation of texts *per se* in Ezekiel 18:9, 17.

But it is possible to suggest that Ezekiel has the Holiness Code in mind because of the similarity to Lev 26:3: "If you walk in my statutes (*ḥuqqôt*) and observe my commandments (*miṣwôt*) and do them." Lev 26:46 reads similarly, but with *ḥuqqîm*: *'ēlleh haḥuqqîm wěhammišpāṭîm wěhattôrōt*, "these are the statutes, the ordinances, and the instructions." If Leviticus 26 is the so-called "canonical" context within which Ezekiel 18 functions, the word *tôrâ* is problematic by its absence in 18:9. Perhaps to use *tôrâ* in connection with an allusion to a canonical standard would point too clearly to the Deuteronomistic concept of *tôrâ*. And the word *ḥuqqîm* (common in Deuteronomy but not in the Holiness Code) in Lev 26:46 is notable by the occurrence of the feminine plural *ḥuqqôt* in Ezek 18:9. I suggest that Lev 26:46 represents a widely accepted formulaic expression which Ezekiel 18 avoids. Instead, what we find in Ezek 18:9 is the characteristically Priestly *ḥuqqôt* of Lev 26:3, together with the word

---

[55] So Greenberg, *Ezekiel 1-20*, 330.

[56] Ibid., 330.

[57] To change *'mt* to *'tm* in Ezek 18:9 would make the similarity even more striking. So Greenberg, ibid.

mišpāṭîm of Lev 26:46. In this situation we see linguistic similarity and a preference for Priestly rather than Deuteronomic terminology.

What, then, can be said about the word *tôrâ*? The word occurs seven times in Ezekiel.[58] In 7:26 *tôrâ* is said to vanish from the domain/vocation of the priest. In 22:26 priests are said to have done violence to "my *tôrâ*." In 43:11, 12 we read of the "*tôrâ* of the temple," which may be a way of distinguishing this *tôrâ* from other *tôrâ*. In 44:5 the *tôrâ* of Yahweh's temple marks those who are to be admitted or excluded from the sanctuary. In 44:24 the priests will be those who "keep my laws and my statutes."[59] One wonders whether Ezekiel has a reason for not using *tôrâ* more often, especially since *mišpāṭ* occurs forty-three times (primarily plural with first person pronominal suffix), *ḥōq* occurs six times (four plural form), and *ḥuqqâ* (plural) occurs twenty-two times.[60] In that connection it is striking that *miṣwâ* does not occur in Ezekiel, but it is a common Deuteronomic expression. It is possible that *tôrâ* and *miṣwâ* connoted a traditional connection with which the Ezekiel tradition did not wish consciously to identify. Where *tôrâ* is used it bears a polemical tone or it is used to identify an alternative *tôrâ* tradition.

Those observations can be clarified by considering the terminology more closely. Note that *ḥōq* occurs primarily in the singular in Leviticus, with the plural form *ḥuqqîm* only in Lev 26:46 (a summary statement) and Lev 10:11. In Ezekiel the plural form *ḥuqqîm* occurs primarily in "negative" contexts and/or formulaic expressions. In 11:12 it occurs in an indictment as a formulaic expression, "you have not walked (*hlk*) in my statutes (*ḥuqqîm*), nor executed ('*śh*) my ordinances (*mišpāṭîm*)." It occurs in a divine speech with a negative tone in 20:18, "And I said to their children in the wilderness, Do not walk (*hlk*) in the statutes (*ḥuqqîm*) of your fathers, nor observe (*šmr*) their ordinances (*mišpāṭîm*), nor defile yourselves with their idols." In 36:27 the formulaic expression occurs again as "I will cause you to walk (*hlk*) in my statutes (*ḥuqqîm*) and be careful to observe my ordinances (*mišpāṭay tišmĕrû wa'ăśîtem*)." And in 20:25 the expression is especially telling: "I gave them statutes (*ḥuqqîm*) that were not good and ordinances (*mišpāṭîm*) by which they could not have life." Aside from those formulaic occurrences with the verbs *hlk*, *šmr*, and '*śh*, the only other occurrence of the plural, in 20:25, employs two Deuteronomisms, "good" and "life."[61] Those expressions reflect the blessings of keeping the Deuteronomic *tôrâ* along with the Deuteronomistic formula *ḥuqqîm*

---

[58]7:26; 22:26 43:11, 12 (2x); 44:5, 24.

[59]The first person pronominal prefixes in 22:26 and 44:24 are in keeping with the usage of the pronoun in Ezekiel.

[60]*ḥōq*: 11:12; 16:27; 20:18, 25; 36:27; 45:14. *ḥuqqôt*: 5:6 (2x), 7; 11:20; 18:9, 17, 19, 21; 20:11, 13, 16, 19, 21, 24; 33:15; 37:24; 43:11 (2x), 18; 44:24; 44:5; 46:14.

[61]Weinfeld, *Deuteronomy and the Deuteronomic School*, 345-46.

wĕmišpāṭîm (Deut 4:1, 5, 8, 14; 5:1; 11:32; 12:1; 26:16). Thus, Ezekiel uses huqqîm only once outside of a formulaic usage, and that in a context that probably reflects a polemic against Deuteronomistic tôrâ (the occurrence in 20:18 belongs to the same context). By contrast, huqqîm occurs throughout Deuteronomy. Ezekiel's usage, therefore, reflects the vocabulary of the Priestly tradition with its use of huqqôt.[62]

The specific expressions šmr mišpāṭîm and 'śh mišpāṭîm occur throughout Leviticus and Deuteronomy and do not belong to any particular legal tradition.[63] In this Ezekiel participates in the common fund of linguistic formulations. When Ezekiel speaks of the rejection of the mišpāṭîm, however, Ezekiel uses the verb m's as in Lev 26:15, 43.[64]

Given those observations, several comments on alternative views are in order. According to G. Liedke, "Im Dtn, beim Dtr., Chr., in H und Ez begegnen hōq und huqqâ meist im plural und in Reihungen mit anderen Termini für Gebot und Gesetz. Alle Termini sind völlig niveliert und bezeichnen synonym das Ganze oder Teile der Anordnungen und Gebote Jahwes."[65] That statement needs clarification, however, in the light of Ezekiel's specific use (or avoidance) of tôrâ. The pair huqqîm/mišpāṭîm is characteristic of Deuteronomy,[66] whereas the pair huqqôt/mišpāṭîm is typical of the Holiness Code and Ezekiel.[67]

Most of the occurrences of huqqâ in Ezekiel are with mišpāṭîm. H. Ringgren suggests a slightly nuanced reading of the linguistic data. He writes:

This pair of words "defines sufficiently and clearly for Ezekiel . . . the entire content of what Yahweh requires." In Ezk 43:11f. and 44:5, the words

---

[62]Lev 18:3, 4, 5, 26, 30; 19:19;, 37; 20:8, 22, 23; 25:18; 26:3, 15, 43. The dominant form of huqqôt in Ezekiel (sixteen out of twenty-two occurrences) is with the first person singular pronominal suffix, "my statutes." The dominant form of huqqôt in Ezekiel is with the first person singular pronominal suffix, "my statutes." Only once does that form occur in chapters 40-48 (44:24), although the plural itself occurs five times (four in chaps. 43-44 and once in 46:14). huqqôt does occur in Deuteronomy, but only in combination with miṣwôt (6:2; 10:13; 28:15, 45; 30:10) and in formulaic uses with miṣwôt and mišpāṭîm (8:11; 11:1; 30:16).

[63]šmr mišpāṭîm: Lev 18:4; 19:37; 20:22; 25:18; Deut 5:1, 31; 7:11-12; 8:11; 11:1, 32; 12:1; 26:16-17; 30:16. Also in Ezek 11:20; 18:9; 20:18ff.; 36:27. 'śh mišpāṭîm: Lev 18:4; 19:37; 20:22; 25:18; Deut 4:1, 5, 14; 5:1, 31; 6:1; 7:11-12; 11:32; 12:1; 26:16; Ezek 5:7-8; 11:12, 20; 18:17; 20:11, 13, 19, 21; 36:27.

[64]Ezek 5:6; 20:13, 16; cf. 20:24 huqqôtay mā'āsû. m's does not occur in Deuteronomy.

[65]"hqq, einritzen, festsetzen," THAT 1 (1971) 631-32; So also Liedke, "špṭ, richten," THAT, 2 (1976) 1009.

[66]Deut 4:1, 5, 8, 14, 45; 5:1, 31; 6:1, 20; 7:11; 11:32; 12:1; 26:16, 17.

[67]Liedke, "špṭ, richten," 1009; Lev 18:4, 5, 26; 19:37; 20:22; 25:18; 26:14-15, 43; Ezek 5:6-7; 11:20; 18:9, 17; 20:11, 13, 16, 19; 37:24; 44:24.

ḥuqqôt and *tôrôt* are clearly used as terms for regulations governing the cult and the temple. In 18:9, we find *ḥuqqôt* and *mišpāṭîm* in a context suggesting that we are dealing with "the two major domains of covenant legislation, the cult and civil law" (cf. vv. 19, 21). In summary, we can say that Ezekiel uses *ḥuqqâ* and *tôrâ* for cultic regulations and *mišpāṭ* for the legal norms governing life in society.[68]

That use of *mišpāṭ* would certainly describe the occurrence in Ezek 18:8, but not necessarily when combined in a formulaic expression as we find it in 18:9. In Ezek 44:24 that distinction between civil and cultic seems to apply. But of the occurrences of *mišpāṭîm* (plural) in Ezekiel, only 7:27 occurs without the parallel *ḥuqqôt/ḥuqqîm*.[69] Their "ways" that will be judged "according to their own judgments" are both cultic and civil crimes.

In conclusion, *ḥuqqôt* and *mišpāṭîm* are used most often in a bound formula, and may well connote elsewhere a distinction between cultic and civil law. But Ezekiel is at pains to indicate that both crimes against Yahweh's cultic order and crimes against human social order have the same consequences. Never in lists of laws in Ezekiel is a distinction made. The metaphor of adultery encompasses both crimes of violence against society and crimes of violence against the sanctuary and its traditions (chaps. 16; 23). For Ezekiel the central offence has been committed against Yahweh, the holy divine presence. All moral infractions are viewed against the standard of the Priestly notion of holiness, which encompasses obligation to divine and human spheres of order. Above all, imitation of Yahweh's character determines the standard of holiness. The community composed of persons who "walk in my statutes and observe my ordinances" will experience life that is blessed by God's holy presence. Anything less is considered an abomination.

Commits abominable deeds
tô'ēbâ 'āśâ (18:12)

This phrase occurs only in the list of vv 10-13, but the plural form of *tô'ēbâ* occurs also in vv 13 and 24, each time with the verb *'āśâ*. In 18:24 the wicked (*rāšā'*) is said to do abominable things. The expression *tô'ēbâ/ôt 'asa* occurs elsewhere in Ezekiel in various formulations (16:47,

---

[68]"*ḥāqaq*," *TDOT* 5 (1986) 145-46. Ringgren's statement includes a citation from R. Hentschke, *Satzung und Setzender: Ein Beitrag zur israelitischen Rechtsterminologie* (BWANT, 83; Stuttgart: Kohlhammer, 1963) 85, 88.

[69]Another plural form occurs in 16:38, but that may correspond to a singular in a similar text condemning adultery in 23:24.

50, 51; 22:11; 33:26; etc.). The word *tôʿēbâ* occurs forty-three times in Ezekiel, more often than in any other book.[70]

The singular form in 16:50 may well refer to the sins of pride and excess (vv 49-50). In 22:11 *tôʿēbâ ʿāśâ* is clearly a sexual sin that harms the sanctity of family relationships. In 33:26 the expression is part of the second of two series of three sins each. It falls between "you resort to the sword" and "each of you defiles his neighbor's wife." After each series the rhetorical question is addressed, "Shall you then possess the land?" The plural *tôʿēbôt* occurs in all the other occurrences in Ezekiel.[71]

It is interesting to note that the term does not occur in the Book of the Covenant, and occurs only six times in Leviticus (18:22, 26, 27, 29, 30; 20:13). The references in Leviticus refer primarily to sexual offenses that are intolerable within Israelite community. For Ezekiel the *tôʿēbâ* is an act that defies the identity of the Israelite community. Although it is not necessarily related to sexual offenses, Ezekiel uses the sexual metaphor of adultery related to *tôʿēbâ* ten times in chaps. 16 and 23 (16:2, 22, 36, 43, 47, 50, 51, 58; 23:36). The imagery, however, is symbolic of breaking the exclusive covenant with Yahweh (8:6, 9, 13, 15, 17). The context of Leviticus 18 adds another dimension that is relevant to Ezekiel's usage. Lev 18:26 makes the connection clear: "You shall keep my statutes and my ordinances and do none of these abominations . . . lest the land vomit you out." The punishment is stated in other terms in Lev 18:29, "For whoever shall do any of these abominations, the persons that do them shall be cut off from among their people." Ezekiel clearly subordinates his wide-ranging moral offenses under the overarching metaphor of adultery, which receives the recompense of being cut off from the community, and more particularly, of being expelled from the land.[72] That connection between *tôʿēbâ* and exclusion or being cut off is found in Ezek 14:8, where the person who does not change and turn away from abominations will be "cut off from the midst of my people." Similarly in 8:6, except that it is Yahweh who is driven far from his sanctuary because of the *tôʿēbâ* of the people. In chap. 20 the present generation's actions are likened to the *tôʿēbôt* of their fathers, whom

---

[70]According to E. Gerstenberger ("*tʿb*, verabscheuen," *THAT* 2 [1971] 1051-52), the word occurs seventeen times in Deuteronomy and twenty-one times in Proverbs. The singular form occurs in Ezek 16:50; 18:12; 22:11; 33:26. All other occurrences are the plural. See also P. Humbert, "Le substantif *tôʿēbâ* et le verbe *tʿb* dans l'Ancien Testament," *ZAW* 72 (1960) 217-37.

[71]Ezek 5:9, 11; 6:9, 11; 7:3, 4, 8, 9, 20; 8:6, 9, 13, 15, 17; 9:4; 11:18, 21; 12:16; 14:6; 16:2, 22, 36, 43, 47, 51, 58; 18:13, 24; 20:4; 22:2; 23:36; 33:29; 44:13.

[72]None of that sentiment is found in Deuteronomy's use of *tôʿēbâ*. There the word is primarily used in conjunction with idolatry and associated practices. Only three times is a more general meaning discernible (22:5; 24:4; and 25:16).

Yahweh did not allow to enter the land he had promised to them. *Tôʻēbâ* and the land (or sanctuary) are mutually exclusive.

According to Gerstenberger, *tôʻēbâ* is whatever is excluded by the inherent character of the subject, and therefore anything that is considered dangerous or harmful to the definition or character of the subject. The use of the term in Ezekiel, therefore, integrates theological and ethical conceptions: "Gewisse Dinge sind mit dem Wesen Jahwes unvereinbar und werden von ihm abgelehnt."[73] Gerstenberger summarizes well the function of the term, which takes on particular significance in Ezekiel as a cipher for Israel's actions that do not conform to the character of Yahweh and hence to the character of Yahweh's people.

> Die Ablehnung oder Ausscheidung des Wesensfremden hat offensichtlich den Zweck, die Homogeneität und Funktionsfähigkeit der Gruppe zu sichern. Kult- und Rechtsgemeinschaften, Verwandtschafts- und Wohngruppen sind vor allem daran interessiert, dass das Fremde . . . als *tôʻēbâ* gekennzeichnet und damit ausgeschlossen wird. . . .
> Das Wort *tôʻēbâ* bezeichnet also ursprünglich das, was aufgrund von Gruppennormen als gefährlich und darum angst- und ekelerregend geltend muss. Vielleicht hat die kultische Verwendung die rechtliche und ethische nach sich gezogen; vielleicht ist das Wort aber auch in mehreren Lebensbereichen gleichzeitig zur Abwehr des Fremden gebraucht worden.[74]

Ezekiel stands in the Priestly tradition by linking the identity and character of the community of faith with the character of Yahweh, with the possession of the land, and with the presence of God in the sanctuary. The threefold repetition of *tôʻēbâ* in Ezekiel 18 is best understood as a cipher for whatever is contrary to the character of Yahweh and his community. The itemization of specific laws in the chapter serves, in part, to characterize both the *ṣaddîq*, for whom a certain way of being fosters life, land, and presence of God, and the *rāšāʻ*, for whom the opposite way leads to exclusion and death.

We turn now to a discussion and a summary of the function of law in Ezekiel 18.

---

[73]"*tʻb*, verabscheuen," 1053.

[74]Ibid., 1054-55. I understand "Das Fremde" to be what is considered foreign to Yahweh's character. That is not to say that the concept does not have other culturally and socially shaped factors. But in Ezekiel it is used as a shorthand for that which is impossible to do and still remain within Yahweh's covenant community.

THE FUNCTION OF TÔRÂ IN EZEKIEL 18

Introduction

In his discussion of the language and forms in Ezekiel Zimmerli noted that in Ezekiel 18 (along with 3:17-21; 14:1-11; 22:1-16; and 33:1-20) a legal argument leads into a summons to repentance. He concluded that "a single formative will of a prophetic nature lies behind the various forms of the adducing of the legal text."[75] It is my interest in what follows to describe that "will" more closely. What are the interests that the text reflects? Is law cited simply to form the backbone of an argument within a disputation speech? Or does the citation of legal traditions in chap. 18 point to larger and more comprehensive interests on the part of Ezekiel or the Ezekiel tradition? How does Ezekiel 18 contribute to our understanding of law as a factor in shaping moral values during the sixth century B.C.E.?

Chapter 4 contains a discussion of models by which the legal lists in Ezekiel 18 have been understood: decalogue-instruction lists, entrance-tôrâ liturgy, confession of integrity, family-clan instruction, and instructions for temple visitors. Each of those models is helpful for providing some insight into the role of law in Israelite society. It is striking that the "list form" continues through the New Testament period, but it is not the decalogue *per se* that survives outside its original locus in the literature. That is, the decalogue is never quoted in its entirety, and when close resemblances are found, only several of the laws are cited. If anything three tendencies prevail. 1) Diverse lists of laws (ten, twelve, or other variant) exist throughout Israelite tradition.[76] 2) Short summaries of the essence of *tôrâ* are common (e.g., Mic 6:8). 3) Lists of laws occur with no specific number. From the way laws are cited and referred to in non-legal literature, we can only conclude that when they are grouped in lists of any length within so-called non-legal texts, the laws themselves are subordinated to the purpose for which they are cited. In Ezekiel 18 the laws have been subordinated to the larger purposes of the disputation speech in which they are found. Yet the laws contribute to the disputation speech to make it unique among disputation speeches. It is the specific contribution of law with which I am here concerned.

---

[75]Zimmerli (*Ezekiel 1*, 35) goes on to argue that "we can therefore hardly deny these sections to the prophet on the grounds of considerations of form." Zimmerli thinks, however, that law has different roles in chaps. 1-39 and 40-48. It may be, however, that in spite of literary historical decisions about the authorship and composition of chaps. 40-48, a compatible vision of law can be discerned in the entire Ezekiel tradition. That concern, however, is beyond the scope of this dissertation.

[76]See von Rad, "The Early History of the Form-Category of 1 Corinthians xiii.4-7."

In the discussion above I suggested several questions that might be considered. 1) Is there a canon of laws to which Ezekiel is referring? 2) What is the connection between the specific laws in chap. 18 and the situation being addressed by the text. 3) Can we draw any conclusions as to the function of these statutes and ordinances in the moral discourses of the book of Ezekiel? Rooted in those concerns are the larger issues of how law was used in moral discourse in Israel, what social function can be discerned in the appeal to law, and whether that appeal was addressed to individuals or to the community.

I am proposing that the Ezekiel tradition appeals to law in a variety of ways, mainly in providing rationale in judgment speeches or allegories of judgment, in providing a hope and a shape for the future, and in instruction that provides a "way" to move from judgment to hope. In what follows I shall argue that law functions in part to articulate and to shape the character of the new community and of those who constitute that community. In the next chapter I shall continue by suggesting that law also serves to justify Yahweh's ways with Israel.

The Contribution of Recent Scholarship

As I noted in Chapter 4, Weinfeld has shown that there is no evidence for a *tôrâ* liturgy in ancient Israel. He also acknowledges no evidence for inscriptions on temple entrances in Israel. But the observations of both suggestions are especially instructive if we forgo the historical question. The literary evidence clearly points to the use of legal lists as character dossiers, as it were, for worshippers at the temple. In its literary location in the book of Ezekiel such lists function in the absence of the physical temple, and in a similar manner. The physical temple is replaced by a visionary one, in which law continues its function as before. The connections I have noted between Ezekiel 18 and the Priestly and Deuteronomistic traditions illustrate that the Ezekiel tradition favours the Priestly theology of divine presence. But the allusion to Deut 24:16 and the emphasis on repentance demonstrate an independence in Ezekiel 18 that seeks to map out new territory in exilic Israel.[77]

Gerstenberger's proposal that the laws originate in the family and clan also contributes to our understanding of law in Ezekiel. That model helps to illustrate the instructional function of law. Even prior to the Priestly role, the authority figures in the family/clan were the protectors and the

---

[77] I am not certain whether Ezekiel's role or office as law-speaker is to be read into the legal material here, as Reventlow (*Wächter über Israel*) argues. I agree with Weinfeld ("Instructions for Temple Visitors") that the original setting in life of the laws is less significant for Ezekiel than is the function of the laws in the literary setting or in actual moral discourse.

disseminators of the law. They bore a responsibility to fulfill their obligation. As Gerstenberger writes,

> in Ägypten und Mesopotamien wie in Israel stellt die konkrete Rechtsordnung die göttlich sanktionierte, kosmische Ordnung dar, der jedermann unterworfen ist. Die Sippenordnung, mündlich weitergegeben und jedermann bekannt, ist *die* Lebensordnung für alle.[78]

Although only implicitly, the relationship of father and son in chap. 18 may be a mirror of the parental educational responsibilities. Perhaps that responsibility has been abrogated.[79]

Gerstenberger continues by stating that one can hardly speak of this order as profane or secular, somehow independent of Israel's theocentric worldview.

> Der Gedanke, dass die Gottheit selbst Wächter über die Lebensordnung sei, findet sich überall und wird nicht zuletzt aus der Tatsache deutlich, dass die Sünden- und Unschuldsbekenntnisse direkt auf die alten Ordnungen und ihre Verbote zurückgreifen. Über die Entstehungsweise dieser Ordnung wird jedoch kaum reflektiert. Sie existiert! Ob empirischen oder göttlichen Ursprungs: Diese Frage ist irrelevent und kann so gar nicht gestellt werden.[80]

The issue that arises from Gerstenberger's analysis as it applies to our discussion is this. Certainly the law existed and functioned before it was expressed orally or literarily in lists of 10, 12, or an indeterminate number. Thus, Gerstenberger's contribution to the discussion is to show the significance of law at the most elemental stages of the formation of social structures. One does not need to posit well-defined cultic or political institutions in order to have a place for law/tôrâ. Another point that arises from Gerstenberger's comments has to do with the distance between the origin of law and the texts that we normally deal with on the form of law lists (Psalm 15; 24; Isa 33:14-16; etc.). Our question in the discussion of Ezekiel 18 is not the origin of laws *per se*, but the origin and function of law lists such as we find there.

The issue that Gerstenberger addresses here is important because of the problem we face with respect to Ezekiel 18 of making the connection between origin and meaning. It seems to me that origin of the legal lists is not the issue. More important is the fact that Ezekiel assumed a cosmic-

---

[78]*Wesen und Herkunft*, 141.
[79]See discussion on kinship terminology in Chapter 5.
[80]*Wesen und Herkunft*, 141-42.

moral order that was circumscribed in part by Israel's legal traditions.[81]
What was disputed, however, was just how that order functioned.   For
Ezekiel the question was significant in the face of the major concerns in the
book: the vindication of God's justice; the destruction of Jerusalem and the
temple; and the existence and preservation of the people of God in a foreign
land.

In addition to the articulation of the divine order, law functioned also
to preserve social order. In other words, the "order" as expressed in "law"
was a means of holding society together.[82] So also in Ezekiel 18 the issue
is the preservation of the social world. It is not, however, the clan, or even
the worshipping community in the temple, but the exiled community in
Babylon (or the community under judgment in Jerusalem) about whom and
for whom law is appealed to in the book of Ezekiel. Yet for Ezekiel the
family/clan is the starting point from which to foster growth of a new
community.

Now with Weinfeld's hypothesis we have another matter to consider.
If the lists in Ezekiel 18 are closely linked with the entrance requirements
written on the gates/entrance of the temple, then the chapter as a whole is
best understood to function *rhetorically* as a sermon given at the entrance
to the temple. The formal allusions can explicitly point the reader to a
temple setting and still allow the text to be rooted in a Babylonian context.
The strength of the formal allusion functions as a pointer to what does not
exist in exile—the worshipping community blessed by the presence of God
in the Temple.

Thus, if the community is to be reconstituted, it must be done in either
of two ways. 1) The community exists without the temple in a foreign land,
but in fellowship with Yahweh. Thus, the requirements that used to signify
injunctions for temple visitors are now adapted to a situation where no
temple exists but where the community of faith continues to search for its
identity in relation to Yahweh. Since the cultic institution no longer exists
(in the same form, at any rate) the chapter is intended to create a movement
from lack of hope to hope through a reapplication (or transferrence) of the
older instructions for visitors to requirements for belonging to the people of
Yahweh who await divine aid in the near future. 2) The community shall
be reconstituted back in the land of Judah with a restored social order there,

---

[81]That is not to say that the sages did not also play a role in discerning that order, but their
quest was more wide ranging and yet not altogether outside legal circles or influence. That
holds true especially if the scribal class and the wisdom tradition were closely aligned, as
Weinfeld argues in *Deuteronomy and the Deuteronomic School*. See also H. H. Schmid,
Gerechtigkeit als Weltordnung.

[82]As Gerstenberger (*Wesen und Herkunft*, 142) notes, "der Gebrauch der Prohibitive in der
alten Sippengemein-schaft war recht umfassend. . . . In allen drei Funktionen, der
erzieherischen, regulierenden und juristischen, erhält die Ordnung die Sippengemeinschaft."

including a temple in renewed fellowship with Yahweh. To evaluate this suggestion we have to ask about Ezekiel's response to the experience of exile. Ezekiel did not, like Jeremiah, counsel the people to "build houses, dwell in them" (Jer 29:5, 28).

Ezekiel uses the legal forms in a foreign land where there is no temple, yet the instructions for temple visitors are still valid, but they serve a different purpose. The allusion to the instructions for temple visitors can also now be expanded to include entrance to the land. If that transference is possible, then the preparations for the new temple in chaps. 40-48, including the description of the partitioning of the land, are significant for making the connections between Ezekiel 18 and the hope for the future depicted in the book of Ezekiel. If the temple is the dwelling place of Yahweh, and if the land has become defiled (according to Ezekiel), then the entrance to the land in which Yahweh will dwell and where he will be known becomes dependent on the character of the people. That holiness is expressed in undifferentiated terms, as both ethical/historical and material/spatial concepts (that is to say, the two are completely integrated). In that case chapter 18 is an exhortation to the people in exile to qualify for the return, which will include both temple and land in the presence of Yahweh.

The Function of Law

Law and Covenant in Ezekiel

Although the word "covenant" is not used in connection with the "new heart" texts in Ezekiel 11 and 36, we should note the relationship between the use of the legal tradition and Ezekiel's understanding of covenant.[83] The broken covenant is depicted in chaps. 16 and 17 as despising the oath.[84] Taking the MT of 20:37 as stating that Yahweh will "lead you into the obligations of covenant," Greenberg comments that "after sifting the people, God will impose his covenant obligation on those who survive the selection; this is the future counterpart of the past imparting of laws and rules in the desert (vss. 11f.)."[85] In Ezek 30:5 *běrît* is a political term associated with formal relationships between nations. It is not unlike the previous uses, since Yahweh is depicted in Ezekiel as Israel's covenant Lord. Breaking oath with Yahweh and with the king of Babylon are

---

[83]*Běrît* is used in Ezek 16:8, 59, 60 (2x), 61, 62; 17:13, 14, 15, 16, 18, 19; 20:37; 30:5; 34:25; 37:26 (2x); 44:7.

[84]That connection may well tie the two chapters together with chap. 18 in the book of Ezekiel.

[85]*Ezekiel 1-20*, 373. The LXX reads: "I will let you go in by number" (RSV).

virtually synonymous political acts (17:16, 18). In Ezek 34:25 we encounter the expression "covenant of peace" for the first time. It occurs again in 37:26 as a restored "everlasting covenant," as in 16:60 (cf. also 44:7). Ezekiel's theological orientation is rooted in the covenant tradition. He focuses particularly on the exodus-law-land connection of the Sinai covenant, but he does not exclude the Davidic connection, as is evident in chap. 37. Kingship, however, is subordinated to the kingship of Yahweh (chap. 34), who will enable the people to dwell securely. This is surely an allusion to the united monarchy under David and Solomon. Of significance is the remarkable promise to Solomon in 1 Kings 6, to which the Ezekiel tradition may be responding in the wake of Yahweh's apparent abandonment of his people in exile: "if you walk in my statutes . . . I will dwell among the children of Israel, and I will not forsake my people Israel" (1 Kgs 6:11-13).

For Ezekiel, therefore, citation of Israel's legal tradition and mention of covenant perform similar rhetorical functions. As Gerstenberger writes,

"nichthalten der Gebote" meint sofort und radikal: Bruch, Auflösung des Bundesverhältnisses. Der Bund manifestiert sich in den Geboten. Die Gebote, im Kontext des Bundes verstanden, sind Ausdruck der personalen Beziehung, des personalen Treueverhältnisses. Es ist nicht möglich, die Gebote vom Bund zu subtrahieren und die reine Gottesgnade übrigzubehalten. Die Bundesgebote sind Ausdruck des guten Gotteswillens, der schützt und erhält, der die Gerechtigkeit und das Gute in der bedrohten Welt hochhält. . . . Bund meint im Alten Testament Lebensgemeinschaft, und als solche ist der Bund zugleich Anspruch und Zuspruch, Hilfe und Forderung, Evangelium und Gesetz.[86]

Ezekiel's articulation of that hope is different from Jeremiah's in that the covenant of peace is integrally connected to a series of specific expectations. Those include a unified Israel under a single king, ordinances and statutes that will characterize the covenant community's life, and a community living in the land, with Yahweh dwelling in his sanctuary in

---

[86]*Wesen und Herkunft*, 146. Hauerwas (*Peaceable Kingdom*, 23-24, 116-21) also applies this insight to his discussion of the ethics of character. He writes: "certain prohibitions of a community are such that to violate them means that one is no longer leading one's life in terms of the narrative that forms that community's understanding of its basic purpose. For the *telos* in fact is a narrative, and the good is not so much a clearly defined 'end' as it is a sense of the journey on which that community finds itself. In political terms it means that the conversation of community is not *about* some good still to be realized, but the conversation *is* the good insofar as it is through the conversation that the community keeps faithful to the narrative" (119).

their midst (37:21-28). Thus, breaking of covenant and renewal of covenant encompass a full range of Israel's theological and symbolic traditions.

Tôrâ and the Way of Yahweh

Ezekiel 18 clearly integrates "doing what is just and right" with "the way of Yahweh." As Greenberg notes, "'doing what is just and right' defines the divine and royal standard of conduct. It is 'the way of YHWH' (Gen 18:19); it is how he acts and what he desires (Jer 9:23; Ps 99:4)."[87] Unlike Jeremiah, who seems to place great hope in that royal ideal (Jer 22:3, 15-17; 23:5; 33:15), Ezekiel's royal person (45:8, 9) is overshadowed by the royal presence of Yahweh and the democratization of the royal ideal. Ezekiel's integration of observing huqqôt and mišpāṭîm with the derek of Yahweh is a way of conveying to the exilic community that that ideal had not been lost in the disasters of recent experience. Whereas the stipulations of Ezekiel 18 have affinities with all three Pentateuchal law codes, only the Deuteronomic code mentions royal obligation. Although we may only draw inferences here, it is possible that the emphatic application of legal stipulations to "the house of Israel" in the book of Ezekiel may be a way of awakening the democratic royal ideal and perhaps signals a move away from a Deuteronomic tôrâ with its interest in human kings.[88] We note Greenberg's comment again: "The priest-prophet's orientation toward torah meant that for him the ancient ideal would be embodied in torah-like individual stipulations."[89]

As I have noted in Chapters 4 and 5, the option of "life" in Ezekiel 18 was understood as a cipher for reconstitution of the community of the faithful who would enjoy God's blessing of land and divine presence. The rhetorical movement of Ezekiel 18 toward that option of life was noted in Chapter 3. Given that plea in the disputation, I suggest that the laws serve as pointers, or signs, of what constitutes the communal experience of life. Although Ezekiel 18 disputes a particular perception of human experience,

---

[87]Ezekiel 1-20, 343.

[88]In chap. 22, for example, it is "the city" that is addressed. "In you" becomes the locus for transgression against the breach of covenant by abominable deeds. Even the princes are listed only as part of the total portrait.

[89]Ezekiel 1-20, 344. A further dimension of tôrâ's function with respect to Yahweh highlights another aspect of the disputation in chap. 18—the comprehensibility of Yahweh's way (18:25, 29). The relationship of tôrâ-keeping and Yahweh's way will be discussed in the next chapter. To anticipate that, I suggest tôrâ also functions as an affirmation of divine justice. The lists in chap. 18 presuppose that someone either is, could, or should be righteous. What is asserted matter-of-factly is that Yahweh is righteous. The empirical evidence would point in the opposite direction, as the citation in v 2 indicates.

it moves beyond that to envision alternatives. In that respect the laws have a pedagogical purpose.[90] The task remains, however, to describe how such pedagogy may have functioned in the exilic context.

Law and Pedagogy

I shall begin by suggesting, with Greenberg, that Ezekiel's appeal to law as a way of "epitomizing the virtues of a godly life" is pedagogic in that it functions as "the definition of membership in the community of YHWH's devotees."[91]   The laws in chap. 18 function as address to individuals in community.   The laws present a selective dossier of the character of the community as that community reflects the character of its members.   The use of kinship relationships in the chapter (and elsewhere in Ezekiel) locates the heart of community not in its social and religious hierarchy but in its people. Thus, the "house of Israel" is addressed here, as elsewhere in Ezekiel, as community under construction. Ezekiel's use of law both judges the community (e.g. chap. 22) and offers alternatives that lead to life (chap. 18).   In either case, law is pedagogical in that it fosters the formation of a community of character. It does that by identifying what it means to be *ṣaddîq*, and how the *ṣaddîqîm* shape the identity of the community.

This use of law is consonant with how the legal codes functioned in moral suasion. As Dale Patrick suggests, "the lawbooks were intended not for judicial application but for instruction in the values, principles, concepts, and procedures of the unwritten divine Law." Rather, the legal traditions in written form served to inculcate

> the values and principles of the legal community. One might say that biblical law sought to create the conscience of the community. The auditors were being instructed in the sense of justice and right expected by their divine sovereign and embedded in the structure of the community.[92]

The fact that Ezekiel 18 does not quote written laws is compatible with the view that divine order is the foundation of which all cited law is a subset.

---

[90]So Greenberg, ibid., 345-46.
[91]Ibid., 346.
[92]*Old Testament Law* (Atlanta, GA: John Knox, 1985) 198, 200.

Law and Social Order

Those suggestions can be strengthened by considering another dimension of the function of law besides its pedagogical function. As mentioned above, law functioned to order society—providing its *Grundstruktur*. That foundational order was expressed in terms of covenant. According to Ezekiel and his audience, two factors threatened to tear away that foundation. For Ezekiel the sins of the "house of Israel" past and present forced the evacuation of both people and Yahweh from the land. For Ezekiel's audience, exile threatened the foundational relationship with Yahweh. Their counter-accusations against Yahweh in chap. 18 highlight the connection between law/covenant and theodicy. Ezekiel appeals to law, therefore, in order to demonstrate the validity of *tôrâ* as a means of social stability in a situation where land, temple, and monarchy no longer serve a stabilizing function. He hopes for a new thing, but the new land, temple, and covenant can only be assured through the practice of the virtues of the community as circumscribed by its *tôrâ*. We can infer, then, that without the legal tradition as an intrinsic part of the Book of Ezekiel, the book remains a torso.

Part of the problem we face in dealing with the function of law in Ezekiel is the bias imposed on the study from the outset by the history of scholarship of legal traditions in the Hebrew Bible. According to Noth, for example, it is first in Cyrus's reign that sacral law became civil law. Only in the period after Ezra do laws become conditions for covenant and for community. Although there certainly was a development of the function of law, Noth's assumption is derived from an inadequate evaluation of the relationship of the individual and the group, and from an excessive institutionalization of law.[93] For Noth, after the exile the individual act was stressed so that law became detached from a specific community.[94]

---

[93]This critique is based on the suggestions of E. Gerstenberger (*Wesen und Herkunft*), whom I have cited often.

[94]"The Laws in the Pentateuch: Their Assumptions and Meaning," *The Laws in the Pentateuch and other Studies* (London: SCM, 1966) 80. Noth has a section called "The survival of the law within the framework of future expectation" (65-70). He writes: "After the cessation of the old order, this clinging to laws whose validity was really in abeyance had no meaning, except in connection with the confident expectation of a restoration looming in the immediate future" (67). Although I agree with Noth's view of law as forward looking, I disagree that "the cessation of the old order" brought about a radical shift in how law functioned. To say that law had no meaning *except* insofar as it enabled the community to look forward to restoration reflects a static view of the relationship between law and social order. Law functions to preserve order as well as to shape the character of the community and its members. Thus its visionary function is not rooted only in civil contexts but in contexts in which the group is in the process of shaping its identity according to its foundational narrative

Aside from the specific analysis of Ezekiel 18, Bentzen suggests that that was not exactly the case. All ancient states were both "states" and "congregations." We cannot separate state laws from sacral laws.[95] In Ezekiel, therefore, legal discourse serves to reconstitute the congregation, which in Israel is primary and to which state is subordinate. This is especially true of the prophetic perception, which comes to a focus in Ezekiel when political identity is shattered. There is no question but that Israel must be reconstituted according to the foundation of covenant embodied in ancient codes of conduct and belief.[96]

Law in Relation to the Individual and the Community

The question remains, however, as to how law effects that reconstitution.

First, laws are used partly in the service of larger topics of concern. Greenberg notes that couching prophetic oracles in the form of case law was "an invention of Ezekiel designed as a vehicle for stating principles of God's dealing with [people], or, in other words, theological doctrines. Case law was the only available literary form of discourse about particulars on an abstract, generalized level."[97] Thus, law transcends its individual focus by addressing matters of corporate concern.

Second, the individualistic tenor of case law lends itself to interpret Ezekiel as being more interested in individuals than in the community. Greenberg observes that although biblical case law is usually voiced in the singular, "the ideal audience of the lawgiver is the people at large." Often, however, legal texts are a mixture of singulars and plurals. That, Greenberg suggests, belongs to the habit of the legal scribe who does not discriminate between the individual and the collective. Ezekiel, therefore, works within the tradition of the Israelite legal tradition, which addressed individuals, but within a corporate narrative tradition.[98] The keeping of *tôrâ*, in other words, could only be practiced in the *tôrâ* community.[99] Similarly, those

---

tradition (*tôrâ*).

[95]Bentzen, *Introduction*. 1. 231-32.

[96]Koch, *The Prophets*. 2. 98.

[97]Drawing on the *tôrâ* literature, Ezekiel generalized about several subjects: "14:4-11—on the denial of oracles to the idolatrous-minded; 14:12-20—the inability of the righteous to save their (unrighteous) sons from a general doom; ch. 18—the 'atomization' of retribution; and 33:1-20—the possibility of repentance" (Greenberg, *Ezekiel 1-20*, 94-95). We might add that in chap. 22 law is used to justify judgment on the city.

[98]Ibid., 95.

[99]Greenberg (ibid., 95) notes: "The Torah laws, whose style Ezekiel imitates, use the singular in particular cases without intent to oppose the individual to the collective; the

not characterized by *tôrâ*-keeping could not be considered part of the community.

Third, the question of individual responsibility in chap. 18 is clarified by Ezekiel's metaphor of the watchman in chaps. 3 and 33, along with his use of legal discourse. The prophet is a watchman "for the house of Israel" (3:17; 33:7). In chap. 33 the watchman is to announce warning to the town as a collective. How then, asks Greenberg, are we to understand the prophet's task as addressing wicked and righteous individuals?

> It is a manner of speaking: the division of responsibility between the lookout and his clients is discussed in terms of a single client; such simplified abstraction is useful for clarifying the principle. But no one would infer from this that the lookout was charged with warning each and every townsman individually. The same holds true for the application to the prophet: "wicked man" and "righteous man" are abstractions for classes within "the house of Israel." There is no intent to oppose individuals to the collective. The prophet is a lookout and gives his warnings to all; their various responses, however, are conveniently discussed in terms of single persons.[100]

Fourth, "the house of Israel" is the central concern of Ezekiel. In chaps. 14 and 18, texts that draw on the legal tradition to discuss the question of responsibility, the ideal audience is the *tôrâ* community. Both texts begin and end with explicit reference to "the house of Israel" (14:5, 6, 11; 18:2, 3, 30), with singular cases discussed in the body of the text. B. Lindars suggests that the father/son discussion in chap. 18 is "allegorical" in that the terms must refer to the generations as collective groups in Israel. "Even though Ezekiel's real concern is the fate of the nation as a whole, the way in which he uses this legal language as if he were speaking about the fate of individuals is . . . a striking feature of his teaching."[101]

Thus, law functions to integrate individual and community. But more than that, law not only describes one who *behaves* in a certain way, law also shapes character and identity. That shaping takes place, however, not by the recitation of rules, but by imaginative engagement with the community's narrative tradition.

---

signification of the singular is, rather, each and every individual in the collective. The same appears true of Ezekiel's usage."

[100]Ibid., 95-96.

[101]"Ezekiel and Individual Responsibility," 461; So also Greenberg, ibid., 96.

The Constitutive World of Legal Discourse

For Ezekiel the keeping of Yahweh's statutes and ordinances determines the character and shapes the identity of the community. As Koch writes, "these traditional rules show clearly whether someone is or is not living as a *saddîq*, which means acting in faithfulness to the community and being potentially destined for salvation."[102] Although acting in accord with the statutes and ordinances is rooted in individual acts, Koch suggests that

> what are presented as divine edicts have nothing to do with a catalogue of the virtues required for individual salvation; nor do they offer instructions as to how to acquire particular religious merit. What Ezekiel appeals to might rather be called the common law of past centuries, which the exiled community has now gathered together in the form of set principles. . . . In cases of conflict, *mišpāṭîm* clarify what it means to act in accordance with the community between God and human beings, and the community of men and women with one another. They also initiate a favourable correlation between action and destiny. God has communicated these *mišpāṭîm* so that through them men and women may find life.[103]

Against the history of religions school earlier in this century, Koch suggests further that the conditions of the exile compel us to adopt a positive estimation of the place of law in social construction.

First, the social context of exile demanded that earlier Israelite moral norms be preserved in order to sustain the fabric of community and to protect against arbitrary claims and group interests.[104]

Second, law functions in those social contexts to offer alternatives to disorder and social dissolution. They do not primarily function in Ezekiel 18 as a basis for judgment. "What they do is to stress *the alternative of life or death*. The person who gives effect to *mišpāṭ* creates the room to live for himself and his society."[105] That does not deny that judgment belongs to the sphere of law, since chap. 18 clearly states that the person who does not order his or her life according to divine *tôrâ* "shall surely die—his blood shall be upon himself" (18:13). Ezekiel aims here to clarify: (1) that human actions and consequences are intimately connected; (2) that that connection is not something Yahweh can tamper with, for he wishes for all to live

---

[102]*The Prophets.* 2. 96.

[103]Ibid., 98.

[104]Koch (ibid. 2. 99) notes: "The anthropological necessity of law becomes the subject for reflection as soon as a social order with a long tradition begins to crumble." This is not, however, to say the same thing as Noth suggested (see note 94 above).

[105]Ibid., 2. 100.

(18:23, 32); and (3) that Yahweh is not removed from the process, but ensures that the consequences of human action ("way") cannot be rationalized away by passing the responsibility off on God (18:25, 29). This text asserts that the human community is fundamentally responsible for its own destiny (18:30-31).

But saying that the laws in Ezekiel 18 offer "set principles" is not adequate. Koch's view that legal discourse evokes an alternative dimension needs to be sharpened. Without undue anachronism, I shall cite the contemporary sociologist Peter Berger, who suggests that law is a means of organizing reality, it is a "society-building enterprise."[106] If that is so, then *tôrâ* in ancient Israel has too long been interpreted exclusively as a religious enterprise. The bifurcation of reality into religious and secular has clouded the sociological function of law. Although we can say that laws reflect the covenant obligations of Israel before its covenant Lord, we ought also to keep in mind that those laws had social significance. In investigating the laws in Ezekiel, therefore, we should try to imagine a social entity in need of social coherence. But to speak of social reality alone would be reductionistic in reverse. Rather, law in Ezekiel participates in a constructive discourse by which the prophet seeks not only to shape the character of a new community, but to offer modes of perceiving reality that are both in keeping with the sacred tradition that shapes the identity of the community, and that engender new options for life in the present.[107]

Tôrâ in Eschatological Perspective

Thus, in Ezekiel laws are cited not so much to describe reality as to create and evoke a new reality. In that respect Ezekiel 18 belongs not only to the judgment oracles of Ezekiel 1-24 (and 25-32), but to the vision of the divine purpose of reconstituting a community of character. That vision is embodied throughout the book of Ezekiel and shows up in chap. 18 in the call to repentance. The plaintive cry of Yahweh expressing divine sorrow at human failure (18:23, 32) summons the community to become faithful to its own character as a covenant people. The call to "get yourselves a new heart and a new spirit" is an invitation to participate in the process of

---

[106]*The Sacred Canopy* (Garden City, NY: Doubleday, 1967) 19. See also P. Berger and T. Luckman, *The Social Construction of Reality* (Garden City, NY: Doubleday, 1966).

[107]J. Barton ("Approaches to Ethics in the Old Testament," *Beginning Old Testament Study* [ed. J. Rogerson; Philadelphia: Westminster, 1983] 128) observes that both laws and narratives "suggest the pattern or shape of a way of life lived in the presence of God." *Tôrâ* is, therefore, also a form of spirituality, "a system by which to live the whole of life in the presence of God, rather than a set of detailed regulations to cover every individual situation in which a moral ruling might be called for."

becoming.[108] Ezekiel calls the community of faith to engage in the eschatological act of God even in the midst of judgment. He envisions a future that is already in process, for the processes that bring death and those that bring life are already at work in the experience of the community. To be a community that is faithful to *tôrâ* is to bring the *tôrâ*-keeping of the future into the present. In that way the alternative of life begins to take effect even as death takes its toll on the community through war and exile. Ezekiel is therefore addressing not *ṣaddîqîm per se*, but potential repentant ones. For them the list of laws functions as a dossier, a list of virtues that characterize the repentant ones, the ones on whom the new community will be built.[109]

Although the concept of polarities is sometimes taken to extremes, a case can also be made for *tôrâ* functioning to provide a counterbalance between judgment and the utopian vision for the future. Just as judgment may be a hyperbolic presentation of Israel's past and present apostasy, so also the future is presented as an fantastic vision of peace and security in the land, at the heart of which stands the renewed temple cult. Both the judgment and the vision of the future are based somewhat loosely on Israel's legal traditions. At the heart of the transformation from apostasy to restoration stand two motifs: the positive dimension of law as the means by which the divine order in the world is manifest, and the renewing power of Yahweh who will bring the people back to life, thereby restoring the glory of Yahweh and the holiness of the people.

SUMMARY AND CONCLUSIONS

From the function of law in Ezekiel we conclude that law is a form of discourse that can emerge in a variety of loci. Law has the diverse roles of shaping character and moral suasion, as well as shaping corporate identity and social coherence.   Law is highly flexible, and although there are differences and similarities between Ezekiel and other legal traditions in Israel, they do not stem so much from different sources or borrowing from documents, but from a flexible and changing body of law—one that developed analogously to the growth of ancient Israelite narrative and prophetic traditions.

Law functions differently in different settings. It is not bound by textuality. *Tôrâ* is as open to interpretive rereading as are narratives and

---

[108]See the next chapter for a discussion of the divine participation in that process.

[109]On this I agree with J. Blenkinsopp (*A History of Prophecy in Israel* [Westminster: Philadelphia, 1983] 200) who notes that "the general impression gained by a reading of the book as a whole is that moral guidelines are related directly to the kind of community Israel was intended to be."

prophetic oracles. For Ezekiel, who incorporates legal discourse into his prophetic discourses, *tôrâ* functions uniquely to provide a distinct shape to the impact of the entire discourse. It is that impact that has not adequately been explored.

When the community of faith needs definition and boundaries have to be drawn, then lines of demarcation must become clearer. Where syncretism or apostasy threaten, self-definition and identity become a major concern of those who believe themselves in charge of preserving the sacred trust of the community. The interests of those who held the authority of law (priests) may well be seen in the emphasis on law in the book of Ezekiel. That emphasis reflects the attempt by the Ezekiel tradition to preserve the integrity of the community in exile.[110] Part of that quest for integrity may be seen in a cryptic polemic against other *tôrâ* traditions that Ezekiel finds inadequate for his situation.

Finally, Ezekiel uses law to re-envision both the expression of the divine order or will, and the shape of the community of faith. Law as moral discourse forms the heart of that revisioning. Therefore, as Patrick writes, "the law is a gift of grace." Yahweh's "commandments are of a piece with his saving acts, for both create community."[111] Law is used in Ezekiel, therefore, as a way of appealing to the generative power of Israel's tradition.

We turn now to consider how Ezekiel construes Yahweh's involvement as a moral agent with Israel's movement toward the new community of faithful people.

---

[110]That estimation of the sociological context of *tôrâ* in Ezekiel does not require the conclusion that the legal dimension derives from later centuries, for apart from the history of legal forms in the book, *tôrâ* as a phenomenon is not out of place in the sixth century. Although my aim has not been explicitly to refute redaction-critical work on Ezekiel, comments such as this have been scattered throughout the dissertation. I have sought, however, to make a positive case for the function of the legal material in Ezekiel in the exilic context.

[111]*Old Testament Law*, 233.

7

THEOLOGY AND ETHICS IN EZEKIEL: AN INTEGRATIVE ANALYSIS

THE RELATIONSHIP BETWEEN GOD AND ETHICS

But the house of Israel says: The way of the Lord is arbitrary.
Are my ways not fair, O house of Israel?
Is it not that your ways are erratic? (Ezek 18:25, 29)

The relationship between God and ethics has already been explored in various ways so far in the discussion. The close relationship has been observed in the discussions concerning the individual and the community, and concerning the function of law as expressing and shaping the character of the moral community. The relationship between God and ethics in the Hebrew Bible has generally been viewed in terms of divine judgment and retribution, and the associated question of divine justice in human experience. Zimmerli phrases the questions this way: "Was there a righteous Governor of the universe? Or was there only meaningless catastrophe?"[1]

In 18:25-29 the people's rebuttal is cited twice, and both times the question is thrown back in their faces. The divine response is as abrupt as the accusation. The people question Yahweh's ordering of the world, as Zimmerli suggests, and Yahweh turns the question back to challenge the moral ordering of the people's lives.[2] Vv 26-28 reflect the first rebuttal, which is framed by the two question-answer statements of vv 25 and 29.

This is a most significant element of the text since the dialogue reflects, in Zimmerli's words, "bitterness," "despair," "cynicism," and "a feeling of hopelessness which could no longer see God's righteousness in face of all that they had suffered."[3] But in response to the seriousness of the theodicy question, Zimmerli states that this "particular feature of Ezek

---

[1]*Ezekiel 1*, 386. Pfeiffer (*Introduction*, 548) suggests that "Ezekiel was concerned primarily with the justification of Jehovah's acts and with the creation of the right religious and ethical conduct in those who constituted the seed of the new Israel."

[2]Ibid., 385-86.

[3]Ibid., 386.

18 lies in the fact that this question, as an audit looking backwards, really only stood at the fringe." Zimmerli admits that it is "not an unimportant question," but "it is not the urgent message for the hour of despair (33:10) and for Israel's cynical resignation (18:2)."[4]

I think Zimmerli is correct when he affirms that the message of life stands at the centre of Ezekiel 18. I have already explored the implications of that message for the reconstitution of peoplehood and the shaping of the community's character. I wish to explore here the theodicy question and to suggest that it does not stand at the fringe but at the centre of Ezekiel's entire project. The call to life and transformation that the chapter affirms cannot be appropriated in the crisis of exile unless the God question is allowed to stand. And the questions that I have explored on the identity of the community and the individual (Chapter 5) and on the shaping of character by means of the narrative covenant and law (Chapter 6) finally cannot stand alone apart from this one. Clearly the text does not address the theodicy question first; it begins with the articulation of character formation (the identity of the community of *ṣaddîqîm* through the formative function of *tôrâ*). But given the impact of the Priestly vision on Ezekielian ethics, the question of how God and ethics are interrelated must be addressed, for at the heart of Ezekiel's ethics is the assumption that the character of the people must correspond to the character of Yahweh. Ezekiel perceives that the disruption of that correspondence ("you shall be holy for I am holy") is fundamental to his explanation of the present, and to his prospect for reconstitution of peoplehood in the future.[5]

---

[4]Ibid., 387. The issue is more forcefully stated by Mendenhall ("The Relation of the Individual to Political Society," 104) who states that "the biblical faith knows nothing of the rights of man against God—it is a false issue." He remarks in a footnote (104, n. 52.) that "the Book of Job raises the question only to reject the idea." Similarly, J. Muilenburg ("Ezekiel," *Peake's Commentary on the Bible* [rev. ed.; ed. M. Black and H. H. Rowley; New York: Nelson, 1962] 570) thinks that theodicy is not a great issue to Ezekiel: "His overwhelming sense of the reality of God, of his righteousness and holiness, and of the absolute justice of his ways prevent him from feeling the acuteness of the dilemmas." But is it not the case that Ezekiel's overwhelmingly powerful depiction of Yahweh is itself a way of overcoming the dilemma that he faces given the facts of the exile and the religious sentiments of his audience? We must distinguish, if we can, between the actual feelings and experiences of the prophet and the way those feelings are depicted to address the theodicy question in the text of Ezekiel. Thus, May ("Individual Responsibility and Retribution," 117) understands Ezekiel's concern to be "the justice rather than the mercy of God." Cooke (*Ezekiel*, 195) also states that "to vindicate God's justice is the prophet's chief concern."

[5]R. Slenczka ("Sozialethik und Theodizee," *KD* 18 [1972] 82-99) argues that ethics and theodicy are intimately related. He writes: "Der Schritt von der Theodizee zur Ethik is nicht gross. Im Grunde umschliesst jede Behandlung der Theodizeefrage ein ethisches Problem, nämlich die freie Selbstbestimmung des Handelns." He describes the relationship this way: "Gemeinsam sind in Theodizee und Sozialethik die Wirklichkeitsdeutung und Daseinsbewälti-

In this chapter I shall therefore explore several specific and interrelated concerns that have a bearing on Ezekiel's view of God in relation to the moral life: 1) Ezekiel's portrayal of Yahweh as moral agent; 2) holiness as a dynamic centre; 3) integrity and character. I shall then discuss two related facets of Ezekiel's discourse: divine enablement and human responsibility; and the relationship between theodicy and the experience of exile in the moral argument of Ezekiel. I shall conclude the chapter with observations about the relationship between judgment and the knowledge of Yahweh.

A Revised Understanding of Yahweh as Moral Agent[6]

It has often been stated that for Ezekiel the universe is theocentric. It is the violation of Yahweh's holiness that led to his departure from the Temple, and only a restoration of that holiness will restore Yahweh's presence among his people. The restoration will be for the sake of Yahweh's name. Alongside the affirmation of theocentricity, however, we recognize that Yahweh's attention is always toward the prophet and the people. Since in most of the book of Ezekiel it is Yahweh who speaks in the first person, addressing the human community ("house of Israel"), the focal point of the book is on human actions, judgment on account of those actions, and hope for the human community after judgment.

I suggest, therefore, that for Ezekiel the moral universe is shaped by personal agents. The ultimate personal statement is "Yahweh is there" (48:35). Thus, the centre of Yahweh's holiness is Yahweh's presence manifested in the community. The presence of Yahweh without the human community is impossible, and although Yahweh can act apart from human agency, this God cannot be honoured without human agency and

---

gung. Doch die Wege scheinen sich zu scheiden, insofern es bei der Theodizee um das Verhältnis von Welterfahrung und Gotteserfahrung geht, während es bei der Sozialethik um das Verhältnis von Geschichte und Gesellschaft auf der einen und menschlihen, christlichem Verhalten auf der anderen Seite geht. Dies könne heissen: *Die Theodizee beginnt an der Grenze des Handelns, die Sozialethik hingegen hat die Möglichkeit des Handelns als Voraussetzung.* Doch gerade in dieser Differenz liegt das Verbindende. Denn es geht ja dann um die Grundfrage, wann überhaupt eine Situation oder ein geschichtlich-gesellschaftlicher Prozess ethisch in der Weise qualifiziert werden kann, dass er sich in seiner Kausalität unter die Kategorien von Tat und Verantwortung einordnen lässt" (96, emphasis mine).

[6]On moral agency see the discussion in Chapter 5 and Hauerwas, *Peaceable Kingdom*, 38-44. For Ezekiel, Yahweh is a moral agent not because he causes things to happen, but because his action is located within an ongoing history of a particular community. Yahweh is a participant in the story and, as such, is also affected by the agency of others. This makes the theodicy question truly a dialogue between covenant partners.

involvement. The human community living in ordered harmony is a prerequisite for Yahweh's holiness to be visible in the world. In other words, Yahweh's presence depends on interpersonal action defined according to the framework for undergirding reality, namely, holiness embodied in peoplehood. In that way Ezekiel 18 provides a conceptual hinge between (or, out of the midst of) judgment and transformation of the new community. Ezekiel 18 is a hinge between Yahweh's departure from the temple and his return. The chapter, along with other legal aspects of the book, marks the beginnings of a "moral architecture" that parallels the temple architecture in the last part of the book of Ezekiel.

Holiness as a Dynamic Centre

Thus, it is precisely the holiness of Yahweh that makes him not merely a transcendent deity but a personal moral agent. Holiness is a category that shapes as well as expresses reality. Thus, to be holy means that Yahweh must express that holiness in the real world of human community. And because that is so, Ezekiel takes great pains "to establish the working of God in Israel on fixed rules of divine behavior."[7] Yahweh is a moral agent, for on no other basis could Ezekiel argue for Israel's judgment *and* for its restoration. To posit such a God is to begin to find ways of living with the ambiguity inherent in Ezekiel.

Zimmerli asserts, however, that "the concept of holiness is important for Ezekiel in a different way than for H." He goes on to say that "the connection of the demand for holiness from the people with the whole range of social and human conduct in Israel, which is characteristic of H and particularly of Leviticus 19 and which is emphasized against the background of Yahweh's holiness, is completely lacking in Ezekiel."[8] Zimmerli supports his statement by noting that: (1) differences between laws in Leviticus 19 and legal emphases in Ezekiel suggest that Ezekiel is not modelling his theology of holiness on that chapter; and (2) comparison between the marriage regulations for priests in Lev 21:7-8 21-22 and Ezek 44:22 show that in the Ezekiel text "we miss . . . the theology of sanctification which is so characteristic of H." Although we cannot appeal to "a hasty formula for the mutual relationship of H and Ezekiel,"[9] we ought to be able to suggest a reason for the differences.

---

[7]Greenberg, "Prolegomenon," xxvii.
[8]*Ezekiel 1*, 48, 49.
[9]Ibid., 51.

G. Bettenzoli moves beyond Zimmerli and argues for recognizing two contradictory traditions within the book of Ezekiel.[10] For Bettenzoli the concept of holiness (*qdš*) has been altered in the Book of Ezekiel. The Ezekiel tradition has been divided so that "Der begriff *qdš* erreicht in der Tat bei ihnen eine theologische Tragweite, die unterschiedlich ist und sogar widersprüchliche Züge annimmt." He goes on to state the presupposition:

> Die Unvereinbarkeit der Vorstellungen der verschiedenen Traditionen bringt auch eine unterschiedliche Verfasserschaft für die Schriften des Buches Ezechiel mit sich: der Prophet konnte in sich keine widersprüchlichen Vorstellungen verbergen, sondern nur die Einheitlichkeit seiner Persönlichkeit äussern, die allein von einem bestimmten Denken geprägt war.[11]

Thus, Bettenzoli tries to show, on the basis of comparison with the Holiness Code, that the *qdš* concept is represented differently by two streams of Israelite tradition, and that those two streams have had a hand in the composition of the Book of Ezekiel. One of those streams, the sacral law (*sakralrechtliche*) tradition, perceives holiness and the divine-human relationship in terms of an historical orientation that is worked out in the socio-religious reality of the community. The other stream is the cultic, which thinks in dualistic categories and perceives holiness as a sign of the sacred realm in which the divine-human relationship is expressed only in the cult. According to Bettenzoli, Ezekiel belonged to the first of those. Over against the cultic tradition, which was determined by spatial categories, Ezekiel belonged to the *sakralrechtliche* tradition, which was "auf geschichtliche Kategorien angewiesen und ethisch charakterisiert."[12]

---

[10]*Geist der Heiligkeit: Traditionsgeschichtliche Untersuchung des QDS-Begriffes im Buch Ezechiel* (Quaderni di Semitistica 8; Florence: Istituto di Linguistica e di Lingue Orientali Università di Firenze, 1979).

[11]Ibid., 13.

[12]Ibid., 227-28. According to Bettenzoli, the cultic tradition is reflected in the following texts: 5:7-13; 6:1-14; 14:1-11; 18; 20; 23:1-20; 36:16-32; 40-48. As Bettenzoli (233) writes: "Im Buch Ezechiel stehen zwei verschiedene religiöse Auffassungen, kultische und sakralrechtliche, nebeneinander, die aber entgegengesetzte Charakteristika aufweisen: sie können keine Synthese bilden.

Das Verständnis der Heiligkeit und des Verhältnisses Gott-Mensch beruht auf verschiedenen Denkkategorien und Voraussetzungen, die nicht vereinbar sind. Die prophetische Botschaft Ezechiels wurde kultisch interpretiert, aber dadurch wurde sie zugleich in ihrer ursprünglichen Tragweite aufgehoben; Gott wurde nicht mehr auf die Geschichte bezogen und das religiöse Leben fiel nicht mehr unter die Kategorien der Gerechtigkeit und der Treue: das Verhältnis Gott-Mensch bekam vielmehr die Bedeutung einer kultischen Frömmigkeit, die im Dualismus sakral-profan begründet ist und eine ethische Verantwortung für die soziale Wirklichkeit ausschliesst."

Bettenzoli's fragmentation of the Ezekiel tradition does it a disservice by assuming that the cultic and ethical-historical traditions are radically incompatible.[13] The Ezekiel tradition seeks to present a holistic, if somewhat overdrawn, synthesis that both historicizes the cult and sacralizes ethics. Holiness is characterized by the interactive dynamic of the divine-human relationship expressed through the community in the world and the community at worship. The one without the other is inconceivable in the eyes of the Ezekiel tradition.

My argument here offers an alternative to the views of Zimmerli and Bettenzoli. Implicit in the Book of Ezekiel is the Priestly injunction of Lev 19:2, "You shall be holy; for I the Lord your God am holy." In both Priestly and Ezekiel traditions, holiness is undifferentiated in terms of ethical and cultic actions.[14] Ethical and moral purity are subsets of the larger notion of character, which in Yahweh's case are indistinguishable. Similarly, Ezekiel's judgment on Israel, especially in the expulsion from the land and Yahweh's departure from the sanctuary, corresponds to the Priestly notions of Yahweh's judgment (Leviticus 26). Although the word *qdš* occurs only rarely in the first twenty-four chapters of Ezekiel, the judgment corresponds to the tragic failure of the injunctions in Lev 20:7-8 and 7:26. The Priestly understanding that Yahweh "sanctifies" Israel (Exod 31:13) is reversed in Ezekiel's understanding by Israel's "rebellion" (Ezek 2:3, 8).[15] Thus, only Ezekiel 20 emphasizes the concept of "holiness" in that the chapter bears striking similarity to the Holiness Code in its notion of sabbath as a sign of Yahweh's sanctifying of Israel. The rest of the judgment oracles of Ezekiel demonstrate Israel's actions, which serve to reverse or nullify Yahweh's sanctifying endeavors. Holiness as a reconstructive process emerges in Ezekiel as a part of the complex of judgment and salvation in which Yahweh vindicates his holy name (Ezek 20:41; 28:23, 25; 36:23; 38:16; 23). Part of that process involves a restoration of covenant relationship between Israel and Yahweh, in which Israel is sanctified (Ezek 20:12; 37:28). Of course chapters 40-48 contain the most occurrences of *qdš*, where the reconstruction vision is articulated symbolically as a paradigm of holiness. The architecture of the temple and redistribution of the land form two symbolic structures according to which holiness will take shape.[16]

---

[13]Herzog (*Die ethische Anschauungen*) argued against this in 1923.

[14]H.-P. Müller, "*qdš*, heilig," *THAT* 2 (1976) 599.

[15]As in Leviticus 26, Ezekiel 2 includes the present generation along with the "fathers" as "house of Israel."

[16]See David Hildebrand, "Israel's Cultic Structure as a Paradigm of Holiness in the Inter-Temple Period (597 B.C.-516 B.C.)" (Th.D. diss., Wycliffe College, Toronto School of Theology, 1984).

Integrity and Character

The tension that Bettenzoli perceives in Ezekiel can be appreciated positively if God and human beings are viewed as partners in the cosmic drama.[17] If, for example, the Priestly teaching of the image of God has moral dimensions that are expressed in the holiness metaphor, would not divine action also have a moral dimension?[18] The notions of election, judgment, and restoration are ways of comprehending that issue in the book of Ezekiel. In election Yahweh acts faithfully, and in restoration he acts faithfully. Thus, for Ezekiel, in judgment, the middle ground, Yahweh also acts in keeping with his name. It is an issue of Yahweh's integrity that Ezekiel addresses. And that is, in fact, the same issue that he addresses regarding the people of Israel.

In Ezek 12:21-25 we find Yahweh responding to a citation of the people, which asserts that the prophetic vision is not being realized. Ezekiel perceives the ridicule against himself as mockery of Yahweh. Thus, in v 23 he announces that fulfillment is at hand. Again in v 25 Yahweh announces, "I will speak the word and perform it." The problem was not that the word was not being spoken, but that the performance was somehow hindered. There was a perceived hiatus between the word and its realization. G. Fohrer comments: "Denn wie für den Israeliten Wort und Tat miteinander verbunden sind und das Handeln aus dem Reden folgt, so gilt dies erst recht für Gott."[19] This further confirms my thesis that for Ezekiel, and indeed for all the prophets, Yahweh is construed and understood as a personal moral agent. The fact is confirmed also by the parallel accusation against the people in Ezek 33:31-32 in which Yahweh

---

[17]The metaphor is developed by S. J. De Vries in *The Achievements of Biblical Religion: A Prolegomenon to Old Testament Theology* (Lanham, MD: University Press of America, 1983) passim. Specifically De Vries states that biblical religion views both human beings and God "as responsible, effective actors in the cosmic drama" (326). This is not a particularly new idea. As D. A. Knight writes ("Old Testament Ethics," *Christian Century* 99 [1982] 57), "This divine/human drama lies at the center of the Bible."

[18]This is an implication of the Israelite understanding of God in covenant relationship with the human community. De Vries speaks of the relational character of the biblical God as "personalistic dualism" (ibid., 63-64), or "covenant personalism" (384). Speaking of the problem of theodicy in the book of Job, De Vries writes: "In the deepest sense, this book represents covenant personalism in an ultimately intensive form. It is simply developing the deepest implications of this notion, wrestling with the meaning of human freedom within the context of the divine responsibility and the divine commitment. According to Israel's highest tradition, Yahweh is answerable. He is answerable not because [humankind] demands it, but because he makes himself answerable" (384).

[19]*Die Propheten des Alten Testaments. Band 3. Die Propheten des frühen 6. Jahrhunderts* (Gütersloh: Gerd Mohn, 1975) 81.

again cites the people who mockingly call one another to hear the words of Yahweh through the voice of the prophet. The response to their mockery is "they hear what you say but they will not do it; for with their lips they show much love, but their heart is set on their gain" (v 31b). As Rost writes: "Für Ezechiel ist es entschieden: Jahwe tut, was er redet. Denn für ihn ist das Wort Jahwes eine fest formulierte, von aussen an den Propheten herangebrachte Gegebenheit, die genau, wortgetreu, ohne Abstrich und Zusatz weiterverkündigt werden muss."[20] And that, I think, is what he is also calling for within the human community—a restored peoplehood that acts out its confessional commitment with integrity, a commitment that is articulated in the framework of the moral order embodied in tôrâ-covenant stipulations.

Although the scope of this project does not lend itself to a full exploration of this subject, one way to break new ground in this matter is to try to articulate the central convictions reflected in the book as a whole. The whole approach to Ezekiel 18 needs to be put on a foundation that includes the integration of the concepts of God and ethics. The God concept in the book of Ezekiel and the concept of human being and human community participate in a collage of intersecting concepts—a conceptual world. To articulate the intersection of God and ethics we must discover the points of integration of concepts such as temple, land, sacred space, law, and justice. Several comments on that are in order.

Ezekiel is temple oriented. The tradition itself has been shaped and molded by a temple group that understood the tension between maintenance *and* critique from within. Within the book of Ezekiel critique (chaps. 8-11) and reconstruction (chaps. 40-48) frame the tradition.[21]

Moreover, Ezekiel is intent on restoring a functioning community that exists on the basis of commonly accepted norms. The entire history of Israel is perceived as a history of tô'ēbâ. That has resulted not only in the expulsion of the people from their land, but Yahweh has also abandoned the sacred space and has given the people over to experience the consequences of their actions. Yahweh has not, however, abandoned peoplehood in principle. At the root of Ezekiel's revisioning of reality is a new work of Yahweh that will enable Yahweh again to dwell with the people in the land. People and land are inseparable just as Yahweh and people are inseparable. Both are responsible agents whose actions can be challenged, and who have bound themselves to covenant interdependence.

---

[20]"Gesetz und Propheten," 30.

[21]See J. D. Levenson (*Sinai and Zion: An Entry into the Jewish Bible* [Minneapolis, MN: Winston, 1985] 170) for a critique of P. D. Hanson's rigid portrayal of the Priestly temple group in *The Dawn of Apocalyptic: The Historical and Sociological Roots of Jewish Apocalyptic Eschatology* (rev. ed.; Philadelphia, PA: Fortress, 1979).

Given the possibility of understanding Yahweh as a moral agent, how does Yahweh participate in the drama of human community? Specifically, are there norms that bind Yahweh? Are there norms by which Yahweh and the human community find themselves responsible to one another? And are there ways to mediate differences of opinion?

In Ezekiel 18 the people accuse Yahweh of not acting according to principle, or not conforming to rule.[22] Yahweh is not acting with integrity; his character is arbitrary. Is this citation simply a rhetorical strategy for asserting the prerogative of a more authoritative voice? On the surface the citation and the rebuke that follows seem not only harsh, but insensitive—hardly what one might expect in an attempt to influence attitudes and actions.

All of Ezekiel 18 taken together is about character. It calls for perceiving the possibilities for restoration on the other side of judgment. The *tôrâ* orientation is hortatory, pedagogical, and formative. And it hardly needs stating that Ezekiel, in other judgment oracles, allegories, and discourses, seeks to implicate the entire community as participants in the actions that drove both Yahweh and people out of the land. Yet if we read the *tôrâ* orientation of Ezekiel 18 as applying to the Israelite community in exile, it is certainly also the intent of the text to draw Yahweh into the dynamic of the *tôrâ* community. Unlike the assumption of the accusation, which criticizes Yahweh for acting out of character and in a manner that defies scrutiny, the disputation places Yahweh's ways and the people's ways as subject to the same standards of scrutiny and evaluation. The point of identification emerges where divine pathos is expressed in vv 23 and 32. That outburst points out the possibility that Yahweh may well be powerless to effect a unilateral reversal of the consequences of human actions. Yahweh does offer, however, an alternative.

DIVINE ENABLEMENT AND HUMAN RESPONSIBILITY[23]

Unlike the often remembered affirmations in Ezek 11:19-20 and 36:26-27 (cf. Jer 31:31-34), Ezek 18:31 speaks the language of responsibility: "Get yourselves a new heart and a new spirit!" That is the

---

[22]Fishbane (*Biblical Interpretation*, 338) understands the verb *yittākēn* in vv 25 and 29 as derived from *tkn*, "to measure." Greenberg (*Ezekiel 1-20*, 333) states that the word "means 'determine' the measure, content, or character of something."

[23]For the most recent and thorough discussion of this matter see P. M. Joyce, *Divine Initiative and Human Response in Ezekiel*.

alternative that is offered in chap. 18, but it is not clear how that motif functions in the chapter and in the book.[24]

The parallelism in Ezek 18:30-31 provides the first clue for determining the function of the new heart/new spirit motif in the chapter. Verse 30a, beginning with *lākēn*, "therefore," announces that Yahweh will judge the "house of Israel," for the behaviour of the community members. Verse 30b abruptly issues a call to repent and turn from transgression and iniquity. Verse 31a reverses the pattern and begins with an elaboration of v 30a. Verse 31b asks the question, "Why will you die, O house of Israel?", which corresponds to v 30a. The acquiring of a new heart/new spirit, then, corresponds to the act of repentance. It is the act of the human community that makes possible the alternative for life. These verses do not assume that this human act will enable the community to avoid the judgment mentioned in v 30a. But it will permit the possibility that death is not the outcome of judgment, but rather that life will flourish in its stead. That is the cry from the heart of Yahweh that is voiced in v 32. The new heart/new spirit motif in chap. 18 emphasizes that the option for viable existence as a community involves decisive human action.

The other occurrences of that motif in Ezek 11:19 and 36:26, however, suggest that the new heart/spirit will be part of Yahweh's restorative work "in his creating his people as an obedient and law-abiding people."[25] Commenting on 11:19, Zimmerli suggests that "the heart, the seat both of thought and of the will, must be changed."[26] The new spirit here seems to nuance the parallelism to suggest a holistic personhood. In Ezek 11:5 and 20:32 *rûah* refers to the "intellectual centre" or place where thoughts arise. In other texts *rûah* is "the organ of decision of the will about the way to be taken."[27] But the specific parallelism in 11:19; 18:31; and 36:26 reflects the broader notion of "character."[28] The most common use of *rûah* in Ezekiel, however, is in relation to Yahweh. In Ezek 37:1-14 the prophet calls on the wind from four directions, which is at the same time Yahweh's spirit (*rûhî*), which gives "life" to the dry bones. The result of "life" is interpreted as "I shall place you in your land" (36:14). In Ezek 36:26-27 the promise of Yahweh's spirit (*rûhî*) is interpreted as "I will insure that you walk in my statutes and observe my laws and do them."[29]

---

[24]Ackroyd (*Exile and Restoration*, 108-9) states: "When God takes action to restore, it is the expression of his will. But the response is never automatic, even if the precise relationship between divine action and human response is never fully defined."

[25]Zimmerli, *Ezekiel 1*, 65. Note that 11:19 reads "one heart," whereas 18:31 and 36:26 have "new heart."

[26]Ibid., 262.

[27]Zimmerli, *Ezekiel 2*, 566. So also Ezek 1:12; 10:17.

[28]So Zimmerli, ibid., 567.

[29]Ibid.

Yahweh's spirit, then, effects a transformation that has moral impact in real space (land).

The heart/spirit motif is therefore a holistic personal-moral category that encompasses both keeping *tôrâ* and living in community. That is so especially if land is understood both in literal/spatial terms and in metaphorical terms. Although return to the land is a significant part of Ezekiel's restoration program, that restoration, with its equal divisions of the land, will not look at all like the land that Israel has known before. New land symbolizes, therefore, a reordering of the socio-political ethic. "Land of Israel" and "house of Israel" are co-terminous. If so, "land of Israel" in 18:2 may be more of an allusion to "the physical pledge of the people's election by God."[30] Thus, peoplehood is not possible without place. So keeping *tôrâ* in community, symbolized by identity in a place/land, are possible in Ezekiel's conceptual world only by uniting *tôrâ*-keeping and land in the moral categories of heart/spirit. In that way Ezekiel grounds his ethical and theological vision in the notion of the character of a specific earth-bound community.

By calling on the community in chap. 18 to fashion (*'śh*) for themselves a new heart/spirit, the chapter contributes to the moral discourse of the Book of Ezekiel by fostering an element of responsible human action in the context of enabling divine action. By offering the human alternative in chap. 18, in the midst of judgment, the prophet suggests that divine intervention beyond the present experience is not the only option for the exilic community. By fashioning its own character as a *tôrâ*-keeping peoplehood, Israel in exile is already participating in the divine intention of restoration.[31]

But does Ezekiel place much hope in that human alternative? Does the human moral community ever amount to anything in Ezekiel's estimation? Do not the citations of the people in 33:10 and 37:11 reflect a lack of hope in human potential? The answer to those questions must be found again in the dialogical and covenantal dimension of discourse in Ezekiel. After the lament of 33:10 the prophet recapitulates the argument of chap. 18. The fact that people are not capable of responding faithfully does not disqualify the validity or significance of the discourse. And the fact that divine initiative is emphasized in chaps. 34 and 36 does not

---

[30]Zimmerli (*Ezekiel 1*, 204), commenting on Ezek 7:1-4.

[31]D. A. Knight ("Jeremiah and the Dimensions of the Moral Life," *The Divine Helmsman: Studies on God's Control of Human Events, Presented to Lou H. Silberman* [ed. J. L. Crenshaw and S. Sandmel; New York: KTAV, 1980] 93) suggests that when Jeremiah recognizes that the people do not respond to his challenge (see 4:4 and 9:25-26), "there appears to be no other hope but that YHWH himself will act to change the people's hearts (31:33)." According to Knight, this is also what Ezekiel expects. I suggest below that Ezekiel's covenantal understanding does not allow him to cancel the human element.

eliminate the significant place given to the call to moral responsibility. The dual focus in Ezekiel reflects the covenantal reality that undergirds Ezekiel's moral vision. Divine enablement does not cancel the covenantal partnership to which the human community has been committed. On the contrary, the hope of divine enablement (and it always remains a hope for Ezekiel and for the postexilic community) becomes rather a part of the narrative that shapes the moral character of the community. This Yahweh is part of a story, the end of which is not limited by the present experience of the community. The community is called, therefore, to live in the middle of time. And that is why Ezekiel 18 is a hinge text, offering a way of being in the liminal moment between judgment and transformation.

THEODICY, EXILE, AND THE MORAL ARGUMENT OF EZEKIEL[32]

The Authority of Yahweh and Divine Pathos

If there is a significant place for human action in the Book of Ezekiel, one does not get that impression from the interaction of the prophet and the divine word. The human voice surfaces in the Book of Ezekiel only in citations of the prophet's audience and in occasional dialogues between Yahweh and the prophet.[33] Yet it is precisely the total blending of prophetic and divine word that provides an additional clue to the intersection of human and divine action and responsibility. The relationship between the prophet and Yahweh suggests a model for the divine-human drama.

Although Ezekiel 18 is a disputation speech, the audience seems to be a foil for the divine discourse, which argues that Yahweh does not act arbitrarily. But the *māšāl* itself is not primarily concerned with arbitrariness. The citation of the *māšāl* suggests that consistency is exactly what the people expected. The question remains: does the implied audience of chap. 18 have in mind the injustice of their situation? Or do they lament the justice of their situation? Are they themselves engaging in an "inner-biblical" debate by presupposing the generational pattern of retribution? And does the prophet counter that pattern? Is it such a straightforward opposition that we encounter here?

In 18:25, 29 Yahweh asserts that it is the people's behaviour, not Yahweh's, that is under scrutiny. Matthews understands the assertion to

---

[32]On theodicy and ethics see L. Perlitt, "Anklage und Freispruch Gottes: Theologische Motive in der Zeit des Exils," *ZTK* 69 (1972) 290-303; C. S. Rodd, "Shall not the judge of all the earth do what is just? (Gen 18:25);" R. Slenczka, "Sozialethik und Theodizee;" M. Weber, *Ancient Judaism* (New York: Free Press, 1952) 297-335.

[33]On citations in Ezekiel see H. W. Wolff, "Das Zitat im Prophetenspruch"; and Clark, "The Citations in the Book of Ezekiel."

reflect a question of equity. Yahweh states, in effect: "My ways are according to the standard of measurement." Matthews continues, "It was the belief of the prophet that the universe at heart was ethically sound."[34] Although that may well be, the prophet does not simply resolve the theodicy question that way.

Ezekiel addresses the theodicy question by insisting on three things: first, that God does not desire the death but the repentance of the wicked; second, that the present generation is both free and responsible (11:17-20; 18:23, 30-32; 33:11); and third, that the present generation is not in bondage to the past. If human freedom is radically affirmed, how can God's justice be questioned?

What can we say, then, about Ezekiel's authority? Are his statements in 18:25 and 29 arbitrary assertions? Is his defense of God in chap. 18 simply counterstatement without grounding in commonly accepted conventions of morality? If what I have argued above is cogent, that Yahweh is viewed in Israel as a moral agent, a participant in the ongoing narrative of his people, then Ezekiel is appealing to conventions by which Yahweh is held accountable. Those conventions are not anthropocentric but emerge out of an understanding within the book of Ezekiel itself, that Yahweh's norms are his own holiness and name. But above all, the divine pathos reflected in 18:23, 32 adds an element of ambiguity to the divine character. Yahweh is not the sole causal agent in history. Yahweh is an interactive moral agent. Certainly Ezekiel's perception is that Yahweh's actions are beyond reproach, but they do not fall outside the norms of covenant commitment.

The Social Function of Theodicy

We can take the discussion beyond the actual language of Ezekiel by paying attention to the question of how theodicy functions in social contexts. Peter Berger has noted that

> the problem of theodicy appears most sharply in radical and ethical monotheism, that is, within the orbit of Biblical religion. If all rival or minor divinities are radically eliminated, and if not only all power but all ethical values are ascribed to the one God who created all things in this or any other world, then the problem of theodicy becomes a pointed question directed to this very conception. Indeed, more than in any other religious constellation, it may be said that this type of monotheism stands or falls with its capacity to solve the question of theodicy, "How can God permit?"[35]

---

[34]*Ezekiel*, 67.
[35]*Sacred Canopy*, 73.

This question is at the heart of Ezekiel's concern.

But I am interested in more than articulating *that* Ezekiel is concerned with the theodicy problem. How does Ezekiel's argument function to resolve the tension between the experience of reality and the covenantal confession of faith in Yahweh? A place to begin is with Berger's three-fold typology for "intermediate theodicy," that is, between irrational and rational explanation: 1) messianic-millenarian, emphasizing this-worldly resolution; 2) other-worldly, focusing on immortality/reversal, or resolution that is hidden in the world; 3) dualistic, in which struggle between good and evil explains the tension.[36]

The reason the matter is so pressing for the interpreter of Ezekiel is that theodicy and social reality are inextricably connected. According to Berger,

> theodicy directly affects the individual in his concrete life in society. A plausible theodicy (which, of course, requires an appropriate plausibility structure) permits the individual to integrate the anomic experiences of his biography into the socially established nomos and its subjective correlate in his own consciousness.[37]

Theodicy, therefore, provides meaning, not happiness. And meaning is the issue for Ezekiel's context.

Although Berger refers here to the individual, he also states that

> entire collectivities are thus permitted to integrate anomic events, acute or chronic, into the nomos established in their society. These events are now given 'a place' in the scheme of things, which consequently is protected from the threat of chaotic disintegration that is always implicit in such events.[38]

For Ezekiel's community the exile must be integrated into the "scheme of things." Ezekiel invites his community to a new scheme, corresponding to a covenantal *nomos*, a new order of faithfulness.

Berger uses the expression the "gains" of theodicy.[39] That expression is significant because interpreters have seldom articulated the positive social and theological function of theodicy. I am suggesting that refocusing the question of God and ethics in Ezekiel with special reference to theodicy helps to gain clarity on the message of the book and the social context of exile. Theodicy is at the heart of Ezekiel precisely because of the social and theological disintegration in the community. And theodicy

---

[36]Ibid., 68-72.
[37]Ibid., 58.
[38]Ibid., 58-59.
[39]Ibid., 58.

aims to address that disintegration directly. Because Yahweh is a moral agent and covenant partner, theodicy is not simply railing against a wall. Similarly, Yahweh's response to the accusations is not the arbitrary assertion of an authoritative voice. Divine pathos in Ezekiel does not allow for a disinterested and dispassionate God.[40]

Thus, both the human accusation and the divine response seek to deal with the problem of a crumbling world. Does the theodicy in Ezekiel serve to legitimate the powerful in exile, the Priestly school? Berger suggests that one of the social functions of theodicy is to explain "socially prevailing inequities of power and privilege." Thus, theodicy provides for "world-maintenance" and often the maintenance of particular institutional orders.[41] I suggest, however, that Ezekiel's theodicy functions slightly differently. It opens a way for world-construction. Thus, it is not ultimately about maintenance, but about revisioning and reconstruction.

If we perceive the theodicy to be about maintenance, then certainly the social order mediated by the Priestly tradition in the religious community would have to be maintained. But if we perceive theodicy in Ezekiel to be about construction, then the Priestly tradition can be allowed to be part of the agency seeking *nomos* and ordering. The old order could not be maintained, since all the constituent parts of that order had fallen by the way. Certainly the Priestly tradition was still "alive," but so were the sages and the prophets. The human being, bound to the community's narrative and tradition, continued to make meaning and to find congruence. As I have suggested, Ezekiel attempts to synthesize the old traditions in order to envision a new reality on which to build a new community, a faithful peoplehood. To face theodicy honestly in the context of exile involved Ezekiel in an authoritative redescription of Yahweh's presence and moral agency, and in a redescription of the relationship between the individual and the community. Those concerns need not be new or novel, but social construction needs to include those aspects of reality.

In his redescription, and in his facing of the theodicy question, Ezekiel opts neither for a irrational theodicy, nor for a rational theodicy. The

---

[40]I am indebted to D. A. Knight for the observation that Yahweh is not understood as a moral agent in the sense that he could do wrong, or that he could choose or discern the good. I doubt that Ezekiel ever entertained that possibility. But the power of theodicy is that it works from the bottom up. It articulates the mood and experience of the weaker partner in the covenant relationship. And it is based on the assumption that Yahweh, people, and land are an integral unity. That point is developed by Christopher J. H. Wright (*An Eye for An Eye: The Place of Old Testament Ethics Today* [Downers Grove, IL: InterVarsity, 1983]) in what he calls "the ethical triangle." Knight ("Old Testament Ethics," 57) suggests that in ancient Israel "God is normally pictured as the supreme practitioner of the morality which humans must follow."

[41]Berger, *Sacred Canopy*, 59.

irrational theodicy is about absorption: "self-transcendent participation in the collective." The rational theodicy is about rigid act-consequence correspondence:

> The life of the individual is only an ephemeral link in a causal chain that extends infinitely into both past and future. It follows that the individual has no one to blame for his misfortunes except himself—and, conversely, he may ascribe his good fortune to nothing but his own merits.[42]

On the surface there are elements of the rational theodicy in Ezekiel. It seems as though Ezekiel 14 and 18 argue from that perspective. I shall show, however (with Berger), that Ezekiel stands between the two options. He sees the impossibility of the extreme positions and posits another. Berger calls this "the eschatological or messianic-millenarian" theodicy.[43] This terminology does not suit Ezekiel, as will become evident.

For Berger the eschatological-millenarian type of theodicy looks to the future for a resolution of the tensions in present experience.

> Anomic phenomena are legitimated by reference to a future nomization, thus reintegrating them within an over-all meaningful order. This theodicy will be rational to the extent that it involves a coherent theory of history. . . . It will be actually or potentially revolutionary to the extent that the divine action about to intervene in the course of events requires or allows human co-operation.[44]

Thus, it is not simply a rejection of the present, but a looking to the future for an orientation. One might say that this kind of theodicy begins its resolution by reading history backwards, beginning with the future prospects and proposals. This kind of eschatological theodicy is not ultimately other-worldly, but this-worldly in that it has revolutionary potential—it bears within it the possibility for change in human history and human experience.[45] This kind of theodicy, therefore, allows a place for human participation in the shaping of the future. In theological terms, it does not limit the possibilities for the future to divine action—although that will certainly play a large part.

Another important matter pertaining to theodicy and ethics is J. L. Crenshaw's assertion that saving God's honour sacrifices human integrity. In a variety of ways theodicy not only results in a loss of human dignity, but also constitutes an "immense sacrifice: of the present, of reality itself,

---

[42]Ibid., 63-65.
[43]Ibid., 69.
[44]Ibid., 69.
[45]Ibid., 70.

of personal honor, and of the will."[46] I agree that for Ezekiel sacrifice is indeed necessary, but it is not the sacrifice of integrity. The call to integrity is, in fact, that which binds human community and God together in interdependent mutuality. Yahweh cannot act in keeping with his character (name and holiness) without the corresponding action of the human community.

Therefore we need to say that Ezekiel saves both God's honour and the honour of the human community by offering both the freedom to act according to the character of the covenantal narrative tradition. That allows Ezekiel to do justice to the tension between human and divine interdependence and responsibility. As Koch writes, through covenant both Yahweh and peoplehood find their "identity" or "authenticity." "Yahweh is not truly a God until he is surrounded by a people faithful to him. And Israel cannot really call itself a people as long as it is not continually and entirely governed by the divine power which guarantees its continuance and solidarity as a people, beyond any injury it can suffer."[47] Also, Ezekiel is able to take seriously the problem of human evil and its power to destroy. More than any other prophet, Ezekiel faces evil head on and allows for no compromising positions on Israel's past. That is what makes the book so terrifying, and what makes it seem to sacrifice the human for God's sake.

Popular Questioning of the Justice of God

But the question of the justice of God is not unique to Ezekiel.[48] Crenshaw argues that many voices called the justice of God into question.

The dogma of individual retribution, far from being a concoction of the egocentric populace, was coined by the religious leaders of Israel. Prophet, priest, and sage contributed to the popularity of the dogma, so that one must

---

[46]"Introduction: The Shift from Theodicy to Anthropodicy," *Theodicy in the Old Testament*, (ed. J. L. Crenshaw; Issues in Religion and Theology 4; Philadelphia, PA: Fortress; London: SPCK, 1983) 7. More specifically concerning Ezekiel 18, Crenshaw argues that "the poverty of rational defense of God surfaces in Ezekiel's feeble efforts to persuade his opponents that God's ways were just and the people's not just (18:19-29). Here assertion alone is deemed adequate, when claim and counter-claim exist. What makes the prophet's word more credible than theirs?" (15, n. 36).

[47]*The Prophets.* 2. 110-111.

[48]The justice of God is attacked in other prophetic disputations as well as the book of Job (See Ezek 12:22; 18:21; 33:10-11; Mal 2:17-3:5; 3:13-21; Isa 29:15-16; Mic 2:6-11; Isa 28:23-29; 40:27-31; 49:14; Lam 3:42-44).

conclude that the doctrine of individual retribution was endorsed by institutional religion.[49]

Crenshaw states that the prophetic view that God controlled history supported the idea that virtue is rewarded; Priestly religion asserted that "the deity repays those who contribute to his well-being by sacrifice or conduct"; and the sages' presupposition was that God created a moral universe in which "those who abide by the principle by which the world coheres" will be rewarded. Crenshaw finds a tension here between the question of individual responsibility and retribution, and the principle of grace.[50] In spelling out the issue in this way, Crenshaw concludes that "the dogma of individual retribution was positively criminal in its effect, even if based on the assumption that the Creator fashioned the universe so that accord with the principle of justice was rewarded."[51]

Crenshaw's comments spell caution to those who would too readily hear the powerful divine words in Ezekiel without entertaining the possibility that Ezekiel's scathing judgment on the exilic generation may have been excessive. The dominant voice in Ezekiel is not that of complaint, but of harsh castigation. Yet Crenshaw's concern for the imbalance between justice and grace is evident in the book of Ezekiel. As I have suggested, Ezekiel does not stand simply against the human community. Both the human and the divine are interactive partners. Neither Yahweh nor the human community is independent of the other.

Our exploration of the book of Ezekiel would add to Crenshaw's three possible responses in Israel to the injustice of God: "(1) human beings are innately evil, so that whatever their lot it is less odious than they deserve; (2) the gods are unjust; and (3) man's knowledge is partial, since the gods are hidden."[52] The fourth option, which Ezekiel espouses, is that God and the human community are interdependent actors, and that the realms of the divine and the human are not mutually exclusive. The question of the transcendent and the imminent do not fully apply in Ezekiel's case, even though Yahweh is depicted in transcendent categories in part of the book. In large part Yahweh is depicted metaphorically and anthropomorphically, but above all personally.[53]

---

[49]*Prophetic Conflict: Its Effect Upon Israelite Religion* (BZAW 124; Berlin/New York: de Gruyter) 36.

[50]Ibid.

[51]Ibid., 35.

[52]Ibid., 38.

[53]That is why I do not think Greenberg's depiction of Ezekiel's rigidity is a fully adequate explanation for the theodicy question. He writes: "The pre-fall prophecies have as their aim not the averting of doom, but the establishment of a record that it was predicted. This record is the foundation of the future hope. Ezekiel predicts the fall, gives a full account of its causes,

Ezekiel's Place in the Old Testament Traditions

Ezekiel's own response to the question of theodicy can be seen more clearly when it is set in the context of the larger debate within the Hebrew Bible.[54] The discussion of the relationship between ethics and theodicy must begin with the paradigmatic text of Gen 18:25, where Abraham chides Yahweh: "Far be it from thee to do such a thing, to slay the righteous with the wicked, so that the righteous fare as the wicked! Far be that from thee! Shall not the Judge of all the earth do right?" That critique of the divine justice comes after Yahweh thinks that he will not withhold anything from Abraham: "I have chosen him, that he may charge his children and his household after him to keep the way of the Lord by doing righteousness and justice; so that the Lord may bring to Abraham what he has promised him" (18:19). That is probably the most explicit statement on the intersection of ethics and theodicy in the Hebrew Bible.

According to Deut 10:17-19, a text that resonates with Deut 24:16, Yahweh is a God who is not partial but who executes justice for the fatherless and the widow.[55] Yahweh's actions have as their goal the ultimate reference point of interhuman justice. Both the judgment and the vision of Ezekiel 18 ought to be seen in the light of that. By returning the people are to seek a renewed justice in inter-human affairs. To get a new heart will mean to take initiative to become the moral community.

How is it, then, that Ezekiel allows so openly to raise the question of Yahweh's justice? Although it is only through the voice of the audience citations, we find a probing that is as significant as that of Abraham in Genesis 18. It is exactly the problem of exile that has raised for Ezekiel and his tradition the question of theodicy. Although Ezekiel does not himself raise the question, it is one of the functions of the audience citations to allow the question to be raised, to bring it to the forefront for discussion. We ask, then, about the way Yahweh responds and provides an answer to the accusations.

---

emphasizes the principle of God's judgment—individual, just recompense. All is set forth with ruthless clarity, with iron-clad certainty. Nothing is left to the irrational realm of mercy or love. . . . That is so because he aims to establish the working of God in Israel on fixed rules of divine behaviour. He seeks to catch all history in a net of inevitability. That is his comfort in the bitter present and his promise of hope for a brighter future. His generalizations, his sweeping programmatic chapters—all contribute to the conception of history as that which must be so" ("Prolegomenon," xxvii).

[54]The larger question is explored fully in J. L. Crenshaw, "Popular Questioning of the Justice of God," *ZAW* 82 (1970) 380-95.

[55]Another text that affirms the justice of Yahweh is 2 Chron 19:7, "take heed what you do, for there is no perversion of justice with the Lord our God, or partiality, or taking bribes." Here is a much later tradition that echoes the same language as Deut 10:17-19.

The books of Job (21:19) and Ecclesiastes also address the question. In the book of Job the theodicy question is raised as an open accusation against God.[56] That is exactly what is happening in Ezekiel 18, and perhaps throughout the book of Ezekiel. Berger, however, groups theodicy and masochism together. In Ezekiel quite a different assertion appears. Yahweh states "I do not wish for any to die" (18:32). Yahweh is a God of pathos.

CONCLUSION:JUDGMENT AND THE KNOWLEDGE OF YAHWEH

The complete domination of the book by the voice of Yahweh is meant to resolve the question of the prophet's authority.[57] The prophetic call and the modes of discourse demonstrate the validity of the judgment that Ezekiel announces. But judgment performs a larger function in the rhetorical strategy of the book.

In 23:49 the prophet suggests "that the people will be brought to know their covenantal Lord (again) *in and through* the judgments."[58]   As Zimmerli has noted, "knowledge of Yahweh" represents a fulcral concern in Ezekiel and his circle. He expands that by asserting the following:

> Their highest concern is neither the restoration of a healthy people nor the reestablishment of social balance within the people; rather it is above all the adoration that kneels because of divinely inspired recognition, an orientation toward the one who himself says 'I am Yahweh'.[59]

But as I have argued, that knowledge is incomprehensible without the reconstitution of peoplehood. "Bowing the knee" also happens, according to Ezekiel, only in the congregation of worshippers in community.

The point at which the recognition formula connects with ethics and theodicy is this. Zimmerli rightly states that "the strict recognition formula is apparently never concerned with Yahweh's self-contained being, but rather with his coming self-manifestation and demand for obedience." In

---

[56]I disagree with Berger (*Sacred Canopy*, 74), who states that "the questioner is radically challenged as to his right to pose the question in the first place. . . . The implicit accusation against God is turned around to become an explicit accusation against man. In this curious reversal the problem of theodicy is made to disappear and in its turn appears a problem of anthropodicy. . . . The question of human sin replaces the question of divine justice." Although human sin is a factor in the discussion, the Yahweh speeches do not call into question Job's right to ask the justice question, nor do they focus on human sin.

[57]See R. R. Wilson, "Prophecy in Crisis: The Call of Ezekiel," *Int* 38 (1984) 126-27.

[58]Fishbane, "Sin and Judgment," 139.

[59]"Knowledge of God," 88.

referring then to Numbers 16 and Moses, Zimmerli suggests further that "the recognition process . . . encompasses both the acknowledgment of Yahweh as Lord and the acknowledgment [of the one] that speaks for Yahweh."[60] The rhetorical function of the recognition formula, therefore, is to make the connection between the eschatological imagination that fuels Ezekiel's theodicy and the ethical responsibility that fuels the prophet's task of moral discernment and the shaping of a community of character. I disagree with Zimmerli, therefore, when he suggests that "knowledge of Yahweh" is not connected primarily to restoration and social reconstruction. Certainly Zimmerli is correct in affirming the "adoration that kneels" before the one who speaks "I am Yahweh." But that fulcrum ought not to be divorced from the social function of theodicy with which Ezekiel is engaged.[61]

Chap. 20 may help to clarify the matter. The chapter affirms repeatedly that Yahweh acts for the sake of his name and that the present generation is judged for profaning YHWH's holy name (20:39). V 44 makes it clear that in the future restoration Yahweh will deal with Israel for his name's sake, "not according to your evil ways, nor according to your corrupt doings." Ezekiel is presenting two stages in Yahweh's work. In the first stage, he presents a past work in which Yahweh acted for the sake of his name, yet which included judgment but not eradication. In the second stage he presents a future work in which Yahweh will act for the sake of his name, a work of grace not based on the merit of actions nor according to the consequences deserved. The present, however, he sees as an evil time, like the past, which will also experience judgment. The knowledge of Yahweh involves, therefore, a recognition of the justice of judgment, and an envisioning of new possibilities.

Thus, the theme of "knowing Yahweh" has, in part, a hortatory intent.

> It means to exhort the exiles to a consciousness of the fact that they will, in the future, have the knowledge, *which is now lacking*, that YHWH is a god of power who fulfills his doom predictions *as announced*. The people in exile will, moreover, know—as will all later readers of Ezekiel's visions and oracles—that the destruction of Jerusalem is not because an impotent god has "abandoned the land," but is rather because a providential and powerful Judge has left his shrine and land in revulsion of the abominations performed there.

---

[60] Ibid., 50.

[61] Fishbane ("Sin and Judgment," 147-48) takes a similar approach, according to which Ezekiel's "primary concern was not to call the people of Jerusalem to repentance but to expound in various ways upon the justice of YHWH *to the exiles*."

Relatedly, since the dooms are described in advance, the addresses have *in the present* a proleptic intimation of this future knowledge.[62]

The rhetorical function of Ezekiel 18 (along with the question of 33:10 and the response there) again addresses the liminal moment and the question about what to do in the meantime. The moral vision of Ezekiel 18 is based on the ancient traditions, yet its focus is on the shaping of a moral community that moves into its future through the reality of judgment. The theodicy question is answered by allowing the tension between human initiative and divine interaction to stand. The future is open, and not closed.

That is precisely because the relationship between theodicy, ethics, and the knowledge of Yahweh has another side—the pathos of God. Israel's God communicates a desire to be known, to be in covenant relationship with a peoplehood. The irony of Ezekiel's message of doom is that he must live with the tension between a God who judges and a God who calls for and initiates relationship in community.[63]   And even when that new work of God arrives, when the new heart and new spirit are given, the word of Ezekiel 18 must still be heard and heeded: Get yourselves a new heart and a new spirit.

---

[62]Ibid., 149. Fishbane suggests also that theoretically the rhetorical effect of the doom oracles might be to bring people to that conclusion on their own.

[63]As Fishbane (ibid., 150) puts it, "for Israel . . . Ezekiel's ultimate lesson is that there is no escaping the covenantal judgment and providence of YHWH, who will be made known to them even against their will."

8

CONCLUSION

THE RHETORICAL SHAPE OF ETHICS IN EZEKIEL 18

Most North American readers of Ezekiel cannot enter the agony of Ezekiel's own moment in history. The terror of losing all the foundations and structures for social identity and religious vision is scarcely comprehensible. In the context of the historical crisis of the sixth century B.C.E., Ezekiel's language reaches to the extremes in search of explanation and possibility.

This dissertation has focused on the analysis of that language—the rhetoric of moral discourse. Ezekiel 18 is an attempt to shape a moral community through the creative use of language. It envisions the possibility for transformation and reconstitution. Its task is to nurture the formation of a peoplehood.

The text engages in a dispute with the community. That dispute functions rhetorically to engage the audience and to call for response. Although the text may not reflect an actual dialogue, it takes seriously the reality of debate. The debate, both the citations and the responses, intersects with Israel's narrative *tôrâ* tradition.

Taking its lead from a proverb in common use, the text utilizes various forms of speech and subordinates them to a larger intention: to shape the virtuous life, to establish responsibility for moral choice, and to motivate the transformation toward a new and cohesive social order. The disputation seeks to change perception and shape a vision. And its context is clearly the transformation of the community, the "house of Israel."

The disputation based on the proverb (about actions and consequences) is the feature that shapes the rhetorical impact of the text. But the question of who is righteous (*saddîq*) cuts like an undercurrent through the disputation. Is it the audience, or is it Yahweh? Alongside the movement of that question runs another: is it of any value to be *saddîq*? The dispute asserts, although not in a simple and comforting way, that being *saddîq* is not only possible but necessary in order for the community to experience life in the presence of God. The possibility of transformation is heightened by the interplay between standards of judgment and the reality of divine order. The dispute concludes by affirming that the *saddîq* is plainly evident, as is the wicked one. The moral order is not evident primarily in the consequences of actions, but in the choices one makes to orient one's life,

219

and ultimately the life of the community, toward *tôrâ*. One is free, therefore, to act in keeping with one's character. Such a conclusion vindicates God's judgment. But the exercise of human freedom for transformation toward what is right and just will lead to a new experience of life in the community of *saddîqîm*. The *saddîq* is therefore characterized by an orientation toward change (repentance) that is expressed in doing what is just and right in community.

THE FUNCTION OF TRADITION
AND THE RHETORIC OF MORAL DISCOURSE

Ezekiel clears a place for himself in distinction from his precursors and contemporaries, which include tradents in both Priestly and Deuteronomistic traditions. Understanding that dynamic in the book of Ezekiel may help to integrate diachronic and synchronic analysis by suggesting new angles of vision. I began by assuming that the text of Ezekiel was composed as part of an historical process that has been informed and shaped by a larger hermeneutical interest. Ezekiel 18 belongs to an inner-biblical, and even inner-Ezekielian dialogue on the ultimate questions of the life and death of a community. World-mending is no easy task; the answers do not always sound the same. Ezekiel offers trajectories of hope within the traditional options. He creates a fresh and vibrant, if shocking, synthesis in the dialogue of possibilities.

The text draws on linguistic and cultural worlds and creates a unique pattern of interactions, either conforming to or breaking away from the traditional world out of which it was formed. That heritage is not an intellectually amorphous entity, however, but is integrally rooted in particular groups of people who bear the tradition. Since traditional material is located in socially identifiable groups, it is of interest for traditio-historical investigation not only to identify elements of tradition common to Ezekiel and, for example, the Priestly or Deuteronomistic traditions, but also to determine the unique formulations and functions of tradition within the structure and message of the book of Ezekiel.

I have argued that Ezekiel articulates a program by which his community might find its identity in the world. He taps the shared goals of Israel's traditions by means of a shared language in order to foster the practice of community in spite of the threat to the legitimacy of the community's basis for existence posed by the question of theodicy. One of the primary means of overcoming that potential disruptive force is his attention to the legal dimension of Israel's traditions, which he uses as the ground of his new community of interpretation. At the root of community, then, is a chosen centre of interpretation around which personal and corporate identity can be reconstructed—Israel's narrative *tôrâ*. Ezekiel's task, therefore, is to reconstitute a hermeneutical community around a hermeneutics of responsibility.

All the traditional conventions utilized in Ezekiel 18 participate in that common task. The formulaic expressions, the proverb, the legal forms, and the call to conversion all conspire to place Ezekiel's audience in the imagined world between judgment and transformation, between chaos and order. The suasive power of the text lies, in part, in its refusal to offer easy solutions. Ezekiel's solution is both critical and constructive. And the traditional conventions of discourse draw the audience into the fabric of Israel's narrative *tôrâ* traditions and in so doing compel them to begin articulating again the questions of identity and vocation.

The reception formula, the formula for a divine saying, and the oath formula work together in the text to validate the authority of the prophetic voice, which here functions to present Yahweh as an interactive presence with the exilic community. The use of traditional formulae already begins to make Yahweh known in the chaos; the words of Yahweh's agent are already laying out options for ordering a meaningful existence.

The declaratory formulae function both to clarify the character of the moral agent and to call the human community to responsible choice. They raise the question of who the righteous are, and at the same time, they challenge all to recognize that divine justice and human transformation are not incompatible. The interaction between the formulae of life and death along with the emphasis on consequences for action presents to the community the radical possibility of alternatives. In other words, judgment persists wherever alternatives are not considered viable.

The proverb itself evokes a new reality, for in its very citation it both articulates an experience and calls it into question. Its very performance in this context invites interaction and evaluation. It raises the theodicy question, and at the same time challenges the perception on which the proverb is based. The proverb is roundly denied as having validity, but at the same time the text suggests a series of parabolic or metaphoric possibilities that continue to evoke response through the rhetorical citation of audience response. The text has been shaped by the tension inherent in the observation that the proverb describes. And in the end the text hints that the people themselves are the paradigm of divine presence.

The legal forms, and in particular the legal lists, give concrete shape to the moral character of the community. Originally functioning as the character dossier of the *tôrâ* community, the lists here become significant reminders of the specific shape of faithfulness of those called to live in the presence of Yahweh. Lists that have affinities with instruction to temple visitors are used in exile, where no temple exists, and where people are searching for how life can be ordered outside the ordered space of temple and land. For Ezekiel, commitment to the narrative tradition embodied in specific obligations provides a way of understanding both what it means to be the Yahweh community and of discerning the mode of divine presence.

Thus, the exhortation to repentance is a statement of human responsibility in a cosmos where both the human community and God have a significant part in ordering the future.

THE SHAPING OF A COMMUNITY OF CHARACTER

The focus on the individual in Ezekiel 18 is in the service of the reconstitution of Israel as the people of God. Ezekiel is calling for a restored peoplehood that acts out its confessional commitment, which is articulated in the framework of the moral order embodied in covenant stipulations.

In this regard Ezekiel is revisionist. He engages in an inner-Biblical dialogue about actions, consequences, and retribution. In doing so he interacts with a community that has been shattered and is without a will to act one way or another. Ezekiel's place in the dialogue is to reject the theology of intergenerational transference of punishment and to advocate generational responsibility as an option for salvation. Land remains the organizing space in which faithfulness is ultimately embodied in peoplehood, but the shaping of the moral community is a prior act. That is a courageous assertion in the face of Ezekiel's recognition of Israel's past failures. The present generation has the bold option of imagining and choosing a future that has no precedent. And in so doing it will act out the failure of the *māšāl*.

That act of social imagination is built on the use of traditional language. Yahweh is known as Lord of the "house" of Israel. Yet the old language fosters a new mode of perceiving reality. It envisions the creation of a community of character in the midst of the wilderness of empire, and it summons the people to see that community as the sacred place in which Yahweh is known.

THE NARRATIVE CHARACTER OF PEOPLEHOOD

That character is articulated most clearly by Israel's *tôrâ* traditions. Although Ezekiel seems to avoid using *tôrâ* explicitly, perhaps to maintain some distance from the Deuteronomistic tradition, his entire social vision is based on the conviction that community is formed through common identification with a narrative tradition. That tradition carries with it certain obligations that are inherent in being the people that the story presents. *Tôrâ* is the means of social stability and a way of envisioning options for the future. But most significant for understanding Ezekiel 18 is the place of law in prophetic discourse in the present. This is one of the few texts in Ezekiel that is hortatory, that calls on the people to take action in the present. Judgment we can understand; even the vision for salvation and the utopian portrait of the restored Israel is comprehensible in the light of the prophetic task. We find Ezekiel holding out a dream for a peaceable world to come. But what makes the connection between the two? Surely chapter 18 is essential to make the movement complete. Without it the overall Ezekiel tradition would be incomplete, two polarities without the dimension of human possibility. Ezekiel 18 bridges the gap between resignation after recognizing the necessity of judgment, and visionary hope for divine intervention and deliverance. The human factor in between, the life in the meantime, is the context to which this chapter speaks. It is the ethical dimension that must be addressed as the people find a way of being in the world, their world, not the past or the future world. Chapter 18 is the *via media* by which the holy God comes to dwell with a holy people. That possibility both enables "life" and is "life" in the presence of God.

Ezekiel's use of *tôrâ*, therefore, is a way of appealing to the generative power of Israel's tradition.

THE INTEGRATION OF THEODICY AND ETHICS

Yet that very tradition also bore within itself the seeds of disillusionment. For Ezekiel and his community the question of theodicy is never far from the questions of ethics. As the citations in chap. 18 and in 33:10 demonstrate, questions about the ordering of the world have a bearing on how one lives, and on whether one is even capable of imagining creative possibilities for action. If divine ways are not discernible, what options for human discernment and choice are available? Especially in view of Ezekiel's Priestly orientation, that concern stands at the forefront. The human community experiences the divine presence when it imitates the character of the holy God.

Yahweh is an interactive personal agent who has a stake in the fate of the people. This God cannot be known apart from embodiment in the life and character of the peoplehood. And this God is affected by the actions of that people. Thus, the actions of the community have consequences not only in the historical experience of Israel, but also the community's actions have driven Yahweh from his land. Ezekiel 18 therefore addresses the theodicy question by suggesting that the moral architecture of the world is known in the real world of human community.

What is at stake in the God question for Ezekiel is the question of integrity, both divine and human. The focus on *tôrâ* in Ezekiel 18 assumes the Priestly notion of character, the character of the *saddîq*. But what of the character of Yahweh? Chap. 18 addresses primarily the options available for decisive human action, and in so doing underscores the conviction that the ethical and theological vision can only be grounded in a specific earth-bound community. That is to say that the theodicy question cannot be separated from ethics. The integrity of the community and the integrity of

Yahweh are bound together inseparably. Enabling divine action and responsible human action are rooted in the covenant reality and moral vision of Israel's narrative tradition. And that conviction is shaped by a profound awareness of the pathos of God.

Thus, the theodicy question adds a sharpness to the text because it addresses the experience of social disintegration within the covenant partnership. And it refuses the option of a disinterested and dispassionate God. Rather, by allowing the theodicy question to stand out boldly as it does, Ezekiel allows the human community a significant place in shaping the future. The present possibilities for creative movement into the future are not limited by the necessity for divine intervention. In this way Ezekiel saves both God's honour and the honour of the human community by offering both the freedom to act according to the character of the covenantal narrative tradition.

The boldness, and perhaps brashness, of Ezekiel's vision reflects also an openness to face the problem of evil directly. He offers no simple solutions. The call for decision in chap. 18 is not nullified by other assertions of divine enablement. Ezekiel's response to evil is to envision a time when Israel and all nations will recognize Yahweh in the reality of human experience of community. Ezekiel's eschatological imagination is fueled by both questions of theodicy and moral responsibility in the context of a community of character.

Ezekiel 18 stands as a testimony to the liminal moment between Ezekiel's harsh announcements of judgment and his bold eschatological vision. The text is rooted in an awareness of divine pathos in partnership with the human community. Its goal is the reconstitution of peoplehood among whom the divine presence is known and made known through the integrity of character in the practice of justice and righteousness. Ezekiel refuses to allow for uncomplicated solutions. The call addressed to the human community is still heard; it refuses to go away: get yourselves a new heart and a new spirit.

BIBLIOGRAPHY

Ackroyd, Peter R. *Exile and Restoration: A Study of Hebrew Thought of the Sixth Century B.C.* OTL. Philadelphia, PA: Westminster, 1968.

Alt, Albrecht. "The Origins of Israelite Law." *Essays in Old Testament History and Religion*, pp. 101-171. New York, NY: Doubleday, 1967.

Auvray, P. "Le prophète comme guetteur (Ez xxxiii, 1-20)." *RB* 71 (1964) 191-205.

Baltzer, Dieter. *Ezechiel und Deuterojesaja: Berührungen in der Heilserwartung der beiden grossen Exilspropheten.* BZAW 121. Berlin/New York: de Gruyter, 1971.

Bardtke, H. "Der Prophet Ezekiel in der modernen Forschung." *TLZ* 96 (1971) 721-34.

Barth H. and O. H. Steck. *Exegese des Alten Testaments: Leitfaden der Methodik.* 9th ed. Neukirchen-Vluyn: Neukirchener Verlag, 1980.

Barton, John. "Understanding Old Testament Ethics." *JSOT* 9 (1978) 44-64.

_____. "Approaches to Ethics in the Old Testament." *Beginning Old Testament Study*, pp. 113-30. Edited by John Rogerson. Philadelphia, PA: Westminster, 1983.

Baumgärtel, Friedrich. "Die Formel *ně'ûm jahwe*." *ZAW* 73 (1961) 277-90.

Begrich, J. "Das priesterliche Heilsorakel." *ZAW* 52 (1934) 81-92.

_____. "Die priesterliche Tôrâ." *Werden und Wesen des Alten Testaments*, pp. 63-88. Edited by P. Volz, F. Stummer and J. Hempel. BZAW 66. Berlin: Töpelmann, 1936.

Bentzen, A. *Introduction to the Old Testament.* 2 Volumes. Copenhagen: Gad, 1958.

Berger, Peter. *The Sacred Canopy.* Garden City, NY: Doubleday, 1967.

Berger P. and T. Luckman. *The Social Construction of Reality.* Garden City, NY: Doubleday, 1966.

Bergren, Richard V. *The Prophets and the Law.* Monographs of the Hebrew Union College 4. Cincinnati, OH: Hebrew Union College, 1974.

225

Bertholet, A. *Das Buch Hesekiel.* Kurzer Hand-Kommentar zum Alten Testament 12. Freiburg/Leipzig/Tübingen: Mohr-Siebeck, 1897.

Bertholet, A. and K. Galling. *Hesekiel.* HAT 13. Tübingen: Mohr-Siebeck, 1936.

Bettenzoli, Giuseppe. *Geist der Heiligkeit: Traditionsgeschichtliche Untersuchung des QDŠ-Begriffes im Buch Ezechiel.* Quaderni di Semitistica 8. Florence: Istituto di Linguistica e di Lingue Orientali Universita di Firenze, 1979.

Blenkinsopp, Joseph. *A History of Prophecy in Israel.* Philadelphia, PA: Westminster, 1983.

Block, Daniel I. "Israel's House: Reflections on the Use of *byt ysr'l* in the Old Testament in the Light of its Ancient Near Eastern Environment." *JETS* 28 (1985) 257-75.

Boadt, Lawrence. "Rhetorical Strategies in Ezekiel's Oracles of Judgment." *Ezekiel and His Book: Textual and Literary Criticism and their Interrelation*, pp. 182-200. Edited by J. Lust. Leuven: Leuven University Press/Peeters, 1986.

Brownlee, William H. *Word Biblical Commentary. Volume 28. Ezekiel 1-19.* Waco, TX: Word, 1986.

Budd, P. J. *Word Biblical Commentary. Volume 5. Numbers.* Waco, TX: Word, 1984.

Bueckers, H. "Kollektiv- und Individualvergeltung im Alten Testament." *TGl* 25 (1933) 273-87.

Burrows, Millar. *The Literary Relations of Ezekiel.* Philadelphia, PA: Jewish Publication Society, 1925.

Buss, Martin J. "The Idea of *Sitz-im-Leben*—History and Critique." *ZAW* 90 (1978) 157-70.

————. "Political Exegesis." *Encounter with the Text*, pp. 139-52. Semeia Supplements. Edited by M. Buss. Missoula, MT: Scholars Press, 1979.

Calès, J. "Rétribution individuelle, vie des justes et mort des pécheurs d'après le livre d'Ezéchiel." *RSR* 11 (1921) 363-71.

Carley, Keith W. *Ezekiel Among the Prophets: A Study of Ezekiel's Place in Prophetic Tradition.* SBT, Second Series, 31. Naperville, IL: Allenson, 1975.

Carreira, José Nunes. "Raizes da linguagem profética de Ezequiel. A proposito de Ez 18, 5-9." *EstBib* 26 (1967) 275-86.

Cassuto, Umberto. "The Arrangement of the Book of Ezekiel." *Biblical and Oriental Studies*, Vol. 1, pp. 227-40. Jerusalem: Magnes, 1973.

Childs, Brevard S. *Introduction to the Old Testament as Scripture.* Philadelphia, PA: Fortress, 1979.

Cholewinski, Alfred. *Heiligkeitsgesetz und Deuteronomium: Eine vergleichende Studie.* AnBib 66. Rome: Biblical Institute Press, 1976.

Clark, Douglas R.. "The Citations in the Book of Ezekiel: An Investigation into Method, Audience, and Message." Ph.D. Dissertation, Vanderbilt University, 1984.

Clements, Ronald E. *A Century of Old Testament Study.* Guildford/London: Lutterworth, 1976.

_____. "The Ezekiel Tradition: Prophecy in a Time of Crisis." *Israel's Prophetic Tradition: Essays in Honour of Peter R. Ackroyd*, pp. 119-36. Edited by R. Coggins, A. Phillips, and M. Knibb. Cambridge/New York: Cambridge University Press, 1982.

_____. "The Chronology of Redaction in Ez 1-24." *Ezekiel and His Book: Textual and Literary Criticism and their Interrelation*, pp. 283-94. Edited by J. Lust. Leuven: Leuven University Press/Peeters, 1986.

Cooke, G. A. "New Views on Ezekiel." *Theology* 24 (1932) 61-69.

_____. Review of *Hesekiel: der Dichter und das Buch*, by G. Hölscher. *JTS* 27 (1925-26) 201-203.

_____. *A Critical and Exegetical Commentary on the Book of Ezekiel.* ICC. New York: Scribner's, 1937.

Cornill, C. H. *Das Buch des Propheten Ezechiel.* Leipzig: Hinrichs, 1886.

Crenshaw, J. L. "Popular Questioning of the Justice of God." *ZAW* 82 (1970) 380-95.

_____. *Prophetic Conflict: Its Effect Upon Israelite Religion.* BZAW 124. Berlin/New York: de Gruyter, 1971.

_____. "Introduction: The Shift from Theodicy to Anthropodicy." *Theodicy in the Old Testament*, pp. 1-16. Edited by J. L. Crenshaw. Issues in Religion and Theology 4. Philadelphia, PA: Fortress; London: SPCK, 1983.

Cross, Frank Moore. *Canaanite Myth and Hebrew Epic: Essays in the History of the Religion of Israel.* Cambridge, MA: Harvard University Press, 1973.

Daube, David. *Studies in Biblical Law*. Cambridge: Cambridge University Press, 1947.

Davidson, A. B. *The Book of the Prophet Ezekiel*. The Cambridge Bible. Cambridge: Cambridge University Press, 1896.

Davies, E. W. *Prophecy and Ethics: Isaiah and the Ethical Tradition of Israel*. JSOTSup 16. Sheffield: JSOT, 1981.

Delorme, J. "Conversion et pardon selon le prophète Ezéchiel." *Mémorial J. Chaine*, pp. 115-44. Bibliothèque de la Faculté catholique de Lyon 5. Lyon: Facultés Catholiques, 1950.

De Vries, Simon J. *The Achievements of Biblical Religion: A Prolegomenon to Old Testament Theology*. Lanham, MD: University Press of America, 1983.

Dion, Paul E. "Une Inscription Araméenne En Style *Awilum Sha* et Quelques Textes Bibliques Datant de l'Exil [Lev 17-26; Eze 18]." *Bib* 55 (1974) 399-403.

Douglas, Mary. *Purity and Danger: An Analysis of Pollution and Taboo*. London/Boston/Henley: Routledge & Kegan Paul, 1966.

Driver, S. R. "The Worth of the Individual: Ezekiel xviii.2-4." *The Ideals of the Prophets*, pp. 62-72. Edinburgh: T. & T. Clark, 1915.

_____. *Introduction to the Literature of the Old Testament*. New York, NY: Meridian, 1956.

Eagleton, Terry. *Literary Theory: An Introduction*. Minneapolis, MN: University of Minneapolis Press, 1983.

Eichrodt, Walther. *Theology of the Old Testament*. 2 Volumes. OTL. Philadelphia, PA: Westminster, 1961, 1967.

_____. "Das prophetische Wächteramt: Zur Exegese von Hesekiel 33." *Tradition und Situation: Studien zur alttestamentlichen Prophetie* (FS A. Weiser), pp. 31-41. Edited by E. Würtwein and O. Kaiser. Göttingen: Vandenhoeck & Ruprecht, 1963.

_____. *Ezekiel: A Commentary*. OTL. Philadelphia: Westminster, 1970.

Eissfeldt, Otto. *Der Maschal im Alten Testament*. BZAW 24. Giessen: Töpelmann, 1913.

Fairman, H. W. "A Scene of the Offering of Truth in the Temple of Edfu," *Mitteilungen des deutschen Archaeologischen Instititut Abteilung Kairo* 16/II (1958) 86-92.

Fensham, F. C. "Widow, Orphan, and the Poor in Ancient Near Eastern Legal and Wisdom Literature." *JNES* 21 (1962) 129-39.

Fish, Stanley. *Is There a Text in This Class? The Authority of Interpretive Communities*. Cambridge, MA: Harvard University Press, 1980.

Fishbane, Michael. "Sin and Judgment in the Prophecies of Ezekiel." *Int* 38 (1984) 131-50.

_____. *Biblical Interpretation in Ancient Israel*. Oxford: Clarendon, 1985.

Fohrer, Georg. *Die Hauptprobleme des Buches Ezechiel*. BZAW 72. Berlin: Töpelmann, 1952.

_____. *Ezechiel*. 2nd ed. HAT 13. Tübingen: Mohr-Siebeck, 1955.

_____. "Das Symptmatische der Ezechielforschung." *TLZ* 83 (1958) 241-50.

_____. "Zehn Jahre Literatur zur alttestamentlichen Prophetie (1950-1960), VIII. Ezechiel." *TRu* 28 (1962) 261-67.

_____. *Die Propheten des Alten Testaments. Band 3. Die Propheten des frühen 6. Jahrhunderts*. Gütersloh: Gerd Mohn, 1975.

_____. "Neue Literatur zur alttestamentlichen Prophetie." *TRu* 45 (1980) 109-32.

Fontaine, Carole R. *Traditional Sayings in the Old Testament: A Contextual Study*. Bible and Literature Series 5. Sheffield: Almond, 1982.

Fox, Michael. "The Identification of Quotations in Biblical Literature." *ZAW* 92 (1980) 416-31.

Fraine, J. de. "Individu et Société dans la religion de l'Ancient Testament." *Bib* 33 (1952) 324-55, 445-75.

Friedman, Richard E. *The Exile and Biblical Narrative: The Formation of the Deuteronomistic and Priestly Works*. HSM 22. Chico, CA: Scholars Press, 1981.

Frymer-Kensky, Tikva. "Tit for Tat: The Principle of Equal Retribution in Near Eastern and Biblical Law." *BA* 43 (1980) 230-34.

Galling, K. "Der Beichtspiegel: Eine Gattungsgeschichtliche Studie." *ZAW* 47 (1929) 125-30.

Gammie, John. "The Theology of Retribution in the Book of Deuteronomy." *CBQ* 32 (1970) 1-12.

Gamoran, H. "The Biblical Law against Loans on Interest." *JNES* 30 (1971) 127-34.

Garscha, J. *Studien zum Ezechielbuch: eine redaktionskritische Untersuchung von Ez 1-39.* Europäische Hochschulschriften 23. Bern: Herbert Lang; Frankfurt: Peter Lang, 1974.

Gerstenberger, Erhard. *Wesen und Herkunft des 'Apodiktischen Rechts'.* WMANT 20. Neukirchen-Vluyn: Neukirchener Verlag, 1965.

_____. "*t'b*, verabscheuen," *THAT* 2 (1976) 1051-55.

Geyer, John B. "Ezekiel 18 and a Hittite Treaty of Mursilis II." *JSOT* 12 (1979) 31-46.

Gill, R. B. "The Moral Implications of Interpretive Communities." *Christianity and Literature* 33/1 (1983) 49-83.

Goldingay, John. *Approaches to Old Testament Interpretation.* Downers Grove, IL: InterVarsity, 1981.

Gordis, Robert. "Quotations as a Literary Usage in Biblical, Oriental, and Rabbinic Literature." *HUCA* 22 (1949) 157-219.

Gottwald, N. K. *All the Kingdoms of the Earth.* New York, NY: Harper & Row, 1964.

Graffy, Adrian. *A Prophet Confronts His People: The Disputation Speech in the Prophets.* AnBib 104. Rome: Biblical Institute Press, 1984.

Greenberg, Moshe. "The Hebrew Oath Particle ḥay/ḥe." *JBL* 76 (1957) 34-39.

_____. "Prolegomenon." *Pseudo-Ezekiel and the Original Prophecy*, by C. C. Torrey, pp. xi-xxxv. Library of Biblical Studies. New York: KTAV, 1970.

_____. "Ezekiel." *EncJud* 6 (1971) 1078-95.

_____. "What are Valid Criteria for Determining Inauthentic Matter in Ezekiel?" *Ezekiel and His Book: Textual and Literary Criticism and their Interrelation*, pp. 123-35. Edited by J. Lust. Leuven: Leuven University Press/ Peeters, 1986.

_____. *Ezekiel 1-20.* AB 22. Garden City, NY: Doubleday, 1983.

Gross, Heinrich. "Umkehr im Alten Testament: In der Sicht der Propheten Jeremia und Ezechiel." *Zeichen des Glaubens. Studien zu Taufe und Firmung. Balthasar Fischer zum 60. Geburtstag*, pp. 19-28. Edited by H. auf der Maur and B. Kleinheyer. Zürich: Benziger; Freiburg: Herder, 1972.

Gruenthaner, M. J. "The Old Testament and Retribution in this Life." *CBQ* 4 (1942) 101-110.

Gunkel, Hermann and Joachim Begrich. *Einleitung in die Psalmen*. 2nd ed. Göttingen: Vandenhoeck & Ruprecht, 1966.

Gunkel, H. "Einleitung: Die Propheten als Schriftsteller und Dichter." In H. Schmidt, *Die Grossen Propheten*. 2nd. ed. Die Schriften des Alten Testaments II/2. Göttingen: Vandenhoeck & Ruprecht, 1923.

Haag, H. *Was lehrt die literarkritische Untersuchung des Ezechieltextes?* Freiburg in der Schweiz: Paulusdruckerie, 1943.

Hals, Ronald M. "Methods of Interpretation: Old Testament Texts [Ezekiel 18]." *Studies in Lutheran Hermeneutics*, pp. 271-82. Edited by John Reumann. Philadelphia, PA: Fortress, 1979.

Hammershaimb, Erling. "De Sure Druer: Nogle Overvejelser til Ez Kap 18." *DTT* 43 (1980) 225-34.

Hanson, P. D. *The Dawn of Apocalyptic: The Historical and Sociological Roots of Jewish Apocalyptic Eschatology*. Rev. ed. Philadelphia, PA: Fortress, 1979.

Haran, Menahem. "The Law Code of Ezekiel XL-XLVII and its Relation to the Priestly School." *HUCA* 50 (1979) 45-71.

_____. *Temples and Temple-Service in Ancient Israel: An Inquiry into the Character of Cult Phenomena and the Historical Setting of the Priestly School*. Oxford: Oxford University Press, 1978.

Harrelson, W. *The Ten Commandments and Human Rights*. OBT. Philadelphia, PA: Fortress, 1980.

Harvey, J. "Collectivisme et individualisme, Ez 18,1-32 et Jér 31,29." *ScEccl* 10 (1958) 167-202.

Hauerwas, Stanley. *A Community of Character: Toward a Constructive Christian Social Ethic*. Notre Dame, IN: University of Notre Dame Press, 1981.

_____. *The Peaceable Kingdom: A Primer in Christian Ethics*. Notre Dame, IN: University of Notre Dame Press, 1983.

Havice, Harriet Katherine. "The Concern for the Widow and the Fatherless in the Ancient Near East: A Case Study in Old Testament Ethics." Ph.D. Disssertation. Yale University, 1978.

Hempel, Johannes. *Das Ethos des Alten Testaments*. 2nd ed. BZAW 67. Berlin: Töpelmann, 1964.

Henry, Marie-Louise. "'Tod' und 'Leben': Unheil und Heil als Funktionen des rechtenden und rettenden Gottes im Alten Testament." *Leben angesichts des Todes: Beiträge zum theologischen Problem des Todes (FS. H. Thielicke)*, pp. 1-26. Tübingen: Mohr-Siebeck, 1968.

Hentschke, R. *Satzung und Setzender: Ein Beitrag zur israelitischen Rechtsterminologie.* BWANT 83. Stuttgart: Kohlhammer, 1963.

Herbert, A. S. "The 'Parable' [*māšāl*] in the Old Testament." *SJT* 7 (1954) 180-96.

Herntrich, Volkmar. *Ezechielprobleme.* BZAW 61. Giessen: Töpelmann, 1932.

Herrmann, Johannes. *Ezechielstudien.* Beiträge zur Wissenschaft vom Alten Testament 2. Leipzig: Hinrichs, 1908.

Herrmann, Siegfried. *Die prophetische Heilserwartungen im Alten Testament: Ursprung und Gestaltswandel.* BWANT 85. Stuttgart: Kohlhammer, 1965.

Hertzberg, H. W. "Die Entwicklung des Begriffes *Mišpāṭ* im Alten Testament." *ZAW* 40 (1922) 256-87 and 41 (1923) 16-76.

Herzog, Patricius. *Die ethischen Anschauungen des Propheten Ezechiel.* ATAbh 9/2,3. Münster i. W.: Aschendorffschen Buchdruckerei, 1923.

Hildebrand, David. "Israel's Cultic Structure as a Paradigm of Holiness in the Inter-Temple Period (597 B.C.-516 B.C.)." Th.D. Dissertation. Wycliffe College, Toronto School of Theology, 1984.

Hoffmann, H. W. "Form—Funktion—Intention." *ZAW* 82 (1970) 341-46.

Hoffner, H. A. "*hābāl.*" *TDOT* 4 (1980) 179-84.

Holladay, William L. *The Root Šûbh in the Old Testament, with Particular Reference to its Usages in Covenantal Contexts.* Leiden: Brill, 1958.

Hölscher, Gustav. *Hesekiel: der Dichter und das Buch.* BZAW 39. Giessen: Töpelmann, 1924.

Horst, L. *Leviticus xvii-xxvi und Hezekiel: Ein Beitrag zur Pentateuchkritik.* Colmar: Barth, 1881.

Hossfeld, F. *Untersuchungen zu Komposition und Theologie des Ezechielbuches.* FB 20. Würzburg: Echter Verlag, 1977.

Hubbard, Robert L. "Is the 'Tatsphäre' Always a Sphere?" *JETS* 25 (1982) 257-62.

Humbert, P. "Le substantif *tô'ēbâ* et le verbe *t'b* dans l'Ancien Testament." *ZAW* 72 (1960) 217-37.

Hunter, A. Vanlier. *Seek the Lord! A Study of the Meaning and Function of the Exhortations in Amos, Hosea, Isaiah, Micah, and Zephaniah.* Baltimore, MD: St. Mary's Seminary and University, 1982.

Hurvitz, Avi. *A Linguistic Study of the Relationship Between the Priestly Source and the Book of Ezekiel: A New Approach to an Old Problem*. CahRB 20. Paris: Gabalda, 1982.

_____. "The Evidence of Language in Dating the Priestly Code: A Linguistic Study in Technical Idioms and Terminology." *RB* 81 (1974) 24-56.

Hutton, Rodney R. "Declaratory Formulae: Forms of Authoritative Pronouncement in Ancient Israel." Ph.D. Dissertation. Claremont Graduate School, 1983.

Illman, Karl-Johan. *Old Testament Formulas About Death*. Medde-landen Från Stiftenlsens för Åbo Akademi Forskningsinstitut 48. Åbo: Åbo Akademi, 1979.

Irwin, W. A. "Ezekiel Research Since 1943." *VT* (1953) 54-66.

Jacob, E. *Theology of the Old Testament*. New York, NY/ Evanston, IL: Harper & Row, 1958.

Janssen, Enno. *Juda in der Exilszeit: Ein Beitrag zur Frage der Entstehung des Judentums*. FRLANT, NF 51. Göttingen: Vandenhoeck & Ruprecht, 1956.

Jepsen, Alfred. "ṢDQ und ṢDQH im Alten Testament." *Gottes Wort und Gottes Land. Festschrift H. W. Hertzberg*, pp. 78-89. Edited by H. G. Reventlow. Göttingen: Vandenhoeck & Ruprecht, 1965.

Johnson, Aubrey R. *The One and the Many in the Israelite Conception of God*. Cardiff: University of Wales Press, 1942.

_____. *The Vitality of the Individual in the Thought of Ancient Israel*. Cardiff: University of Wales Press, 1949.

_____. "*MŠL*." *Wisdom in Israel and in the Ancient Near East*, pp. 162-69. VTSup 3. Edited by M. Noth. Leiden: Brill, 1955.

Joyce, Paul M. "Individual Responsibility in Ezekiel 18?" *Studia Biblica 1978: Papers on Old Testament and Related Themes*, pp. 185-96. JSOTSup 11. Edited by E. A. Livingstone. Sheffield: JSOT, 1979.

_____. *Divine Initiative and Human Response in Ezekiel*. JSOTSup 51. Sheffield: JSOT, 1989.

_____. "The Individual and the Community." *Beginning Old Testament Study*, pp. 74-89. Edited by John Rogerson. Philadelphia, PA: Westminster, 1983.

_____. "Ezekiel and Individual Responsibility." *Ezekiel and His Book: Textual and Literary Criticism and their Interrelation*, pp. 317-21. Edited by J. Lust. Leuven: Leuven University Press/Peeters, 1986.

Junker, H. "Ein Kernstück der Predigt Ezechiels." *BZ* NF 7 (1963) 173-85.

Kaufmann, Y. *The Religion of Israel: From Its Beginnings to the Babylonian Exile.* Chicago, IL: University of Chicago, 1960; reprint ed., New York, NY: Schocken, 1972.

Kautzsch, E. *Gesenius' Hebrew Grammar.* 2nd English Edition. Revised by A. E. Cowley. Oxford: Clarendon, 1910.

Klein, Ralph W. "Yahweh Faithful and Free: A Study in Ezekiel." *CTM* 42 (1971) 493-501.

_____. *Israel in Exile: A Theological Interpretation.* OBT. Philadelphia, PA: Fortress, 1979.

_____. *Ezekiel: The Prophet and His Message.* Studies on Personalities of the Old Testament. Columbia, SC: University of South Carolina Press, 1988.

Klostermann, A. "Beiträge zur Entstehungsgeschichte des Pentateuchs." *Zeitschrift für lutherische Theologie und Kirche* 38 (1877) 401-45 = "Ezechiel und das Heiligkeitsgesetz." *Der Pentateuch*, pp. 368-418. Leipzig: Deichert, 1893.

Knierim, Rolf. *Hauptbegriffe für Sünde im Alten Testament.* Gütersloh: Gerd Mohn, 1965.

_____. "Old Testament Form Criticism Reconsidered." *Int* 27 (1973) 435-68.

Knight, Douglas A. *Rediscovering the Traditions of Israel.* Rev. ed. SBLDS 9. Missoula, MT: Scholars Press, 1975.

_____. "The Understanding of 'Sitz im Leben' in Form Criticism." *Society of Biblical Literature Seminar Papers I*, pp. 105-25. Edited by G. MacRae. Cambridge, MA: Scholars Press, 1973.

_____. "Jeremiah and the Dimensions of the Moral Life." *The Divine Helmsman: Studies on God's Control of Human Events, Presented to Lou H. Silberman*, pp. 87-105. Edited by J. L. Crenshaw and S. Sandmel. New York, NY: KTAV, 1980.

_____. "Old Testament Ethics." *Christian Century* 99 (1982) 55-59.

Koch, Klaus. "Is There a Doctrine of Retribution in the Old Testament?" *Theodicy in the Old Testament*, pp. 57-87. Edited by James L. Crenshaw. Issues in Religion and Theology 4. Philadelphia, PA: Fortress; London: SPCK, 1983. Originally published as "Gibt es ein Vergeltungsdogma im Alten Testament?" *ZThK* 52 (1955) 1-42.

_____. "Wesen und Herkunft der 'Gemeinschaftstreue' im Israel der Königszeit." *ZEE* 5 (1961) 72-90.

———. "Tempeleinlassliturgien und Dekaloge." *Studien zur Theologie der alttestamentlichen Uberlieferungen*, pp. 45-60. Edited by R. Rendtorff and K. Koch. Neukirchen: Neukirchener Verlag, 1961.

———. "Der Spruch 'Sein Blut bleibe auf seinem Haupt' und die Israelitische Auffassung von Vergossenen Blut." *Um das Prinzip der Vergeltung in Religion und Recht des Alten Testaments*, pp. 432-56. Wege der Forschung 125. Edited by K. Koch. Darmstadt: Wissenschaftliche Buchgesellschaft, 1972. Originally published in *VT* 12 (1962) 396-416.

———. *The Growth of the Biblical Tradition.* New York, NY: Scribner's, 1969.

———. "*sdq*, gemeinschaftstreu/heilvoll sein." *THAT* 2 (1976) 507-30.

———. "*hāta'*." *TDOT* 4 (1980) 309-19.

———. *The Prophets.* 2 Volumes. Philadelphia, PA: Fortress, 1982, 1984.

König, Ed. "Die letzte Pentateuchschicht und Hesekiel." *ZAW* 28 (1908) 174-79.

Korosec, Viktor. "Die Kollektivhaftung in hethitischen Recht." *Archiv Orientalni* (Praha) 18/3 (1950) 187-209.

Kosmala, Hans. "His Blood on Us and on Our Children." *ASTI* 7 (1970) 94-127.

Kraetzschmar, R. *Das Buch Ezechiel.* HKAT. Göttingen: Vandenhoeck & Ruprecht, 1900.

Krüger, Thomas. *Geschichtskonzepte im Ezekielbuch.* BZAW 180. Berlin/New York: de Gruyter, 1989.

Kuhl, C. "Zur Geschichte der Hesekiel-Forschung." *TRu* 5 (1933) 92-118.

———. "Neuere Hesekiel-Literatur." *TRu* 20 (1952) 1-26.

———. "Zum Stand der Hesekiel-Forschung." *TRu* 24 (1956-57) 1-53.

Kuschke, Arnulf. "Die Menschenwege und der Weg Gottes im Alten Testament." *ST* 5 (1951) 106-18.

Kutsch, Ernst. *Die chronologischen Daten des Ezechiel-buches.* OBO 62. Freiburg: Universitätsverlag; Göttingen: Vandenhoeck & Ruprecht, 1985.

Lambert, W. G. "Literary Style in First Millennium Mesopotamia." *JAOS* 88 (1968) 123-32.

Landes, G. M. "Jonah: A *Māšāl?*" *Israelite Wisdom: Theological and Literary Essays in Honor of Samuel Terrien*, pp. 137-58. Edited by J. G. Gammie, W. A. Brueggemann, W. L. Humphreys, and J. M. Ward; New York, NY: Scholars Press/Union Theological Seminary, 1978.

Lang, B. *Kein Aufstand in Jerusalem: Die Politik des Propheten Ezechiel.* SBB. Stuttgart: Katholisches Bibelwerk, 1978.

_____. *Ezechiel: Der Prophet und das Buch.* ErFor 153. Darmstadt: Wissenschaftliche Buchgesellschaft, 1981.

Lescow, T. "Die dreistufige Tora." *ZAW* 82 (1970) 362-79.

Levenson, Jon D. *The Theology of the Program of Restoration of Ezekiel 40-48.* HSM 10. Missoula, MT: Scholars Press, 1976.

_____. *Sinai and Zion: An Entry into the Jewish Bible.* Minneapolis, MN: Winston, 1985.

Levine, B. A. *In the Presence of the Lord: A Study of Cult and some Cultic Terms in Ancient Israel.* SJLA 5. Leiden: Brill, 1974.

Lichtheim, M. *Ancient Egyptian Literature.* 3 Volumes. Berkeley, CA/Los Angeles, CA/London: University of California Press, 1973, 1976, 1980.

Liedke, Gerhard. *Gestalt und Bezeichnung alttestamentlichen Rechtsätze: Eine formgeschichtlich-terminologische Studie.* WMANT 39. Neukirchen-Vluyn: Neukirchener Verlag, 1971.

_____. "*ḥqq*, einritzen, festsetzen." *THAT* 1 (1971) 626-33.

_____. "*špṭ*, richten." *THAT* 2 (1976) 999-1009.

Lindars, Barnabus. "Ezekiel and Individual Responsibility." *VT* 15 (1965) 452-67.

Lindsay, Roger. "Rules as a Bridge between Speech and Action." *Social Rules and Social Behaviour*, pp. 150-73. Edited by Peter Collett. Oxford: Blackwell, 1977.

Lisowsky, G. *Konkordanz zum Hebräischen Alten Testament.* 2nd ed. Stuttgart: Würtembergische Bibelanstalt, 1958.

Liwak, Rüdiger. "Überlieferungsgeschichtliche Probleme des Ezechielbuches: eine Studie zu postezechielischen Interpretationen und Kompositionen." D.Theol. Dissertation, Ruhr-Universität Bochum, 1976.

Loewenstamm, S. E. "*m/trbyt* and *nšk*," *JBL* 88 (1969) 78-80.

Löhr, Max. *Sozialismus und Individualismus im alten Testament.* BZAW 10. Giessen: Töpelmann, 1906.

Lust, J. "Introduction." *Ezekiel and His Book: Textual and Literary Criticism and their Interrelation,* pp. 1-3. Edited by J. Lust. Leuven: Leuven University Press/ Peeters, 1986.

McConville, J. G. "Priests and Levites in Ezekiel: A Crux in the Interpretation of Israel's History." *TynBul* 34 (1983) 3-31.

McKane, W. *Proverbs: A New Approach.* OTL. Philadelphia, PA: Westminster, 1970.

McKeating, H. "Sanctions Against Adultery in Ancient Israelite Society, with some Reflections on Methodology in the Study of Old Testament Ethics." *JSOT* 11 (1979) 57-72.

Macholz, G. C. "Noch einmal: Planungen für den Wiederaufbau nach der Katastrophe von 587." *VT* 19 (1969) 322-52.

Maloney, R. P. "Usury and Restrictions on Interest-Taking in the Ancient Near East." *CBQ* 36 (1974) 1-20.

March, W. Eugene. "Prophecy." *Old Testament Form Criticism,* pp. 141-77. Edited by J. H. Hayes. Trinity University Monograph Series in Religion 2. San Antonio, TX: Trinity University, 1974.

Matthews, I. G. *Ezekiel.* An American Commentary on the Old Testament. Philadelphia, PA: The American Baptist Publication Society, 1939.

May, Herbert G. "Individual Responsibility and Retribution." *HUCA* 32 (1961) 107-20.

Mays, J. L. "Justice: Perspectives from the Prophetic Tradition." *Int* 37 (1983) 5-17.

Mendenhall, G. E. "The Relation of the Individual to Political Society in Ancient Israel." *Biblical Studies in Memory of H. C. Alleman,* pp. 89-108. Edited by J. M. Myers, O. Reimherr, and H. N. Bream. Locust Valley, NY: Augustin, 1960.

_____. "The Conflict Between Value Systems and Social Control." *Unity and Diversity: Essays in the History, Literature, and Religion of the Ancient Near East,* pp. 169-80. Edited by H. Goedicke and J. J. M. Roberts. Baltimore, MD/London: Johns Hopkins University Press, 1975.

Merkelbach, R. "Ein Agyptischer Priestereid." *Zeitschrift für Papyrologie und Epigraphik* 2 (1968) 7-30.

Milgrom, J. *Cult and Conscience: The Asham and the Priestly Doctrine of Repentance.* SJLA 18. Leiden: Brill, 1976.

Miller, John W. *Das Verhältnis Jeremias und Hesekiels sprachlich und theologisch untersucht.* Assen: Van Gorcum, 1955.

Miller, P. D., Jr. *Sin and Judgment in the Prophets: A Stylistic and Theological Analysis.* SBLMS 27. Chico, CA: Scholars Press, 1982.

Mosis, R. "Ez 14,1-11—ein Ruf zur Umkehr." *BZ* 19 (1975) 161-94.

_____. *Das Buch Ezechiel. Teil I. Kap. 1:1-20:44.* Geistliche Schriftlesung 8/1. Düsseldorf: Patmos, 1978.

Mowinckel, S. *Le Décalogue.* Paris: Alcan, 1927.

_____. "Zur Geschichte der Dekaloge." *ZAW* 55 (1937) 218-35.

_____. *Psalmenstudien V: Segen und Fluch in Israels Kult und Psalmendichtung.* Amsterdam: Schippers, 1924.

_____. *The Psalms in Israel's Worship.* 2 Volumes. New York/Nashville: Abingdon, 1962.

Mozley, J. B. "Visitation of the Sins of the Fathers Upon the Children." *Ruling Ideas in Early Ages and Their Relation to Old Testament Faith,* pp. 104-25. London: Longmans, Green, & Co., 1906.

Muilenburg, J. "Ezekiel." *Peake's Commentary on the Bible.* Rev. ed. Edited by M. Black and H. H. Rowley. New York: Nelson, 1962.

_____. "Form Criticism and Beyond." *JBL* 88 (1969) 1-18.

Müller, H.-P. "*qdš,* heilig." *THAT* 2 (1976) 589-609.

Murray, D. F. "The Rhetoric of Disputation: Re-Examination of a Prophetic Genre." *JSOT* 38 (1987) 95-121.

Neufeld, E. "The Prohibitions against Loans at Interest in Ancient Hebrew Laws." *HUCA* 26 (1955) 355-412.

Neumann, P. K. D. "Das Wort, das geschehen ist." *VT* 23 (1973) 171-217.

North, Robert. *Sociology of the Biblical Jubilee.* AnBib 4. Rome: Pontifical Biblical Institute, 1954.

Noth, M. "The Laws in the Pentateuch: Their Assumptions and Meaning." *The Laws in the Pentateuch and Other Studies,* pp. 1-107. Edinburgh/London: Oliver & Boyd, 1966.

_____. "The Jerusalem Catastrophe of 587 B.C. and its Significance for Israel." *The Laws in the Pentateuch and Other Studies,* pp. 260-80. Edinburgh/London: Oliver & Boyd, 1966.

Olmo Lete, G. de. "Estructura literaria de Ez 33,1-20." *EstBibl* 22 (1963) 5-31.

Overholt, T. "Prophecy: the Problem of Cross-Cultural Comparison." *Semeia* 21 (1981) 55-78.

Oyen, Hendrik van. *Ethik des Alten Testaments.* Geschichte der Ethik 2. Gütersloh: Gerd Mohn, 1967.

Pareira, Berthold A. *The Call to Conversion in Ezekiel and Biblical-Theology.* Rome: Pontificia Universitas Gregoriana, 1975.

Park, Joon Surh. "Theological Traditions of Israel in the Prophetic Judgment of Ezekiel." Ph.D. Dissertation. Princeton University, 1978.

Parunak, H. Van Dyke. "Structural Studies in Ezekiel." Ph.D. Dissertation. Harvard University, 1978.

_____. "Transitional Techniques in the Bible." *JBL* 102 (1983) 525-48.

_____. *Linguistic Density Plots in Ezekiel.* The Computer Bible, Vol. XXVII-A. Wooster, OH: Biblical Research Associates, 1984.

Paton, L. B. "The Holiness Code and Ezekiel." *Presbyterian and Reformed Review* 7/25 (1896) 98-115.

Patrick, D. "Political Exegesis." *Encounter with the Text: Form and History in the Hebrew Bible*, pp. 139-51. Semeia Supplements. Edited by M. J. Buss. Philadelphia, PA: Fortress; Missoula, MT: Scholars Press, 1979.

_____. *Old Testament Law.* Atlanta, GA: John Knox, 1985.

Pedersen, J. *Israel: Its Life and Culture.* 2 Volumes. London: Oxford University Press; Copenhagen: Brannerog Korch, 1926.

Perlitt, L. "Anklage und Freispruch Gottes: Theologische Motive in der Zeit des Exils." *ZThK* 69 (1972) 290-303.

Pfeiffer, Robert H. *Introduction to the Old Testament.* Rev. ed. New York, NY: Harper & Brothers, 1948.

Polk, T. "Paradigms, Parables and *Měšālîm*: On Reading the *Māšāl* in Scripture." *CBQ* 45 (1983) 564-83.

Porter, J. R. "The Legal Aspects of the Concept of Corporate Personality in the Old Testament." *VT* 15 (1965) 361-80.

Rabenau, K. von. "Die Entstehung des buches Ezechiel in formgeschichtlicher Sicht." *Wissenschaftliche Zeitschrift* (Halle) 5 (1955-56) 659-94.

Rad, Gerhard. von. *Old Testament Theology*. 2 Volumes. London: SCM, 1965.

_____. "The Early History of the Form-Category of 1 Corinthians xiii. 4-7." *The Problem of the Hexateuch and Other Essays*, pp. 301-17. New York, NY: McGraw Hill, 1966.

_____. "Faith Reckoned as Righteousness." *The Problem of the Hexateuch and Other Essays*, pp. 125-30. New York, NY: McGraw Hill, 1966.

_____. "'Righteousness' and 'Life' in the Cultic Language of the Psalms." *The Problem of the Hexateuch and Other Essays*, pp. 243-66. New York, NY: McGraw Hill, 1966.

Raitt, T. M. "The Prophetic Summons to Repentance." *ZAW* 83 (1971) 30-49.

_____. *A Theology of Exile*. Philadelphia, PA: Fortress, 1977.

Rautenberg, Willy. "Die Zukunftsthora des Hesekiel." *ZAW* 33 (1913) 92-115.

Rendtorff, R. *Die Gesetze in der Priesterschrift: Eine gattungsgeschichtliche Untersuchung*. FRLANT 62. Göttingen: Vandenhoeck & Ruprecht, 1954.

_____. "Zum Gebrauch der Formel *nĕ'ûm jahwe* im Jeremiabuch." *ZAW* 66 (1954) 27-37.

_____. "Botenformel und Botenspruch." *ZAW* 74 (1962) 165-77.

Reventlow, H. Graf. "Sein Blut komme über sein Haupt." *Um das Prinzip der Vergeltung in Religion und Recht des Alten Testaments*, 412-31. Wege der Forschung 125. Edited by K. Koch. Darmstadt: Wissenschaftliche Buchgesellschaft, 1972. Originally published in *VT* 10 (1960) 311-27.

_____. *Wächter über Israel: Ezechiel und seine Tradition*. BZAW 82. Berlin: Töpelmann, 1962.

Ringgren, H. "*ḥāqaq*." *TDOT* 5 (1986) 139-47.

Robinson, H. W. *The Christian Doctrine of Man*. Edingurgh: T. & T. Clark, 1911.

_____. "The Hebrew Conception of Corporate Personality." *Werden und Wesen des Alten Testaments*, 49-62. BZAW 66. Edited by P. Volz, F. Stummer, and J. Hempel. Berlin: Töpelmann, 1936.

Rodd, C. S. "Shall not the judge of all the earth do what is just? (Gen 18:25)." *ExpTim* 83 (1972) 137-39.

Rogerson, J. W. "The Hebrew Conception of Corporate Personality: a Re-examination." *JTS* 21 (1970) 1-16.

_____. *Anthropology and the Old Testament*. Atlanta, GA: John Knox, 1978.

Ross, B. L. "The Individual in the Community: Personal Identification in Ancient Israel." Ph.D. Dissertation. Drew University, 1979.

Rost, L. "Die Schuld der Väter." *Studien zum Alten Testament*, pp. 66-71. BWANT 101. Stuttgart: Kohlhammer, 1974.

_____. "Gesetz und Propheten." *Studien zum Alten Testament*, pp. 9-38. BWANT 101. Stuttgart: Kohlhammer, 1974.

Rowley, H. H. "The Book of Ezekiel in Modern Study." *BJRL* 36 (1953/54) 146-90.

_____. *The Faith of Israel*. London: SCM, 1956.

Sakenfeld, K. D. "Ez 18:25-32." *Int* 32 (1978) 295-300.

Scalise, Pamela D. J. "From Prophet's Word to Prophetic Book: A Study of Walther Zimmerli's Theory of Nachinterpretation." Ph.D. Dissertation. Yale University, 1982.

Scharbert, J. "Formgeschichte und Exegese von Ex. 34,6f und seiner Parallelen." *Bib* 38 (1957) 130-50.

_____. "Unsere Sünden und die Sünden unserer Väter." *BZ* 2 (1958) 14-26.

_____. *Solidarität in Segen und Fluch im Alten Testament und in seiner Umwelt. Band I: Väterfluch und Vätersegen*. BBB 14. Bonn: Hanstein, 1958.

Schenker, A. "Saure Trauben ohne stumpfe Zähne: Bedeutung und Tragweite von Ez 18 und 33:10-20 oder ein Kapitel alttestamentlicher Moraltheologie." *Mélanges Dominique Barthélemy: etudes bibliques offertes à l'occasion de son 60e anniversaire*, 449-70. Edited by P. Casetti, O. Keel, and A. Schenker. OBO 38. Fribourg, Suisse: Editions Universitaires; Göttingen: Vandenhoeck & Ruprecht, 1981.

Schmid, H. H. *Gerechtigkeit als Weltordnung: Hintergrund und Geschichte des alttestamentlichen Gerechtigkeitsbegriffes*. BHT 40. Tübingen: Mohr-Siebeck, 1968.

Schmidt, W. H. *Zukunftsgewissheit und Gegenwartskritik: Grundzüge prophetischer Verkündigung*. BibS(N) 64. Neukirchen-Vluyn: Neukirchener Verlag, 1973.

Schulz, H. *Das Todesrecht im Alten Testament: Studien zur Rechtsform der Mot-Jumat-Sätze*. BZAW 114. Berlin: Töpelmann, 1969.

Schüpphaus, J. *"gāzal."* *TDOT* 2 (1975) 456-58.

Seeligmann, I. L. "Lending, Pledge and Interest in Biblical Law and Biblical Thought." *Studies in Bible and the Ancient Near East Presented to Samuel E. Loewenstamm on His Seventieth Birthday*, Volume 2, pp. 183-205. English Abstract, Volume 1, pp. 209-210. Edited by Y. Avishur and J. Blau. Jerusalem: Rubenstein, 1978.

Simian, Horacio. *Die theologische Nachgeschichte der Prophetie Ezechiels: Form- und traditionskritische Untersuchung zu Ez 6; 35; 36*. FB 14. Würzburg: Echter Verlag, 1974.

Skinner, J. *The Book of Ezekiel*. The Expositor's Bible. New York: Armstrong, 1895.

Slater, J. R. "Individualism and Solidarity as Developed by Jeremiah and Ezekiel." *The Biblical World* 14 (1899) 172-83.

Slenczka, Richard. "Sozialethik und Theodizee." *KD* 18 (1972) 82-99.

Slotki, I. W. "Ezek 18:10." *AJSL* 43 (1926-27) 63-66.

Smend R. *Der Prophet Ezechiel*. 2nd. ed. Kurzgefasstes exegetisches Handbuch zum Alten Testament 8. Leipzig: Hirzel, 1880.

Soggin, J. A. *"māšāl."* *THAT* 1 (1971) 930-33.

Spadafora, F. Leni di. *Collectivismo e individualismo nel Vecchio Testament*. Quaderni Esegetici 2. Rovigo: Istituto Padano di Arti Grafiche, 1953.

Stalker, D. M. G. *Ezekiel: Introduction and Commentary*. London: SCM, 1968.

Steck, O. H. "Theological Streams of Tradition." *Tradition and Theology in the Old Testament*, pp. 183-214. Edited by D. A. Knight. Philadelphia, PA: Fortress, 1977.

Suter, D. *"Māšāl* in the Similitudes of Enoch." *JBL* 100 (1981) 193-212.

Talmon, S. and M. Fishbane. "The Structuring of Biblical Books: Studies in the Book of Ezekiel." *ASTI* 10 (1976) 129-53.

Thiel, W. "Erwägungen zum Alter des Heiligkeitsgesetzes," *ZAW* 81 (1969) 40-73.

Tsevat, M. "The Neo-Assyrian and Neo-Babylonian Vassal Oaths and the Prophet Ezekiel." *JBL* 78 (1959) 199-204.

Vetter, D. *Seherspruch und Segensschilderung.* Calwer Theologische Monographien 4. Stuttgart: Calwer, 1974.

Vogt, Ernst. *Untersuchungen zum Buch Ezechiel.* AnBib 95; Rome: Biblical Institute Press, 1981.

Vriezen, T. C. *An Outline of Old Testament Theology.* 2nd ed. Oxford: Blackwell, 1970.

Wächter, L. *Der Tod im Alten Testament.* Arbeiten zur Theologie II/8. Stuttgart: Calwer, 1967.

Wagner, G. "Umfang und Inhalt der *môt-jûmāt*-Reihe." *OLZ* 63 (1968) 325-28.

Wagner, V. *Rechtssätze in gebundener Sprache und Rechtssatzreihen im israelitischen Recht: Ein Beitrag zur Gattungsforschung.* BZAW 127. Berlin/New York: de Gruyter, 1972.

Weber, M. *Ancient Judaism.* New York: Free Press, 1952.

Westermann, C. *Basic Forms of Prophetic Speech.* Philadelphia, PA: Westminster, 1967.

Wevers, John W. *Ezekiel.* NCB. London: Nelson, 1969.; reprint ed., Grand Rapids, MI: Eerdmans; London: Marshall, Morgan & Scott, 1976.

Weinfeld, M. *Deuteronomy and the Deuteronomic School.* Oxford: Clarendon, 1972.

_____. "Instructions for Temple Visitors in the Bible and in Ancient Egypt." *Egyptological Studies*, pp. 224-50. Scripta Hierosolymitana 28. Edited by S. Israel-Groll. Jerusalem: Magnes, 1982.

Whitelam, K. W. *The Just King: Monarchical Judicial Authority in Ancient Israel.* JSOTSup 12. Sheffield: JSOT, 1979.

Wiesel, Elie. "Ezekiel." *Congregation: Contemporary Writers Read the Jewish Bible*, pp. 167-86. Edited by David Rosenberg. San Diego, CA/New York, NY/London: Harcourt, Brace, Jovanovich, 1987.

Williams, R. J. *Hebrew Syntax: An Outline.* 2nd ed. Toronto/Buffalo/London: University of Toronto, 1976.

Wilson, Robert R. "Form-Critical Investigation of the Prophetic Literature: The Present Situation." *Society of Biblical Literature Seminar Papers I*, pp. 100-127 Edited by G. MacRae. Cambridge, MA: Scholars Press, 1973.

_____. *Prophecy and Society in Ancient Israel.* Philadelphia, PA: Fortress, 1980.

_____. "Prophecy in Crisis: The Call of Ezekiel." *Int* 38 (1984) 117-30.

Wolff, H. W. "Das Zitat im Prophetenspruch: Eine Studie zur prophetischen Veründigungsweise." *Gesammelte Studien zum Alten Testament*, 2nd ed., pp. 36-129. TBü 22. Munich: Kaiser, 1973.

_____. "Das Thema 'Umkehr' in der alttestamentlichen Prophetie." *Gesammelte Studien zum Alten Testament*, 2nd ed., pp. 130-150. TBü 22. Munich: Kaiser, 1973.

_____. *Anthropology of the Old Testament*. Philadelphia, PA: Fortress, 1974.

Yoder, P. *From Word to Life: A Guide to the Art of Bible Study*. Scottdale, PA: Herald Press, 1982.

Zimmerli, W. "Die Eigenart der prophetischen Rede des Ezechiel: ein Beitrag zum Problem an Hand von Ezech. xiv 1-11." *ZAW* 66 (1954) 1-26.

_____. "'Leben' und 'Tod' im Buche des Propheten Ezechiel." *TZ* 13 (1957) 494-508.

_____. "The Special Form- and Traditio-Historical Character of Ezekiel's Prophecy." *VT* 15 (1965) 515-27.

_____. *The Law and the Prophets*. Oxford: Blackwell, 1965; reprint ed., New York, NY: Harper & Row, 1967.

_____. Review of *Das Todesrecht im Alten Testament*, by H. Schulz. *TLZ* 95 (1970) 891-97.

_____. "Deutero-Ezechiel?" *ZAW* 84 (1972) 501-16.

_____. *Ezechiel: Gestalt und Botschaft*. BibS(N) 62. Neukirchen-Vluyn: Neukirchener Verlag, 1972.

_____. *Ezekiel 1*. Hermeneia. Philadelphia, PA: Fortress, 1979.

_____. "Knowledge of God According to the Book of Ezekiel." *I Am Yahweh*, pp. 29-98. Edited with an Introduction by W. Brueggemann. Atlanta, GA: John Knox, 1982.

_____. *Ezekiel 2*. Hermeneia. Philadelphia, PA: Fortress, 1983.

_____. "Das Phänomen der 'Fortschreibung' im buche Ezechiel." *Prophecy: Essays Presented to G. Fohrer*, pp. 174-91. Edited by J. A. Emerton. BZAW 150. Berlin/New York: de Gruyter, 1980.

Zyl, A. H. van. "Solidarity and Individualism in Ezekiel." *Studies on the Book of Ezekiel*, pp. 38-52. Pretoria: Die Out Testamentiese Werkgemeenskap in Suid-Afrika, 1961.